Praise for *West of the Ghetto*

"A fascinating study of Californian Jewish women who smash every stereotype. Radicals, institution builders, snappy reporters, and socialist shapeshifters, the writers that Lori Harrison-Kahan has rediscovered—Emma Wolf, Bettie Lowenberg, Harriet Lane Levy, Miriam Michelson, and Anna Strunsky—lead us to a more expansive American Jewish literary landscape."

—Josh Lambert, Sophia Moses Robison Professor of Jewish Studies and English, Wellesley College

"Harrison-Kahan's pioneering study is a significant corrective and exciting intervention into several intersecting areas of literary study focused on religion, ethnicity, race, gender, and class. Harrison-Kahan at once provides an alternative geography of Jewish literary production, focused on the far west and San Francisco in particular, and at the same time introduces a cluster of overlooked and obscured women writers whose fascinating and diverse work provides a window into the complex reformist and progressive politics of the turn of the twentieth century."

—Rachel Rubinstein, dean of the School of Arts and Sciences, Springfield College

"The romance of the American West is rarely associated with Jews—much less Jewish women—but *West of the Ghetto* provides an important corrective through an all-star cast of cosmopolitan Californian Jewish women writers whose lives and writings expand our understanding of the Gilded Age, antisemitism, and Jewish experience in America."

—Rachel Gordan, Shorstein Professor of American Jewish Culture and Society, University of Florida

West of the Ghetto

WEST OF THE GHETTO

Jewish Women, Old San Francisco, and American Literary Culture

LORI HARRISON-KAHAN

WAYNE STATE UNIVERSITY PRESS
DETROIT

ISBN 9780814352328 (paperback)
ISBN 9780814352311 (hardcover)
ISBN 9780814352335 (ebook)

Library of Congress Control Number: 2025942244

On cover: Market Street, San Francisco, 1900. Image courtesy of Detroit Photographic Co., Library of Congress. Cover design by Elke Barter.

Published with the assistance of a fund established by Thelma Gray James of Wayne State University for the publication of folklore and English studies.

Wayne State University Press rests on Waawiyaataanong, also referred to as Detroit, the ancestral and contemporary homeland of the Three Fires Confederacy. These sovereign lands were granted by the Ojibwe, Odawa, Potawatomi, and Wyandot Nations, in 1807, through the Treaty of Detroit. Wayne State University Press affirms Indigenous sovereignty and honors all tribes with a connection to Detroit. With our Native neighbors, the press works to advance educational equity and promote a better future for the earth and all people.

Wayne State University Press
Leonard N. Simons Building
4809 Woodward Avenue
Detroit, Michigan 48201-1309

Visit us online at wsupress.wayne.edu.

Contents

Acknowledgments

West of the Ghetto has been over a decade in the making, and I am indebted to the friends, family, colleagues, and institutions who have supported me over the course of this long journey.

In 2011, shortly after finishing my first book, I was invited to contribute a chapter on turn-of-the-twentieth-century Jewish American fiction to *The Edinburgh Companion to Modern Jewish Fiction*. I am grateful to the editors of that volume, David Brauner and Axel Stähler, for encouraging my inclination to look beyond canonical texts. The seeds of this book can be found in that chapter.

West of the Ghetto became more of a reality in 2016 when I received a Summer Stipend Award from the National Endowment for the Humanities, a Research Travel Award from the Modernist Studies Association, an International Fellowship in Jewish Studies from the Memorial Foundation for Jewish Culture, and a Robert E. Levinson Fellowship from the Bancroft Library at the University of California, Berkeley. These awards and fellowships made archival research possible—as did the staffs at the Bancroft Library, the Stanford University Library, the Huntington Library, the Beinecke Library, the Yale University Archives, the New York Public Library, and the Center for Jewish History. With the aid of Anne Kenny and the interlibrary loan staff at Boston College, I was also able to do a good deal of research for this book from home, sitting in front of my computer. Thank you to Albert Bennett and Christopher Walling, who graciously shared family lore with me; to Laura Sheppard for her insights about Harriet Lane Levy; and to Joan Michelson for carrying on the spirit of her great-great aunt Miriam.

I am incredibly grateful to the Hadassah-Brandeis Institute (HBI) at Brandeis University, where I began writing this book in earnest as a scholar in residence in spring 2016. Thank you to Shulamit Reinharz, Lisa Fishbayn Joffe, Sylvia Barack Fishman, Debby Olins, and Amy

Powell. While at Brandeis, I benefited from opportunities to discuss my research with Joyce Antler, Jonathan Sarna, and Stephen Whitfield. A Faculty Fellowship from Boston College gave me an additional semester of research and writing time. In the latter stages of this book, the Association for Jewish Studies provided crucial assistance through a Contingent Faculty and Independent Scholar Research Grant and its Summer Writing Workshop for Women, Transgender, and Nonbinary Scholars. Thank you to Sarah Abrevaya Stein, who facilitated the workshop, and to my writing group members, Ayelet Brinn, Naomi Taub, Stefanie Fischer, and Jacqueline Adams.

A Cashmere Subvention Award in Jewish, Gender, and Women's Studies from the Gender Justice Caucus of the Association for Jewish Studies helped cover the cost of indexing and gave me the push I needed at exactly the right time. Special thanks to Laura Levitt, who does so much for the profession. The Dean's Office at Boston College's Morrissey College of Arts and Sciences assisted with additional costs of indexing; thank you to Dean Gregory Kalscheur, S.J., and English Department Chair Min Song for supporting this book's publication.

I am fortunate to be publishing my fourth book with Wayne State University Press, which has proved its commitment to scholarship in Jewish Studies and on Jewish women's writing. Thank you to my editors, Sandra Korn and Emily Gauronskas, and to the rest of the staff at the press who ushered this book through production.

While working on this book, I collaborated with other scholars on projects related to Jewish American literature, Jewish women writers, and American women's writing. Those collaborators have had a significant influence on my thinking about the writers, texts, and literary history I consider herein. Thank you to Josh Lambert, Karen E. H. Skinazi, Barbara Cantalupo, Jessica Kirzane, Annie Atura, Ashley Walters, and Jane Carr.

An earlier version of chapter 1 appeared as "'A Grave Experiment': Emma Wolf's Marriage Plots and the Deghettoization of American Jewish Fiction" in *American Jewish History* (January 2017). An additional thank you goes to Josh Lambert, who edited that special issue on New Literary Histories, for including my essay. Keith Newlin, Adam Mendelsohn, and Jonathan Sarna invited me to contribute essays on Emma Wolf to edited volumes, ensuring that this important but largely forgotten Jewish American woman writer receives the recognition she deserves.

Other scholars generously shared their feedback on parts of this manuscript along the way, including Rachel Gordan, Tahneer Oksman, Ava Kahn, Laura Fisher, and Amy Feinstein. Thanks are also due to colleagues who offered feedback on papers at conferences sponsored by the Society for the Study of American Women Writers, the American Literature Association, the Association for Jewish Studies, and the American Jewish Historical Society. Thank you to Kirsten Fermaglich, who invited me to participate in a conference on Gender, Women's Suffrage, and Political Power at Michigan State, and to Keren Hammerschlag, who invited me to participate in Georgetown University's conference on the Modern Jewess: Image and Text. Keren also edited a special issue of *Shofar* on the same topic, to which I contributed an earlier version of chapter 3 titled "Through the Bay Window: Harriet Lane Levy's *920 O'Farrell Street* as Modernist Memoir." I am appreciative, too, of the anonymous reviewers who took the time to offer thoughtful and extensive feedback.

My research has benefited tremendously from the Undergraduate Research Fellowship Program at Boston College and from the eagle eyes of my research assistants; thank you to Marena Cole, Marianna Sorensen, Karen Choi, Grace Denny, Maggie McQuade, Sophia Pandelidis, Christine Lenahan, Riane Lumer, Erin Dooling, Sydney Luciano, Sierra Hyman, and Emmbrooke Flather. Thank you, too, to Arianna Unger, who was my research assistant during my semester at HBI. Among my many wonderful Boston College colleagues who have cheered me on, I would like to give special shout-outs to Lynne Anderson and Elizabeth Graver. I would also like to honor the memory of Judith Wilt, a dear English Department colleague and an advocate for this book in its early stages.

Ilyon Woo has been an amazing "art friend," even as she has tried to lure me away from academic writing; with her work as inspiration, I may get there yet. I am grateful for the decades-long friendship of Emily Burg; the generosity of Darren Gobert and Ross Gascho, who welcomed me into their home when I most needed a break; and the continued camaraderie of my former dissertation-writing group members Jessica Lang, Jennifer Sartori, and Katie Kendall.

This book would not be possible without my writing partners. My deepest gratitude goes to Kimberly Chabot Davis and Elif Armbruster for all of their feedback and emotional support. Writing retreats with Kim,

Elif, and Shilpa Davé provided the companionship I needed to cross the finishing line.

Finally, I thank my family for their love and support—and for always being up for a trip to the West Coast. Cuyler, Amory, and Bailey have grown up with this book and, in the process, have taught me so much about the many meanings of Jewishness. *West of the Ghetto* is dedicated to them.

Introduction

In her autobiography *My Portion* (1925), Rebekah Bettelheim Kohut narrates her coming of age in late nineteenth-century San Francisco, mapping the formation of Jewish American identity onto a Western landscape. The chapter titled "Westward We Go" employs mythic tropes of manifest destiny to describe her father's decision to move his family across the continent to settle on the West Coast. "The state of California was at its period of greatest romantic appeal, and the glamour of the Golden Gate, radiating over the entire country, touched my father, too," Kohut writes. "The West allured with the many tales of the land flowing with milk and honey. To be a pioneer, or almost a pioneer, was a pleasing thought. He saw as his own duty in such a world not the hewing of roads and the building of houses for people to dwell in, but the building of a spiritual house in which souls might dwell."[1] Through her biblical allusion to a "land flowing with milk and honey," Kohut envisions San Francisco as a divinely ordained home for the Jewish people. This formulation of the Golden Gate City as a new Promised Land, an "American Jerusalem," recurs in other autobiographical writings by nineteenth-century Jewish women from California. In her memoir *920 O'Farrell Street* (1947), for instance, Harriet Lane Levy recalls her father's playful revision of the Passover Haggadah's final line: "Next Year in Jerusalem"—the messianic hope that the following year's seder would find the Jewish people back in the Holy Land—becomes "Next Year in San Francisco." The substitution of the ancient city with the modern urban haven of San Francisco expresses the Levy family's contentment with its lot and suggests how the attainment of an American homeland curtailed diasporic yearnings.[2]

As Kohut continues her spatial rendering of Jewishness elsewhere in *My Portion*, San Francisco also functions as the site of the spiritual struggle that dominated her adolescent years—even as she went on, later in life, to distinguish herself as a Jewish community leader, anointed "American Jewry's First Lady."[3] In Kohut's telling, her most intense questioning of her faith took place during "botany excursions" accompanied by Emma Wolf, a fellow Jewish classmate at San Francisco Girls' High School. Later to become the "brilliant authoress" of *Other Things Being*

Equal (1892) and *Heirs of Yesterday* (1900), among other novels, Wolf turned to fiction to explore how Jews in nineteenth-century San Francisco navigated tensions between religious allegiances and pressures to assimilate into mainstream American society. In her autobiography, Kohut describes how she and Wolf debated such questions in their girlhood, voicing the "spiritual growing pains of adolescence" as they "roam[ed] the sand hills together," collecting flowers. The setting of their conversations is imbued with meaning. The natural landscapes on the outskirts of the still-developing city provided Kohut and Wolf with a liminal space in which to negotiate their own self-formation, weighing the "sacrifices" they must make to maintain Judaism's "separate ideals" and whether it was preferable to "choose the easier way and be like all the rest."[4]

Reviewers of Kohut's *My Portion* frequently remarked on the uniqueness of its setting and regional specificity—exemplified in the above episode by the distinct coastal landscape and the "new specimens of flowers" the girls collect on their walks. Hailing Kohut's memoir as a work of "feminist literature" for its depiction of a woman's ability to balance public life as a writer, reformer, and educator with "the utmost devotion to husband, children and parents," *The Menorah Journal*'s reviewer, Ruth Sapin, noted how the text expanded representations of Jewishness beyond those currently dominating Anglophone letters. "American readers, who know the Jewish home only from ghetto fiction and the autobiographies of immigrant Jewesses, will find in Mrs. Kohut's book pictures of Jewish family life of quite a different sort," Sapin wrote.[5]

Sapin was not the only reader to contrast *My Portion* with ghetto literature, a genre that gained tremendous popularity at the end of the nineteenth century with Jewish writers such as Israel Zangwill in Britain and Abraham Cahan in the United States depicting the lives of poor immigrants dwelling in the slums of London and New York. A review of Kohut's autobiography in *The New York Times* cautioned: "To those who have observed Jewish life through the pages of Zangwill and are accustomed to regard it as a pageant of quaint customs and exotic color, Mrs. Kohut's story will be a surprise and, at first perhaps, a disappointment." The *Times* reviewer assured readers, however, that the book has much to offer Jewish and non-Jewish audiences, describing it as a "human document" that is at once "strongly Jewish" and "intensely American."[6] The autobiography's introduction by Hadassah founder Henrietta Szold similarly emphasized how Kohut "strike[s] a new note" in her portrayal of "the California period [which] palpitate[s] with pioneering memories," but "does not carry us away from the Jewish milieu."[7] The text's sustained focus on Judaism—via Kohut's charting of her spiritual return, marriage to a prominent rabbi, and lifelong commitment to her people as a religious authority in her own right—offsets more familiar assimilationist trajectories that had come to dominate Jewish American writing, and especially immigrant autobiography, in the early twentieth century.

Kohut's autobiography was not as anomalous as it first appears. *West of the Ghetto: Jewish Women, Old San Francisco, and American Literary Culture* uncovers an archive of writings by Jewish women who were based in San Francisco during the Gilded Age and Progressive Era and whose works were shaped, in varied ways, by their California context: the landscape, local culture, and national myths of the American West. This book broadens our current understanding of a foundational moment in Jewish American literary history by examining the careers of five overlooked Western women writers—Emma Wolf (1865–1932), Bettie Lowenberg (1845–1924), Harriet Lane Levy (1866–1950), Miriam Michelson (1870–1942), and Anna Strunsky (1877–1964)—as well as the fiction, autobiography, and literary journalism that they produced. This fuller account of turn-of-the-twentieth-century Jewish literary production in the United States complements and complicates the established canon of Jewish American literature by adding multifaceted perspectives on gender, class, progressivism, regionalism, and transnationalism, as well as interreligious, interethnic, and cross-racial relations.

That this monograph is one of the few to focus on Jews and Western American literary culture speaks to the New York-centrism of existing scholarship in the field and the way that the ghetto tale has long exerted a hold over the American cultural imagination. Writing in *The Menorah Journal* in 1932, the novelist Albert Halper lamented that the terrain of Jewish American literature was largely confined to the New York ghetto.[8] Enjoining Jewish writers to look for source material somewhere other than in the tenements, factories, and pushcarts of the Lower East Side, Halper complained that Jewish American fiction had become "a row of shacks without a single skyscraper to break the stubby level of novels that fall into a limited number of patterns."[9] Scholarship today continues to conflate early Jewish literary production in the United States with the ghetto tale and thus with working-class, eastern European immigrant experiences. For example, Cahan and Anzia Yezierska, whose characters dream of rising from the New York slums, are the only early twentieth-century Jewish American fictionists to have received sustained attention from scholars, while Mary Antin's *The Promised Land* (1912), an "up from the ghetto" narrative charting its author's Americanization, remains the best-known autobiography of the period.

The positioning of such authors and texts as the genesis of a Jewish literary tradition in the United States has yielded a simplified, linear trajectory of literary history, in which Jewish American writers have moved further from the ghetto and into the cultural mainstream. Correspondingly, this version of literary history has contributed to a monolithic notion of American Jewishness; authenticity and belonging are often determined by the tracing of roots back to arrival from eastern Europe and to a Yiddish-speaking immigrant culture. In his introduction to a special issue of *Studies in American Jewish Literature* titled "Before the Flood," Michael P. Kramer contends that this simplified version of Jewish American literary history was due to the "Eastern European provenance and predilections of the postwar founders of the field" who "fashioned [it] in their own image." As a corrective, Kramer and other contributors to the special issue extend the historiography of Jewish American literature further back in time, "before the flood" of eastern European immigration, considering works in a variety of genres from the seventeenth, eighteenth, and nineteenth centuries. This book similarly challenges the single "master narrative" that has come to dominate Jewish American literary history.[10] It does so, however, by extending the field's regional, rather than temporal, boundaries, excavating a neglected West Coast–based Jewish literary culture that was coterminous with the emergence of the ghetto genre.

From the time it solidified as a genre in the late nineteenth century, the ghetto tale has been the subject of critique by writers, critics, and publishers, as well as religious and secular leaders, all of whom viewed literature as a means of defining Jewish identity and forming community in America. Of particular concern was the ghetto genre's potential to reinforce antisemitic tropes and stereotypes through the portrayal of Jews as a "peculiar people," set apart by exotic difference and their association with Old World values and customs.[11] The dominance of the ghetto tale thus threatened to obscure the heterogeneity of modern Jewish life in America and circumscribed the parameters of Jewish American literature, as indicated by Halper's concern that fiction by Jewish authors fell "into a limited number of patterns." But it was not true that early twentieth-century Jewish writers in the United States failed to move beyond the ghetto. Instead, this sense of a limited terrain was, and continues to be, the product of critical blind spots and cultural gatekeeping that sidelines women's writing, especially works that do not conform to ingrained expectations about American Jews and Jewish American literature. While the ethnic turn in literary studies made some space in the canon for Jewish writing, it simultaneously reinforced the primacy of ghetto literature. Featuring bilingual, working-class protagonists in the process of acclimating to American society, the ghetto genre adhered to familiar tropes of immigrant writing and thus fit neatly into broader ethnic studies paradigms. This selective inclusion, I argue, flattened Jewish American literature and came at the expense of the rich variety of Jewish literary works emerging at the turn of the twentieth century—notably those produced and consumed by women, many of whom were native-born Americans from middle-class backgrounds.

To be sure, women writers have been fairly well represented in early Jewish American literature, as the canonization of Antin and Yezierska suggests. At the same time, however, most framings of Jewish American literary history have centered patriarchal figures. The privileging of New York-centric, Yiddish-influenced literary culture as an origin point, for example, hinges on the towering presence of writer Abraham Cahan and his role as founder and editor of the *Forverts*.[12] Similarly, in the mid-twentieth century, male writers such as Philip Roth, Saul Bellow, and Bernard Malamud were credited with ushering in the so-called golden age of Jewish American literature, with nods to token women such as Cynthia Ozick.[13]

In contrast, the Jewish literary culture that emerged in the American West at the end of the nineteenth century was not anchored by male luminaries. Instead, women were *the* principal players, as both readers and writers. Their ascendancy is a key reason that the California period has failed to receive attention from scholars. Like most turn-of-the-twentieth-century American women writers, those in this study forged careers within male-dominated institutions, overcoming gender barriers and benefiting from partnerships with men. But the flourishing of Jewish literary culture in the West was also made possible by women's literacy practices and institutions such as the Philomath Club, San Francisco's first Jewish women's literary society, whose founding by novelist and reformer Bettie Lowenberg is discussed in chapter 2. Jewish life in the San Francisco Bay Area gave rise to woman-centered networks sustained by bonds of women's friendships and intimate relationships, including sisterhood and other familial ties.

West of the Ghetto unearths this obscured tradition of women's literature by looking toward the far West as a region of Jewish settlement and cultural production. In so doing, it surveys a more expansive terrain, illuminating not only the diversity of the Jewish experience in America but also the diverse ways that Jewish writers have contributed to American culture. The writers discussed in this book do more than supply alternatives to the ghetto genre; they also exhibit the heretofore unacknowledged breadth of Jewish writing in Gilded-Age and Progressive-Era America. At the turn of the twentieth century, Jewish women writers produced an extraordinary array of prose in multiple genres and various print media: domestic and social purpose novels that employ conventions of the nineteenth-century marriage plot, magazine writings that range from serialized stories for juvenile audiences and an early feminist utopian novella to genteel realism and sensation fiction, essays and literary journalism published in daily newspapers and the Jewish press, and experimental forms that include modernist autobiography and a collaboratively authored epistolary novel.

Despite significant differences in form and genre, the careers of the writers in this study share a common thread: all were shaped by their experiences as Jewish women in the American West. Their literary productions, in turn, constitute a provocative but neglected archive of engagement with ethno-religious, class, and gender discourses circulating in turn-of-the-twentieth-century America. The archive assembled here also offers opportunities to consider how Jewish women writers engaged with the racial thinking of their era and participated in processes of comparative racialization. Documenting the ethnic and racial diversity of the American West, some of these works challenge cultural myths undergirding US expansionism, settler colonialism, and anti-Asian racism, while others activate cultural logics that reify racial hierarchies, claiming space, rights, and privileges for Jews as American citizens by aligning Jewishness with whiteness.[14]

Kohut's treatment of Indigeneity in her autobiography provides an illustrative example. Describing her family's overland journey from the East Coast to San Francisco, undertaken when she was a child of ten, Kohut recalls how her brothers, indoctrinated in "harrowing tales of Indian warfare," spent the train ride on the lookout for Indians. She goes on to reveal:

> As a matter of fact their apprehensions came true; on two different occasions Indians discharged arrows at the train—probably a gesture of resentment rather than a desire to do definite harm. Yet the act had its effect upon us. I was convinced that the Indians were as ferocious as I had been told. Later my notions were upset in a distressing manner. I was left without my perfected design of the universe when we found other Indians peacefully selling beads at Cheyenne and other stations.[15]

Mimicking the curves of the railway, this passage traces the process of comparative racialization as it follows the twists and turns in Kohut's thinking about the land's Indigenous people and her relationship to them. At first attributing the fear and nervous excitement to her brothers alone, Kohut masculinizes the mythic encounter between Native people and settlers, who are represented, in her initial telling, by a group of men. As the passage continues, however, pronouns shift to include Kohut herself; her "brothers" becomes "us" and then "I." At the same time, perceptions of "the Indians" shift from sentence to sentence. "As a matter of fact" suggests a reversal of expectations, implying that Kohut attributes her brothers' fears of Native people to overstimulated imaginations. While the arrows legitimate her brothers' "apprehensions," Kohut seems to overturn stereotypes of Indians as barbaric aggressors in explaining that they were "resentful over the many new railway lines that cut through their stamping-grounds" and "probably" did not "desire to do definite harm."[16] Yet, in the next breath, she confesses to imbibing her brothers' notions of Indian savagery ("I was convinced that the Indians were as ferocious as I had been told"), only to have her perception dispelled by the sight of "Indians peacefully selling beads." By adopting a self-mocking tone at the end of the passage ("I was left without my perfected design of the universe"), Kohut gently chastises her younger self for uncritically accepting an ideological narrative in which defenseless and innocent pioneers found themselves at the mercy of uncivilized savages.

Kohut's autobiography thus issues a critique of the frontier myth, even as it participates in that very mythmaking by vanishing Indigeneity from her narrative. Appearing only briefly during the westward journey, Native people are thus depicted as an obstacle to be overcome. As David Koffman writes in *The Jews' Indian: Colonialism, Pluralism, and Belonging in America*, "When Jews cast Indians as foils to build credibility as 'pioneers,' they marked their settler status, their 'settledness' in America, as it were, their deservedness of privilege in the colonial process, and their whiteness."[17] Via the othering and subsequent erasure of Indigenous people, Kohut defines her family's identity in opposition to Indianness. Recording her childhood adventures as "a pioneer"—or, as she writes, "*almost* a pioneer"—brings Kohut into greater proximity to whiteness and seemingly legitimates her family's right to their portion of the "land flowing with milk and honey."[18]

Analyses of texts set in the American West by Jewish women writers such as Kohut thus contribute to scholarship that examines how Jews have used Indianness, among other racial differences, to negotiate their own relationship to Americanness, a project taken up by both historians and literary critics.[19] Part of chapter 4, for instance, attends to the presence of Native people in the work of Miriam Michelson, who incorporated Indigenous characters in her fiction and covered topics such as the Indian boarding school system as a journalist. While Native people figure in Michelson's vision of a multiethnic West, they are absent entirely from texts by other writers considered in *West of the Ghetto*. Similarly, Hispanic people seldom appear in Western Jewish American women's writing, despite the fact that these literary works were written in California and thus on land that was under Mexican control until the middle of the nineteenth century.[20] As exemplified by my reading of the Indigenous presence in Kohut's memoir, such gaps in representation bear meaning. The erasure of Native and Mexican people may have the effect of erasing their historical ties to the West, clearing space for Jews of European descent to reimagine San Francisco as a new Promised Land.

Jews were, of course, one among many migrant groups drawn to the West by the promises of the Gold Rush and the opportunities for commerce and labor that followed in its wake. The texts under consideration in this book offer additional occasions to examine Jewish American writing in the context of comparative race and ethnic studies via portrayals of people of color, especially Chinese immigrants, as well as non-Jewish European immigrants and the aggregate of white ethnicity. In Wolf's fiction, for example, Irish secondary characters supply comic relief, appearing as servants to Jewish protagonists; when contrasted with their employers' unaccented speech, the Irish immigrants' brogue serves as a means of marking assimilated Jews' cultural refinement and ascension into the middle class. In many of Michelson's fictions, in contrast, Jewishness and Irishness become interchangeable. Her most self-consciously autobiographical stories employ a strategy of ethnic substitution, displacing her own experiences growing up in a large Jewish family in Virginia City onto the adventures of an Irish brood known as the "Nevada Madigans."[21]

Several texts examined here, including Michelson's *The Madigans*, juxtapose norms of white ethnicity with marginalized and exoticized Asian difference in order to universalize experiences of European immigrants and their descendants, bolstering claims to American citizenship. While people of European descent are fully developed as characters and autobiographical subjects in works by turn-of-the-twentieth-century Jewish women from the American West, Chinese immigrants are relegated to minor, often stock, roles in both fiction and memoirs. Chinese men are typically cast as either subservient menial laborers or cunning criminals, and Chinese women are rarely seen outside the context of prostitution. Such Orientalizing patterns of representation prompt new evaluations of literary relationships between white-identified Jewish Americans and Asian Americans. Much of the existing scholarship on the interethnic imagination focuses on Asian-Jewish confluences, attributing them to model minority discourses that emerged in the mid-twentieth century.[22] In contrast, these early twentieth-century texts foreground how some Jews of European descent sought to distinguish themselves from Chinese immigrants and to dispel associations between Jewishness and Orientalism, often by calling upon racial, gendered, and spatial discourses to delineate Chinatown as a place of vice, sexual depravity, and disease.[23] In the process of deghettoizing Jewish American literature by considering alternatives to the ghetto narrative, this book simultaneously illuminates literary conventions—exemplified, for instance, by the popular genre of the Chinatown tale—that contribute to the ghettoization of Chinese Americans and Asian American culture. The use of racist tropes and conventions circumscribing representations of Asian characters made possible, in turn, couplings of Jewishness with whiteness—a racial construct that continues to have bearing on Jewish communities today, which often come under critique for their failure to include and recognize Asian Jews and other Jews of color.[24]

Again, *My Portion* supplies an apt illustration of how such comparative racial dynamics are imbricated with gender via Kohut's references to the Chinese immigrant population residing in San Francisco's Chinatown. In a passage intended to convey teenage angst and rebellion, a theme also explored in her dialogue with Emma Wolf, Kohut maps her adolescent turmoil onto the racialized space of the city:

> My first year at high school was a period of torment to me. The junior class of high school was located in a building only two blocks away from Chinatown. The proximity to this quarter, then branded as dangerous for young girls, aroused in me a peculiar spirit. I hated everything that made it necessary for me to go near that morbid part of the city. I hated the school, the teachers, the educational system, the hilly streets I had to trudge, while well-to-do friends rode. . . . School, once a haven, became a prison to me.[25]

Rather than asserting an identification with Chinatown's residents as fellow immigrants, Kohut attempts to shore up spatial and racial borders in order to differentiate herself from non-white people. Chinese Americans are noticeably absent from this passage; instead, they are conflated with the segregated neighborhood of Chinatown. That Kohut expresses Sinophobia as an anxiety about "proximity" to a racialized space suggests fears of contagion, and she heightens her vulnerability through gendered and sexual discourse. The fact that the Chinese quarter had been "branded as dangerous for young girls" evokes Orientalist myths of innocent white women under sexual threat from Asian men who embody the "yellow peril." In her bourgeois aspirations, expressed as a resentment of "trudg[ing]" the streets near Chinatown while "well-to-do friends rode," Kohut draws on racist tropes to ally herself with idealized white femininity.

My analysis of the ways that Kohut's autobiography maps her spiritual journey and racial formation onto a Western landscape previews the various case studies that make up this book. Conversant with an important body of scholarship that examines the racial imaginaries of Jewish American writing, *West of the Ghetto* fills gaps in the scholarship on whiteness and comparative racialization by centering gender as a category of analysis and drawing upon literary texts by women as its primary archive.[26] As the first full-length work of literary scholarship to consider a cohort of Jewish women writers from the American West and fin de siècle San Francisco as a site for the production of Jewish literary culture, this book expands the regional parameters of Jewish American literature.[27] It builds upon books by scholars such as Rachel Rubinstein, whose *Members of the Tribe* examines texts set in the West via Jewish writers' engagement with the figure of the American Indian, and Michael Hoberman, whose *A Hundred Acres of America: The Geography of Jewish American Literary History* looks at frontier and rural landscapes to consider how Jewish writers cultivated a sense of place in America. In addition to its intervention in the field of Jewish American literature, *West of the Ghetto* joins a larger interdisciplinary conversation in Jewish Studies, complementing a still-growing body of scholarship by historians and religious studies scholars who have pushed beyond familiar immigrant patterns and written about Jews in the American West.[28] Such works provide historical grounding for the chapters that follow.

Jews, Fin de Siècle San Francisco, and Literary Antisemitism

Three of the writers discussed in this book—Emma Wolf, Harriet Lane Levy, and Miriam Michelson—were born and raised in the American West. Two others—Bettie Lowenberg and Anna Strunsky—migrated to the Bay Area in their teenage years; these women thus spent the most formative period of their lives in the region, whether San Francisco became a permanent home (in Lowenberg's case) or a temporary one (in Strunsky's). The oldest of these writers, Lowenberg, was born in Prairie Bluff, Alabama, in 1845, while Strunsky, the youngest and the sole immigrant, was born in Babinots, Russia, in 1877. Of Ashkenazi heritage, these women comprise a range of national backgrounds; the American-born women's families immigrated to the United States from France, Prussia, Germany, and Poland. Despite variation in their ages and points of origin, all five women were swept up in the surge of cultural creativity that overtook San Francisco at the turn of the twentieth century. All began producing writing in the 1890s, propelled by the artistic and social momentum of the Gilded Age, and continued to do so throughout the Progressive Era—although a few (Levy and Lowenberg) would not publish book-length works until late in their lives.

Products of a particular time and place, these women belonged to a group of second-generation Jewish San Franciscans whom historian Fred Rosenbaum labels "rooted cosmopolitans" in his book *Cosmopolitans: A Social and Cultural History of the Jews of the San Francisco Bay Area.*[29] That these women had opportunities to immerse themselves in art and culture and to create literary works and institutions was due in no small part to the generation that preceded them. Migrating West during the mid-nineteenth-century California Gold Rush, first-generation Jewish pioneers helped build the city of San Francisco and accrued success in mercantile businesses, which ensured stable financial futures for their children. Given that daughters were not expected to continue the family business, a responsibility conferred primarily upon sons, this economic stability gave these women leisure to devote to creative and intellectual pursuits; some would go on to make their own independent livings with their pens, contributing materially to the support of their families.

In *Cosmopolitans*, Rosenbaum explains how and why Jewish cultural production in the Bay Area differed significantly from that on the opposite coast. "The rich and lively culture on the East Coast was largely an expression of immigrant life," he states. As a result, Jewish American texts by New York writers bore some uniformity in form and in style, as indicated by the emergence of ghetto realism as a distinct genre beginning in the 1890s. In contrast, there is much less thematic and stylistic uniformity present among West Coast Jewish writers of the period, and no overarching literary genre can categorize and encapsulate their writings. As Rosenbaum notes, "[T]he California Jewish imagination of this era resists easy definition."[30] Instead, the writings discussed in this book display remarkable range and are reflective of the diversity and heterogeneity of turn-of-the-twentieth-century American Jewishness.

In the succeeding chapters, I discuss distinct cultural contexts that shaped these women's lives and careers, contrasting, for example, the bourgeois elitism that defined Lowenberg's and Wolf's milieu with the bohemian subculture that exerted its pull on Strunsky, who grew up in a home of socialist intellectuals. Despite such differences, certain historical themes and forces supply common ground for the case studies that follow, situating this group of writers as an interconnected literary cohort. They may have operated within different social, cultural, and professional circles, but on the Venn diagram of turn-of-the-twentieth-century San Francisco, those circles had significant overlap. The interrelated currents that characterized Jewish life in fin de siècle San Francisco and influenced how these women carved out places for themselves within American literary culture include: (1) a sense of openness and freedom associated with both the realities and mythologies of the West, which liberated many Jews and women from some of the traditions and conventions constraining their counterparts in the East; (2) looser attitudes toward religion and religious observance, which were exemplified by California synagogues becoming innovators of Reform Judaism and led some of these women to view Jewishness as a minor difference or even an irrelevant factor in their identities; (3) less virulent forms of antisemitic exclusion, prejudice, and discrimination as compared to elsewhere in the country; (4) class demographics of a region in which the most visible Jewish population consisted of affluent, Americanized, English-speaking elites rather than recently arrived, working-class immigrants living in poverty, as was the case in New York at the turn of the twentieth century; and (5) a symbiotic relationship between literary endeavors and activism, demonstrated by the involvement of these writers in a variety of social reform movements across the political spectrum.

Historians such as Ava Kahn and Robert Levinson have traced the origins of Jewish life in California back to the Gold Rush, whose promises of economic opportunity lured Jews to the West, where most made their livings as merchants. As pioneering settlers, Jews created businesses that helped sustain and grow what would become the city of San Francisco, which began as a "population of 462 people 'living in tents, shanties and adobe huts' in 1847" and "became, in three years' time, a city of 21,000 people."[31] Although New York eclipsed all other cities as the locus of Jewish life in the United States by the twentieth century, in the second half of the nineteenth century, San Francisco was well on its way to becoming New York's West Coast counterpart, an epicenter of the Jewish diaspora, drawing Ashkenazi and Sephardi Jews from many different national backgrounds. According to the documentary *American Jerusalem: Jews and the Making of San Francisco*, by 1870, Jews constituted more than 10 percent of the city's population of 150,000 people, making San Francisco "the largest Jewish population outside of New York."[32] Scholars of California Jewish history have emphasized the symbolic nature of the West Coast in American Jewish life of the period. Moses Rischin, for instance, characterizes the Golden State as a place that "more than any other appeared from the outset to project—as seen from a Jewish perspective—a sense of America at its most promising, open, and refreshing."[33]

In her introduction to *Jewish Voices of the California Gold Rush: A Documentary History, 1849–1880*, Kahn captures the vibrancy of San Francisco Jewish life, as early settlers contributed to the development of numerous cultural institutions, both Jewish and ecumenical:

> San Francisco became the center of Jewish life, as it did of California life. By the 1870s, a distant, drowsy California outpost had become "the City," a center of Jewish journalism and publication second only to New York City, as well as home to debate and literary societies, clubs, libraries, an orphan home, and a host of fraternal and benevolent organizations. . . . [S]ynagogue leaders in California became more independent than their eastern counterparts and had no inhibitions about speaking up or standing out. At times the community was nonconformist in its practices . . . , reflect[ing] an ability to synthesize Jewish traditions with a new, American way of life. . . . They joined with coreligionists to form the Concordia and other social clubs, to found literary and debating societies, and to establish . . . fraternal organizations. In these associations, small merchants could meet independent of the religious and family constraints of the synagogue.[34]

Kahn depicts the metropolis as a welcoming environment for Jews and as a place of innovation, where a synthesis between American and Jewish life could be forged, opening the way for new formulations of American Jewishness as cultural and religious identity. As Shari Rabin asserts, Jews on the frontier often eschewed the rigidity of tradition and instead created flexible and adaptive versions of Judaism and Jewishness in which religion became "a mobile assemblage of resources for living."[35]

The flexibility and freedoms associated with the West held special meaning for women, as Jeanne Abrams demonstrates in her book *Jewish Women Pioneering the Frontier Trail*. "Jewish women's experience in the West fostered significant opportunities for expanded female roles," writes Abrams. She shows how Jewish women in San Francisco and other Western outposts were "disproportionately" visible in public and civic life, participating in community-building and enlarging "the parameters of a woman's sphere."[36] The career of Rachel "Ray" Frank (Litman) (1861–1948) serves as a high-profile example of the ways Jewish women found unprecedented license in the West. The daughter of Orthodox immigrant parents who settled in the Bay Area, Frank, a journalist and Sabbath school educator, rose to a prominent position of religious leadership when she gave a Yom Kippur sermon in Spokane, Washington, in 1890, becoming the first Jewish American woman to preach from a synagogue pulpit. Although Frank was never ordained, the popular press billed her as "the girl rabbi of the Golden West"—a designation that speaks to how her fame as a forerunner is tied to the environment that made her breakthrough possible.[37] Each of the writers discussed in this book corroborates Abrams's thesis that the West afforded Jewish women occasions to broaden the terms of womanhood and femininity, whether they radically challenged gender roles and fought for women's rights, as Michelson did, or expanded women's sphere through the conservative ideologies of "domestic feminism," as was the case for Lowenberg.

In part, Abrams attributes Jewish women's expanded opportunities in the West to a "muted" antisemitism, and other historians concur that Jews on the frontier were not as hobbled by prejudice and discrimination as those in the East.[38] "Because Jews were pioneers among pioneers, there was little overt anti-Semitism," observes Edward Zerin, "They were welcomed into the social life of the community, winning the respect of their fellow citizens."[39] Marc Dollinger elaborates upon the reasons that Jews found fewer obstacles on the West Coast: "The rapid population growth, lack of preexisting Anglo power structure, and trade skills enjoyed by Jewish arrivals combined to create unprecedented Jewish social mobility," leading "San Francisco Jews [to] count . . . the 'City by the Bay' as one of this nation's most friendly." Dollinger goes on to explain that, as a result, the city's "Jewish residents tended to resist the temptation to live in cloistered Jewish enclaves, enjoying instead the opportunity to live and socialize among the larger non-Jewish community."[40] The acceptance that Jews found in San Francisco was exemplified by the prominent leadership of Adolph Sutro, a German American Jew who was elected as the city's mayor in 1895.

Turn-of-the-twentieth-century Jewish American literature by California women at once supports and complicates such historical accounts. Rather than discounting or downplaying antisemitism as a force shaping San Francisco Jews' cultural productions, *West of the Ghetto* offers a nuanced consideration of the varied forms and effects of antisemitic discourse. The literary careers and texts comprising this book further a view of San Francisco as a haven for members of a minority religion, a place where they could be integrated into the social, economic, political, and cultural life of the city. However, many of these authors and their literary works simultaneously reveal the tentative and precarious nature of such social acceptance. Wolf's novels *Other Things Being Equal* (1892) and *Heirs of Yesterday* (1900), for instance, depict San Francisco as a fairly inclusive environment for Jews, but do not shy away from examining themes of genteel antisemitism and social exclusion due to religious difference. Despite claims from historians that the Golden State eliminated restrictions Jews faced in Europe and on the East Coast, the impulse toward assimilation—the "spiritual" struggle that Kohut articulated in the passage from her autobiography quoted earlier—is typically a response to societal prejudice and to external pressures that Jews conform to the Christian majority rather than maintain "separate ideals."[41]

For several of these writers, decisions *not* to represent Jews in their works simultaneously speak to a more religiously tolerant and inclusive society—that is, the sense that Jews are so fully woven into the national fabric as to be indistinguishable from other Americans—*and* to anxieties about openly expressing ethno-religious difference. Michelson, for example, chose not to pigeonhole her fictional characters as Jews when she drew upon her own family's story for her novel *The Madigans*, filtering Jewish identity through Irishness. While this choice suggests the interchangeability of white ethnic immigrant identities, positioning Jewish and Irish people as universal rather than particular types, it also raises the possibility that Michelson opted to steer clear of controversies around ethnic representation that frequently accompanied portrayals of Jews. Similarly, as I discuss in chapter 5, the absence of explicit references to Jewishness in *The Kempton-Wace Letters*, the 1903 epistolary novel that Anna Strunsky coauthored with Jack London, disguises the fact that their literary experiment came about precisely because of London's eugenicist beliefs and racial biases, which ignited the pair's disagreement about the viability of intermarriage between Anglo-Saxons and Jews.

When considering historians' claims about the absence or mildness of religious discrimination in San Francisco society, it is also important to keep in mind that antisemitism was not only a local or regional phenomenon. Because antisemitism insinuated itself into so many aspects of the national culture and circulated through the media (notably, via theater, literature, and periodicals), San Francisco was not immune. From productions of Shakespeare's *The Merchant of Venice* to the dialect comedy of vaudeville, fin de siècle theater trafficked in Jewish stereotypes; the stage Jew, whose hooked nose portended the evils of unchecked materialism, was easily recognizable to American audiences.[42] Antisemitic representations were also pervasive in print culture. Popular periodicals regularly published dialect stories and ghetto tales in which Jews appeared as one-dimensional caricatures, as well as cartoons and jokes whose punchlines depended on the audience's familiarity with Jewish stereotypes.[43] Ghetto literature by Jewish writers such as Zangwill and Cahan received critical acclaim for realistic depictions of immigrant life, but it also engendered debate and controversy due to fears that it promoted stereotypical representations that did a disservice to fellow Jews.

While some non-Jewish American writers voiced respect and sympathy for Jews, leading at times to complex literary portrayals, scholars such as Donald Pizer have exposed the extent of antisemitic representation in the work of canonical turn-of-the-twentieth-century writers—including San Francisco's own Frank Norris.[44] In his 1899 novel, *McTeague: A Story of San Francisco*, Norris describes the character of Zerkow, a Polish Jewish junk dealer, in demonic and animalistic terms: "a dry, shriveled old man" with satanically red hair; "eager, catlike lips of the covetous; eyes that had grown keen as those of a lynx from long searching amid muck and debris; and clawlike, prehensile fingers—the fingers of a man who accumulates, but never disburses." Zerkow's "inordinate, insatiable greed" leads him to marry a poor Mexican charwoman, Maria Macapa, in order to get his hands on a set of gold dishes that her family purportedly owned.[45] By the end of the novel, Zerkow's lust for gold turns murderous, and he kills his wife in pursuit of the illusory dishes. As Elisa New writes, "Norris' depiction of the greedy Jew reflects a particularly American anti-Semitism that was very much of the 1890s and was shared by other naturalist writers."[46]

At the same time that the 1890s gave rise to literary antisemitism and anti-immigrant rhetoric fueled by the influx of immigrants from eastern Europe, the decade also proved a watershed moment in Jewish American literature. The publication of short stories and novels by Jewish American fiction writers became a regular occurrence at the end of the nineteenth century, prompting essayist and book critic Josephine Lazarus to observe, "To-day we have almost a new Jewish literature of our own, springing up in our midst, dealing not with foreign conditions and circumstance, but with the facts as they are here and now among us."[47] Lazarus's prescient essay "Judaism, Old and New," written in 1894, illuminates the confluence of historical and literary factors that fertilized Jewish American literary culture at the turn of the twentieth century. As Lazarus notes, the coming of age of American-born children of mid-nineteenth-century Jewish immigrants coincided with the late nineteenth-century mass migration of eastern European immigrants to the United States. Today, most studies of Jewish American literature of this period have focused on the latter group of writers, privileging the socialist Yiddish literary culture of New York with Abraham Cahan at its helm. This book, in contrast, brings attention to a cohort of "cosmopolitan" California women who have been largely overlooked, even as their writings offer important counter-representations to the literary antisemitism of naturalist writers like Norris as well as alternatives to the ghetto realism of writers such as Cahan. Through the recovery of understudied women writers who emerged at this formative moment in Jewish American literary history, *West of the Ghetto* unsettles long-ingrained scholarly paradigms, expanding and complicating understandings of

Jews, Jewishness, and Jewish literature in the turn-of-the-twentieth-century United States.

Recovering Jewish American Women's Literature

As a literary recovery project, *West of the Ghetto* follows in the footsteps of feminist literary scholars who, since the 1970s, have used archival methods to rediscover the works of forgotten women writers, to contextualize their oeuvres and careers, and to bring visibility to their writings through critical analyses, reprints, and digital editions. This ongoing project of repopulating and renegotiating literary canons has proven generative for American literary history, injecting new life and energy into the field, especially through attention to the work of Black American, Asian American, Indigenous, and Latina women writers.[48] Jewish American women writers have been part of the larger project of literary recovery since feminist scholars began "diving into the wreck"—to cite the title of Adrienne Rich's 1973 poem, which became a mantra for scholars seeking to counteract historical erasure. Tillie Olsen (1912–2007), a Jewish writer who was born in Nebraska and spent most of her adult life in Northern California, spurred some of the earliest efforts of literary recovery when she rediscovered and republished Rebecca Harding Davis's novella *Life in the Iron Mills* (1861) in the 1970s. In 1978, Olsen published *Silences*, a groundbreaking work of feminist literary criticism, which sought to explain gendered and class constraints on the production of women's writing as well as the absence of women from the literary canon.[49]

It was also in the 1970s that historian Alice Kessler-Harris rescued the writer Anzia Yezierska from literary obscurity, a process that began with the republication of Yezierska's 1925 novel *Bread Givers* in 1975. Claimed as a foremother of Jewish American literature, Yezierska became the best-known early Jewish American woman writer and continues to be frequently taught and studied.[50] Through the 1980s and 1990s, such efforts continued with the publication of several monographs examining Jewish American women's writing and Ann Shapiro's reference book *Jewish American Women Writers: A Bio-Bibliographical and Critical Sourcebook*.[51] More recently, in the twenty-first century feminist scholars have upended the field of Yiddish literature by translating the work of Yiddish women writers into English, yielding new literary genealogies and "defy[ing] . . . received hierarchies and narratives of genre, geography, and gender."[52]

By examining understudied women writers and illuminating women-centered literary networks, *West of the Ghetto* participates in projects of feminist literary recovery and builds upon such scholarship of Jewish American women's literature as Diane Lichtenstein's *Writing Their Nations: The Tradition of Nineteenth-Century American Jewish Women Writers*—the only other monograph thus far to trace Jewish women's writing in the United States back to the nineteenth century. My aim is not simply to insert women's perspectives into a male-dominated canon; instead, by returning to a formative moment in the construction of Jewish American literary history, *West of the Ghetto* operates from the premise that women writers have been crucial to the development of Jewish American literature since its inception and testifies to the ways literary history has been constructed through "the distorting lenses of patriarchy and misogyny."[53] As Allison Schachter writes, "Recovering [the] voices [of women writers] is not merely an additive project, but rather a generative enterprise that requires transforming our narratives of literary and cultural history—and of modernity itself—to include their capacious visions."[54] It is my hope that the "capacious visions" of Wolf, Lowenberg, Michelson, Levy, and Strunsky will alter existing narratives and generate future scholarship—both on these writers themselves and on other Jewish American writers from varied backgrounds and regions.

The first two chapters of this book focus on domestic novels, building upon previous efforts to recover Emma Wolf as an important turn-of-the-twentieth-century fiction writer while also introducing Bettie Lowenberg, who has mostly escaped the attention of scholars.[55] Examining how Wolf used the conventions of the marriage plot as a means of negotiating Jewish sameness and difference in relation to gentile America, the first chapter begins with an analysis of her novels *Other Things Being Equal* (1892) and *Heirs of Yesterday* (1900). Set in the San Francisco Reform community and featuring cultured, professional, well-off Jews who could not be differentiated from their non-Jewish neighbors except in their religious practices, Wolf's novels challenge the dominant critical paradigms established by literary critics who have addressed the relationship between intermarriage and assimilation in early Jewish American fiction. In Wolf's work, interfaith union is not a means of assimilation, but instead "a grave experiment" in social equality between Jews and Christians.[56] In my analysis of Wolf's fiction, I further demonstrate her importance to transatlantic literary history and theories of ethnic identity by examining her correspondence with Israel Zangwill; I argue that Zangwill's 1908 play, *The Melting Pot*, which popularized the concept of the "melting pot" as a potent metaphor for American identity, borrowed from Wolf's symbolic use of the interfaith marriage plot.

The next chapter takes up the case of Lowenberg, a prominent California clubwoman and reformer. I discuss her contributions to turn-of-the-twentieth-century letters as the leader of literary and cultural societies that allowed middle- and upper-class Jewish women to participate in the social and intellectual life of San Francisco and to devote themselves to patriotic and charitable causes. In the last decades of her life, Lowenberg combined her commitment to civic ideals with her literary inclinations as the author of novels that employed tragic marriage plots in the service of social reform. Set in a Midwestern town, her 1908 novel, *The Irresistible Current*, for instance, used the complicated entanglements of interfaith romance to advocate the elimination of religious barriers between Jews and Christians. I argue that Lowenberg's plea for universal religion imagines alternatives to the pluralist and assimilationist stances prevalent in canonical early Jewish American fiction set in the urban Northeast.

Chapter 3 further expands the regional parameters of Jewish American literature by analyzing an autobiographical narrative about growing up Jewish in nineteenth-century Northern California: Harriet Lane Levy's modernist memoir *920 O'Farrell Street* (1947). Analyzing Levy's use of the Victorian house as a structuring device, I argue that *920 O'Farrell Street* alters current understandings of Jewish American literary history by mapping Jewishness onto the geographic and architectural sites of Old San Francisco and displacing the ghetto as the sole locus of Jewish life and literature in the United States. Jewish American literary scholarship's New York-centrism and its privileging of the ghetto tale have obscured the pivotal role played by California Jewish women in the early stages of the modernist movement. As a corrective, I preface my close reading of the memoir with background on Levy, placing her in the context of a group of remarkable women—including Gertrude Stein, an Oakland resident in her youth, and Alice B. Toklas, Levy's O'Farrell Street neighbor—who moved between the middle-class Jewish communities of the Bay Area and the Left Bank of Paris in the early twentieth century.

Chapter 4 considers the wide-ranging oeuvre of Levy's cousin, Miriam Michelson, a journalist, suffragist, and author of feminist fiction. This chapter begins by offering a literary-biographical overview of Michelson's career; through a reading of her autobiographical novel, *The Madigans* (1904), I demonstrate that her work is a product of her experiences as a Jewish girl on the nineteenth-century multiethnic frontier, which shaped her attitudes toward gender, race, and class. I go on to argue that the interplay between Michelson's journalistic and fictional work—especially in her 1905 episodic novel *A Yellow Journalist*—enriches our understanding of turn-of-the-twentieth-century American literature in terms of gender, ethnicity, and cross-racial representations. I examine how Michelson drew on her experiences as a newspaper reporter for San Francisco's top dailies to create popular magazine fiction and bestselling novels with audacious, slang-speaking New Women protagonists. Set in the West, Michelson's fiction was populated by Irish, Black, Chinese, Hawaiian, and Native American characters. Her work thus testifies to the ways that Jewish writers captured the regional and ethno-racial diversity of American life and were engaged with cultures and traditions other than their own—an aspect of literary history sometimes forgotten among the New York ghetto tales that currently make up the early Jewish American canon. Unearthing Michelson's fiction and nonfiction as artifacts of turn-of-the-twentieth-century literary and periodical culture, I restore this fascinating woman writer to her rightful place in feminist literary history. Far from being limited to the ghetto (per Halper's quibble), Michelson's experiments with place, time, and genre exhibit the extraordinary range of first-generation Jewish writing in America and enrich our understanding of American women writers' contributions to journalism, magazine culture, and activism.

The book's final chapter turns to Anna Strunsky, a Russian immigrant woman who was part of the late nineteenth-century migration of eastern European Jews that was responsible for producing the genre of ghetto literature. While Strunsky's socialism links her to many of the New York writers of the period, her politics found expression in genres other than ghetto fiction, and her career attests to the ways Jewish immigrant writers were involved in varied artistic movements. This chapter addresses Strunsky's early life as a socialist activist and writer in bohemian San Francisco, offering an in-depth interpretation of her first book, *The Kempton-Wace Letters* (1903), an epistolary novel written in collaboration with Jack London that is partially set in Northern California. I situate the text and its production history in the context of Strunsky's real-life correspondence with London, the eugenicist beliefs that kept London from marrying his Jewish collaborator despite their erotically charged intellectual partnership, and critical debates about women's literary production and the meaning of intermarriage in the American cultural imagination. Although Strunsky rarely wrote explicitly about Jewishness or Jewish topics, I demonstrate how her literary interests and political passions were shaped by her background as a Russian Jewish immigrant woman reared on the freedoms of turn-of-the-twentieth-century intellectual life in San Francisco.

Part literary criticism, part cultural history, and part collective biography, *West of the Ghetto* draws on a wide variety of print and archival sources—newspapers, magazines, novels, memoirs, letters, diaries, scrapbooks, and unpublished manuscripts—to present case studies of Jewish women whose lives and work have long been obscured. Resisting the New York-centrism that dominates scholarship on Jewish American literature and culture, this book explores the newspaper offices, universities, bohemian cafés, synagogues, and Jewish neighborhoods of turn-of-the-twentieth-century San Francisco, while also taking excursions around the globe to the salons of avant-garde Paris and the anti-annexation protests in late nineteenth-century Hawaii. The writings of Wolf, Lowenberg, Levy, Michelson, and Strunsky serve as proof that, despite the dominance of the ghetto tale, there is no single story of Jewish life in America. By situating their careers alongside each other, I further demonstrate that there was no single path by which fin de siècle Jewish women entered the public sphere and exercised their creativity to propel the nation out of Victorianism and into modernity. My analysis of the varied representations of unconventional women in the fiction and nonfiction of these pioneering writers brings to light their significant contributions to American literary culture, which have had far-reaching implications beyond the Gilded Age and Progressive Era.

1
Marriage Plots and Melting Pots

Deghettoizing American Jewish Fiction

Most scholars of American literary history are familiar with William Dean Howells's championing of ghetto fiction, especially the work of immigrant writer Abraham Cahan, for the way such writing exemplified the aesthetic principles of realism. For Howells, writers of "the Hebraic school" such as Cahan, Montague Glass, and Fannie Hurst displayed an "instinct for reality," and the streets of New York provided them with raw material that lent itself well to being rendered in gritty detail.[1] The fiction of ghetto writers succeeds because they "persuade us that they have told the truth," explained Howells.[2] Yet literary scholars have paid considerably less attention to realist Jewish American writers whose work is set outside the ghetto. This chapter considers one such writer, Emma Wolf, whose novels about middle-class Jewish life in late nineteenth-century San Francisco offer important alternatives to the ghetto genre, demonstrating not only the diversity of the Jewish experience in the United States but also the diverse ways that Jewish writers have contributed to understandings of race, ethnicity, and religion in American culture.

Despite Howells's praise of ghetto fiction, the genre had its fair share of detractors in its day. In both the mainstream and Jewish press, critics accused Jewish writers of sacrificing truth for caricature and exoticism in their depictions of ghetto life, betraying their own people as well as the very principles of realism that Howells extolled. The debate about whether or not the ghetto was a fit subject for literary art initially came to a head over the publication of Cahan's 1896 novella *Yekl: A Tale of the New York Ghetto* and the 1899 play *Children of the Ghetto*, an adaptation of the novel by British writer Israel Zangwill, whose stories of the London ghetto and subsequent drama about American immigrants, *The Melting Pot* (1908), profoundly influenced many Jewish American writers.[3]

The dissenters were often upper-class Jews from German and Sephardic backgrounds who wanted to distance themselves from their newly arrived eastern European coreligionists and feared that they would be associated with such lowly literary representations of ghetto Jews, with their broken English, unrefined manners, and outdated traditions. In *The American Israelite*, for instance, Julius Wise, a prominent Chicago physician who wrote under the pseudonym "Nickerdown," issued a scathing attack on Cahan, accusing him of "intentionally exaggerat[ing] what is worst among his own class of people," labeling him "a scoundrel [who lies] for the sake of a few dollars" and calling for a boycott of magazines that publish his "vile lucubration."[4]

A more measured critique came from the pen of writer Annie Nathan Meyer. A Sephardic Jew who dated her family's American heritage back to the Revolution and a public advocate of women's education and other causes, Meyer was known for founding Barnard College. While acknowledging the "genius" of Zangwill and Cahan, Meyer summarized the concerns of her affluent, professional class in this way:

> They realize perfectly that the foreign-looking, strange-speaking Hebrew of the Ghetto, with Talmudic lore at the end of his tongue, and a frayed *talith* at the end of his shoulder, is infinitely better "copy" than the Talmudically ignorant Americanized Hebrew, who drives in his automobile or sits with his Gentile brethren on charitable boards and missions. The Americanized Hebrew is growing a little tired of this reiteration of the Ghetto type which the Gentile world find so interesting within the covers of a book. After all, when the good American used to be piqued because the cowboy filled the horizon of literary London, it was given him to point to some novels dealing with the average American banker who prefers to take his promenades without his six-shooter. But to the Americanized Hebrew is denied *in toto* the luxury of pointing to any literature that pretends to describe him seriously . . . [T]here is implanted in the breast of the Jew, quite as well as in the breast of his Gentile brother, the . . . desire . . . to hold up his resemblances rather than his differences. The Jew is doing his best to show off his fine Oxford cloth coat of latest cut, while the public persists in looking for the gabardine.

Meyer's response goes deeper than the anger voiced by Wise. The common representation of the ghetto Jew is not simply an "academic question of Art," she writes, but also "a very real social problem." Given Jews' history of exile and the antisemitism that continued to plague even upper-class Jews who found themselves "bracketed with 'dogs and other nuisances' at some select hotels and apartment houses," she asked if it was not wiser for Jewish writers to promote their similarities to, rather than their differences from, gentiles.[5]

While Meyer occasionally gave voice to what she called "the unwritten-up Jew" in her own fiction, California novelist Emma Wolf offered the most sustained articulation of Jewishness through the lens of genteel, rather than ghetto, realism.[6] Two of Wolf's novels, *Other Things Being Equal* (1892) and *Heirs of Yesterday* (1900), feature cultured, professional, well-off Jews who could not be differentiated from their gentile neighbors except in their religious practices and affiliations. Both are domestic novels relying on the conventions of the marriage plot, but with a Jewish twist. They are thus successors to George Eliot's Victorian novel *Daniel Deronda* (1876) and antecedents to Edith Wharton's realist *The House of Mirth* (1905), part of an Anglophone literary tradition in which characters' Jewish backgrounds complicate resolutions to the marriage plot. In *Other Things Being Equal*, Wolf's first novel, the cultural taboo against intermarriage presents an obstacle for a Jewish protagonist in love with a Christian man, while the would-be lovers at the center of *Heirs of Yesterday*, although both Jewish by birth, find themselves divided over whether they should continue to identify as such.

In its front-page review of *Heirs of Yesterday*, *The Jewish Messenger* identified Wolf as "one of the rare exceptions to the general rule" in the recent explosion of Jewish fiction. "She is to be expressly omitted from the category of Jewish novelists who exploit their religion and special class of people and call the result literature," the article stated, going on to note that Wolf's "delicacy, spirituality, [and] intellectuality are not restricted to Jewish subjects, although she has written with power and suggestiveness on certain Jewish character-studies and problems."[7] The fact that Wolf did not limit herself to Jewish subjects drew notice from other critics as well. In his review of *The Joy of Life* (1896), one of Wolf's novels without Jewish characters, Zangwill described "the Jewish Authoress" as much more than a "popular 'lady novelist.'" Her work "stands out luminous and arrestive amid the thousand-and-one tales of our overproductive generation," wrote Zangwill, while another review of *The Joy of Life* concluded with this declaration: "Emma Wolf is not only the best Jewish fiction writer of America, but the peer of the best novelists."[8]

Largely overlooked today even by scholars of American Jewish fiction, Wolf's writings, as well as her background, compel a reevaluation of early Jewish American literary history, which has positioned eastern European immigrant writers as its forefathers and foremothers and New York as its cultural epicenter.[9] In surveying the roots of Jewish American literature, scholars have gravitated toward writers such as Cahan and Anzia Yezierska, whose dialect-speaking characters and ghetto settings better fit the broader paradigms of ethnic literary studies. The work of eastern European immigrants set in the tenements has much in common with well-known texts by African American, Asian American, and Latinx writers, which similarly represent working-class characters and experiences. In late nineteenth-century San Francisco, however, the largest and most visible part of the Jewish population was middle class, and Jews with money rarely qualify as "ethnic." Wolf's work played a significant part in shaping notions of ethnic American identity despite the author's middle-class, Western background. Her novels offer opportunities to deghettoize American Jewish fiction, expanding our understanding of fin de siècle Jewish literary culture in the United States in terms of gender, class, and region.

It is not incidental that Wolf's first novel utilized an intermarriage plot. Though most closely associated with the Victorian novel in Britain and domestic and sentimental fiction in the nineteenth-century United States, the marriage plot continued to have resonance for Progressive-Era writers, many of whom used it to explore gender and class politics, to mark the breakdown of separate-spheres ideology, and to agitate for matrimonial reform.[10] Intermarriage, meanwhile, has long been one of the most prevalent themes in American fiction by and about Jews, as well as one of the most hotly debated topics in American Jewish life. As Jews and Christians increasingly intermarried in the nineteenth century,[11] the topic entered the public discourse, with, on the one hand, rabbis sermonizing against it and, on the other, eugenicists fueling nativist fears by warning of the threat to Anglo-Saxon purity. Because Jewishness was viewed as an ethno-racial difference as well as a religious one, the debate over marriage between Christians and Jews was part of a larger discourse about interracial coupling and miscegenation.[12] Intermarriage, then, was a loaded trope, a means for those within and outside Jewish communities to express and explore anxieties about immigration and assimilation, intermixing and racial purity, and loss of religious faith and tradition in a modern, increasingly secular world. Fiction provided a relatively safe space in which to imagine tragic consequences, not only of intermarriage, but also of the prohibition on interethnic romance. It also provided a space in which to imagine the possibilities that intermarriage held for the betterment of Jewish lives and American culture in the future.

Wolf's intermarriage plot differs in significant ways from the more familiar ones that have entered the canon of Jewish American fiction, and it thus defies many of the critical paradigms established about interethnic relations. Most tellingly, although Wolf's *Other Things Being Equal* explores controversies about intermarriage, it ultimately offers a mostly harmonious vision. Rather than cautioning that exogamy may signal the demise of the Jewish people, Wolf's novel pushes for acceptance of intermarriage as a barometer of social equality and a testament to the sacredness of love between soulmates. In this respect, Wolf's views differ from those of many other Jewish writers and prominent religious leaders.[13] Some of Wolf's optimism about intermarriage may be attributed to differences of gender; because liberal and traditional Judaism of the time determined descent matrilineally, Jewish women who intermarried did not necessarily threaten the continuance of their people. However, Wolf's vision of intermarriage as an ideal also bears notable similarities to one of the most famous male-authored representations of interethnic romance in American culture: the passionate relationship between Jewish composer David Quixano and Christian settlement worker Vera Revendal in Zangwill's *The Melting Pot*. Using the Quixano-Revendal union to represent America as a "fusion" of different races, Zangwill's 1908 play popularized the concept of the "melting pot" as an enduring, if contested, metaphor for American identity in the twentieth century. As this chapter shows, Wolf actively stirred the pot that produced that potent metaphor.

In my analysis of Wolf's fiction, and by considering her relationship with and to Zangwill, I demonstrate her importance to theories of

American ethnic identity and her centrality to transnational American literary history. Though Wolf and Zangwill never met in person, their correspondence and reviews of each other's books provide evidence of their mutual influence on one another—and, in turn, on American culture. This chapter begins by providing background on Wolf and examining how she used the conventions of the marriage plot as a means of negotiating Jewish sameness and difference in relation to gentile America. I argue that Wolf challenges the dominant critical paradigms established by literary critics and historians such as Leslie Fiedler, Frederic Cople Jaher, and Adam Sol, who have addressed the relationship between intermarriage and assimilation in early Jewish American fiction. In Wolf's work, interfaith union is not a means of upward mobility, but instead an experiment in social equality between Jews and Christians. Wolf's plea for religious tolerance is imbricated with her characters' negotiations of white American identity, which occur in relation to other ethno-racial groups and, in *Heirs of Yesterday*, against the backdrop of late nineteenth-century expansionism. In extending the scope of Progressive-Era Jewish literary history beyond the ghetto tale, Wolf's fiction complicates the relationship between Jewish texts and ethnic studies, offering new insights into processes of comparative racialization and opening space for considerations of Jewish cultural engagements with US imperialism.

"A Grave Experiment": Intermarriage in *Other Things Being Equal*

According to established genealogies of Jewish literary history, modern Jewish American fiction began with the ghetto tale.[14] But Wolf, one of the earliest Jewish American women novelists to achieve renown, was no child of the ghetto.[15] Born in San Francisco in 1865, she grew up in a large family of French-Alsatian pioneers. Among the first Jewish settlers in the Bay Area, her father, Simon Wolf, was a successful businessman who established cigar and general merchandise stores in San Francisco and Contra Costa County. The Wolfs belonged to Temple Emanu-El, a congregation founded by traders and merchants during the Gold Rush of 1849. By the late nineteenth century, Emanu-El, under the leadership of Rabbis Elkan Cohn and Jacob Voorsanger, had become one of the nation's leading Reform synagogues, initiating looser interpretations of religious law in order "to remake the Jewish liturgy, ritual, and credo to suit the values of the New World."[16]

As Marc Lee Raphael has demonstrated, Voorsanger, who was appointed rabbi of Emanu-El in 1886, one year after the Pittsburgh Platform, strongly emphasized the progressive potential of Reform Judaism by drawing links to the American belief in "manifest destiny" and its implied assumption of white superiority. A proponent of assimilation in all matters but religion, Voorsanger was concerned that the influx of newly arrived eastern coreligionists with their "'meaningless, Oriental rites'" would "chain Jews to the ghetto," going so far as to support immigration restrictions to ensure that Jews who were already settled in the United States would not be deemed backward and racially inferior by association. According to Raphael, Voorsanger's convictions resulted in a "general rejection of all which stood between Judaism and the non-Jewish world" for many Emanu-El members.[17] Thus, in accordance with the Pittsburgh Platform, practices that would have interfered in Jews' ability to socialize and conduct business with their gentile counterparts, such as kosher dietary laws or strict Sabbath observance, were largely abandoned. Members of Emanu-El formed an elite society of Jews who had emigrated from central Europe in the mid-nineteenth century and who lived as neighbors in upper-middle-class Pacific Heights, the setting for Wolf's novels. Although the Jews of Emanu-El modeled their community and social lives on those of their gentile neighbors, they continued to identify publicly as Jews, believing that the practice of liberal Judaism created "alternatives to assimilation," in the words of one historian of the American Reform movement.[18]

Wolf's work was shaped by the late nineteenth-century Reform movement as well as by personal and familial circumstances. Her writing career began at an early age, coinciding with her father's sudden death, most likely from a heart attack as he returned from a business trip in 1878.[19] The death of a father comes to play a symbolic role in many of her works, and, especially in the Jewish-themed texts, it represents a break with tradition and serves as a catalyst for the children to marry and form families of their own. Wolf herself was born with a physical disability, which enabled her to become a woman of letters. An undeveloped left arm prevented her from following the conventional route for women of her social echelon and thus freed her from expectations of marriage, childbearing, and other domestic duties.[20] From this vantage point, she became a careful observer of her seven sisters' courtships and marriages, which provided her with raw material for her domestic tales. Constance Herriott, the heroine of her 1894 novel, *A Prodigal in Love*, for example, devotes her life to ensuring the happiness and well-being of her five younger sisters following the death of their parents. True to her name, Constance goes so far as to sacrifice her own love for the writer Hall Kenyon, who has also claimed the heart of the second eldest sister, Eleanor. In a reversal of Jane Austen's novel of sisterhood *Sense and Sensibility* (1811), Wolf's Eleanor is "sensibility" to Constance's "sense," and the resulting marriage between Eleanor and Kenyon leads to heartbreak and estrangement before resolving in love and understanding.

Emma Wolf in 1913. Courtesy of Donald Auslen and Barbara Cantalupo.

Wolf favored realistic depictions of love and marriage, often incorporating references to fairy tales to juxtapose her realism with the earlier romantic tradition of idealized love. Her short story "One-Eye, Two-Eye, Three-Eye"—which, though it appeared in *The American Jewess* in 1896, is devoid of explicitly Jewish content—directly acknowledges and then rejects the fairy tale on which it is based to contrast the love lives of three sisters. "Fairy tales are impossible nowadays," the story begins. "Fact is quite interesting enough at this epoch . . . Formerly we saw as through a glass darkly, now face to face."[21] As for other women writers of the era, including Wharton, Charlotte Perkins Gilman, and Kate Chopin, realism–or, seeing "face to face"—allowed Wolf to offer intertwined, if more understated, critiques of romanticized domesticity and patriarchy. Her fiction may conclude with domestic happy endings, but the bonds of matrimony, at least initially, restrict women's intellectual and artistic inclinations and ambitions, a theme she derived from observing members of her family. For example, one of Emma's sisters, Alice S. Wolf, a contributor of short stories to the San Francisco literary magazine *The Argonaut* and other periodicals, saw her career as a writer come to an end when she wed Colonel William MacDonald, by whom she had been employed as a private secretary. Alice's one novel, *A House of Cards* (1896), published two years before her wedding, dealt with a woman who reluctantly chose marriage over a career as a teacher.[22] It was left to Emma, the single sister, to document stories of women who sought "fulfillment"—as her last novel, published in 1916, was titled—in intellectual activities rather than primarily in love and marriage.[23]

As in better-known fiction by Gilman, Wharton, and Chopin, the duties of marriage conflict with women's intellectual and professional aspirations in the writings of the Wolf sisters. But Emma's first novel, *Other Things Being Equal*, centered instead on a different obstacle to marriage: religious differences. The heroine, Ruth Levice, the beloved only child of prosperous French Jewish immigrants who mix freely with their Christian neighbors, finds love and intellectual companionship with a Unitarian, Dr. Herbert Kemp. Ruth's father, however, objects to their marriage on the grounds of the "great difference between the Jewish race and traditions, and the Christian," fearing that his daughter, and her future children, would face a lifetime of social ostracism from both religious communities.[24] By the end of the novel, however,

Mr. Levice is persuaded by the force of their love to overturn his objections. Stricken ill while doing business on the East Coast, he returns home to San Francisco, where his daughter and Dr. Kemp grant him his deathbed wish, marrying that very day so that he can bless their new life together and publicly sanction their union as "a grave experiment" in social equality.[25] In taking her protagonist's name from the Book of Ruth, Wolf alludes to a biblical precedent for treating mixed marriage as viable for the Jewish people.

Through its deployment of the intermarriage theme, *Other Things Being Equal* challenges several critical paradigms in the scholarship on early American Jewish literature. In a 1958 survey tracing the American Jewish novel from its inception in the nineteenth century through the 1920s writings of Ben Hecht and Ludwig Lewisohn, Leslie Fiedler noted the prevalence of the "erotic-assimilationist" theme in which the male protagonist's love affairs take on symbolic meaning in relation to his social ascent.[26] According to Frederic Cople Jaher, the eroticization of assimilation reached its apotheosis in post–World War II fiction and was closely associated with the trope of the self-hating Jew; in novels by writers such as Philip Roth, the male protagonist's lust for a non-Jewish woman, often referred to with the Yiddish word *shiksa*, was equated with a desire to rid himself of Jewish difference and to elevate his status in order to be accepted by the gentile majority. "Gentile women represent tickets of entry into middle- and upper-class WASP society; they are trophies of success," states Jaher, juxtaposing the fantasy of "the genteel, elegant, Anglo-American goddess" with the stereotype of the unattractive, unrefined, and often vulgar "Jewess."[27]

While Fiedler and Jaher exclusively draw their evidence from interfaith relationships in fiction by men, scholars who also include women writers in their analysis have noted a similar dynamic, albeit one that reverses gender roles, portraying unions between Jewish women and gentile men (*shaygets* in Yiddish). In the fiction of Anzia Yezierska, taking a gentile lover or husband functions as an escape route from the ghetto. Sonya Vrunsky, the protagonist of Yezierska's 1923 novel, *Salome of the Tenements*, for example, orchestrates an elaborate performance, making herself look "Fifth-Avenue born," in order to win the heart of the millionaire philanthropist John Manning and flee her working-class, immigrant roots.[28] But if Sonya and Manning are to provide the prototype, then interfaith, interclass unions are cross-cultural experiments doomed to failure. Sonya comes to realize that "just as fire and water cannot fuse, neither could her Russian Jewish soul fuse with the stolid, the unimaginative, the invulnerable thickness of [her] New England puritan" husband.[29] She divorces Manning, and by the end of the novel, finds compatibility, if not passionate love, with a Jewish husband. As Adam Sol observes, intermarriage in early Jewish American fiction represents a "problematic solution to the temptations of assimilation," indicating that a fully Americanized identity is unattainable—and undesirable—for Jewish immigrants.[30] In favoring endogamy over exogamy, the works thus far discussed by critics conform to ingrained expectations about ethnic literature—namely, that ethnic literature would detail the *process* of Americanization, exploring the allure of, and obstacles to, assimilation while ultimately expressing regret about the loss of cultural heritage.[31]

Wolf's novel may explore the obstacles to a union between individuals of different faiths, but it ultimately depicts intermarriage as an attainable ideal rather than a "problematic solution." Although *Other Things Being Equal* offers little insight into the couple's married life together, concluding as it does with the solemnity of Ruth's mourning for her father, it promises a future of matrimonial happiness and harmony. "We are everything to each other," Ruth tells Kemp adoringly in the novel's final pages. "We are—all the world to each other. We are—the past, present, and future to each other—we are husband and wife."[32] Importantly, Ruth's attraction to Kemp does not reflect a desire to eradicate Jewish difference in order to achieve acceptance by mainstream society. Instead, as the title, *Other Things Being Equal*, suggests, intermarriage functions as a public affirmation of a social equality that has mostly been achieved. The "erotic-assimilationist" novel depends upon the attraction of opposites; difference itself is eroticized. Cultured, refined, and well-mannered, products of the same affluent social milieu, Ruth and Kemp are drawn to each other due more to their similarities than to their differences. Ruth's father explains this in describing how he overcame his opposition to the couple's marriage:

> I grasped your two images before me and drew parallels: Socially—in my opinion society is a mutual drawing together of resemblances—socially, each was as fair as the other. Mentally, the

woman was of the same stratum as the man. Physically, both were perfect types of pure, healthy blood. Morally, both were irreproachable. Religiously, both held a broad, abiding love for man and God. I stood convicted. I was in the position of a blind reactionary who, with a beautiful picture before him, fastens his critical, condemning gaze upon a rusting nail in the wall behind—a nail even now loosened, and which, some day, please God, shall fall.[33]

Ruth's father reverses his initial judgment, replacing it with a "beautiful picture" of equality that derives foremost from commonalities in social environment. When set in the ghetto, narratives of interethnic romance necessitate spatial crossings. Inhabiting distinct social environs, the lovers must transcend segregated space, moving, for instance, between uptown and downtown; thus, as exemplified by Yezierska's *Salome of the Tenements*, ethno-religious difference becomes inextricable from class difference. In *Other Things Being Equal*, in contrast, socioeconomic class brings the lovers together; they reside in the same middle-class neighborhood, fortuitously discovering early on that they live only "a few blocks" apart from one another.[34]

While social class easily justifies the rightness of the couple's mutual attraction, Mr. Levice's speech must work to overwrite other differences that interfere in the image of equality—differences of religion, race, and even gender. Rather than identifying along conventional gender lines with her mother, a "nervous and hysterical" woman whose primary interests are shopping and society affairs, Ruth is closer in temperament to her studious father, an "intellectual, self-made man" who enjoys his hard-earned prosperity by indulging in books.[35] Mr. Levice takes great pride in his daughter's intellect, believing that her cerebral qualities—rather than traditionally domestic and feminine traits—make her a fitting mate for Kemp. Religious differences, too, are rendered insignificant, as Mr. Levice emphasizes their shared monotheistic, Judeo-Christian values. Perhaps the most interesting aspect of the speech, however, is the father's assertion that Ruth and Kemp were "both perfect types of pure, healthy blood," affirming the description of each "as fair as the other" and seemingly rejecting his earlier concern about insurmountable racial differences.

Even as they evoke a popular scientific belief in eugenics, which categorized "types" according to biological ancestry in the service of improving the racial quality of future generations, Mr. Levice's words speak to the mutability of racial categories and discourse. As Eric Goldstein has argued, in the late nineteenth and early twentieth centuries, American Jews used shifting terms of language as they "negotiated their place in a complex racial world."[36] In the 1890s, most American Jews viewed their racial distinctiveness in positive terms; racial language and imagery—especially that of blood—were means of preserving identity in the diaspora. It is significant, then, that Mr. Levice does not claim that Ruth and Kemp are "of one blood." His language allows for Jewish racial distinction, while asserting that his family's biological make-up is equally "pure" and "healthy." As Goldstein has shown, intermarriage was an especially fraught site in turn-of-the-twentieth-century America because "a definition of Jewishness grounded in blood and ancestry often set the limit of social interaction with non-Jews at marriage."[37] Mr. Levice gets around such limitations by arguing that intolerance toward intermixing was a product of outmoded thought. While dramas like *The Melting Pot* would later sanction intermarriage, at times unwittingly fostering the belief that "racial amalgamation was a prerequisite to becoming true Americans,"[38] Wolf's novel leaves open the question of "amalgamation," or race-mixing, by sidestepping further discussion of Ruth and Kemp's offspring, children whom Mr. Levice will not live to see. The novel concludes with only the vaguest of glances forward: "And so the future took them."[39] As uncertain as the ending is, by virtue of having a Jewish female protagonist, Wolf's novel allows for a future that may include Jewish children, a possibility foreclosed by texts like *The Melting Pot* that depict unions between Jewish men and Christian women.

Mr. Levice's change of heart may depend upon his ability to rationalize away differences between Christians and Jews, but Wolf's representation of intermarriage does not adhere to the conventional paradigms of assimilationist literature, in which the desire for sameness is aligned with Jewish shame and self-hatred. Ruth's love for Kemp also leads to soul-searching on the daughter's part, as she comes to a deeper understanding of herself as a Jewish woman. Just as Ruth's father reverses his "reactionary" position against intermarriage for a more modern vision of social equality, Ruth comes closer to seeing her father's supposedly old-fashioned point of view. Although she earlier questioned her father's objections to her marriage, reminding him that he "taught [her] to look upon my Christian friends as upon my Jewish," she later concedes that his claims of Jewish difference were not completely unfounded.[40] The prospect of marriage to a Christian provides an occasion for Wolf's heroine to express pride in the ethno-religious identity that sets her apart. Horrified, for example, by her father's suggestion that her marriage would be perceived by others as a renunciation of Judaism, Ruth declares, "I am a Jewess, and will die one."[41] Her father's argument against intermarriage also allows Ruth, seemingly for the first time in her life, to entertain the possibility that she herself could be subjected to prejudice based on imagined notions of racial difference and inferiority. "Involuntarily the Christian mind always rears its ghettoes," she tells Kemp in response to his insistence that there is no distinction between Christian and Jew. "And in that mental ghetto, I want you to know, I belong—and proudly."[42] In "erotic-assimilationist" novels, a union with a gentile is usually understood as an act of distancing oneself from one's Jewishness; only through the repudiation of such a union could the protagonists reclaim their Jewish selves. In *Other Things Being Equal*, however, Ruth comes to embrace her Jewish identity through her union with a Christian man, acknowledging its distinctiveness in a way that she did not when her loyalty to her faith and people went unchallenged.

In the familiar immigrant tale of the era, the "foreign-looking, strange-speaking Hebrew of the Ghetto" provided the local color; he was a part of his surroundings, and his surroundings were a part of him.[43] In contrast to the physical and material barriers present in "erotic-assimilationist" novels, the Jewish "ghetto" in Wolf's fiction is a mental construct, a means of articulating elusive differences—differences that become a source of pride rather than anxiety. Spatial "ghettos" do exist in Wolf's Old San Francisco, but, significantly, they do not contain Jews. Observe, for instance, Wolf's description of Ruth's excursion into the city's "foreign and picturesque" quarters, where, early in the novel, she is sent by Kemp on errands of good will: "So immersed was she in this call of her deeper being, she walked on, . . . [past] the old gray Greek church with its dome and minarets, the long flights of wooden steps leading up to the tinder-box homes with their spindly balconies, the Italian fishermen and bambinos, the Negroes and gayly-garbed Negresses, the blue-smocked Chinese with their queues, trotting along imperturbably—the whole motley bouquet of the Latin quarter." Though she supposedly remains "unconscious of her . . . surroundings,"[44] this array of racial and ethnic types sharply contrasts with Ruth's gentility and reminds the reader of the heroine's lack of "foreignness." The portrayal of Ruth as charitable do-gooder, soulmate to the similarly selfless Dr. Kemp, further emphasizes the protagonist's affinity with the Christian majority, especially through her adherence to the doctrine of brotherly love, but without compelling her to sacrifice her religion or her family.

It is notable, however, that the novel promotes such "resemblances" between Jews and their Christian brethren at the expense of cross-racial and interethnic solidarity. *Other Things Being Equal* may allow for a successful interreligious union, and it effectively upends Jewish stereotypes, but it does so by reinforcing exotic stereotypes, and the hierarchical "ghettoization," of other racial and ethnic groups. The contrast of Ruth with Black Americans and Chinese immigrants, as well as with newer European immigrants, reverberates with Mr. Levice's characterization of his daughter as pure-blooded, a description that deems her more fit to reproduce with Anglo-Saxons. The multiethnic setting of this episode lends support for Goldstein's claim that Jews actively negotiated their whiteness in relation to other racial minorities. Positioning its Jewish characters outside—and as outsiders to—the ghetto, *Other Things Being Equal* anticipated Annie Nathan Meyer's call for fiction that describes Jews "seriously . . . [by] hold[ing] up . . . resemblances rather than . . . differences." It did so, however, by using, rather than debunking, the logic of race and blood as grounds for equality.

Wolf's imaginative resolutions to the American quandary of difference versus equality did not satisfy all of her readers. Some took issue with the novel's representation of mixed marriage. In an 1896 speech before the New York Section of the National Council of Jewish Women (NCJW), for instance, Annie Josephine Levi, a fellow writer who became best known for her book of devotional literature, *Meditations of the Heart: A Book of Private Devotion for Old and Young* (1900), acknowledged her respect for Wolf's "charmingly told story," but she warned that Wolf's "unsatisfactory solution of the intermarriage problem, wherein religious sympathy is a minor consideration," might "sow dangerous seeds in the minds of youth."[45] Despite, or perhaps because of, these concerns, Wolf's intermarriage novel remained a popular success, read and discussed, for example, by Jewish women's clubs around the nation.[46] For many readers, the novel "untangled a knotty problem," as the *San Francisco Chronicle* reported in a story on Wolf, adding that although the author had received many thank-you notes accompanied by wedding announcements, she "has no idea how many marriages her story is responsible for."[47] While the novel has largely escaped attention by critics today, it is worth consideration not only for the way it influenced historical attitudes toward interfaith marriage, but also for the way its "unsatisfactory resolution of the intermarriage problem" productively unsettles established paradigms of Jewish American and ethnic literature.

"If You Are Jewish, Must I Not Too Be Jew?": *Heirs of Yesterday* and the Melting Pot

Contrary to the received wisdom that exogamy necessarily attenuates Jewish identity, the intermarriage plot in *Other Things Being Equal* sets in motion a journey that brings Wolf's protagonist closer to her Jewishness, one that at the same time compels a redefinition of what it means to be Jewish and American. Wolf's next two novels, *A Prodigal in Love* (1894) and *The Joy of Life* (1896), similarly rely on the conventions of the marriage plot, even as they eliminate Jewish characters and themes. It would be a mistake, however, to read these two works as evidence of the author's turning away from her own Jewishness.[48] On both the local and national levels, Wolf was a part of an emergent Jewish literary scene that coincided with the rise of the woman's club movement in the 1890s. As a member of the Philomath Club, which was described by founder Bettie Lowenberg as "the first club composed of Jewish women with a regularly adopted constitution in the world" (and which will receive further attention in the next chapter), Wolf met to discuss literary and social issues with other Jewish women in San Francisco.[49] In the club's luxurious meeting space at the Palace Hotel, she would have attended lectures on German and English literature by Stanford University professors and delivered papers herself.[50] She published fiction and poetry in *The American Jewess*, a journal founded in 1895 by editor Rosa Sonneschein to serve as an unofficial promotional organ for the recently formed NCJW.[51] Wolf also reviewed works of ghetto fiction by Israel Zangwill and Martha Wolfenstein in the Jewish press. When Wolf returned to explicitly Jewish subject matter with her 1900 novel, *Heirs of Yesterday*, she once again mobilized a marriage plot as a means of exploring the shifting meanings of Jewishness in predominantly Christian America. Read in the context of Wolf's relationship with Zangwill, *Heirs of Yesterday* proves an important addition to transnational American literary history, demonstrating that turn-of-the-twentieth-century Anglophone Jewish fiction need not rehearse familiar ghetto tropes in order to contribute to our understanding of ethnicity and American culture.

In 1896, Wolf sent Zangwill a copy of *The Joy of Life*, initiating a correspondence between the two writers that lasted for at least four years.[52] The fact that Wolf reached out to a fellow Jewish writer, the best-known in the Anglo-Jewish world, indicates that she saw herself and her writing as part of a Jewish literary tradition. With *Children of the Ghetto: A Study of a Peculiar People* (1892), published in the same year as *Other Things Being Equal*, Zangwill had risen to fame on both sides of the Atlantic; his career as an author also gave him a platform for his political activism, which ranged from Zionism to women's suffrage.[53] Zangwill had not yet read Wolf's writing (her work had not been published in Britain), but he knew of her "vaguely—through [her] previous book on the intermarriage problem." Though the novel she sent him was absent of Jewish content, his letters indicate that he identified with her as a fellow Jewish writer. Thanking Wolf for the letter and book, which "enabled [him] to become aware of surely the most promising Jewish writer of the younger generation," Zangwill anoints her "the best product of American Judaism since Emma Lazarus."[54] Publicly, Zangwill also praised *The Joy of Life*, reviewing it in *The Jewish Chronicle* with the premise of introducing a "new" Jewish American novelist to readers on his side of the Atlantic.[55] In a brief item in *Cosmopolitan*, Zangwill described *The Joy of Life* as "remarkably virile, incisive and thoughtful, but full of the promise of still finer things to come."[56]

As for what those "finer things" might be, Zangwill had a specific idea in mind. Although he had not yet read *Other Things Being Equal*, he encouraged Wolf to return to Jewish themes. "Why not write the Jewish story which is stirring in your subconscious?" he asked. Recommending the Jewish Publication Society as an American publisher as long as the imprimatur would not "cramp" her, he urged honesty: "You must say exactly what you think about Jews & Judaism."[57] Zangwill also offered to help Wolf find a British publisher for her previous work, but when he read the copy of *Other Things Being Equal* she sent for this purpose, he came away less impressed, admitting privately to her that he "did not like [her] Jewish work as well [her] American." Though he credited his preference to the fact that *The Joy of Life* was the more "mature work," Zangwill's "tempered" praise for *Other Things Being Equal* can also be understood as a critique of what he saw as Wolf's failure to adhere to the tenets of realism. Suggesting that her characters were "vague idealisation[s]" rather than "types studied from . . . life," Zangwill revealed his discomfort with the way her work defied expectations for fin de siècle Anglo-Jewish fiction—namely, the conventions of ghetto realism that his own stories had helped to establish.[58] Contrary to Zangwill's critique, Wolf's characters were, in fact, drawn from the life she knew as a middle-class Jewish woman living in San Francisco. In this sense, Wolf's writing provided Zangwill with both an early awareness of the range of Jewish life in America and an entrée into the intricacies of the American "melting pot," which he would later come to experience firsthand when visiting the United States.

In his early assessment of Wolf's literary career, Zangwill divided her work into separate categories—"Jewish" or "American"—but, as her characterizations suggest, it is unclear that Wolf herself would have made so rigid a distinction. The book that she produced next, *Heirs of Yesterday*, took aim at exactly such divisive thinking. While she appeared to have followed Zangwill's advice, turning once again to American Jewish life, she also framed her new novel as a response to the ghetto tradition, with its tendency to play up Jewish difference—that is, the notion of Jews as a "peculiar people." Given the direction in which Zangwill's own work matured, cresting in 1908 with his melodramatic treatment of intermarriage and American Jewish life in *The Melting Pot*, the relationship between Zangwill and Wolf seems to be more than a unidirectional case of "transatlantic mentorship" (as Barbara Cantalupo has categorized it). Instead, the two writers had a reciprocal influence on the development of each other's work—and, in turn, on one of the most resonant concepts in American ethnic studies.

In his paradigm-defining study *Beyond Ethnicity: Consent and Descent in American Culture* (1986), Werner Sollors demonstrates how strongly Zangwill's *The Melting Pot* influenced sociological narratives about ethnicity, even those, like Horace Kallen's theory of cultural pluralism, which supposedly opposed Zangwill's assimilationist principles.[59] As Sollors argues, the concept of the "melting pot," as popularized in Zangwill's play, contributed to an understanding of American identity that privileged "consent" over "descent," one in which immigrants, regardless of their identities at birth, could transform themselves into Americans by choosing to embrace national ideals. Unlike most of Zangwill's stories about Jewish life in London, which take place in the East End ghetto, *The Melting Pot* is primarily set in a "non-Jewish borough of New York," home to the Quixanos, a family of Russian Jewish immigrants whose residence is "a curious blend of shabbiness, Americanism, Jewishness, and music."[60] The play's narrative conflict is the star-crossed love affair between Christian settlement worker Vera Revendal, herself a Russian immigrant, and Jewish composer David Quixano, whose idealistic rhetoric provides the central voice and motif of the play. In the play's most-quoted speech, David rhapsodizes about his adopted nation, the inspiration for his musical composition:

> America is God's Crucible, the great Melting-Pot where all the races of Europe are melting and reforming! Here you stand, good folk, think I, when I see them at Ellis Island, here you stand in your fifty groups, with your fifty languages and histories, and your fifty blood hatreds and rivalries. But you won't be long like that, brothers, for these are the fires of God you've come to—these are the fires of God. A fig for your feuds and vendettas! Germans and Frenchmen, Irishmen and Englishmen, Jews and Russians—into the Crucible with you all! God is making the American.[61]

The play's marriage plot puts David's idealism to the test, especially his belief that national "feuds and vendettas" could be left behind in the Old World. The conflict over the couple's religious differences is heightened by the discovery that state-sponsored antisemitism had violently intertwined their Russian pasts: Vera's father, Baron Revendal, was responsible for the murder of David's parents in the Kishinev pogrom of 1903. In the play's last act, which takes place at the Fourth of July premiere of the immigrant composer's American symphony, David and Vera—"Jew and Gentile"—overcome their differences and break free of the familial histories that threaten to drive them apart. Their union becomes the embodiment of the melting pot ideal. The play concludes with a dramatic image of their embrace as they stand upon the roof of the settlement house against the backdrop of the Statue of Liberty, as "the sound of voices and instruments joining in 'My Country, 'tis of Thee'" rises from below. Fulfilling David's prophecy for the American "Crucible," interfaith love brings about amalgamation, the "melt[ing]" and "fus[ing]" of "all nations and races" to form a new American identity.[62] In Sollors's words, the play's intermarriage plot "sacralizes loving consent as the abolition of prejudices of descent."[63]

Sollors's perceptive reading of the play accounts for antecedents to Zangwill's melting pot metaphor. He does not, however, fully consider sources for Zangwill's equally important use of a marriage plot. Although Zangwill reverses the gender positions of his interfaith couple and sets his play in New York, his symbolic use of intermarriage is indebted to Wolf's *Other Things Being Equal*. Like Kemp and Ruth, David and Vera do not reject their religious backgrounds. To her father's accusation that she has "become a Jewess," Vera replies, "No more than David has become a Christian. We were already at one."[64] Zangwill's prophesy of universal religion and racial amalgamation takes Wolf's vision of ethno-religious equality a step further. Instead of sidestepping the question of the next generation, as Wolf does, the play's ending paves the way for the coming of the future American, the "unborn millions, fated to fill this giant continent." With its evocations of manifest destiny, David's final "benediction" reaches westward, beyond the environs of New York to the rest of the nation.[65] For Zangwill, marriage—the bringing together of individuals to form "one"—provides a model of a consensual, rather than a consanguineal, relationship. By *choosing* to wed oneself to another, or by choosing to embrace the ideals of a new nation, the individual's identity is reformed, as he or she becomes part of a greater union.

Zangwill's use of marriage as a metaphor for consensual transformation also owes a debt to *Heirs of Yesterday*. "I have read 'Heirs of Yesterday' with much pleasure," Zangwill wrote to Wolf in December 1900, "not only on account of its art but of its information. The exact place of the Jew in the 'Republic of human brotherhood' is a point that interests me exceedingly. Apparently it is just above the coloured folk." With *Heirs of Yesterday*, Zangwill believed that Wolf was "sinking [her] shaft much deeper than" in her previous Jewish-themed novel.[66] Unlike the religious differences that separate Ruth and Kemp, the couple at the center of *Heirs of Yesterday*'s marriage plot are both Jewish according to the laws of descent, but they differ in terms of consent. The notion that endogamy and descent do not necessarily provide the groundwork for a harmonious union, and can even be divisive in a culture that prides itself on freedom of choice, is at the heart of *Heirs of Yesterday*. Set in the hills of Pacific Heights, where "the tide of Jewish social culture runs its mimic parallel alongside" the rest of San Francisco society, the book uses a love story to engage with questions of difference and equality central to the project of American democracy.[67]

By the time Wolf published *Heirs of Yesterday*, ghetto fiction had firmly secured its niche in Anglo-Jewish letters. Wolf thus explicitly positions *Heirs of Yesterday* as a response, distancing her writing from the trope of the slum-dwelling immigrant Jew while simultaneously acknowledging Zangwill, one of the originators of the genre. The novel's epigraph comes from "A Child of the Ghetto," the short story that introduces Zangwill's *Dreamers of the Ghetto* (1898), a book that Wolf had reviewed for *The American Jewess*: "For something larger had come into his life, a sense of a vaster universe without, and its spaciousness and strangeness filled his soul with a nameless trouble and a vague unrest. He was no longer a child of the Ghetto."[68]

Transposed from the conclusion of Zangwill's late nineteenth-century tale of a Venetian youth to the opening of Wolf's novel, published at the dawn of a new century, these lines characterize Philip May, the male protagonist of *Heirs of Yesterday*. A young physician who had trained in the East, Philip returns to the San Francisco home of his Yiddish-speaking father, Joseph May, a widowed merchant, and announces his intention to dissociate from the Jewish community and live his life as a gentile. Philip rejects his Jewishness for practical reasons—"I have discovered that to be a Jew, turn wheresoever you will, is to be socially handicapped for life"—as well as ideological ones: "I consider Judaism a dead letter, a monument to the past." Summarizing "a noted English litterateur, himself a Jew," presumably Zangwill, Philip describes the plight of Jews who have achieved economic and professional success: "hung between the Ghetto it has outlived and the Christian society it can neither live with nor without," the Jewish middle class is adrift, isolated by the "racial prejudices" that persist in the gentile mind.[69] As in *Other*

Things Being Equal, the ghetto is not a spatial entity that segregates Jews, but a mental construct, a metonym for ethno-religious difference and a vestige of the Old World that inhibits movement into modernity.

Heirs of Yesterday is notable for using the literary trope of "passing," a genre most often associated with African American literature, in which fair-skinned, mixed-race protagonists cross the color line to take on a white identity. Yet Fiedler and other critics have understood the genesis of Jewish American literature in terms of assimilation, not passing. The fiction of Cahan and Yezierska, for instance, depicts assimilation as a gradual process in which ties to the past and to religion are shed slowly as characters become more American. Wolf, in contrast, narrates the experiences of middle-class Jews who have achieved economic stability and, with that, a degree of social equality. In African American passing narratives, mixed-race characters' performances of whiteness work to expose the social construction of racial differences (via the one-drop rule, for example). Wolf similarly uses the passing narrative to challenge notions of Jewish racial difference. Yet, it is equally important that *Heirs of Yesterday*—like many of the African American passing narratives that have entered the ethnic literary canon—rejects passing as a means of attaining equality. The novel instead redefines Jewishness in terms that prioritize consent over descent, supplanting the passing narrative with a marriage plot. This redefinition of Jewish identity is enabled by two late nineteenth-century historical developments: the rise of Reform Judaism, which sought alternatives to secularization by adapting religious practice to an American context, and American military interventionism abroad, which provided opportunities for Jews to display their allegiance to the United States. Over the course of Wolf's novel, these historical forces work in concert to render the strategy of passing unnecessary.

Philip May's initial decision to pass as gentile does not take place in San Francisco, where Jews historically experienced less antisemitism than in other parts of the country. Instead, Philip decides to pass after experiencing social isolation while at school in Boston. He explains his reasoning in a long speech to his father:

> I was an American—with a difference. I hated the difference. I wanted to be successful—successful socially as well as

> professionally. I resolved to override every obstacle to obtain that perfect success.
>
> The opening came at Harvard. Thanks to you I have been endowed with a name which tells no tales, thanks to my mother my features are equally silent. I was thrown in with a crowd of young Bostonians . . . who, through the fact that I had been seen in the Unitarian church, took me for one of their own persuasion. It was a suggested evasion of an unfit shackle. There was no preconceived deception. I simply filled the bill.[70]

Philip does not wholly renounce his parentage, but instead cherry-picks aspects of his familial lineage—his father's name, his mother's features—that make him similar to rather than different from those around him. What is further notable here is the effortlessness of Philip's passing. He does not need to *work* to become American; he does not need to achieve what Cahan calls, in *The Rise of David Levinsky*, a "convincing personation" or to premeditate acts of deception and illusion, as Sonya Vrunsky does in *Salome of the Tenements*.[71] Instead, he "*simply* filled the bill" (italics mine). In these respects, *Heirs of Yesterday* may answer Meyer's call for fiction that emphasizes resemblances to rather than differences from the Christian majority. However, it is also important that *Heirs of Yesterday* does not erase Jewish particularity. Instead, the Jewish characters ultimately choose to identify as Jewish, even when class status and other factors deem it unnecessary; they reclaim Jewish difference as a source of pride and a sign of American individualism. By the end of *Heirs of Yesterday*, Philip May appears to be converted to the view that his decision and desire to pass were ill-founded, and this conversion takes place through a marriage plot—this time between individuals born to the same faith.

Upon his return to San Francisco from the East, Philip falls in love with a Jewish woman, Jean Willard. Jean lives next door to his father with her uncle, Daniel Willard, who is Joseph May's neighbor and closest friend. A talented pianist, Jean is a sought-after companion in her circle of young intellectuals and artists. Jean's "religion," we are told, "had always lain lightly upon her" and she "belonged to none and to all of the finely demarcated circles which go to make Jewish society."[72] Such descriptions suggest that Jean's Jewishness is more external than internal, with an elasticity that neither confines nor fully defines her. Jean is depicted as a fervid individualist who openly, if quietly, speaks her mind and resists being hemmed in by others. Most tellingly, early in the novel, she refuses to pose for the antisemitic painter Stephen Forrest, who later, and without her consent, transforms his memory of her image into his portrait of "The Jewess." Though Forrest, in his desire for the beautiful pianist, assures Jean that her "sex unsects" her,[73] she correctly intuits that modeling for him would fix her as a distinct "type"; she instead perceives her own art as a means of self-definition. As an orphan, Jean is seemingly released of the filial obligations that bind Philip, but she chooses nonetheless to devote herself to her father's brother, Daniel Willard, and his closest friend, Joseph May. Calling both of them "Uncle," she defines kinship by bonds of love and affection above blood. As with Philip, Jean's name and features "tell . . . no tales." Despite her belief in "the development of individuality at any cost," however, Jean—like Ruth in *Other Things Being Equal*—holds fast to her Jewishness, and Jean and Philip are kept apart by their conflicting attitudes toward their Jewish identities.[74] Accusing Philip of violating the fifth commandment, Jean views her would-be lover as responsible for the death of his own father, her adopted "uncle." Joseph May dies heartbroken at the idea that his son, in rejecting Judaism in order to become "a self-made man," had also rejected his father.[75]

Orphaned, like Jean, and disinherited by his father, who revises his will upon hearing of his son's intent to pass as gentile in order to promote his career and gain membership in the city's best social club, Philip seems free of the "unfit shackle" that threatened to confine him. But both his attraction to Jean and the death of his father propel Philip into a reencounter with Judaism and an opportunity to find new meaning in the religion he once wrote off as "a monument to the past." It is Jean who begins Philip's course of enlightenment, introducing him to the versatile doctrine of Reform Judaism when he finds himself a reluctant guest at the Willards' Passover seder. In a conversation that positions Jean as Philip's intellectual equal, she shares with him her religious philosophy: that Judaism is not an ancient practice, but an evolving one—"a becoming" is how she describes it, appropriating Philip's own words. In language evocative of frontier mythology, Jean views Jewish thought as "singularly free, unhampered, broad, open to the light of every day"—a far cry from

Philip's association of his abandoned religion with the cramped confinement of the ghetto.[76] Jean's lessons are reiterated by her uncle, Daniel, who accompanies Philip to Temple for Friday night services during his father's shiva. There, Philip experiences Judaism "robbed of provincialisms and anachronisms." As Daniel explains to the man who aspires to become his nephew-in-law, "the Talmudic idea—was that the Law was never to be a sealed matter—that it was always to remain open to the interpretation of the search-light of progress."[77] Functioning similarly to intermarriage in *Other Things Being Equal*, Reform Judaism is depicted as an open "experiment," with the potential to forge a reconciliation between religious belief and modernity.

Philip may maintain some of his skepticism, but, by the end of the novel, he comes to accept, if not Judaism, then love as his religion. "You have become my religion," he tells Jean in an effort to win her back. "If you are Jewish, must I not too be Jew?"[78] Though Jewish according to the logic of matrilineal descent, Philip proves that law "open to interpretation" and reinvents himself as a Jew by choice. He comes to see himself as Jewish not because his parents were, but rather because the woman to whom he hopes to bind himself is. If *The Melting Pot* "sacralizes loving consent as the abolition of prejudices of descent,"[79] *Heirs of Yesterday* similarly uses modern love and marriage—a union of equals and of individualists, brought together by erotic choice—as a vehicle for consensual identification and citizenship. Where the violent, "seething"[80] alchemy of Zangwill's melting pot threatens a loss of individuality (and thus threatens democracy, as Horace Kallen famously proposed), Wolf's marriage metaphor, underwritten by the modern tenets of Reform Judaism, offers a resolution to the American dilemma, a way to moderate difference and to progress into the future without completely relinquishing Jewish ideals.

Although Wolf, while in the process of working on *Heirs of Yesterday*, wrote to Zangwill of her intent to "make [her] story end happily for love's sake," the published novel ends on a much more ambiguous note than initially planned.[81] When Philip asks, "If you are Jewish, must I not too be Jew?," Jean does not answer his question with words. Instead, an image of the two of them "walk[ing] on together over the hill," in the direction of the horizon, echoes *Other Things Being Equal*'s vague glance toward the future.[82] This time, however, Wolf takes a more dramatic and unexpected turn. *Heirs of Yesterday* does not end with the neat resolution of the marriage plot. Instead, the domestic novel zooms outward to the national and world stage, as the historical backdrop of the Spanish-American War overtakes the lives of Wolf's fictional characters.

The Spanish-American War was a pivotal moment in Jewish American history. As Jeanne Abrams's analysis of the war's coverage in *The American Israelite* demonstrates, the Reform community in particular saw its interests as Jews aligned with its interests as Americans and supported the nation's efforts to expand its borders and spread democracy. Military service abroad and Red Cross service at home became means for Jewish men and women to show the "compatibility of Jewish and American ideals in matters of government and humanitarian diplomacy," to answer antisemitic attacks by illustrating "that Jews were just as brave and patriotic as any other group of Americans," and to ensure that Jews would take part in the bounty of manifest destiny.[83] As the United States' first major international conflict after the Civil War, the war with Spain was viewed as an opportunity for Americans of all races and backgrounds to unite against a common foreign enemy, deflecting some of the stigma of ethno-racial difference away from Jewish and Black Americans and on to the people of the Philippines, Cuba, and Puerto Rico.

In *Heirs of Yesterday*, the opening of chapter 15 explicitly shifts from the quiet intimacy of the marriage plot to the bold national headlines of recent history. Wolf describes the sinking of the USS *Maine* in Havana Harbor on February 15, 1898, the event that famously fueled the war cries of the yellow press:

> But whatever Philip May, or any other, was battling with in silence of heart, was presently lost, swallowed up, in the shock which shook the whole nation to its foundations, when, on a night of February, two hundred and fifty American seamen were hurled, without herald, out of a friendly port into the port of the silent Unknown.
>
> The calamity brought the nation as one man to its feet. . . . [T]here was no longer any individual life—it was all national.[84]

Wolf's "individualist" characters are subsumed into this national narrative. In a show of patriotism, Philip enlists as an army surgeon—likely a historical reference to Colonel Joseph M. Heller, a surgeon who roused Jewish pride when he left a thriving medical practice to become the first man to volunteer following the United States' declaration of war.[85] Jean, meanwhile, devotes herself to the San Francisco Red Cross, preparing packages for soldiers and entertaining them with "patriotic airs." Finding "an absorbing interest beyond self," and giving "herself to it with fanatic zeal," Jean's "face began to wear the white, spiritual light of a devotee."[86]

Jean's religious devotion to the patriotic cause affirms her American identity—whitens her, even—but her nationalism is not free of critique. As a Jew, she remains conscious of national prejudices and the limits of American democracy at home. Attending a Red Cross meeting where "a vote of thanks was offered to all the ladies who had given assistance to the soldiers, especially for the splendid patriotism shown by the Jewish and colored ladies," Jean takes issue with the fact that such "fine distinctions" are made under the banner of the American flag.[87] Although Jean proudly identifies with her Jewishness, observes Jewish rituals such as the Passover seder, and participates in the city's "Jewish social culture," she believes that difference should be a matter of individual choice rather than a "distinction" imposed by others. This reference to "Jewish and colored ladies" may well have influenced Zangwill's interpretation of the novel's social message: the irony that even in the "Republic of human brotherhood," Jews and "coloured folk" are at the bottom.

This brief allusion to San Francisco's Black population, who remain on the novel's periphery, also returns us to an earlier scene in which Jews were tenuously aligned with the "coloured folk," while being more forcefully differentiated from them. At a social gathering of Jewish friends, Jean confesses her fondness for the popular "coon songs" of the day, even as she implies that such music does not meet the highest of "social standards and tastes." The evening ends with Jean enthusiastically providing the piano accompaniment for a fellow guest who sings "song after song . . . with all the jubilant rhythm, the peculiar darky joy, which make the coon-song so unmistakably a song of color."[88] Even if born of a supposed appreciation for Black culture, this performance of racial appropriation "mimics" the fads and anti-Black racism of gentile society. Wolf's language—for example, her reference to "the peculiar darky joy" of the "coon-song"—positions Blacks, not Jews, as the metaphorical "children of the ghetto." Like Ruth's walk through the Latin quarter in

Other Things Being Equal, the scene may at first align Jean with communities of color, but it ultimately serves to downplay her difference, making her and the Jewish society of which she is a part appear whiter in the eyes of Wolf's readers.[89]

The novel's ending also works as an interesting counterpoint to the literary tradition of ghetto fiction. The image of Philip and Jean walking together over the hills and into the future is followed by a coda depicting the Manila expedition departing for the Philippines from San Francisco Bay with Philip on board, and Jean standing with the crowds of Pacific Heights in a patriotic farewell salute. The coda omits any reference to its central characters' names, making them representative of gendered American "types": the brave soldier and the patriotic Red Cross volunteer. Wolf's characters have indeed become part of "a vaster" and more spacious "universe," to refer back to the Zangwill epigraph, but they have done so while reclaiming and redefining, rather than creating greater distance from, their Jewish identities. Nor does a return to Jewish identity require a return to the spatial and metaphorical ghetto, as it often does for Yezierska's protagonists. Instead, Philip's increasing acceptance of his Jewishness coincides with his participation in the project of American expansionism. The novel's ending raises the specter of Philip's losing his life at sea or at war, creating narrative ambiguity about whether Philip will sacrifice himself for his country or return home a hero, sealing his union with Jean through marriage. But, compared to the beginning of the novel, there is less ambiguity about who Philip May is, or who he is "becoming": a Jew and an American, not by birth and blood, but by love and consent.

In both *Heirs of Yesterday* and *Other Things Being Equal*, Wolf used the conventions of the marriage plot as a means of writing Jews into a national narrative. By privileging consensual allegiances above lineage by blood, her novels hold up resemblances between Jewish and non-Jewish white Americans without erasing ethno-religious difference. The significance of these novels' Western settings should not be underestimated. As William Handley argues, "In literature of the American West, the preoccupation with marriage is especially fraught with questions about the identity of American whiteness and the meaning of western history."[90] In the 1890s, as Wolf embarked upon her career as a novelist, the meaning of Western American history was simultaneously being shaped by historian Frederick Jackson Turner, who first introduced his frontier thesis to the American public at the World's Columbian Exposition in Chicago in 1893. Turner's frontier is a place of "perennial rebirth" where the "fluidity of American life, this expansion westward with its new opportunities, its continuous touch with the simplicity of primitive society, furnish[es] the forces dominating American character."[91] Wolf's Jewish characters have imbibed the spirit of the Turnerian frontier, as they strike a balance between nationalism and individualism, forging their identities in ways that bring their Jewishness ever closer to "American whiteness" and widening the gap between themselves and ethnic minorities of color, including colonized people of the newly expanded empire.

In 1916, Wolf published what was to be her last book, *Fulfillment: A California Novel*, in addition to a new edition of *Other Things Being Equal*, a novel whose treatment of intermarriage remained relevant to "a new generation," as Wolf herself pointed out in a foreword to the reissue.[92] Like *A Prodigal in Love*, *The Joy of Life*, and the stories she published in popular magazines such as *The Smart Set*, *Fulfillment* was absent of Jewish themes. Though it relies, as almost all her work does, on the romance of the marriage plot, its book-loving heroine, Gwen Heath, finds her greatest fulfillment in a fledgling career as a writer of children's stories, while her sister, Deborah, remains unmarried, selflessly devoting herself to Gwen's happiness and to her settlement work. Characters such as Gwen and Deborah also bear a sisterly resemblance to Wolf's Jewish heroines, Ruth Levice and Jean Willard, who are similarly defined as much by their artistic, intellectual, and humanitarian pursuits as by their marriage prospects. For Wolf, moving between what Zangwill categorized as "Jewish" and "American" books was another means of drawing parallels between middle-class Jews and non-Jewish bourgeois society.

Announcing the dual publication of *Fulfillment* and *Other Things Being Equal* as two books "of California life," a description that interestingly omits any mention of the latter's Jewish content, the *Chicago Daily Tribune* prophesied, "If the promise of these books is kept up, Miss Wolf will some day rank high among American writers of fiction."[93] The promise of continued literary production was not to be. According to the notice of her death that appeared in the *San Francisco Chronicle* in

1932, Wolf succumbed to the ill health that had plagued her throughout her life and had spent her last fifteen years "virtually confined to her room."[94] But from the last decade of the nineteenth century through World War I, Wolf was a central figure in San Francisco's Jewish literary culture, a writer whose work offers important perspectives on gender, religion, class, region, and ethno-racial identity in Progressive-Era America, and whose influence extended across the United States and beyond its borders, even as she herself rarely left her California home. The side-by-side publication of *Other Things Being Equal* and *Fulfillment* in 1916 was a fitting valedictory for an author who, whether or not she was writing explicitly about Jewish life, broke through misconceptions, past and present, about American Jews, Jewish fiction, and Jewish American writers. Wolf may have admired the work of contemporary ghetto writers like Zangwill for the glimpses they offered into the circumscribed lives of a "peculiar" people, but her own writing, set in cosmopolitan San Francisco, challenged demarcations that set Jews apart from the rest of the nation. It functioned as its own "grave experiment" in how to achieve the American ideal of equality without sacrificing Jewish identity.

2
The Philomaths

Domestic Feminism, the Women's Club Movement, and Jewish Literary Culture

In 1893, San Francisco socialite Bettie Lowenberg traveled to Chicago to visit the World's Columbian Exposition. There she attended the Jewish Women's Congress at the World's Parliament on Religions, where she heard activists such as Hannah Greenebaum Solomon and Sadie American speak about the need to create a national organization.[1] The event famously led to the formation of the National Council of Jewish Women, but it also inspired Lowenberg to take local action. Upon her return to San Francisco, she decided to launch her own women's club. While the NCJW's agenda included religion as well as education and philanthropy, Lowenberg's club began primarily as a literary venture for middle- and upper-class Jewish women. "I was imbued by the idea that there were many intellectual and brilliant Jewish women in San Francisco who lacked the opportunity of development by organization," recalled Lowenberg of her club's inception. In response to this need, she envisioned a "conservative, but progressive" woman's club that would "promote the general culture of its members by the discussion of educational, moral and social topics."[2] The organization's name, the Philomath Club, united its members through their love of knowledge and summed up the club's primary mission: study and learning.

In January of 1895, Lowenberg presided over the Philomath Club's first open meeting, which took place at San Francisco's luxurious Palace Hotel. The meeting featured presentations by two young women who were rising literary stars: Harriet Lane Levy, a recent University of California graduate who was then writing for a San Francisco journal called *The Wave* (and whose career will be the subject of the following chapter), and the novelist Emma Wolf.[3] Wolf's first novel was already a popular success—due, in part, to its controversial intermarriage plot, as I discussed in chapter 1. Influenced by *Other Things Being Equal*'s intermarriage plot, Israel Zangwill later adapted Wolf's story of star-crossed Jewish and non-Jewish lovers to dramatize the conflict between ethnic loyalty and American identity in *The Melting Pot*. In 1908, the same year that the Washington, DC, premiere of Zangwill's play inscribed the "melting pot" in the American lexicon, Lowenberg published her first novel, *The Irresistible Current*. Set in a Midwestern frontier town on the Mississippi River (based on Cape Girardeau, Missouri, where Lowenberg spent her youth), Lowenberg's debut novel—like Wolf's *Other Things Being Equal* and Zangwill's play—uses the complicated entanglements of interfaith romance to make a case for religious tolerance and social equality.

Positioning eastern European immigrant writers as the forefathers and foremothers of Jewish American literature, and New York as its cultural epicenter, scholars have largely overlooked the literary genealogy I have outlined above. Like the previous chapter, this one examines what happens when we shift the regional focus of Jewish American literary history to the West Coast; it also broadens the parameters of Jewish literary culture to include the institutional history of the nineteenth-century woman's club movement and illuminates female reformers' interdependent literacy practices as both readers and writers.[4] The San Francisco women's club movement, I argue, operated as an important site for the production of fin de siècle Jewish literary culture. While Wolf's career as a fiction writer spanned from the 1890s through World War I, Lowenberg did not turn to novel writing until she was in her sixties. Instead, she made her greatest contribution to turn-of-the-century letters as a leader of organizations that nurtured the social, literary, political, and intellectual lives of San Francisco's Jewish women. From the 1890s onward, she devoted her time and considerable financial resources to women's clubs. Lowenberg created a distinctly Western space where her contemporaries, and their children, could overcome the intellectual and social barriers they experienced as women and religious minorities, thus fostering the cultural and institutional conditions that allowed a writer like Wolf to flourish. By tracing the development of Lowenberg's own career from clubwoman to novelist, I show that Jewish women contributed to turn-of-the-twentieth-century American literary culture in varied and interdependent ways: as writers, readers, speakers, thinkers, philanthropists, and reformers.

Bettie Lowenberg, the Philomath Club, and Domestic Feminism

Defying familiar historical narratives of nineteenth-century Jewish life in the United States, Lowenberg's background, as well as her writings, compel a reevaluation of early Jewish American literary history. She was born in Prairie Bluff, Alabama, on December 11, 1845, to William and Pauline (Levy) Lilienfeld, immigrants from Prussia and Germany. When Bettie was six years old, the Lilienfelds moved to Cape Girardeau, Missouri, where she was educated at the Convent of St. Vincent—an experience that supplied the seeds for her first novel.[5] Lured farther west by the economic opportunities of the Gold Rush, the Lilienfelds migrated to Carson City, Nevada, where they were one of the few Jewish pioneer families.[6] By 1860, when she was fifteen, Bettie had made San Francisco her permanent home. In 1862, the same year that her mother gave birth to the Lilienfelds' only son, Bettie married Prussian immigrant Isidor Lowenberg. Born in 1836, Isidor had arrived in the United States in 1853, eight years after the birth of his American-born wife. Along with his partner, banker Lewis Meyerstein, who had married Bettie's sister, Jane, in 1861, Isidor started a successful menswear business, first as distributors and later as manufacturers of denim, making them competitors of Levi Strauss. In 1887, Meyerstein & Lowenberg became Lowenberg & Company, run by Isidor and his son, Albert, who was born in 1864.[7] A daughter, Ruby, had also been born to Bettie and Isidor in 1872. A younger sister of Bettie's, Emma (Lilienfeld) Wineburgh, who became a poet and member of Los Angeles's Shakespeare Club, a woman's club devoted to studying works of the bard, also lived for a time in the Lowenbergs' San Francisco home prior to her marriage in 1882.

Beginning in the 1890s, the Lowenbergs' names regularly appear in the society pages of publications such as *The San Francisco Call*, *The Argonaut*, *The Wasp*, and *The Wave*. Ruby's 1896 wedding to Abraham Lincoln Brown, officiated by Rabbi Voorsanger of Temple Emanu-El, for example, was reported in sumptuous detail in *The Call* and *The Wave*, the latter noting that the bride's father was "reputed" to be a millionaire.[8] Most of these references, however, document Bettie's career as a leading figure in San Francisco's civic life, active in a variety of cultural and benevolent societies, both Jewish and nonsectarian. The 1916–17 volume of *Who's Who in America* lists some of her many positions and involvements: the women's board of the 1915 Panama-Pacific International Exposition and first vice president of the Congress of Authors and Journalists (the idea to include an exhibit of leading literary figures at the exposition originated with Lowenberg), the American Red Cross (of which she chaired the Hospitality Committee during the Spanish-American War), the State Commission on Marriage and Divorce, and the California Prison Commission. She also served as president of a number of women's organizations, including the California Federation of Women's Clubs, the Pacific Coast Women's Press Association, the Laurel Hall Club (San Francisco's oldest women's literary club), and the Philomath Club, the club that Lowenberg founded and which, as she proudly noted, had "the distinction of being the first club composed of Jewish women with a regularly adopted constitution in the world."[9]

In *The Clubwoman as Feminist: True Womanhood Redefined, 1868–1914*, Karen Blair demonstrates that the woman's club movement was a key moment in feminist history. The clubs brought women together, allowing them to organize as a group and work toward their "intellectual and social self-improvement." Made up of middle- and upper-class women, the clubs were often seen as a conservative force devoted to the maintenance of women's sphere and to the feminine ideals of "proper" womanhood. Blair argues, however, that progressive and even radical ideas brewed under this "ideological cover" as the women supported, if not suffrage and gender equality, then at the very least, "Domestic Feminism"—the notion that the woman's sphere of the home could be extended further to have a positive moral influence on public affairs.[10] Thus, even as women's clubs seemed to maintain separate spheres, they created pathways for women to enter public life. In this Progressive-Era context, the literary and cultural interests of club members often operated dialectically with social and political endeavors such as reform and charity work. In her investigation of women's clubs' "literacy practices," Anne Ruggles Gere explores how clubwomen made "their own history and defin[ed] their own cultural identity." Through symbiotic acts of reading and writing, the clubs "provided spaces where women could exert some *control* over the terms of their representations," first collaborating in their "critiques of the dominant culture" and then "developing and implementing alternatives to the status quo."[11]

Scholars of Jewish women's clubs have noted similar trends, but for Jewish women, the clubs' promotion of bourgeois feminine ideals took on additional layers of meaning, as it did for African American clubwomen who mobilized a "politics of respectability" to shape how they were seen by others.[12] By emulating the genteel practices of white Christian society, upwardly mobile women on the ethno-racial and religious margins displayed their attributes as "ladies" and proved themselves deserving of respect. According to Selma Berrol, for "bourgeois Jewish matron[s]," women's clubs, and the literature they produced, were a means of "emulating the folkways of the WASP community," a community that was usually not welcoming to them. Women's clubs tended to be exclusionary, dividing along religious, class, and racial lines.[13] Although there were Jewish women who belonged to clubs affiliated with the General Federation of Women's Clubs, "many white Protestant groups barred [Jewish women], borrowing from the construction of Jews as nonwhite and the ready fund of anti-Semitism." Economic class, and even great wealth, did not entirely shield middle- and upper-class Jewish women from social exclusion. American-born, bourgeois Jews were often "classed" with recent immigrants and seen as "not fully American" despite the fact that they viewed themselves as superior to and certainly more American than their newly arrived eastern European coreligionists, many of whom did not yet speak English.[14] Jewish women used club "literacy practices" to combat such perceptions of them as "foreign," both by undertaking programs of study that exhibited their knowledge and veneration of Anglo and Western art and literature and by working toward the uplift and education of newly arrived immigrants as volunteers at settlement houses. Lowenberg's own career provides evidence of the effectiveness of such strategies. She went from founding a club specifically for Jewish women to serving in various official capacities for the California Federation of Women's Clubs and for its umbrella organization, the General Federation of Women's Clubs.

At a time when women could not participate directly in government, clubs were not only a means of Americanization but also a means for them to *contest* Americanization and redefine what it meant to be American. Given that religious morality and piety were important components of nineteenth-century bourgeois femininity, most Jewish clubwomen were reluctant to forgo their Judaism. This created a conundrum since they were simultaneously invested in the project of Americanization. Jewish clubwomen thus had to negotiate the tension "between fostering acculturation and avoiding total assimilation." Ultimately, Gere argues, Jewish and other minority clubwomen moved "beyond the national fantasy toward an Americanization of their own making, one that included greater respect for diversity and an appreciation for the contributions of *all* citizens."[15] Lowenberg's career shows how Jewish clubwomen were not simply emulating non-Jewish elite society but also shaping national ideology by holding on to the ethno-religious identity that made their clubs distinct from others *and* forming alliances with other clubs across religious lines. These interreligious alliances, however, further entrenched class differences and often came at the cost of interethnic and cross-racial solidarity with other minority groups.

The tension between the desire to maintain a distinct identity and the desire to assimilate is evident in the formation of the Philomath Club. Writing about the club's founding, Lowenberg drew attention to the Philomath's status as a pioneer in the club movement, a first of its kind for Jewish women, while also emphasizing its similarities to comparable non-Jewish institutions, the fact that her club would exist "side by side, with the brilliant literary associations of the day."[16] Lowenberg had indeed tapped into a need among affluent Jewish women, and, from its beginnings, the Philomath Club was a great success. A news item on the club's first "open meeting" at the Palace Hotel on January 15, 1895, lamented the fact that "a more commodious hall was not chosen, as the Maple room proved inadequate to meet the requirements of the large number of society people who turned out."[17]

The phrase "society people" is, of course, telling. Lowenberg designed the club with exclusivity in mind and not only because the Philomath was only open to Jewish women. Although it is unclear how the selection process worked, the club was limited to 150 to 175 members, and, in the club's later years, Lowenberg took pride in the fact that it had a waiting list. As much as she dedicated her own life to club work, Lowenberg believed that clubs were not for all women. She was aware of the fact that her club involvement was made possible by her economic position and her age; having joined the club movement after her own children were grown, Lowenberg cautioned that clubs should not detract from women's domestic duties, especially child-rearing. "It should be understood that it is only the woman of leisure who can constantly respond to a club's call," she stated. "To the woman of family without abundant means the club should only be a diversion, smoothing out worries and composing the nerves, so that she can take up home duties with a fresh mind."[18] In fact, Lowenberg did not believe that mothers "without abundant means"—that is, the means to hire servants who would care for their children—should take part in the club movement, as revealed by her anecdote about a young woman on her way to a "mother's club": "I never saw so striking an instance of [the fact that clubs are not for everyone] as when I noticed a mother crossing a crowded street with one child, almost a baby, hanging on to her skirts, and others, in danger of their lives, trying to follow. . . . The proper mother's club for her to attend was at home instead of dragging little children away from home while she should be told how to take care of them."[19]

Critics of the club movement voiced fears that the organization of women would lead to the neglect of their domestic responsibilities. In *Harper's*, political cartoonist Charles G. Bush depicted a meeting of the Sorosis Club in which men sat on the stairs off to the side, caring for babies, while their wives' attempts to follow parliamentary procedure devolved into chaos.[20] Lowenberg's statements—especially her hyperbolic alarm that attending a club meeting puts children "in danger of their lives"—would have been reassuring to critics who viewed the club movement as a threat to the social order. Privileging domesticity above women's communal identity and mental well-being, Lowenberg affirmed the clubs as a supplement to and extension of the home. On the opposite end of the spectrum, critics, including feminist scholars, have taken women's clubs to task for reinforcing the status quo. As much as they created a sense of unity among certain groups of women, shoring up political power, club leaders like Lowenberg participated in the policing of clubs along class lines, in part by adhering to conservative gender ideologies. There is some evidence to suggest that Lowenberg did what she could to make the clubs more inclusive. Believing that nonsectarian clubs should be open to Jewish women who met the requirements of class, Lowenberg extended her vision of ethno-racial inclusivity to African Americans as well. At a 1902 meeting of the State Federation of

Women's Clubs, where Lowenberg was elected vice president of the San Francisco district, she supported a resolution that would allow African American women's clubs to join the general federation. Her advocacy for Black women, however, put her in the minority, and the delegates ended up voting down the resolution out of fear that southern women's clubs would secede from the federation.[21]

In *Forgotten Readers: Recovering the Lost History of African American Literary Societies*, Elizabeth McHenry illustrates how African American clubwomen became "literary activists" through their collaborative engagement with "race literature." Although, as I argue, there is an activist dimension to Lowenberg's career as a clubwoman, the literacy practices of the Philomath Club tended to be more traditional, especially in their content, and, with only occasional exceptions, did not cover Jewish literature or religious topics. At the same time, club activities often put women on the same plane as men, creating opportunities for members to display their intellectual and artistic talents. Offering a broad notion of the "literary," the club's program usually consisted of a variety of presentations, including the reading of papers on topics ranging from "Children" and "Home" to "Ragtime" and "The Idealism of Emerson"; vocal and instrumental performances of classical music; dramatic performances, including *tableaux vivants* and original plays written and acted by members; and recitations of classic and contemporary works of literature.

For outside speakers, the club often extended invitations to male experts, usually professors from the nearby campuses of Stanford and Berkeley. In keeping with Gere's argument that women's clubs "foster[ed] the neo-colonialism of Anglo-Saxonism,"[22] English literature was a frequent topic in the Philomath's early years, and the women heard lectures by noted scholars on Tennyson and Carlyle. Julius Goebel, a Stanford professor known for his work on German immigrants in America, delivered lectures on Faust and "English and German Folk-songs." An art historian gave a talk on Venetian painting and architecture titled "City of the Doges." In 1900, members embarked on the study of American history, led by Professor Clyde Duniway, whose research focused on the history of slavery in California, among other topics.[23]

Speakers were not only drawn from the groves of academe. Congressman Julius Kahn, husband of the Philomath's second president,

Florence Prag Kahn, gave several lectures on local and national politics to the club over the years, leading *The San Francisco Call*'s woman's club columnist to quip, "It has become quite the fashion for generous club presidents to lend their husbands . . . for an afternoon."[24] In 1915, the club hosted Stephen S. Wise, the influential Reform rabbi from New York's Free Synagogue. Steering clear of explicitly Judaic topics, Wise gave a talk titled "The Drama of Our Time" in which he railed against the immorality of "filthy and loathsome plays" that focus on "sex problems" with "frankness" but "little seriousness."[25] During World War I, the club's programming took a decidedly patriotic bent, with, for example, a military chaplain presenting a talk on "The Life of a Soldier" and a screening of the Edison film *The Birth of the Star-Spangled Banner*.[26]

Other examples suggest that the club had a particular interest in hearing from adventurous and accomplished Jewish women. In 1904, socialist activist and Russian immigrant Anna Strunsky—the subject of chapter 5—kicked off a series of talks on Russia, holding club members "spellbound" with a speech on the life of Prince Peter Kropotkin.[27] Later that same year, Polish immigrant Mary Prag—a San Francisco high school teacher, associate member of the club, and mother of Florence Prag Kahn—spoke on "Experiences Among the Mormons in Utah," describing her early married life in Gold Rush-era Salt Lake City, where she and her husband befriended the Mormon leader Brigham Young.[28] And in 1909, the NCJW's executive secretary, Sadie American, whose 1893 speech at the Columbian Exposition had galvanized Lowenberg to organize San Francisco's Jewish women, appeared before the club as part of a West Coast speaking tour and detailed her work with recent Jewish immigrants in New York. Whether a fellow member was presenting a paper or an outside expert was lecturing, the meetings offered opportunities for discussion and debate, with women in the audience asking questions and articulating their own opinions. For well-bred, well-read women who did not have the opportunity to attend college because of their sex, the club filled an intellectual vacuum, allowing them to build upon their secondary or finishing school educations and to participate in public discourse about a wide range of issues.

The club also filled a social need. Convening in the posh function rooms of the Palace Hotel, the meetings were a site of conspicuous consumption. Society-page reports on club gatherings lingered on details of food, floral decorations, and fashionably gowned guests. Gere argues that, far from diminishing the club's educational value and intellectual rigor, the setting, along with communal consumption of food and drink, transformed literacy into a social practice and gave it gendered meaning. In contrast, she notes that "accommodations to the body never appeared in the" more masculine environment of "the classroom, where students occupied hard seats in lined rows, with the figure of the instructor often towering over them . . . and where handwork and refreshments of all sorts were explicitly forbidden." For Gere, the context in which meetings took place played a crucial role in creating "intimacy" among members: "clubwomen's literacy practices embodied their love, liking, and care for one another."[29] Other women's clubs met in members' homes or in communal spaces like libraries or churches. For the women of the Philomath Club, however, "intimacy" and camaraderie were not born from the domestic space of the home or the religious space of the synagogue but from social ties formed through the collaborative enactment of upper-class mores. The hotel setting (and the expenses it incurred) suggests that the women were carving out a public space for themselves at the center of San Francisco's social and cultural life. Lowenberg's lip service to domesticity aside, this was not an informal homey gathering, but an elegant and tastefully orchestrated affair; it offered women an opportunity to show off not only their knowledge and talent, but also their refinement, etiquette, and material prosperity. From its choice of subject matter to its choice of location, the Philomath Club made Jewish women an integral and visible part of secular, bourgeois culture.

The Jewishness of the Philomath Club certainly did not seem to be at the forefront. In fact, while Deborah Grand Golomb argues that Jewish women's clubs should not be seen as feminist because they put their identities as Jews before their identities as women, the Philomath Club took the opposite approach. The club's name obscured the common religious affiliation of its members while highlighting instead women's intellect and literary acumen. This emphasis was similarly reinforced by the club's logo, which featured an owl, a symbol of wisdom, perched atop a heart surrounding an open book. In a 1903 report in *Club Life*, Lowenberg described the group as united by secular principles: "These women are banded together with the diamond and steel of intelligence and with earnestness of purpose for the betterment of conditions and beautifying of surroundings as well as for intellectual culture."[30] Though the broader Jewish community claimed the Philomath as a Jewish institution, covering the club's founding in the Jewish press,[31] the popular press rarely mentioned the club's religious identity when reporting on its activities. Even on the occasion of Strunsky's speech, for instance, *The Call* observed that "it was fitting that the series of talks upon Russia should be opened by a Russian," without noting the speaker's shared religious heritage with her audience.[32]

There were, however, notable exceptions. In 1897, the invited lecturer, Berkeley professor George Holmes Howison, created an uproar at a club meeting when he called his hostesses "heathens" during a theology lecture. In reporting on the event, the Associated Press noted that "the prominent Hebrew ladies" of the club responded to the professor's lecture "with murmurs of disapproval and whispered indignant comments." When one offended woman (identified as the wife of the ex-minister of the United States to Turkey) asked Howison to clarify whether, in calling all non-Christians "heathens," he intended to label her one as well, his affirmative reply generated even more of a stir, causing the speaker to backtrack and claim that he meant the word only in its "etymological sense." The story was picked up by the Jewish press, and made local and national news, with *The Sacramento Bee* editorializing, "We suggest to these good Hebrew women that they pay no attention to this professor, or to any other man who talks to them about 'heathens.' . . . Professor Howison is, in the estimation of three-fourths of the world's inhabitants, a 'heathen,' whose heathenism entitles him to the distinguished honor of roasting forever and a day on the hottest coals in hell. For be it known, good women, that whenever we cannot prove a man's theology to be wrong by argument, we immediately lift up our hands in pitying horror and send him straight to hell."[33] The incident is telling for many reasons: the fact that the press, in a demonstration of religious tolerance, leaped to the defense of the "good Hebrew women" and villainized a respected male scholar, the outrage of the women themselves who banded together in defiance of their guest's prejudiced attack on their religion, and the possibility that the professor did not realize that he was lecturing to a group of Jewish women until the question about their "heathenism" was directly posed to him.

Occasionally, observers did draw attention to the club's unique identity, as when the *San Francisco Chronicle* reported on a "cablegram of sympathy" that Lowenberg, as club president, had sent to the wife of Alfred Dreyfus in September 1899 following his conviction for treason in France. Though the cablegram expressed a gender-based identification with Madame Dreyfus, assuring her that "the women of the Philomath Club appreciate your wifely devotion and courage," the newspaper offered a slightly different interpretation. Implying that the clubwomen's response to the Dreyfus affair was due to religious empathy and underlying fears of antisemitism, it stated that the club's "prominent Jewish women . . . wanted the suffering woman to know that there were many of her faith in the Far West who grieved with her."[34]

Sadie American's 1909 speech at a Philomath meeting also occasioned scrutiny of the club's Jewish identity, exposing a complex and contradictory web of associations among Jewishness, class, gender, and region. Finding herself more enthralled by the audience than by the "young Eastern" speaker "helping to solve the problems of the poor of her race," Harriet Watson Capwell, a writer for the *San Francisco News Letter*, penned an encomium of the clubwomen, including Lowenberg, whom she singles out as "a woman with an unusual equipment of broad mentality." But Capwell's article, solicitously titled "The Philomath Club an Object of Admiration" [*sic*], simultaneously traffics in gendered stereotypes about Jewish American women linked to cultural anxieties about assimilation.[35] Capwell's initial description of the Philomath membership emphasizes their difference from other middle-class women:

> How volatile and emotional the Jewish women are, and how their faces reflect every shade and nuance of their feelings. A gathering of New England women would not act as a sounding board for the most inspired speaker, yet here was a speaker, who would lay no claim to oratorical ability, and her audience smiled and sighed and brushed away a tear and leaned forward or settled back with climax and anti-climax. I doubt if any other woman's club in San Francisco would give anything but attention stiff as buckram. This facile, pliable, emotional interest is not in the average American make-up. . . . The [Philomath women] are not the first generation on this soil, and they have been educated in your best schools, have traveled and lived and loved even as their most fortunate neighbors. And yet they have retained that gracious flexibility of feature,

> that abandon of responsiveness which is a part of the temperament which has given the world so many artists and musicians.

Although she views the Jewish women's demonstrativeness as a positive attribute, noting, for instance, their "gracious flexibility of feature," Capwell's pointed contrasts with comparable groups from both New England and San Francisco suggest that the Philomath women are defined more by innate Jewish difference than by class or regional identity. Her statement does make a distinction between these middle-class women and the new Jewish immigrants who were the subject of Sadie American's lecture by acknowledging that the Philomaths are native-born and educated in American schools (expensive, private finishing schools, no less). However, she maintains that ingrained biological differences, rather than more mutable differences of religious belief and practice, interfere with full assimilation: their racial "make-up" simply differs from that of the "average American." As a strong proponent of Americanization, Lowenberg would likely disagree with this assessment, having "patterned" (in Capwell's word) her club on non-Jewish women's clubs with the purpose not of erasing all difference but of subtly contesting what constitutes the "average American."[36]

Despite the fact that Capwell's ostensibly favorable impressions depict the women as exuding Jewish difference, she does acknowledge that the Philomath Club succeeded in defying some of the more invidious stereotypes about upwardly mobile Jewish women as gaudily and ostentatiously overreaching in their attempt to fit in with high society. "One often hears that Jewish women err on the margin of overdress," she writes, "they are sometimes pictured be-ribboned and be-chiffoned and be-plumed and be-jeweled. Diamonds are said to be as necessary to their make-up as a marrow bone to a good soup." Implying that such negative views are based on hearsay rather than personal experience and using the passive voice ("they are sometimes pictured" and "Diamonds are said") to question the reliability of such representations, Capwell presents her observations of the Philomath Club as a corrective. She notes, for example, that "overdress and decoration" are "vehemently checked" among the clubwomen, offering her readers a first-person testimonial: "At no afternoon gathering have I seen such elegant restraint in apparel. . . . [these women] serve as a rebuke to the notion that over-dressing and jewels go by racial destiny."[37] Unlike her view of the women's emotional and expressive temperament, Capwell's depiction of their outward appearance paints a portrait of successful assimilation made possible by high economic standing and the materiality of dress. Still, antisemitic stereotypes lurk beneath the surface of Capwell's flattering descriptions, since she suggests that the wealth and good taste of this particular group of women allow them to overcome their "racial destiny." They are the exception, not the rule, and they represent not *all* Jewish women, but rather an elite group—a carefully fashioned segment of Jewish society. Here, Capwell also asserts a kind of proprietary regional pride in the city's Jewish community, praising them for being of a better class than East Coast (or even Los Angeles) Jews.[38] Her title, too, conveys this sense of proprietary pride: the Philomath Club is positioned as "an *object* of admiration," rather than an active and integral part of San Francisco society.

Capwell's article offers insight into the Philomath's strategies of self-fashioning, reminding us why the women chose to downplay Jewish identity in their club's self-representation. "Jewishness" was so deeply inscribed with antisemitic and racialized meaning that even supposedly sympathetic observers could not avoid the language of stereotype. Still, for the Philomath women, Judaism and Jewish values remained a point of pride and integrity, even if they were not at the forefront of their club's identity. Reflecting on the roots of the woman's club movement, Lowenberg drew attention to its religious origins. The clubs dated "back to the sewing circles of the New England churches, where neighbors gathered . . . to make aprons and nightcaps for the benighted heathens in some far part of the world," explained Lowenberg. "While busy fingers deftly plied the needle, some read tracts and essays for the benefit of the soul and mind."[39] In contrast to Professor Howison's views of Jewish women as "heathens," Lowenberg situated the Philomath Club in an American tradition of enlightened women doing their part to uplift the uncivilized people of the world. In Lowenberg's version of club history, self-improvement, now central to the work of literary societies, was once secondary; literacy practices supplied spiritual and mental sustenance while women were engaged in the primary task of missionary labor. Increasingly, however, Lowenberg's career as a clubwoman would move in the direction of benevolent aid, whether to American soldiers serving overseas or poor immigrants at home. Attesting to the interplay between literature and reform in the Progressive Era, reading and writing were to remain important components of her charitable undertakings.

Lowenberg did not simply use rhetoric to root the legacy of the club movement in a Judeo-Christian tradition; she also actively forged interreligious alliances with non-Jewish clubwomen. Not content to stop at founding one of the most prominent Jewish women's literary clubs in the nation, Lowenberg rose to leadership positions in a number of nonsectarian clubs. At the same time that she was serving as president of the Philomath, for example, Lowenberg assumed the presidency of the prestigious Laurel Hall Club. Bearing the motto "Life without literature is death," Laurel Hall was San Francisco's first literary club, formed in 1886 by the alumnae of the Laurel Hall Seminary, a girls' finishing school in San Mateo. In 1898, the woman's club section of *The Land of Sunshine* attributed the club's continued success to Lowenberg's "untiring zeal, and loving, tactful guidance."[40]

Lowenberg's essay "The Unsolved Problem," one of the few papers she presented before the Laurel Hall Club that has been preserved in print, offers insight into how the author negotiated her Jewish identity in a Christian framework. The paper, which treats "the unsolved problem" of poverty, opens with a quotation from Mark: "'The poor,' says Jesus 'ye have always with you, and whenever you will you can do them good.'" Lowenberg goes on to reject both Christian and Jewish practices of charity, discarding, in a single sentence, the "religious duty" of Christian almsgiving and the Talmudic prescription of tzedakah as a "right of religious and civil law." Instead, Lowenberg argues that in a secular context where the poor fall under the domain of municipal rather than religious institutions, the solution is to find work for the unemployed, rather than offering handouts.[41] "The Unsolved Problem" was Lowenberg's most widely disseminated paper; printed in *Club Life* in 1903, it was also excerpted in Ella Sterling Mighels's *Literary California: Poetry, Prose and Portraits* in 1918, along with a short selection from Lowenberg's first novel, *The Irresistible Current*. With quotations from Tolstoy, Shakespeare, and Charlotte Brontë, as well as Jesus and Paul, and an erudite, if wordy, prose style, Lowenberg's essay made a case against a social welfare system while subtly creating common ground between Judaism and Christianity by suggesting that the principles of religious altruism were less relevant in a modern age.

Lowenberg also worked to bring the various clubs together around shared interests, increasing, in effect, the size of this female political base. Beginning in 1895, in her capacity as president of the Philomath and Laurel Hall Clubs, she regularly hosted joint events and invited other women's clubs and their leaders to join them in conversation. Under a headline that announced "an array of pretty toilets," *The Call* reported on the "unusual occasion" of a breakfast hosted by Lowenberg at the Palace Hotel for constituents of her clubs as well as the Century and Sorosis, two well-established women's clubs with branches around the nation. According to *The Call*, the "200 handsomely attired ladies" in attendance "represented the wealth, beauty and intellect, at least in a great degree, of the great City of the coast." If class alone did not bind these women to one another, the different groups were united through performative acts of Americanization. At the 1895 breakfast, for example, the papers included a panegyric on the United States, which was followed by the "musicians [striking] up 'America' amid much clapping of hands."[42] Patriotic toasts and music became a standard feature of the gatherings hosted by Lowenberg, who firmly believed that both native-born and naturalized citizens should "owe allegiance to America and to no other country."[43]

Interclub events may have solidified bourgeois Jewish women's place in the nation, seating them side by side with their non-Jewish compatriots, but such gatherings also exposed tensions about gender ideology that simmered beneath the surface of the club movement. At club meetings, the subject of suffrage was often taboo due to the controversy it would engender, even as clubwomen frequently discussed the broader topic of women's progress and the phenomenon of the New Woman. "I would sooner see a man offer me a seat in a streetcar than make me stand because we are equal," stated one speaker at the 1895 breakfast. "I will grant there may be some day equality in the world. But there never can be equality in the home. From the nature of things the woman must have more influence there than the man."[44] The logic of the statement—that gender equality would disrupt the natural order not by threatening male authority, but rather by challenging *women's* superiority in the home—is evidence of what Blair calls "Domestic Feminism."

Of all the San Francisco women's clubs, it was the Philomath that took the strongest stand against suffrage, in deference to its founder's

"The Ladies of the Laurel Hall, Sorosis, Century, and Philomath Clubs at Their Breakfast in the Marble Room." This sketch appeared in *The San Francisco Call* on November 23, 1895, with an article headlined "Club Ladies Breakfast: Mrs. I. Lowenberg Entertains About 200 of Them at the Palace Hotel: An Array of Pretty Toilets: Laurel Hall, Century, Sorosis and Philomath Club Members on Woman's Progress."

ideological beliefs.[45] Outside commentators saw women's clubs as a "disguise for suffrage," where women "band . . . together under a literary and harmless exterior and watch their chance." Lowenberg, however, was no suffragist in disguise. A 1901 profile of the club leader in *The Call*, for example, went so far as to describe her as "unclublike" because of her outspokenness against votes for women. In contrast to many of her contemporaries, who believed that women's moral superiority would purify politics, Lowenberg thought that the vote would corrupt women, expressing the fear that "the polls [would] rub off something of that sweet womanliness which everyone loves and admires."[46] Her role in the club movement may not have been a cover for suffrage activism, but Lowenberg's femininity did operate as a form of masquerade; her adherence to the status quo, at the least on the surface, provided her with a nonthreatening public platform, and thus a way to challenge gender norms, ensuring that women had a voice in local and national affairs. "Mrs. Lowenberg wins out by her womanliness," the profile in *The Call* began, while going on to declare her "one of the cleverest, brainiest, most earnest club women in the city."[47]

Indeed, Lowenberg cut a contradictory figure. Many of her words and her actions resonate with feminist ideas about women's empowerment and the necessity of equal opportunity through education. In contrast to the "myth" of Jewish clubwomen as behind-the-scenes enablers,[48] Lowenberg sought the spotlight, as exemplified by the lavish affairs over which she presided. As further evidence of her prominence as a public figure, the California press regularly turned to her on matters of the sexes. For example, in 1909, she was asked to comment on an article published in *Red Book* by University of Chicago anthropologist Frederick Starr; claiming that women had not made any significant achievements in literature and the arts, Starr dismissed the entire sex as "savages." In her response, Lowenberg quickly turned the tables on him, noting that "every step and advance in our civilization have been marked by women" and expressing her view of men as the true "barbarians."[49] Lowenberg came across as a strong advocate for women's education who believed that women were equal, if not superior, to men in intelligence. "The mind of a well-read person—man or woman—is a thesaurus, which only requires a little tapping to supply necessary wants," she wrote in an 1895 symposium in *The Wave* about whether the "burden of conversation" rested with men or women. "No mind should be allowed to be in a state of inertia."[50] Here and elsewhere, Lowenberg critiqued medical practices that linked female neurasthenia to an excess of intellectual activity, a belief that infamously led to near-disastrous treatment of Charlotte Perkins Gilman with the "rest cure." Lowenberg and other club leaders believed instead that the intellectual stimulation of women's clubs could be a "cure for feminine nerves," a means of relieving "monotony and repression."[51]

Still, unlike Gilman, Lowenberg did not forsake the cult of domesticity. Her 1903 report on the Philomaths in *Club Life* described the club's mission as "intellectual advancement" while stressing its members' shared conviction that "the home 'is the bulwark of civilization.'"[52] A 1900 feature in *The Call* on the "twentieth century girl" included this statement from Lowenberg: "Woman no longer sits down and waits for the recognition of man, but she rises in the dignity of her true womanhood and makes for herself a niche in the world. . . . To-day [woman] is by [man's] side endeavoring to lighten his task as a breadwinner as well as being 'a ministering angel.' And she is more than ever anxious to better the conditions of humanity . . . Woman, though weak physically, is strong mentally . . . Paradoxical as it may seem, woman is stronger and braver than man."[53] Holding on to rather than rejecting the discourse of true womanhood, and stopping short of imagining independent New Women who do not need to be by the side of a man, Lowenberg's words bridged nineteenth-century notions of "the angel in the house" with a vision of a modern twentieth-century woman, who actively participated in public and economic life.

Later in life, Lowenberg herself appeared "more than ever anxious to serve the conditions of humanity." The club movement had honed her leadership skills, providing her with a road map into public affairs, and she eagerly took on more explicit roles in the nation's political scene. She may have opposed suffrage, but once women did have the vote, she was a vocal supporter of Warren Harding in 1920 and Calvin Coolidge in 1924. However, unlike fellow Philomath member Florence Prag Kahn, who went on to serve the nation as a congresswoman from California, Lowenberg was not interested in holding political office, declining, for example, a nomination to run for the lieutenant governorship of California.[54] Yet, she persisted in using her public platform to express her views on law and governance. She spoke out about the need to abolish the Electoral College, presented a plan for six-year presidential term limits, and provided congressional testimony on marriage reform, the cause that she took up in her 1910 novel, *A Nation's Crime*, which used a sensational bigamy plot to advocate state uniformity in divorce law.

At the end of the nineteenth century, Lowenberg had also been caught up in the patriotic fervor of the Spanish- and Philippine-American Wars. As Jeanne Abrams has shown, the nation's military interventionism abroad allowed the Reform community in particular to demonstrate American patriotism by supporting the nation's efforts to expand its borders and spread democracy.[55] Like Wolf's Jewish female characters in *Heirs of Yesterday*, Lowenberg seized upon this opportunity to display her loyalty to her country. She became active in the local and national branches of the Red Cross, hosting benefit teas—this time, not in a hotel, but in her "beautiful home," where the city's Jewish and non-Jewish elite could hobnob with the likes of General Arthur MacArthur, who led the 1899 Battle of Manila.[56]

While her public service grew in new directions, her belief in the power of literacy remained a constant. As chair of the committee of the American library for Manila, for example, Lowenberg's primary objective was to supply books to soldiers serving overseas.[57] Her twin commitments to literacy and America's imperial project were also evident in her involvement with the Panama-Pacific International Exposition, the world's fair held in San Francisco in 1915 to commemorate the completion of the Panama Canal and celebrate the expansion of the nation's global reach.[58] As president of the Pacific Coast Women's Press Association (an office formerly held by Charlotte Perkins Gilman, who ultimately found the organization too traditional for her tastes[59]), Lowenberg proposed the idea for a Congress of Authors and Journalists. With Lowenberg serving as vice president and chairing many of its sessions, the congress celebrated California writers such as Bret Harte and Ina Coolbrith, featured papers that ranged in topic from Japanese and Chinese literature to the influence of Victorianism on modern writers, and included a speech by Temple Emanu-El's Rabbi Martin Meyer on wit and humor in medieval and modern Jewish poetry.[60] Lowenberg's vision for the congress was one of literary diversity, balancing religious and secular texts and regional and national literatures.

Following the lead of its founder, the Philomath Club also grew in the direction of volunteerism and philanthropy. In the pages of *Emanu-El*, San Francisco's weekly Jewish newspaper, Lowenberg published short pieces urging women to combine philanthropy and social service.[61] By 1918, the club listed among its activities the adoption of French war orphans, a variety of scholarships, Americanization programs, and raising money for the Palestinian Restoration Fund, whose goal was to establish a "spiritual center" for Jewry in Palestine.[62] Lowenberg was proud of the fact that, like so many other women's clubs, the Philomath had evolved beyond its literary beginnings. In a speech titled "Then and Now" that she gave to her fellow Philomaths in 1923, two years before her death, she reflected on her long association with the club: "Universities do not train all their students to remain and to be professors, but send them out to grapple with the problems of the world. So when the Founder was told the members of Philomath wished to fly, The founder felt and still feels that was the greatest tribute that could be paid her—To fly from the nest—be ready to go out into the world and do things—fill positions with honor and efficiency—brilliant children of her dreams."[63] Speaking of herself in the third person, Lowenberg employs seemingly contradictory analogies to mark the waning years of the women's club movement: she is at once the capital-F "Founder" of an institution of higher learning akin to the male-dominated university system and a nurturing maternal figure, setting free her "brilliant children," looking on proudly as they spread their wings and "fly from the nest." These gendered analogies define Lowenberg's legacy, fulfilling her vision of a literary club for Jewish women that engaged in rigorous intellectual work and upheld the principles of what scholars have labeled "domestic feminism."

The Philomath Club encourages us to think about Jewish American literature not just in terms of writers and texts but also in terms of institutions and literacy practices. Under Lowenberg's leadership, elite Jewish women of turn-of-the-twentieth-century San Francisco created a vibrant secular literary culture—one that was very different from the Jewish literary culture that flourished at the same time in New York and has dominated scholarship on Jewish American literature of this period. These elite Jewish women of the West Coast wrote speeches, essays, toasts, poetry, fiction, and plays. They studied and debated, researched and read. They undertook these literacy practices in the company of—and for audiences of—other women. They broke intellectual barriers and ethno-religious ones, helping to build a pluralistic community, in which, "other things being equal," they were accepted by the Christian majority.

These women's activities have largely escaped the notice of literary and cultural historians, in part because their intellectual labor took place in bourgeois and woman-centered contexts and in part because most of what they produced never made its way into print. For Lowenberg, however, print culture became one of many ways she worked to disseminate her message and advocate reform. While her early writings appeared in journals such as *Club Life* and *Club Woman*, in the last decades of her life, she sought a broader audience, combining her commitment to reform with her literary leanings as the author of three novels, which, as reviewers were quick to point out, were "written for a definite cause."[64] The first of these novels, *The Irresistible Current*, presented an argument for religious tolerance—an argument that was also woven through her career in the women's club movement, where she worked to cultivate sorority between Christians and Jews and to break down the barriers that kept educated Jewish women of leisure from participating fully in the social and cultural life of the nation. In her fiction, Lowenberg placed considerably less emphasis on this communal network of clubs, where bonds were forged between women; instead, the heterosexual and domestic institution of marriage became the linchpin of her argument.

The Intermarriage Plot and Jewish American Literary History

In April 1896, on the other side of the country, a very different sort of conversation was taking place at a meeting of the New York section of the NCJW, where writer Annie Josephine Levi was presenting a paper on "Intermarriage." "It is with alarm that I notice many of our ranks seeking life-partners from among Gentiles," she noted. Detailing threats to "marital felicity" and the future of Judaism, Levi concluded her speech by urging her audience to "guard" their Jewish "inheritance as a priceless treasure." The speech obliquely referenced the San Francisco Philomaths when Levi called out one of the club's best-known members, Emma Wolf, whose 1892 novel *Other Things Being Equal* was still being read and discussed by women's clubs around the country. While acknowledging her respect for Wolf's "charmingly told story," Levi cautioned that the novel's "unsatisfactory resolution of the intermarriage problem, wherein religious sympathy is a minor consideration" might "sow dangerous seeds in the minds of youth."[65] As Jews and Christians increasingly intermarried in the nineteenth century, most religious leaders in the Jewish community shared Levi's views.[66] Intermarriage was an especially fraught site in turn-of-the-twentieth-century America, according to Eric Goldstein, because "a definition of Jewishness grounded in blood and ancestry often set the limit of social interactions with non-Jews at marriage."[67] Striking at the heart of questions about Jewish identity, and the longevity of Judaism in the diaspora, intermarriage became—and continues to be—one of the most hotly debated topics in American Jewish life.

In the conclusion of this chapter, I turn to *The Irresistible Current* in order to demonstrate how clubs like the Philomath, begun as regional networks of like-minded women, also operated as sites of national literary production. Publishing novels became a way for clubwomen to extend their reach beyond the local and to further solidify the relationship between literature and reform in Progressive-Era culture. For both Wolf and Lowenberg, the intermarriage theme was a stepping stone to other social issues. While the conventions of the marriage plot allowed them to explore the political power of literature in the "womanly" guise of a domestic novel, the *inter*marriage plot allowed them to weave themselves, and other Jews, into a national narrative.

It is more than coincidental that two of the Philomath members who published novels chose intermarriage as the subject of their debuts. Though Wolf, physically disabled and without the resources available to married women like Lowenberg, was not as active in the club movement, Philomath meetings brought the two writers together, providing them with opportunities to encounter the same ideas, learn from each other, read the same books, and discuss each other's work. Even as they shared much common ground, the two women would have likely disagreed on some matters of gender and of religion. Though their first novels have related premises, the narratives play out quite differently. In Wolf's intermarriage ideal, social equality is achieved and Jewish difference preserved. Lowenberg takes Wolf's sympathetic treatment of intermarriage a few steps further. *The Irresistible Current* hypothesizes that harmony can only be attained through the *elimination* of religious differences. Yet, like Wolf's, Lowenberg's novel diverges in important ways from "erotic-assimilationist" fiction in which Americanization often meant marrying a gentile and thus becoming less Jewish and more Christian. Set west of the New York ghetto, in a small frontier community, *The Irresistible Current* makes a case for the transformation of all religious denominations into one, exploring and then rejecting the possibility that Jews could be Christianized, or Christians Judaized, through a tragic marriage plot turned failed conversion narrative.

To great fanfare in the world of San Francisco women's clubs, Lowenberg's literary debut took place in the summer of 1908, just months before Zangwill's *The Melting Pot* opened in Washington, DC. In *The Irresistible Current*, Lowenberg returned to the Missouri of her youth, drawing on her experiences growing up as a Jewish girl at a Catholic convent in a small town on the Mississippi River. With its intersecting plotlines and sentimental style, the novel might be dubbed the *Uncle Tom's Cabin* of interfaith unions, though it was never to reach anywhere near the readership of Harriet Beecher Stowe's abolitionist bestseller. The book was published by the New York–based Broadway Publishing Company, and its author was identified by her husband's name, "Mrs. I. Lowenberg," a propriety to which the clubwoman adhered in social and literary life.[68] The book was advertised in the secular and Jewish press, with an ad in *The American Hebrew and Jewish Messenger*, for example, citing the *San Francisco Examiner*'s comparison to works by Upton Sinclair and Winston Churchill. Advertisements highlighted *The Irresistible Current*'s status as a "purpose novel," whose stated goal was the promotion of "a Universal Religion."[69] While both Zangwill's play and Lowenberg's novel used intermarriage stories to make a case for religious universalism, the two writers took different approaches to a similar problem. Zangwill's play is a comedy, with its last act uniting the star-crossed Jewish and non-Jewish lovers, redeeming them in life as a symbol of the melting pot ideal. Lowenberg's novel ends in tragedy with the death of its heartbroken Jewish heroine, Grace Feld. Whereas Zangwill's melodramatic language swelled national pride (as proven by Theodore Roosevelt's oft-quoted praise of the playwright), Lowenberg's sentimental rhetoric was intended to provoke the shedding of tears that would move its readers to action.[70]

Lowenberg's novel initially treads ground familiar to readers of turn-of-the-twentieth-century Jewish American fiction. The first two chapters focus on Ruth Rheinberg's transatlantic journey to New York to join her brother, Joseph, following the deaths of their parents in Wiesbaden, Germany. The novel takes an unexpected turn in chapter 3, jumping ahead more than eighteen years to find Joseph and Ruth, both now married, settled in a small town on the Western frontier. Joseph makes his living as a merchant, while Ruth's husband, Henry Feld, has acquired substantial wealth by investing in new land. In making this temporal and geographic leap, Lowenberg conveniently skips over the assimilation process. By the time readers catch up with the Rheinberg siblings, they have been acculturated to American ways. Regionalism further attenuates their Judaism, since the small town is devoid of Jewish cultural and religious institutions. Instead, Joseph's and Ruth's daughters, the American-born cousins Letitia Rheinberg and Grace Feld, are preparing to graduate from the local convent school.

The frontier town provides the backdrop for *The Irresistible Current*'s exploration of social exclusions faced by middle-class Jews. In Lowenberg's grandiose description of the setting,

> Civilization had reached the mighty West of the New Continent and had built the town of D——, in Missouri, on the grand Mississippi. Progress had been born there, but struggled feebly for existence. The child was not yet strong enough to strangle the serpent Prejudice, which flourished on the soil and raised its hardy head with pride and insolence.[71]

Though their American belief in religious freedom prevents the non-Jewish settlers from confining Jewish residents "to Ghettos and precincts of old . . . as is still done in Russia," the townspeople try to maintain distinct social circles, expressing the antisemitic belief that Jews are "of that proscribed race whom nothing but conversion can make good."[72] As opposed to fiction set in the ghetto, in which Jewish characters were often defined by spatial segregation, here there is little to separate and distinguish the town's few Jewish families from their Christian neighbors. Those of different religions find themselves in frequent and unavoidable contact.

Interreligious contact is inescapable in part because the Christian townspeople cannot detect who is Jewish. They are surprised to discover that, in both appearance and behavior, Jews resemble their Christian counterparts, rather than ghetto stereotypes. Instead of being "short of stature" with "black, hungry looking eyes, receding forehead, a nose like the beak of an eagle" and "thick lips," for example, the town's Jewish attorney, Mark Anthony Everard, turns out to be a "tall, commanding figure" with "blue eyes," "a pleasant mouth, a fair complexion and no little curls."[73] In defiance of Shylockian caricature, Everard—as his given name suggests—was created in the image of the Roman statesman and lover of the Egyptian Queen Cleopatra. The heroine's name, Grace Feld, similarly signals to readers that she does not comply with antisemitic stereotypes. Graceful in looks and in the ethereal spirituality of her demeanor, Lowenberg's Jewish protagonist recognizes that her appearance would allow her to pass as Christian. "If you did not know we were Jews could you read it in our faces?"[74] Grace asks Everard, in an effort to understand why she was blackballed from a sorority organized by her classmates—a plot detail that takes on heightened meaning in light of Lowenberg's founding of the Philomath Club and her desire for Jewish inclusion in San Francisco's elite women's club culture. Struggling to come to terms with her minority identity, Grace "wish[es] [that] we were out of this detestable place or that God has made us Christians." But her mother prevails upon her to keep her faith in Judaism. Though Grace's mother, Ruth, is not devout in her religious observance, she explains that her "heart is a Jewish one and beats for Judaism." These words echo sentiments expressed by another Ruth, the heroine of Wolf's *Other Things Being Equal*, who refused to renounce her religion, asserting, "I am a Jewess, and will die one."[75]

The Irresistible Current tests its characters' religious faith and the barriers of religious difference through a Victorian marriage plot, juxtaposing the courtships of endogamous Jewish and Christian couples with star-crossed interfaith romances. The "serpent Prejudice" primarily resides in the mansion of sisters Alice and Amelia Hill, whose opposing personalities correspond with those of the Jewish cousins, angelic Grace and mean-spirited Letitia. Over the course of the 558-page novel, Amelia, the snootier and more vocally antisemitic of the Hill sisters, does finally overcome her prejudice when she falls in love with Everard, and puts aside her "religious scruples" to accept his persistent proposals of marriage. The couple is able to resolve their religious differences by finding common ground in universalism. As Everard declares to his wife, "You are no Christian, I no Jew, we are simply Monotheists, believers in God and in immortality."[76] Everard operates as a mouthpiece for Lowenberg's own views. In an interview that appeared in 1905 in *Emanu-El*, the author argued that there is no meaningful difference between Judaic and Christian ideals since both are monotheistic religions, and "monotheism is the most rational and convincing of dogmas."[77]

As in *Other Things Being Equal*, intermarriage in *The Irresistible Current* is not a "problematic solution to the temptations of assimilation." The central Jewish characters in Lowenberg's novel are assimilated and

American-born Jews, not new immigrants striving to become American. Intermarriage is instead represented as a symbolic ideal, an answer not to "the temptations of assimilation," but to the "problem" of inequality and religious prejudice. Furthermore, in Lowenberg's novel, religious difference in general, rather than Jewishness specifically, is construed as an obstacle to love between social equals. In the case of the novel's sentimental heroine, the social taboo of Christian-Jewish marriage leads to suffering and tragedy. Traveling with her parents to New York (a trip that notably includes the daughter's first visit to a synagogue), Grace finds herself torn between two suitors, wealthy William LaValle, who, as her mother puts it, "is of our religion, and is every way a man to be encouraged in respectable families," and Dr. Arthur Montmartre, a Unitarian minister, whose kindness and intellect win Grace's heart.[78] Though Montmartre sees little difference between the liberal Christianity of Unitarianism and the Felds' loose allegiance to Judaism, Grace and her parents are less convinced that even nominal differences in religion can be overcome. When the minister finds himself unable to comply with Grace's request that he convert to Judaism so that they can marry, Grace experiences her first heartbreak, setting in motion a chain of tragic events.

Back in Missouri, Grace comes to accept LaValle, but Letitia, jealous of her cousin's good fortune and future wealth, schemes to break up their engagement. Letitia's machinations lead, in rapid succession, to the financial ruin of the Felds, the suicide of Grace's father, and the death of her mother. Taking refuge at the convent, where she is cared for by her former teachers, the grief-stricken orphan finds comfort in her religious duties and decides to convert to Catholicism. Yet Grace, now the novice-elect Sister Catharine, is unable to reconcile her Jewish identity with her adopted religion; she falls fatally ill and returns to her cousin Letitia's home to wait out her final days. Those who loved Grace put aside their religious differences to join together around her deathbed:

> It was a harmonious, though sad, solemn and impressive scene. Such a closing tableau is seldom witnessed. Here were represented various denominations, the Jew, the Catholic and the Unitarian, supplicating God for one Jewish soul. Oh, Faith, brotherly love and sympathy, after such a concordant exhibition, a millennium on

> earth seems possible. Angels must have smiled over this chorus of religious sentiments, which partook of Divine unison. Such fruits of the reconciliation of different religious beliefs will be the euthanasia of atheism. Truly out of death comes life.[79]

The novel employs a device common to Victorian sentimentalism in which the death of an innocent transfigures the living in an effort to heal earthly divisions. Like the passing of Stowe's Little Eva, whose love for all humankind promised to abolish differences between the enslaved and the free, the death of Grace Feld asserts the need to replace religious difference, and ensuing prejudice, with a universal religion that would create harmony and unity among its believers.

Through universalism, Lowenberg imagines an alternative to the pluralist and assimilationist stances prevalent in early twentieth-century American Jewish fiction. Rather than have her characters fully embrace their Jewish difference or erase their ethno-religious specificity in order to conform to the Christian majority, here the "various denominations, the Jew, the Catholic and the Unitarian" come together to form a new religious ideal. Like *Other Things Being Equal*, *The Irresistible Current* emphasizes similarities rather than differences between Jews and gentiles, but Lowenberg's intermarriage plot takes its argument even further: it makes a sentimental plea for universal religion, contending that the American ideal of equality can only be achieved by removing difference. Montmartre's initial refusal to convert to Judaism and Grace's fatal attempt to take vows as a Catholic also put a spin on the typical conversion narrative. *The Irresistible Current* suggests that national unity—and the "euthanasia of atheism"—demands the spiritual rebirth of all, not simply the conversion of those who are different. In Lowenberg's imaginative solution, institutions, not individuals, need to adapt and change to foster a more tolerant and inclusive society—a philosophy that similarly motivated its author's strategic use of the women's club movement to carve out a space for Jewish women in bourgeois San Francisco.

The reception of Lowenberg's *The Irresistible Current* was lukewarm at best. Some of the harshest criticism appeared in the *Los Angeles Herald*, which called the novel "negligible as literature," finding that its "didactic" tone and "odd mixture of . . . diction" created a "grotesque" effect.[80] The response to *The Irresistible Current* was shaped by readers' and reviewers' assumptions about regionalism and provincialism. Though set in the Midwest, the South, and New York, the novel warranted only minor attention beyond its author's home state of California. *The New York Times* editor who briefly mentioned the novel in an announcement of new releases did not bother to read it, or even its description, assuming that if the author was a woman from the West Coast, the book could be summed up as "a story of California life."[81]

The West Coast Jewish press paid more careful attention to this novel written by one of their own. "One may not agree with Mrs. Lowenberg's view on Judaism or Christianity," stated a review in *The Jewish Tribune* (Portland, Oregon), "yet this novel gives a mass of food for thinking people to digest."[82] An unsigned review in *Emanu-El* concurred: "Whether one may or may not agree with her conclusions . . . [*The Irresistible Current*] is a bold and noble attempt to conciliate the various religious beliefs of the world presented in the form of a novel of which the literary style is above the mediocre." Despite the tepid appraisal of Lowenberg's prose, the reviewer complimented the author for her "remarkable" knowledge of religious subjects, noting that she has "demonstrated in her own person that the enjoyments and attractions of social life incident to wealth and a devotion to philanthropic work are no bar to intellectual pursuits." Lowenberg, the reviewer opined, has "preached a strong sermon in the shape of a love story in which the central figure is a Jewish girl."[83]

Rabbi Marcus Friedlander of Temple Sinai in nearby Oakland was less than pleased with Lowenberg's "sermon." His pan of the novel appeared in a separate issue of *Emanu-El. The Irresistible Current* "undertakes to solve world-perplexing problems, and fails," he wrote. He went on to offer a sharp critique of Lowenberg's negative portrayals of Jewish characters, which neglect to "bring . . . out any of the great virtues the Jew has proved himself capable of"; her tendency to cite biblical passages from the New Testament; her "want of knowledge of Jewish history, Jewish philosophy, and religious criticism"; and her espousal of a "vague" and "mysterious" religious universalism.[84] Friedlander's criticism suggests that the national Jewish press's silence on the book was likely due to Lowenberg's outdated message. By the time the novel was published, even the liberally religious Reform movement, whose leader Rabbi Isaac Mayer Wise had briefly flirted with universalism, had resolutely moved in the direction of Jewish triumphalism.[85]

Lowenberg, however, seemed undeterred by such a negative assessment of *The Irresistible Current*. Not only did she go on to write other novels (albeit ones devoid of explicitly Jewish content), but Friedlander's lengthy review appears in her scrapbook, without comment, alongside reviews from other San Francisco newspapers. That her first novel's warmest reception occurred in San Francisco's secular press speaks to Lowenberg's strong and supportive local following, especially as the critical response was more a show of respect for the author than for the book itself. "In saying complimentary things about 'The Irresistible Current' . . . the reviewer is apt to be charged with loyalty and pride of locality," wrote the San Francisco-based magazine *Overland Monthly*, "for Mrs. Lowenberg is a San Franciscan, well-known socially and for her work in the clubs."[86] *Sunset* magazine's review similarly singled out the author as a "San Franciscan, noted for her public spirit and for her clear thinking and ability to define her position on all questions dealing with civic welfare or public advancement."[87] Upon the novel's publication, Lowenberg was feted by many of the city's women's clubs, who took up her book as a topic of discussion. In the spirit of open debate that the club leader had helped foster, the women invited Lowenberg to "[hear and reply] to friendly criticism."[88] Lowenberg's aim as a writer was to spark a national dialogue, not win literary acclaim. As one reviewer of *The Irresistible Current* pointed out, Lowenberg, at age sixty-three, did not suddenly fancy herself a "budding novelist."[89] Instead, print in general and the novel specifically could potentially broaden her audience beyond the California club movement. Her choice of a sentimental marriage plot suggests that she was particularly interested in reaching other women, who would respond to her message that bigotry and religious intolerance threatened the harmony of the family and the home.

The sanctity of marriage was also the primary concern of her next social purpose novel, *A Nation's Crime* (1910). Just as Wolf had followed *Other Things Being Equal* with a series of domestic novels that were absent of explicitly Jewish characters or themes,[90] Lowenberg's intermarriage novel served as a springboard for the writer to explore non-Jewish content in her fiction. Published two years after *The Irresistible Current*, *A Nation's Crime* used a similarly tragic and intricate domestic plot to argue for reform in marriage law. At the same time that other California Jewish women, such as activist Selina Solomons and journalist-turned-bestselling novelist Miriam Michelson, were organizing one of the first successful suffrage campaigns in the nation, culminating in an amendment to the state constitution in 1911, Lowenberg was presenting verbal and written arguments for a constitutional amendment that would create federal uniformity in divorce law. Her stated goal was to ensure that "the purity and integrity of the home . . . be preserved."[91] In *A Nation's Crime*, Lowenberg appeals to Americans' sense of morality, weaving a sensational story in which the haphazardness of divorce laws tears at the heart of the family structure, leading to charges of bigamy, illegitimacy, contested wills, and suicide. Frequent analogies to the nation's past crime of slavery—including a pointed reminder that without legal divorce "woman was a slave to her husband"—position Lowenberg as a successor to Stowe's protest tradition. In the rousing dialogue that ends the novel, the various characters dedicate themselves to the "abolition" of unequal laws that Lowenberg calls "A Nation's Crime": "The nation which has given liberty and protection to the friendless, to the oppressed, to the persecuted; which has emancipated slavery and placed the laurel on Lincoln's brow, will give the world . . . a Uniform Divorce Law which all nations with a claim to civilization must—will—follow."[92] Like *The Irresistible Current*, the novel ends on a hopeful and regenerative note with the patriotic promise that the United States will prove itself a leader in righting international wrongs.

Lowenberg's third and last novel, *The Voices* (1920), similarly couches its critique in the discourse of American exceptionalism. Published five years before Lowenberg's death, and dedicated to the memory of her recently deceased husband, *The Voices* tackles a host of political and social issues through the character of Joan Lynn, a young stenographer who becomes a modern-day Joan of Arc, galvanizing the masses with her inspirational calls to action. The only novel by Lowenberg to be set in California and to bear the imprint of a West Coast publisher, the book is a barely disguised political platform. Advertisements declared the novel "the herald of the presidential campaign of 1920."[93] *The Voices* appears at first to be a novel in the radical tradition. Its female protagonist is a woman of the people, a union activist and "militant suffragette" so committed to her causes that she vows never to marry. By the end, however, it confusingly veers in other political directions, with the same protagonist spouting nativist rhetoric in an effort to keep "undesirables" from infiltrating the nation's borders.[94] And although the novel deviates somewhat from Lowenberg's previous reliance on the marriage plot for its structure, it ends with the pro-labor protagonist caving and finally agreeing to marry her capitalist boss, whose relentless pursuit smacks of sexual harassment. Despite this, the novel was reviewed favorably in the California press. "No novel more timely or useful could have been written," stated one review. "And that a woman should have written it makes the literary performance all the more remarkable. The feminine intellect does not lack in force brilliancy, but it seldom addresses itself to such a task as the infusion of political economy, practical politics, and ethics in a tale of love, with a happy termination."[95]

For all her talk of the "sanctity" of the home, Lowenberg herself had moved far beyond the domestic sphere. Under the "ideological cover" of "Domestic Feminism," she and other clubwomen entered public life as intellectuals, speakers, reformers, and writers. Through the cultural practices of women's clubs, Lowenberg brokered an intermarriage of sorts, forging close bonds between Jewish and non-Jewish bourgeois women who found common ground in literature and philanthropic service. In April 1925, three months after her death, Lowenberg was eulogized at the San Francisco District Convention of the California Federation of Women's Clubs by one of its past presidents, Dr. Mariana Bertola. A daughter of Italian immigrant parents, obstetrician, and social reformer, Bertola summarized Lowenberg's many accomplishments as evidence that her fellow clubwoman's "work was never bound by creed, color, or nationality." Like many of the obituaries of Lowenberg, Bertola's eulogy noted that one of her last deeds was to establish the Bettie Lowenberg Annual Memorial Christmas Tree Fund at the San Francisco Nursery, where she spent the holiday distributing gifts to homeless children. For Bertola, Lowenberg's final act was not a sign of assimilation, but a "lesson in Tolerance." Indeed, Bertola concluded her eulogy by paying tribute to Lowenberg as a Jew. "We were always impressed with her deep religious feeling, the true love of God within her heart," stated Bertola before offering a reading from a psalm of David, "one of the Great Men of [Lowenberg's] faith."[96]

In an essay on Jewish women and religious identity in the American West, William Toll argues that while nineteenth-century American-born San Francisco women may have passed on only a "rudimentary Judaism" to their children, they generated "a spirit of communal responsibility."[97] This "spirit of communal responsibility" is Lowenberg's legacy. She may not be remembered for producing a great and enduring work of literature, but the intellectual culture that she nourished is worthy of consideration for the way it expanded Jewish women's minds and opportunities. It was against this backdrop, for example, that a writer like Wolf was able to flourish.

With their Western settings and middle-class characters who defy Jewish stereotypes, the novels of Wolf and Lowenberg are many miles away—figuratively and literally—from the ghetto tales that have long dominated scholarship on early Jewish American literary history. For these bourgeois California writers, the West fostered an expansiveness of vision in regard to ethno-religious identity that differs in significant ways from the familiar narrative of the poor, immigrant outsider laboring among sweatshops and pushcarts while striving to become American. Wolf and Lowenberg complicate accepted narratives about immigration and assimilation and challenge national and ethno-racial demarcations between "Jewish" and "American" as well as theological ones between Judaism and Christianity. The writings and careers of these two overlooked women compel a more capacious understanding of what constitutes an ethnic literary tradition, while also speaking to the ways that California Jewish women contributed to debates about some of the most fundamental concepts in ethnic studies, such as the "melting pot." In the following chapter, I examine another writer who was (at least briefly) affiliated with the Philomath Club, Harriet Lane Levy, to demonstrate how Jewish women who came of age in late nineteenth-century California proved to be pioneers in yet another arena: the emerging movements of American and transnational modernism.

3
Between San Francisco and the Left Bank

The Architecture of Modernist Memoir

In her memoir *920 O'Farrell Street*, completed when she was eighty years old, Harriet Lane Levy describes her Jewish upbringing in late nineteenth-century San Francisco. The daughter of religiously observant immigrants, Levy was torn between conflicting expectations: on the one hand, her parents expected her to abide by Victorian gender conventions; on the other, they encouraged her to pursue the education that would lead her to become a modern, independent woman of the new century. Like Rebekah Bettelheim Kohut's 1925 autobiography, *My Portion* (which I discussed in the introduction), *920 O'Farrell Street* garnered favorable comparison to more familiar stories of American Jewish life when it was first published by Doubleday in 1947. "What a pleasant relief to open a book about an orthodox Jewish family and not find the stereotypes of conventional post-Ellis Island stories," wrote reviewer Allen Lesser.[1] Lesser's review appeared in *The Menorah Journal*, which had published two chapters from Levy's book in 1937, identifying them as excerpts from "the story of a San Francisco pioneer family."[2] That Levy's memoir did not conform to the "stereotypes" and "conventions" of traditional immigrant stories helps explain why it languished unpublished for a decade. Lesser admonished "the many publishers . . . including the Jewish Publication Society of America" who "rejected it," suggesting that they "might well profit by a few moments' reflection on the reasons why they missed up on a bestseller."[3] Lesser's criticism speaks to the ways that the institution of publishing has played a significant role in defining Jewishness, ushering certain stories into print and discarding others. *The Menorah Journal*, with its mission to promote secular Jewish culture, saw value in Levy's story, Lesser implies, while the Jewish Publication Society hewed to a more limited, even stereotypical notion of what constituted Jewish life in America.[4]

Lesser's words might give pause for reflection today as well. Despite a reissue by California publisher Heyday Books in 1996 with an added subtitle "A Jewish Girlhood in Old San Francisco," and despite numerous scholarly analyses of Jewish American autobiographical texts like Mary Antin's *The Promised Land* (1912), *920 O'Farrell Street* has continued to languish, untouched by literary critics.[5] This neglect is made more curious by Levy's direct connection to Gertrude Stein, one of modernism's most important and endlessly discussed figures, and by the way *920 O'Farrell Street* is shaped by modernist aesthetics. Levy's experiment with autobiographical form makes for rich comparisons with Stein's autobiographical oeuvre and the prose of other modernist women writers, such as Virginia Woolf, whose use of spatial metaphors to represent the social dynamics of gender, the relationship between past and present, and the shift from Victorian domesticity to domestic modernism have received ample attention from critics.[6] As a modernist memoir set in middle-class, fin de siècle San Francisco, *920 O'Farrell Street* fills a significant gap in the Jewish American literary canon. As I demonstrate through close analysis of Levy's memoir, and in particular her use of the Victorian house as a structuring device, *920 O'Farrell Street* expands the parameters of Jewish American literary history by mapping Jewishness on to the geographic and architectural sites of turn-of-the-twentieth-century San Francisco and displacing the ghetto as the sole locus of Jewish life and literature in the United States.

Jewish American literary scholarship's New York-centrism has obscured the pivotal role played by California Jewish women in the early stages of the modernist movement. As a corrective, I preface my close reading of the memoir with background on Levy, placing her in the context of a group of remarkable women—including Stein, an Oakland resident in her youth, and Alice B. Toklas, Levy's O'Farrell Street neighbor—who moved between the middle-class Jewish communities of Northern California and the expatriate salons of Paris in the first decades of the twentieth century. In a special issue of *Modern Fiction Studies* on "Modernism's Jews/Jewish Modernisms," editor Maren Linett called for more attention to the ways that Jewish writers, especially women, "shaped literary modernism and the intricate ways modernism was in turn shaped by its figuring of Jews and Jewishness."[7] Expanding on the insights of Linett's contributors and building in particular upon recent work by Amy Feinstein, who has demonstrated the centrality of Jewishness for modernist women artists, this chapter shifts the focus from fiction to autobiographical writing and uncovers the distinctly Californian Jewish roots of American and transatlantic modernism.[8]

San Francisco Jewish Women and the Making of Modernism

Born in California in 1866, Harriet Lane Levy was part of a cohort of middle-class, intellectually and artistically minded Jewish women that included Alice B. Toklas, sisters-in-law Gertrude and Sarah (Samuels) Stein, sculptor Annette Rosenshine, and pianist Theresa Erman (later Thérèse Jelenko), among others.[9] As Rosenshine describes in her unpublished memoir, this generation entered a changing world, poised between the "conditioning" of their "middle-class Victorian home[s]" and the educational and professional opportunities newly available to women.[10] This sense of being on the cusp of change was furthered by their positions as American-born daughters of Jewish immigrants. Married in 1858, Levy's parents, Benjamin "Benish" Levy (1826–1900) and Henrietta "Yetta" (Michelson) Levy (1827–1916), had immigrated to the United States from Fordon, Prussia (now a part of Poland), in the middle of the century. Benjamin and Yetta had arrived separately on the West Coast during the Gold Rush, likely meeting in Virginia City, Nevada, where Benjamin worked as a merchant alongside Yetta's brother, Samuel Michelson. The Levys decided to settle in San Francisco, purchasing a home in a newly built residential district. San Francisco offered good schools for their expanding family as well as an emerging Jewish community, which appealed to Levy's religiously observant father. The family belonged to Sherith Israel, the Orthodox synagogue whose congregation was largely made up of Polish Jews, and Benjamin was a member of the First Hebrew Benevolent Society.[11]

Unlike her two older sisters, Adeline ("Addie") and Pauline ("Polly"), whose courtships and weddings are described in *920 O'Farrell Street*, Harriet was focused on education, not marriage, and remained single throughout her life. Levy's father pushed her, if not always kindly, in the direction of intellectual validation. "To spare me the pain of future disappointment, Father prepared me for my destiny. I was bright but plain-looking, and must not expect a marriage of any consequence," she wrote in *920 O'Farrell Street*, adding that "he tapped" her "nose tenderly" and uttered, "*Hassliche Naslein* [ugly little nose]." But Benjamin Levy was clearly proud of his youngest daughter's academic achievements. In 1882, Harriet graduated first in her class from San Francisco Girls' High School, giving an impressive valedictory speech that ended with lines from George Eliot's poem "O, may I join the choir invisible." This scholarly triumph was followed by others. When news of her oratorical feat reached the entertainment committee of Temple Emanu-El, the synagogue invited her to participate in a public debate on the question "Are the Jews Responsible for the Prejudices Existing Against Them?" Despite her confession that, due to a fairly sheltered existence, she "had never encountered prejudice against the Jews from without," she bested her male opponent with a passionate argument against holding the Jewish people culpable for the perpetuation of antisemitism and, in her own words, "exonerated the race."[12]

While most Girls' High graduates of Levy's caliber went on to become teachers (if they did not immediately marry), she took a different route, enrolling at the University of California, Berkeley at a time when few women attended and becoming the first member of her family to pursue a college education. Ignoring warnings from his friends that education would "spoil the chances of a girl" because "men did not like smart wives," Levy's father gave her his blessing, though he offered "sober advice about crossing the bay alone, and presented the disadvantages of intermarriage."[13] Levy excelled at Berkeley, where she befriended classmates with interests in the arts and wrote for the campus newspaper. When she graduated in 1886, she was the only woman from her class to give an oration at commencement exercises, reading an original short story titled "Wanted, a Comedy."[14]

Following graduation, Levy's literary aspirations took her to *The Wave*, where her short stories, society sketches, and theater reviews were published alongside works by Frank Norris and Jack London. Levy also wrote dramatic criticism for *The San Francisco Call*, drawing on the education she had received attending performances as a child with her father, who "in the theater . . . found the richness of the living denied him at home."[15] Though *The Wave*'s editor, John O'Hara Cosgrave, considered her one of the San Francisco journal's "bright hopes" in the early 1890s, Levy's writing seemed to taper off toward the end of the century.[16] Even as her print output diminished, Levy remained involved in San Francisco's literary and social club scene. She presented her original writings to Jewish clubs such as the Harmonie (formerly the Young Men's Hebrew Association) and the Philomath, where she appeared on the program for the exclusive women's club's first open meeting alongside her former Girls' High classmate, novelist Emma Wolf. Along with her cousin, journalist and writer Miriam Michelson (who is the subject of the following chapter), Levy was a member of the Spinners' and Round Table Clubs, where San Francisco's women writers gathered, often over meals at luxury hotels, to discuss literature. Levy's active social life gave her many opportunities to display her wit and talent for public speaking. When the Spinners' Club published *Prosit: A Book of Toasts* in 1904, they included Levy's "To San Francisco" under the heading "Toasts to States" alongside entries from Oliver Wendell Holmes and Charles Dickens. It reads: "Our city, / Once, oh, so fast, / Now quite good caste,—— / A pity!"[17]

Levy's four lines succinctly trace San Francisco's evolution from its rough, Gold Rush beginnings, which lured her parents west, to her own cosmopolitan present. At the turn of the twentieth century, the so-called Paris of the West offered ample opportunities for this daughter of prosperous pioneers to indulge in the genteel pursuit of art and culture. But it had also come time for Levy to spread her wings beyond the Bay Area. Following the death of her father in June 1900, she planned her first trip overseas to Europe, departing in April 1901. In addition to the standard sites for an American tourist, her itinerary included a pilgrimage to the Wagnerian Opera Festival in Bayreuth; a visit with Israel Zangwill in London, who asked her if she was a Zionist before she knew what the term meant; and an auspicious meeting with fellow California transplants Gertrude and Leo Stein in Florence.[18] Soon after Levy's return to the United States, natural disaster struck. Levy records her reaction to the 1906 earthquake in the final pages of *920 O'Farrell Street*:

> In my travels [in Europe] I walked about the ruins of ancient cities, tourist-wise, speculating upon evidence of destruction too vast, too remote, to be actual. I returned home to behold a devastation as great as any I had witnessed, created not by earthquake alone, but

> by the fire which had followed upon it. I had left closely packed city streets; I returned to a barren waste of hills and to isolated buildings in unconvincing locations. Nothing was in its right place; nothing was where it used to be.
>
> I sought reassurance in some remembered landmark which would restore to me my lost identity.[19]

Decades later, Levy would turn to writing to recreate the "remembered landmarks" of her youth, her family's O'Farrell Street home, and her "lost identity."

Although Levy's memoir leaves off at the 1906 earthquake, she recounts her decision to return to Europe in unpublished reminiscences (published posthumously, in 2011, as *Paris Portraits*). This time she was accompanied by a close friend whose life had also been upended by the earthquake, Alice B. Toklas. Toklas, who grew up in San Francisco and Seattle, moved next door to Levy in 1897, living at 922 O'Farrell Street with her maternal grandparents, Louis and Hanchen Levinsky (barely disguised as the Levisons in *920 O'Farrell Street*), following her mother's death. Describing Toklas as "a strange note on the Levison canvas," Levy recalls the two women's early friendship, from passing bouquets of flowers between the windows of their homes to vacationing together at Sherman's Rose, a romantic adobe cottage in Monterey, where Toklas found annual "release" from her "monastic" life of housekeeping for her "tribe of relatives."[20]

Toklas was offered a longer respite from domestic drudgery when Sarah and Michael Stein invited her to travel with them to Europe. Michael, a San Francisco businessman, and Sarah, an amateur painter, were avid collectors who planned to acquire art using profits from family investments in San Francisco streetcars and real estate. Initially resisting Sarah's domineering personality, Toklas declined, sending art student Annette Rosenshine in her stead. After the 1906 earthquake, however, Toklas changed her mind, persuaded by the turn of events in San Francisco and Rosenshine's frequent letters describing the Paris art world, her painting classes with Matisse, and deep conversations about psychology with her new friend Gertrude Stein. Toklas also persuaded Levy, who had initially sworn off traveling due to an injured shoulder, to make the journey with her, arguing "that at worst it would be more diverting to sit behind a window in Paris and see life go by than to observe it from an apartment in San Francisco."[21] Because Toklas was in debt for spending her limited income on clothes, Levy financed both of their trips, loaning her friend $1,000 that would never be repaid. In September 1907, Levy and Toklas arrived in Paris, without setting a date for their return.

As Shari Benstock has demonstrated, by the early twentieth century, Paris's Left Bank had become a haven for women, including many American expatriates. Paris's artistic community offered professional and sexual freedoms, allowing women to lead woman-centered lives, outside the constraints of heteronormativity. The women of the Left Bank played a central role in the development of modernism while ushering in new attitudes toward gender and sexual norms.[22] Whereas Harriet and Alice resided with their families in San Francisco, overseas they lived together, staying at a hotel until they found a four-room apartment on the rue Notre-Dame-des-Champs, in walking distance from Leo and Gertrude's home on the rue de Fleurus. Like the setting of the vacation cottage in Monterey, the city of Paris—and the spaces the women inhabited within—presented alternatives to the outdated norms of Victorian domesticity, embodied by the O'Farrell Street residences Levy and Toklas were leaving behind.

With Paris as their home base, Harriet and Alice led a lively existence, attending the Steins' salons; meeting up-and-coming artists such as Picasso; studying French with his mistress Fernande Olivier; and spending summers in Fiesole, Italy, where they stayed at the Casa Ricci, not far from the Steins' own villa. In Italy, Levy especially enjoyed shopping excursions to Florence with Gertrude, in whose presence "old furniture and pieces of old jewelry . . . would release a beauty invisible to me when I went alone."[23] Influenced by Sarah Stein's passion for Matisse, Levy began collecting paintings. She also saw herself immortalized in art by David Edstrom, a married sculptor who claimed to have fallen in love with her. Toklas, meanwhile, was developing an intimacy with Gertrude Stein. "Day after day [Alice] wept because of the new love that had come into her life," Levy recalled of this time, "Alice used thirty handkerchiefs a day."[24]

While Gertrude and Alice were spending more of their time together, Harriet was bonding with Sarah, who had become a Christian Science practitioner and was treating Levy's physical ailments. Sarah persuaded

Harriet Lane Levy and Alice B. Toklas in Fiesole, Italy, in 1909. Courtesy of Bancroft Library, University of California, Berkeley.

Levy, who was in the midst of a spiritual struggle, to convert to Christian Science. Levy was likely predisposed to the church because her sister, Addie, had been "lured into the enclosure of Christian Science" back in San Francisco.[25] Mary Baker Eddy's religious teachings held particular appeal for middle-class Jewish women at the time, who were attracted by the emphasis on health and happiness as well as to women's central role in the church's leadership. "Christian Science," explains one scholar, "emphasizes the gentler, less aggressive, typically middle class, feminine sort of behavior."[26] Nor did Jewish women necessarily see Christian Science as a renunciation of their Jewish backgrounds. The Levy daughters, for instance, viewed it, in part, as "the modern dress of [their parents'] own familiar faith," providing a way for them to embrace spirituality without feeling tethered to outdated traditions.[27]

As Levy was in the process of exploring her newfound spirituality, attending services twice weekly, she had become an obstacle to Gertrude and Alice's blossoming romance. Alice, who lived on Levy's largesse, remained loyal to her San Francisco friend; she would not move out, as Gertrude wished, so that the couple could set up house in the Steins' apartment on the rue de Fleurus. Gertrude was no stranger to love triangles, and her early works, such as the posthumously published *Q.E.D.*, were structured around such romantic entanglements between women. In a mean-spirited word portrait titled "Harriet," which was not published until 1934, appearing alongside laudatory essays on figures such as Cezanne, Picasso, and Matisse in *Portraits and Prayers*, Stein vented her frustration about Levy: "She said she did not have any plans for the summer. No one was interested in this thing in whether she had any plans for the summer." For three pages, the portrait repeats variations on these phrases, only briefly alluding to the hoped-for abandonment of Levy by Toklas: "It was not easy for her to come to have a plan for the winter, some whom she was needing to have with her would be leaving her."[28] "Harriet" reads less like a character study and more like an incantation, an attempt to wish a rival out of the way. In the end, Gertrude's wish was fulfilled. Levy made plans to return home to the United States, accompanied by Sarah and Michael Stein, who had been called home due to the death of Sarah's father. By the summer of 1910, the society pages of *The San Francisco Call* reported that Levy's San Francisco friends and family were feting her with parties, "anxious to greet her after the long absence abroad."[29]

Despite the circumstances of her leaving Paris, Levy appears to have remained on good terms with Toklas, and the two women corresponded for many years. When Levy's mother died in 1916, Toklas's condolence letter contained warm memories of the O'Farrell Street next-door neighbors who offered her respite from her grandfather's tyrannical household. "She was so kind to me," Toklas wrote of Yetta Levy, "as you all were. I wish I might be able to tell how much I feel for you in your loss—you know Harriet dear how constantly you are in my thoughts."[30] The two women reconnected in person twice in the years after the fateful trip on which Gertrude came between them. In 1912, on a return visit to Europe as chaperone to her niece, Sylvia, Levy had a "joyous" reunion with the Steins in Paris, though she and Sylvia spent most of the year-long trip with Sarah, Michael, and their son, Allen, seeing less of Gertrude and Alice.[31] Levy, at this time, was writing fiction, but with limited success. As she relates, her attempt to show Gertrude a story she was working on was thwarted by the other woman's repeated declarations of her own greatness. In *Paris Portraits*, Levy acerbically recalls, "I never got a chance to read her my story and left Paris eventually enriched only by the knowledge that Gertrude Stein was now great in France."[32] In the mid-1930s, Toklas and Levy briefly reunited in San Francisco, visiting together during Gertrude's lecture tour. In a letter thanking Levy for the visit, Toklas wrote "to say how awfully good you are—and how much I feel it."[33]

Although Gertrude devoted an entire word portrait to Levy and used her as material for portraits of women in "Many Many Women" and *The Making of Americans*, Levy's near-erasure from literary history may be due in part to Stein's most widely read work, *The Autobiography of Alice B. Toklas*. Writing from the perspective of Toklas, Stein refers to Levy as simply a "friend"—and once, in describing Toklas's and Levy's first attempts to understand modern art, as an "ever curious friend."[34] A comparison between Levy's treatment in Stein's *The Autobiography of Alice B. Toklas* and in Toklas's self-authored autobiography, *What Is Remembered* (1963), is especially revealing. Stein's version of Toklas's autobiography leaves Levy unnamed (despite frequent name-dropping of the famous and the ordinary), downplaying the role that she played in Toklas's life. In contrast, the first four chapters of *What Is Remembered* contain many explicit references to Harriet, as Toklas narrates their experiences together during the San Francisco earthquake and in Europe.[35] In one of Harriet's last appearances in the memoir, Toklas tells how she enlisted the help of another San Francisco friend, Caroline Helbing (Blum), who had come to Paris in 1909 on Levy's invitation, ostensibly to help assuage the loneliness she experienced as Gertrude and Alice increasingly excluded her from their outings. In her remembered version of events, Toklas takes Caroline aside and matter-of-factly tells her, "See that when Harriet goes back to America she does not return to Paris because it is already arranged that I should go to stay with Gertrude and Leo at the rue de Fleurus." Comprehending the delicacy of the situation, Caroline successfully executed Toklas's plan: "How she did it I do not know, but Harriet returned to San Francisco . . . and soon wrote to me that I should close the flat and that the pictures," which included Matisse's *The Girl with Green Eyes* (1908), "should be carefully packed and sent to her as she was probably remaining in California."[36]

While Alice certainly conspired with Gertrude behind Levy's back, it was not until Levy's minor success as an author, with the simultaneous publication of *920 O'Farrell Street* and a book of poetry in 1947, that Toklas appears to have lost some of her abiding affection for her longtime friend. "Do you remember Harriet Levy?" Toklas asks in a letter to Louise and Redvers Taylor. "[W]ell, she's eighty years old and has just published her first *two* books and she sent them to me. It has been my exceedingly difficult task to write to her about them because oh dear she should have restrained herself just a little longer. And the worst is she *can* write. It's that she has nothing to say which is a thousand pities as it's nearly always the other way round."[37] Because Toklas does not elaborate, it is unclear why she wished Levy had restrained herself longer. It is likely that Toklas—who tended to be private about her own life, preferring to see Gertrude in the spotlight—objected to being included in *920 O'Farrell Street*, though the portrait is sympathetic and often flattering; whereas Toklas's own family paid her little attention, writing her off as "odd," Levy expresses appreciation for her friend's intelligence, liveliness, and "strange, austere beauty."[38]

Toklas's attitude toward Levy in her correspondence with others is often contradictory. As her praise for Levy's writing ability suggests, Toklas maintained a grudging respect for her friend of four decades. A letter to Mildred and W. G. Rogers reveals Toklas's deeper concern: Levy's publisher, Doubleday, had asked her to write a second memoir about her three years in Paris with Toklas and the Steins. Levy had written asking Toklas to suggest material and to help her recall names. "She has some extraordinary material but she'll never use it," Toklas writes to the Rogerses, as if reassuring herself, "It's not for me to say what she should or shouldn't do—but oh but what a book if she dared. And then again she may—who knows. And will she get it done. It quite fascinates me."[39] This fascination with the prospect of Levy's second memoir and her suggestion that her friend may, unlike before, have something to say, is intriguing in light of Toklas's own struggles deciding whether, and how, to record her life story. The wavering back and forth—"It's not for me to say what she should or shouldn't do—but oh but what a book if she dared. And then again she may—who knows. And will she get it done"—may be easily applied to Toklas's inner conflict about how her own writing could best preserve Stein's legacy.[40] Later, when Toklas reports to friends her decision to begin writing her own book, what would become *The Alice B. Toklas Cookbook* (1954), her announcement is framed as if she is in competition with Levy. "[It is] never too late to commence—eight years earlier than Harriet Levy!" she writes, referring to the age at which Levy published her memoirs as well as the ten-year difference between them. A certain cattiness comes across as well, with Toklas going on to share secondhand gossip about Levy, fashion-forward even in her old age: "It appears that she only appears on great occasions and then in the newest of new looks aided by everything that Elizabeth Arden manufactures and that it is worth the price of admission."[41]

While these words about her octogenarian friend, who would live only one year longer, are less than kind, Toklas—a fierce protector of the reputation of Gertrude Stein, who had died in 1946—did have legitimate cause for concern. Levy had devoted the last years of her life, despite failing health, to working on the memoirs of her Paris days, although they were left unfinished and were not published until 2011, when they appeared under the title *Paris Portraits: Stories of Picasso, Matisse, Gertrude Stein, and Their Circle*. The portrait that Levy draws of Gertrude is not flattering; as indicated in the anecdote about the thwarted attempt to share her writing, Levy took aim at Stein's egotism. At one point, she writes of the Steins, "In spite of my affection for them, I hated them because I never had the courage to tell them to go to hell, as I so often wanted to do."[42] Levy's relationship with the Steins may have had a transformative effect on her life, but they also silenced her, and even her professed desire "to tell them to go to hell" would not appear in print until sixty years after her death. When Levy died on September 15, 1950, a short obituary in *The New York Times* identified her as an "author, art collector, and world traveler."[43] Her collection of modern art proved a valuable legacy. Bequeathed to the San Francisco Museum of Modern Art, it includes works by Matisse and Picasso. Among the pieces are two simple graphite sketches of Levy, which she persuaded Matisse to draw despite his dislike for portraiture. But Levy's collection of art is only a portion of her legacy; it is one piece of a larger story about the role that she and other California Jewish women played in the making of modernism. Until now, Levy's small body of autobiographical writings has served as a source for scholarship in history, art history, and literary biography. In what follows, I demonstrate that her first memoir, *920 O'Farrell Street*, can also be read as a work of modernist art in its own right.

Harriet Lane Levy's House of Autobiography

Although *920 O'Farrell Street* focuses on the period of Levy's life prior to her introduction to modern art, the effects of her engagement with modernism are evident throughout. Just as Stein's *Autobiography of Alice B. Toklas* was based on a conceit that allowed her to experiment with form, including a nonlinear structure and an indirect narrative voice that exposes the artifice of representation (that is, the narrating "I" of *The Autobiography of Alice B. Toklas* is not the same as the "I" of its author), Levy's approach to autobiographical writing is nontraditional.[44] More urban landscape than self-portrait, *920 O'Farrell Street* signals its literary conceit by taking the author's childhood address as its title. Half of its chapters are named for rooms (and, in one case, an architectural feature) of the Levys' Victorian home. In one of her earliest descriptions of the house in the book's first chapter, Levy writes, "O'Farrell Street, to the senses, was solid as a cube. When I turned the corner, my heart quickened at the sight of our white house springing forth from the drabness of its neighbors."[45] With this description, Levy deftly focuses attention on the house while, like a landscape painter, creating a composition that positions the house against the backdrop of a larger community. Her descriptions are surprising because of the contrast between the ornate Victorian architecture of the home and the sparer, modern aesthetic of the prose in which it is represented. As the analogy "solid as a cube" suggests, Levy's style is akin to cubism.[46] Rather than proceeding neatly through her life story in a linear fashion, each chapter of the memoir examines her childhood from a different angle. Many of these perspectives, centering as they do on rooms of the house, take on a geometric quality, becoming part of the larger picture of 920 O'Farrell Street. Levy's multi-perspectival approach is enhanced by shifts between first-person singular, first-person plural, and second person. With these shifts in point of view, Levy examines the past not only through the lens of the self ("I"), but also through the lenses of her family and community ("we"). At times, too, she merges her perspective with that of her readers ("you"), guiding them through the house of memory.

Importantly, at the time Levy wrote her memoir, the house no longer stood, having been destroyed in the San Francisco earthquake and fire of 1906, which she mentions sporadically throughout and narrates in more detail in the final chapter. Thus Levy's book does not have a direct referent in the real, or physical, world; rather, the material objects and physical environment she recreates are accessed only through memory, and their visual representation is available only in language.[47] While each chapter of the book could stand on its own—like a distinct room or city block—the reader is also aware of the interconnections; each part of the house is a fragment of a larger picture, and the house itself is interwoven into a community. In writing the book, Levy breaks down the house at 920 O'Farrell Street into smaller parts, and then reassembles those parts into a new, textual whole: the book, *920 O'Farrell Street*. Levy's memories are represented in an associative rather than a linear fashion. While the book is, to some degree, moving forward in time, from her father's purchasing of the house in San Francisco's "new residence district" to the earthquake that destroys it, the narrative circles around itself—and around descriptions of the various rooms—as Levy looks ahead or backtracks unexpectedly.[48]

These innovations, especially the nonlinear structure, are significant for several reasons. The memoir's subtitle, "A Jewish Girlhood in Old San Francisco," which was added by Heyday Books in 1996, places the work in easily recognizable autobiographical contexts. The reference to "girlhood," for instance, contextualizes the book as a childhood, or coming-of-age, memoir (akin to its fictional counterpart, the bildungsroman), while "Jewish" aligns the work with minority literature, evoking immigrant or ethnic autobiographies that often take the form of assimilation narratives. Narratives of childhood and ethnic assimilation (two genres that, interestingly, overlap) depend on linearity: a protagonist journeys from childhood and adolescence to adulthood, or from immigrant to American. Although elements of these genres are present in *920 O'Farrell Street*, self-development is not the main trajectory of Levy's memoir. The added subtitle is, in a sense, misleading, re-centering the protagonist (that is, a "Jewish girl," Levy herself) rather than the house, as its original, unadorned title did.

Certainly, there are some fairly typical coming-of-age moments in the memoir. For instance, the sixth chapter, titled "Education," narrates Levy's school years, building to her high school graduation and admission to the University of California, Berkeley, and ends with an anecdote that seems, at first, out of place. Levy is sent on an errand to pick up a bill from her father's physician who suggests an exchange of sexual services in lieu of payment. "Let me teach you. Let me show you the way," he says before physically overpowering her in an assault she narrowly escapes.[49] The chapter's closing anecdote consolidates tropes from the female bildungsroman tradition; the narrative of academic initiation—which for Levy, as we know, is a triumphant success—is presented alongside, and narratively superseded by, initiation into patriarchy's predatory use of sexual power, offering an important commentary on the limits of education for women as a means of getting ahead. Despite such moments of gender and sexual formation typical of coming-of-age narratives, however, the "character" who undergoes the most significant change in the narrative is a place: 920 O'Farrell Street, and by extension San Francisco. Furthermore, this transformation is not only about progress, or development, but in many ways, its opposite. The solidity of O'Farrell Street and of Levy's family home is undercut by the end of the memoir, whose final chapter, "The Earthquake," describes the destruction of her neighborhood and the disorienting loss of familiar, contextualizing landmarks.

Just as the text defies the standard narratives of self-formation and progress, Levy's relationship to Jewishness is difficult to chart in a linear manner. Levy frequently discusses her parents' faith and her own estrangement from Judaism, suggesting a first-generation American story of assimilation, which is typically presented in the form of generational conflict between a traditional, Old World father and a modern child who embraces the secular world. Yet the very order of the chapters confuses this familiar narrative, as the book seemingly builds toward, rather than moves away from, religious themes. Chapters 16 and 17, for example, are titled "Rosh Hashona" and "The Synagogue" respectively, and it is here that Levy gives her most detailed accounts of the Jewish New Year and Day of Atonement. Dates are absent entirely, and time is portrayed as more cyclical than progressive; significantly, that cycle adheres most closely to the Hebrew calendar, with references to Jewish holidays such as Yom Kippur, Passover, and Sukkot occurring throughout. While the Jewish calendar provides an underlying temporal structure, the absence of specific dates contributes to the spatial form of the memoir, allowing, in Joseph Frank's famous formulation, the reader to "apprehend" the "work spatially, in a moment of time, rather than as a [narrative] sequence."[50]

Often, when marking the Jewish holidays, Levy expresses her distance from Judaism, which she attributes, in part, to her lack of knowledge of Hebrew. But her treatment of religion turns out to be more complex, especially when considered in relation to space and place. In chapter 5, Levy discusses her father's strict religious observance, describing his practices on Shabbat and other holidays; determined to preserve tradition, Benish Levy "challenged every reform that threatened to alter a tittle of the Law."[51] Yet, when it comes to a description of the family's Passover seder, Levy notes that the "gaiety" of the celebration "softened" her father, leading to an important deviation from the written Haggadah: "When [he] voiced the ancient hope of the nation that the next Passover would find us back in Jerusalem, Father, smiling sheepishly at us, substituted for the Holy City, San Francisco, separating the syllables and drawing out the last '*co*,' letting God know by this exaggeration the jocular nature of the substitution."[52] In fact, the substitution may not be purely "jocular." Levy's father is more modern than he first appears, supporting, for example, his daughter's prioritizing of education over marriage. His imagining of San Francisco as a new Promised Land is in keeping with his progressive attitude, especially toward his children's futures. By mapping Jewishness on to San Francisco's geography and built environments, Levy herself creates a variant text; she enacts her father's revision of the "ancient hope" that Jews of the diaspora would return to the land of Israel, substituting instead the city of her birth. The city of San Francisco serves as both the beginning and end points of Levy's spiritual journey, which culminates in the writing of *920 O'Farrell Street*.

The first chapter of *920 O'Farrell Street* disrupts traditional autobiographical conventions, using a distinctive feature of San Francisco's Victorian architecture—the bay window—to establish the book's complex and multiple perspectives. While even *The Autobiography of Alice B. Toklas* begins with the conventional opening line, "I was born in San Francisco, California," "The Bay Window" does not lead with the expected autobiographical "I" statement, but rather with an image of Levy's father:

> Father sat at his ease in the bedroom bay window, looking down upon the street as from the balcony of a theater, approving the panorama like an old subscriber to the opera. Friends, walking along the sidewalk, looked up to wave a hand to him, or to make words with their lips. Along the block each bay window framed a face.[53]

This opening reinforces the book's central conceit: Levy's mapping of class, ethno-religious difference, and gender onto the space of the city. In this case, houses come to stand in for the identities of various individuals, whose faces are aesthetically framed, like portraits, by the bay windows.

The bay window—a part of the house that at once separates its occupants from the street *and* connects them to the surrounding neighborhood—symbolizes the complex boundaries that Levy explores throughout the book. In her initial survey of the O'Farrell Street environs, Levy is especially attentive to the way space delineates class hierarchies, with her family situated firmly in the middle. She explains that her father "approved of O'Farrell Street" because of its proximity to "the 900 block to Van Ness Avenue, a block with a future."[54] The "grandeur of Van Ness Avenue" gave him something to aspire to; there, the "mansions of the wealthy retired behind deep lawn and gilded iron fence."[55] While the "gilded iron fence" represents the protective barrier of San Francisco's upmost class, O'Farrell Street itself is divided into two sides, the north side, where the Levys live, and the south side: "The south side of 900 broke away from the ordered arrangement of the north side. Small groups of narrow bay-windowed houses served as rented homes to small families. . . . We identified them vaguely as 'the people across the street.' When they walked down their steps on Sunday morning, our minds registered only 'going to church.'"[56] The north side, with its "narrow bay-windowed" houses, may at first appear to mirror the south, but Levy carefully exposes subtle distinctions in class before revealing, through the reference to church, that the social distinctions are based on more than economic status.

Levy depicts distinct social worlds separated by an almost imperceptible barrier.[57] Jews and non-Jews may occupy approximal space, but do not intermingle. "The seclusion of the Gentiles across the street was not distorted into intentional distinction or racial prejudice," she writes in the final lines of the chapter, "No one desired to break through the natural barriers established by difference of race or background. The north side was satisfied that their enjoyment should be heightened by high-toned neighbors who so fortuitously embellished their view, gave distinction to their neighborhood, and provided exciting entertainment by the glamorous variations of their lives."[58] The chapter's concluding lines make a provocative comparison to more familiar representations of Jewish urban space in turn-of-the-twentieth-century America. Here, it is the gentiles, rather than Jews, who experience "seclusion." Furthermore, whereas Levy earlier used first-person plural, describing the north side from the perspective of the Jewish south side (for example, "We identified them vaguely as 'the people across the street'"), her syntax in this final passage obfuscates perspective. Though Levy claims the separation is not "intentional," it is unclear whether the "racial prejudice" she has in mind would be on the part of Jews or non-Jews (though it could also be both). The subject "no one" at first appears to suggest that both groups stick to their own due to a common agreement; however, a closer look at the passage indicates that the Christians on the north side, not the Jews on the south side, would be the ones to desire, or aspire to, crossing over. By the final sentence of "The Bay Window," Levy has shifted to the point of view of the north siders, who, she assumes, were simply "satisfied" to gaze upon their "high-toned" Jewish neighbors.

Levy's representation of Jewish space also becomes increasingly complex in this chapter, as she identifies fractures within the Jewish middle class. At first, the group to which her family belongs appears unified. Observing her father and the other north side men as they leave their O'Farrell Street "homes for their places of business downtown" each day, Levy emphasizes the uniformity in their immigrant backgrounds: "All the men were united by the place and circumstance of their birth. They had come to America . . . and had worked themselves up from small stores in the interior of California to businesses in San Francisco."[59] But as Levy walks along O'Farrell Street in her memory, she recalls how her "spirit automatically drew back" as she approached the homes of the wealthiest Jewish families who snobbishly avoided socializing with her family.[60] Levy had hinted at small fractures as early as the chapter's first paragraph when her "father's glance toward the avenue made an arc excluding" his neighbor at 922 O'Farrell Street. In the following chapter, "Neighbors," we learn that "Mrs. Levison" (Toklas's maternal grandmother, Hanchen Levinsky) looked down upon the Levys, believing her own family to be of a "superior" caste.[61]

In "Neighbors," Levy further reveals her own complicity in maintaining social hierarchies within the Jewish community. She describes the arrival of a new rabbi, whose "greenhorn" status is indicated by his "black-bearded face" and "thick speech," as an "invasion [that] lowered the tone of the block." Rabbi Hirsh's family "poured out [of their house] at any hour of the day," she writes, "They did not come singly but in a rush as if in escape from an immigrant ship, exultant to explore a promised land."[62] Although Levy herself is wary of intragroup prejudice, going so far as to pretend her family is of German rather than Polish origin at school to avoid second-tier status, her language conveys hostility to the new arrivals. While she emphasizes the solidity of her O'Farrell Street house, the Hirsh home, in her analogy, is characterized by impermanence, "an immigrant ship" kept at bay. Yet, as she goes on to show (in part via the eventual destruction of her family's home in the earthquake), even the most stable-seeming structures can be dismantled, and barriers that appear solid prove tenuous.

In mapping the neighborhood, Levy captures its subtle variations and complexities, opening a window to a multidimensional cityscape. One of the few specific anecdotes included in "The Bay Window" exposes the artificiality of class barriers, while offering a reversal of the typical immigrant "rags to riches" story. Levy tells how her mother would task her and her sisters with keeping an eye out for the tax assessors. The moment they were sighted, the women flew around the house, hiding away valuable items and "reduc[ing] the rooms, as far as possible, to a semblance of shabbiness and poverty."[63] Early Jewish American literature typically depicts immigrants orchestrating performances to impersonate "higher-ups," to use Anzia Yezierska's distinctive phrase; we might think, for example, of her *Salome of the Tenements* (1923), in which the protagonist, Sonya Vrunsky, refashions herself and her tenement apartment in an attempt to ensnare her non-Jewish love interest, a millionaire philanthropist. Yetta Levy's performance of poverty works in a similar way to expose the artifice of class, but in using this scene to set the stage, Levy inverts some of the familiar tropes of immigrant literature. The dismantling of the house operates in many ways like the memoir itself, deconstructing a whole in order to examine the complexities of its parts, compelling readers to see the overall structure in a new light. Given Levy's interests in modernism and psychology, it is fitting that one of her readers' earliest glimpses into the interior of 920 O'Farrell Street involves dissembling and disassembling.

In subsequent chapters, Levy breaks down the barrier between public and private space established by the bay window, exposing her parents' intimate lives and idiosyncrasies as she guides readers through "The Parlor," "The Music Room," "The Dining Room," "The Front Bedroom," "The Back Bedroom," "The Kitchen," and "The Basement." If class dynamics are explored by mapping the streets of her neighborhood and describing the exteriors of its homes, the interior of the house, in contrast, becomes a means of probing the psychology of childhood in relation to gender, sexuality, religion, and race. For example, "The Front Bedroom" (which readers come to realize is not simply the "front bedroom," but the author's parents' bedroom) moves from the "sunshine and warmth" offered by the room's southward-facing bay window to the discovery of "disturbing and mysterious objects which it housed." Levy's multivalent autobiographical voice details the room's contents—each stored-away treasured object, every curve of the heavy furniture—in language resonant with sexual imagery. Some of this language is clearly intended to convey a child's curiosity about adult sexuality. Observing her parents' unmade bed in the morning, for instance, Levy writes, "it was uncontrolled, loose, ribald—a fat woman who had chucked her corset," and she cannot help but wonder if her straitlaced mother "yield[s] to its sensuous hollows" and "voluptuous billows" or "lie[s] upon the crest, resisting this appeal."[64]

But for Levy, the front bedroom harbors greater mysteries than sex. ("For of sex I feared only enlightenment," she informs the reader.)[65] These mysteries begin to reveal themselves in another description of the bed: the "slender rectangular columns" of the ornate bedstead are "crowned by festal cupolas, like the ornament of bells upon the white satin cover of the Sephar Torah, the Scroll of the Law, in the synagogue."[66]

In analogizing the bedstead's decorative design to the ornamentation adorning the congregational Torah, Levy may gesture to the sacredness of the marital bed, but she simultaneously imbues the religion that makes up her parents'—and especially her father's—inner lives with a sense of the unknown and the verboten.

The association between religion and the forbidden becomes especially evident in the sexualized description of her father's tefillin, which reside in his closet beside the bed: "In the dark corner of the shelf, *coiled like a snake*, lay the phylacteries. I could not talk about the phylacteries, and my fingers shunned contact with the long, narrow band of black leather that Father wound around and around his upper left arm, and the two narrower bands with the small, square, leather box in the center that he wore every morning in the middle of his forehead while he said his prayers."[67] Through the phallic simile with its biblical invocations of the Garden of Eden, Levy expresses her repulsion toward male sexuality while also limning her distance from her father's religious observance. This distance is represented by "alien objects," as she calls the tefillin, which repel her and render her speechless, "stirring distaste and an unspoken entreaty that they would disappear from Father's closet forever."[68] Finally, in describing the mezuzah nailed to the doorpost of her parents' bedroom, Levy gets at the crux of the matter. Fearful of asking her parents about "the small metal case that clung, as by pores, to the jamb of the door," refusing to look at it with "free eyes," Levy tells us that even its name is anathema to her: "Invasion of our intimate life by an object so estrangingly named—Mezuzah—confirmed the accusation that we were a peculiar people, and I did not wish to be peculiar. I wanted to be like."[69] "The Front Bedroom" uses symbolic descriptions of place—and the material objects contained within—to represent the narrator's relationship to, and estrangement from, Judaism.

Yet, Levy's desire for sameness is tellingly ambiguous; the declaration "I wanted to be like" is missing an object of comparison. Elsewhere, the memoir raises questions about what it means "to be like" in the cosmopolitan space of San Francisco, a city made up of individuals from diverse ethnic and racial backgrounds. Levy's most sustained treatment of San Francisco's ethno-racial dynamics occurs in the chapter titled "The Kitchen." Drawn to the kitchen as a multiethnic, transnational space, Levy writes, "Many nations and races united to furnish us with our supplies. The baker was German; the fish man, Italian; the grocer, a Jew; the butcher, Irish; the steam laundryman, a New Englander. The vegetable vendor and the regular laundryman . . . were Chinese. The Chinamen were the high note of color and piquancy in the kitchen traffic of the day."[70]

Levy's description of the kitchen is rife with contradictions. Although she initially figures the kitchen as a democratic space, claiming that "between us and the tradesmen who came to our door an equality existed," her descriptions of the Chinese vendor and laundryman belie that equality, exposing not only differences of social class but also the Levy family's sense of racial superiority. Her singling out of the Chinese for their "color and piquancy" emphasizes their exotic difference and effectively separates them from white ethnics. In Levy's writing, the Chinese tradespeople are relegated to a separate sentence: she not only uses parallel structure to align Germans, Jews, Irish, and Italians but also suggests an equivalency between European immigrants and transplants from New England. She goes on to note that the Chinese vegetable seller, Chung Lung, does not enter the kitchen itself. Instead, he "remain[s] . . . outside in the alley" while the Levys haggle with him, mimicking his pidgin English. Levy describes their interactions as "playing a game" and declares her love for Chung Lung and the goods he supplies, but her depiction of him with his "eyes screwed into slits," speaking in "a language, unintelligible to any of us but himself" and "showing his three black fangs in merry insistence upon his rights" does not come across as playful or affectionate. It is a racist caricature, reinforced by Levy's informing us that the name of the laundryman was "Hi Lo, but we called him John, our generic name for all male Chinese" and by her use of the slur "Chinamen."[71] In Levy's broader rhetoric, the kitchen is imagined as a pluralistic ideal, where "many nations and races [are] united," but the smaller details that emerge in this chapter expose cracks in the bigger picture. Heightening the racial otherness of the Chinese population through Orientalist tropes, Levy downplays her family's difference, ensuring that Jewishness is read in ethno-religious rather than ethno-racial terms and thus shoring up their position within the *white* middle class.

It is significant that Levy incorporates the Chinese presence into "The Kitchen" since this is also the chapter in which she discusses her family's observance of kosher dietary laws, a religious practice that marks their difference from the Christian majority. Like the mezuzah on her parents' bedroom door, the practice of kashrut "confirmed the accusation that we were a peculiar people" when Levy "wanted to be like."[72] But here, too, is where much of the complexity emerges. While the Chinese presence comparatively constructs the Levys as white (and thus, as not peculiar), Levy's own attraction to the Chinese as "a peculiar people" plays a role in her rebellion against Judaism. Levy sets the stage for her challenge to religious law at the beginning of the chapter, writing, "The kitchen was the temple in which Mother was priest and Maggie Doyle, Levite."[73] A biblical allusion to the twelve tribes of Israel, Levy's metaphor is multilayered. The Levys, as their name indicates and as Levy makes clear earlier in the text, are Levites, descendants of the tribe that served as assistants to the high priests, the Kohanim. Levy's metaphor elevates the status of her mother while their Irish maid, Maggie Doyle, who helps maintain the home's kosher kitchen, becomes a figurative Jew and Levite. Though the Kohanim and Levites traditionally served as religious leaders of the community, in charge of ritual practices such as sacrificial offerings, here the domestic labor of preparing food while ensuring the "gulf" between milk and meat and the purity of the Passover dishes is described as a "priestly office."[74] Given the patriarchal underpinnings of traditional Judaism, women, even if they were members of the anointed tribe, could not perform priestly or Levitical duties. Levy thus employs figurative language that not only transgresses lines of religious identity and caste, but also complicates the way we think about traditional gender roles.

Levy's transgressive metaphor prepares us for her representation of the kitchen as a site of her early apostasy. As the chapter progresses, she describes how her initial fear of violating Mosaic law transformed into pleasure: "If a sudden contraction of my heart gave warning that I had cut into the butter with a meat knife, I turned toward Mother, bent under the effort to cut stars into the cookie dough, and over her back I intercepted in Maggie Doyle's eyes the gleam of amused complicity."[75] In comparison to *The Promised Land*'s famous scene in which Mary Antin, lunching at her teacher's house, devours ham for the first time, "determined to eat more of it than anybody at the table,"[76] Levy's first encounters with trefah do not appear motivated by a need to prove (or overcompensate for) her Americanness, despite her stated desire "to be like." Furthermore, unlike Miss Dillingham, the non-Jewish teacher who serves Antin the non-kosher meat, Levy's coconspirators are not only fellow ethnic minorities, but immigrants, their status as Americans less stable than that of the American-born Levy. In addition to Maggie Doyle's "gleam of amused complicity," which transforms Levy's horror at mixing milk and meat into a bit of harmless, mischievous fun, we find out that Levy would stay outside in the alley with the Chinese vendor Chung Lung so that he "might teach [her] how to twist the tail of the shrimp to make the meat pop out, unbroken." Levy rounds out the encounter thus: "I loved Chung Lung, and when, with a straining of muscle, he lifted the bent pole to his shoulders, and trotted off, a little bowed under the heavy baskets, I called out to him, 'Good-by, Chung, bring me a big peach tomorrow.' 'All light, all light,' he called back."[77]

From Chung's promise of a peach and straining muscles, not to mention the sensuous act of popping out the "unbroken" meat, Levy portrays the scene as an eroticized interracial encounter. Chung's mispronunciation, effectively bringing "light" to a scene that other writers might convey as dark and sinister, indicates that Levy does not view the Chinese man as a sexual threat. Slyly inserting the lesson in shrimp-twisting into "The Kitchen," Levy never says whether or not she ate the shellfish, but it is clear from her tantalizing description that even proximity to non-kosher food could elicit both mental thrill and physical pleasure. Later in the chapter, Levy recalls how her mother would cover "a strip of salt pork" in a flannel stocking and wrap it around her daughter's neck "close against the skin" to treat a sore throat. In a passage that prefigures Alexander Portnoy's masturbatory encounter with raw liver in Philip Roth's novel *Portnoy's Complaint* (1969), she reflects, "To wear so close to the body the flesh that must never enter it was strange excitement. I had faith in pork, for I reasoned that where there was so great a prohibition there must be power."[78] That Levy is linking dietary and sexual prohibitions seems undeniable when we read of her "strange excitement" at coming into contact with "the flesh that must never enter" the body.

As demonstrated by her love for Chung Lung and his shrimp and her "faith in pork," Levy is drawn to the illicit, seeing in the taboo a source of power and an opportunity to disrupt propriety and convention. The final section of "The Kitchen" is especially intriguing in this regard. She sets up the concluding anecdote with a remarkable sentence:

> When the dinner dishes had been washed and put into the closet at night, and the big tin basin and the dark washrag were housed in the cupboard under the sink; when the soap that must never touch a dish because of the interdicted lard in its content had removed every vestige of grease and crumb from the corrugated wooden sink board; when Maggie Doyle, her cheeks glowing with freshness after the thirteen hours of almost uninterrupted work, locked the kitchen door and disappeared in the darkness of the avenue where her beau awaited her coming; when the lights were out and the day was done, then the nightly procession began.[79]

This sentence is itself a "procession," with one clause marching along after the next. As the reader soon learns, "the nightly procession" of which Levy writes is an infestation of cockroaches. Levy does not understand why her mother repeatedly banishes them with boiling water and forbids her daughter from mentioning their presence to anyone outside their house. Rather than being repelled by the bugs, Levy is curious about them, asking endless questions in an attempt to better understand their habits. In the chapter's final line, she confesses, "I liked them [the cockroaches], but I was afraid to say so." As this strange anecdote confirms, Levy often embraces and identifies with what is conventionally undesirable. Her writing may be complicit in reinforcing class and racial hierarchies, but it also subtly reframes social taboos, compelling us to see that which is often associated with darkness and dirtiness in a new light. When she writes, for instance, that the cockroaches "did not get into anything; they just moved about in black designs," she transforms them from an embarrassing and repellent nuisance into a source of aesthetic and scientific fascination.[80]

Throughout *920 O'Farrell Street*, Levy reframes gender and sexual taboos in a similar manner, as exemplified by the chapter titled "The Music Room." Levy describes the music room, with its Steinway piano and frescoed ceiling, as "redolent of gentility." This gentility was closely connected to conventional femininity, to which her sisters adhered, but she defied. The music room is Addie and Polly's domain. While Polly with her "moving contralto voice" is untrained, Addie, the more obedient sister, excels by taking lessons. In contrast to her sisters' abilities to perform and conform, Levy herself is hopelessly unable to stay in tune.

In this chapter, she addresses her lack of conformity to feminine norms indirectly by focusing not on herself but on the music teacher, Miss Tourney, who, she writes, "was single and lived alone. How could she be so old and yet unwed? I knew no other unmarried women of her age."[81] Levy's admiring descriptions of Miss Tourney create a decided contrast with a German song her mother "sang as a warning" to the three daughters; in that song, a woman is doomed to weep alone for "many a day" after spurning a prospective lover. While the song conjures an image of a "solitary figure, standing at an open window, looking forlornly at the world," Miss Tourney does not fit this romantic notion of ill-fated heterosexual love. "Miss Tourney was too bristling for so delicate a setting," Levy writes, "and my imagination could not bend the robust figure and enormous bosom to an appropriate droop of desolation."[82] Given the retrospective nature of this account, written when Levy was at the end of her full life as a single woman, this line could be read as commentary on the author herself. She does not fulfill the archetypal role of retiring old maid, but instead stands "tall, vigorous, huge-bosomed," like the "flowering and redundant" Miss Tourney.[83] Levy provides an implicit answer to the question "How could she be so old and yet unwed?," critiquing its presumption of heteronormativity. By the time she wrote *920 O'Farrell Street*, Levy knew others who chose to live independently of men and, in some cases, with women as their life partners.

In the work of early twentieth-century women writers such as Stein, Virginia Woolf, Djuna Barnes, and H. D., modernist experimentalism is linked inextricably to narrative and linguistic play with conventional codes of gender and sexuality. Scholars have drawn particular attention to the way that Stein's autobiographical writings opened space for the expression of same-sex desire. As Leigh Gilmore writes in her analysis of *The Autobiography of Alice B. Toklas*: "In contrast to the autobiographer bound by traditional laws of gender and genre, Stein reads the technologies of autobiography available at the beginning of the twentieth century for the gaps, discontinuities, and noncoincidences in gendered and sexual 'identity' and reveals there a lesbian space of self-representation."[84] By focusing on the text's "coupled" signature, which attributes the book to both Gertrude and Alice as a collaborative production, Gilmore argues that the *Autobiography* is a "lesbian autobiography" that makes same-sex love central and visible. In a more recent interpretation of the text, Nora

Doyle analyzes the *Autobiography*'s tropes of domesticity, arguing that Stein parodies the genre of the domestic memoir, "a specifically feminine form of autobiography" usually written by the wife of a famous man, in order to "to reflect the contingencies of her own life as a woman, a lesbian, a writer, a Jew, and a self-styled genius."[85] Doyle thus builds upon Barbara Will's work, which examines the ways that Stein's autobiographical self-fashioning allowed her to define herself as a "genius" in part by "emphasiz[ing] her 'maleness' and homosexuality over her femaleness and Jewishness."[86]

On the surface, Levy's memoir may appear more conventional than Stein's inventive approach to autobiography. As I previously suggested, the added subtitle "A Jewish Girlhood in Old San Francisco" deflects from the stylistic innovation of *920 O'Farrell Street*, while seemingly naturalizing Levy's Jewishness and femininity as the primary components of her identity. In light of this misleading subtitle, the space of the Victorian house and the temporality of "Old San Francisco" situate Levy's story within a bygone era, as a record of the past. However, when we read the memoir as a work of literary modernism rather than simply a historical document, it becomes clear that Levy is using the house as a metonym for traditional domesticity in much the same way that Stein uses the genre of the domestic memoir in Doyle's analysis, or Toklas reinvents the form of the cookbook as a basis for her autobiographical writing. Levy's memoir dismantles the foundations of the house to assemble new structures. Thus, as Sidonie Smith writes in reference to *The Autobiography of Alice B. Toklas*, "The very autobiographical recitation that promises to shore up gender identity becomes its very undoing."[87]

As I have shown, Levy's use of the Victorian house as an organizational device defamiliarizes Jewishness and destabilizes the dominant representation of Jewish American life, which was framed by the space of the ghetto. By placing Jewishness in a spatial context that is unfamiliar to many readers, the memoir depicts religion and ethno-racial identity as complex processes of negotiation with meanings that shift in relation to space and time. Similarly, the dismantling and reassembling of the Victorian house deconstruct familiar notions of female domesticity and heteropatriarchy. From its opening sentences, for instance, the book undermines gendered literary tropes. While nineteenth-century literature often conflated domestic space with the woman's sphere, the opening paragraph positions the author's father, rather than Levy herself, behind the glass of the upstairs bedroom's bay window; an isolated figure, observing but cut off from the outside world, he occupies a space commonly reserved for women like the nameless wife who narrates her stifling confinement in Charlotte Perkins Gilman's "The Yellow Wallpaper" (1892). Levy's work can be read as a queer autobiography, one that takes pleasure in subverting behavioral and cultural codes that restrict full gender and sexual expression.

Like the Victorian house in Alison Bechdel's graphic memoir *Fun Home* (2006), which explores her coming of age as a lesbian cartoonist in light of the untimely death, possibly by suicide, of her closeted gay father, the Levy family residence at 920 O'Farrell Street functions as façade and portal. A closer examination of the interior exposes the artifices of gender, sexuality, and traditional heteropatriarchal domestic life. Throughout *920 O'Farrell Street*, Levy hints at alternatives to heterosexual romance and marriage—for example, when she expresses her repulsion from (white) male sexuality as well as her admiration for Miss Tourney, an unmarried woman with a creative profession, and her romantic affection for Alice Toklas. Although the extratextual triangle of Harriet, Alice, and Gertrude can certainly be read in terms of sexual rivalry, Levy's sexuality and the exact nature of her relationship with Toklas remain ambiguous. That Levy's friends and family members have felt the need to justify her single status through anecdotes about thwarted love affairs with married men confirms that she was not open about her sexuality, even as evidence points to her attraction to women.[88] If Gertrude Stein's autobiographical writings are groundbreaking for giving voice and visibility to lesbian desire, Levy appears to be more reticent.[89]

Levy comes closest to addressing her sexual identity directly not in *920 O'Farrell Street* but instead in a chapter from the posthumously published *Paris Portraits* titled "A Beautiful Girl." In this chapter, while writing letters in the lobby of a Paris hotel, Levy is approached and propositioned by "a charming young woman," who suggests that if they are both "alone in Paris" and "free" that they might travel together. Levy's prose turns Steinian in its use of simplistic repetition: "What was she saying to me? I did not know. And at the same time I did know. I knew. And I grew tense with knowing that I must not let her know that I knew. I must not let her suspect that I knew." At the end of the encounter, the woman kisses her hand several times and Levy concludes:

> Nothing had been said.
>
> Yet I was deeply moved. Depths of my being had been stirred.
>
> Stirred by fear of the question which had not been asked.
>
> Then the question arose.
>
> Why had she selected me?[90]

Like the repetitive phrase "I knew," which emerges from the initial denial, the question arises even without being asked. In effect, the previous affirmation of knowledge provides a muted answer to the silence of the question that is at once posed and left unsaid: what can be read as a suppression of lesbian desire is simultaneously its expression. Ambiguity then is precisely the point. What makes Levy's work "queer" aligns with what makes it modernist: the text's resistance to definitive answers and concrete definitions.[91] This resistance extends to the genre of *920 O'Farrell Street*, a text poised between reader's expectations for the conventions of autobiography and the avant-garde aesthetics pioneered by Levy's creative cohort.

In contrast to Stein's most experimental work, which self-consciously promotes itself as high art, often reading as "nonsense" because it is stripped of contextual clues and historical referents, Levy's memoir—the sole full-length work of prose she published in her lifetime—is rooted in history. In the book's final chapter, "The Earthquake," Levy draws upon the event of the great San Francisco earthquake and fire of 1906 to bring her memoir to a close. Because she does not mention the date, however, the earthquake becomes much more than a singular event; rather, it serves as a symbol of larger societal and historical ruptures. Nor does Levy provide a straightforward account of her experiences during the earthquake. Like the rest of the book, the final chapter uses the modernist technique of juxtaposition; it presents a series of loosely related scenes revolving around her father's death and her mother's decision to rent out the O'Farrell Street home alongside Levy's decision to travel to Europe and her attempts to reclaim the familiar sites of her childhood in the aftermath of catastrophe. Each vignette circles back to and provides refractive commentary on previous episodes in the memoir.

For instance, in discussing the selection of a burial plot for her father at Hills of Eternity, the cemetery for members of Congregation Sherith Israel, Levy revisits the motif of class divisions within San Francisco's Jewish community. Noting that Hills of Eternity is next to "Home of Peace, which housed the more aristocratic dust of the members of Temple Emanuel" and that she "felt as ill at ease among the bones of the people buried there as I had felt among their living bodies," Levy points to the absurdity of such social divisions existing even in death. The loss of her father also resurfaces her inner religious conflict, as she vows that instead of being interred in the family plot, she would "have [her] ashes scattered" in violation of the religious law mandating that Jewish remains be buried in the ground.[92]

Subsequent scenes, however, continue to unsettle easy dichotomies pairing Old World immigrant parents with piety and tradition on the one hand and their American-born daughter with apostasy and modernity on the other. Just as Levy's father updated the concluding words of the Passover seder, replacing Jerusalem with San Francisco, Levy credits her mother with moving the family forward into the new century—a move whose symbolism is similarly conveyed in spatial terms. Following the death of her father and the marriage of her sisters, Levy's mother announces her plan to relocate with Harriet to a smaller residence and rent out 920 O'Farrell Street. Given that her mother "had trained [her] to regard the dislodgment of a chair as a violation of a law of God," the announcement takes Levy by surprise. Her surprise is compounded by news of the house's new inhabitants: an unmarried couple, two opera singers identified as Signor X and Signora X. At first, Levy has difficulty wrapping her head around their presence "in our house, in our kitchen where, for years, Saturday upon Saturday, Passover upon Passover, closets and dishes—to the last knife and fork—had been guarded from impurity." But Levy quickly comes around, taking vicarious pleasure in the tenants' moral transgression and reminding herself that her theater-loving father would have "loved to have them in his house."[93] As Levy stands outside her former home, peering into the kitchen for a glimpse of the opera singers, "wait[ing] eagerly for the slow, burning kiss which should climax an illicit love," the scene circles back not only to "The Kitchen" as the site of Levy's earlier flirtations with "impurity," but also to the book's opening, in which Levy's father surveyed the street from inside the house, "approving the panorama like an old subscriber to the opera."[94]

The presence of professional performers in the house and the emission of "bursts of song" in place of "illicit" kisses serve as prelude to the house's final transformation into a work of art, a transformation that is preceded by its destruction. In the last section of the memoir, returning to O'Farrell Street for the first time after the earthquake, Levy writes,

> I descended upon a *waste of land* which reiterated the story of the unimpeded progress of the fire all the way up to Van Ness Avenue where dynamite had halted its advance. Not one building remained to confirm my memory. . . .
>
> [A] whole block—substantial, solid as a cube, guaranteed to wear for generations—had disappeared.
>
> The home of the Benish Levys, the only house with storm doors, the only garden with a gravel walk . . . the house so white it looked like marble, had disappeared as if it had never been, along with a city behind it.
>
> Once again O'Farrell Street had become a stretch of land, 920 a lot, a building site.[95]

The allusion to T. S. Eliot's poem "The Waste Land" makes Levy's modernist themes evident. Here, "unimpeded progress" translates into destruction. The block, once "solid as a cube," has become a blank canvas, and Levy is left to gather the fragments of memory to shore up against the ruins.

In the final sentences of the memoir, Levy abruptly shifts perspective to decades later. Returning again to O'Farrell Street, she discovers that "there is no there there," as Gertrude Stein famously observed when she visited the former site of her Oakland childhood home in the mid-1930s.[96] Urban development has erased all traces of the middle-class Jewish neighborhood in which Levy grew up. The Victorian house has been replaced by that icon of modern technological progress: the automobile dealer. The memoir's final sentence reads, "And today motorcars drive into the repair department of the Cadillac Motor Company over the invisible, spotless, velvet parlor carpet of my 920 O'Farrell Street."[97] Rather than participating in the substitution of tradition with modernity, Levy's final sentence brings 920 O'Farrell Street back into existence. From "invisible" and "spotless" to "velvet," she restores the house's materiality, creating an ambivalent space of art and memory in which tradition and modernity, domesticity and mobility, coexist. The patriarchal "home of the Benish Levys" is now "*my* 920 O'Farrell Street." Levy lays claim to her inheritance by creating a portrait of the artist as a young woman transposed on to the urban landscape.

For scholars of Jewish American literary studies, *920 O'Farrell Street* raises a set of interdisciplinary questions: about the aesthetics and provenance of Jewish modernism; about the turn-of-the-twentieth-century middle-class cultural milieu that produced women like Levy, Toklas, Gertrude and Sarah Stein; and about scholarly blind spots and lacunae that occlude and marginalize certain representations of Jewishness while centering others. Levy's modernist memoir also has much to tell us about the dynamics of Jewish American autobiography. In Hana Wirth-Nesher's introduction to a special issue of *Prooftexts*, she observed that Jewish American autobiography is defined by a "tension between Adamic self-invention and Jewish origins and destiny." According to Wirth-Nesher, "The Jewish-American is moving both toward and away simultaneously."[98] Indeed, movement in Levy's memoir—between past and present, between Jewishness and Americanness—is often multidirectional rather than linear. Levy's modernist experimentation with autobiographical form resists familiar tropes of assimilation and self-development. Instead, Levy maps religion, race, class, gender, and sexuality onto the geographic and architectural spaces of San Francisco, constructing a house of autobiography that allows her to examine tensions between tradition and modernity from various angles.

4
Frontier Feminism

Fiction and Journalism in the Multiethnic West

Although she was considered one of San Francisco's most promising young writers in the 1890s, Harriet Lane Levy's story is one of unrealized ambition: *920 O'Farrell Street*, published in 1947, was the only book of prose she published in her lifetime. In contrast, her cousin, fellow San Francisco writer Miriam Michelson, produced a large body of work in multiple genres: hundreds of newspaper articles, over forty fictional stories in magazines, six novels, a collection of novellas, a history of the Comstock Lode, and a number of plays.[1] A celebrity reporter in the 1890s, at a time when "girl stunt reporters" were putting their unique stamp on journalism history, Michelson went on to become a popular and prolific fiction writer during the first decade of the twentieth century.[2] Playing a pivotal role in feminist literary history and the cultural history of the Progressive Era, she used her fame to advance a variety of causes, especially women's suffrage, both on the lecture circuit and through publications such as *The Superwoman* (1912), a speculative novella that offers a trailblazing vision of a matriarchal utopia.[3]

In her time, Michelson was also recognized as a famous Jewish woman writer—"a California Jewess who has succeeded with her pen," in the words of *The Washington Post*.[4] Today, however, she has escaped the notice of scholars of Jewish American literature. In this chapter, I expand upon my previous claims that the recovery of Michelson's oeuvre fills gaps in multiethnic and Jewish American literary history by examining the relationship among gender, ethno-religious, and ethno-racial representation in her journalism and fiction. As a fiction writer, Michelson drew on her experiences as a reporter for San Francisco's top dailies to create entertaining narratives with audacious, slang-speaking New Women protagonists. Jewish characters occasionally appear in her stories (most prominently in *A Yellow Journalist*, where the reporter-heroine investigates a scandal involving a theatrical family named Lowenthal), but Michelson also populated her writing with Black, Chinese, Hawaiian, Native American, Irish, and French characters. Set in California, Nevada, and the Dakotas, her work testifies to the ways that Jewish writers captured the regional and ethno-racial diversity of American life and were engaged with cultures and traditions other than their own.

This chapter begins by establishing how Michelson's work is a product of her experiences coming of age as a Jewish girl in the nineteenth-century, multiethnic West. In the absence of a substantial archival record, I rely in part on an analysis of her semi-autobiographical novel *The Madigans* (1904) to illuminate how Michelson's engagement with gender, race, religion, and secularism was shaped by her family's westward migration. Set in Virginia City, Nevada, where Michelson spent her childhood, *The Madigans* fictionalizes her family through an Irish ethnic filter and transforms its coed brood into a sextet of tomboyish sisters. The chapter goes on to discuss Michelson's career as a reporter for *The San Francisco Call* and the *Bulletin* in the 1890s, during which time she reported on a host of progressive issues, including the suffrage movement, the experiences of Asian immigrants in Chinatown, anti-Black racism in the US military, and assimilationist policies of Indian boarding schools. The conventions of late nineteenth-century new journalism, as pioneered and practiced by women reporters in particular, allowed Michelson to serve as a mediator between cultures and amplify the voices of those on the margins—as exemplified by her first front-page news story, "Strangling Hands upon a Nation's Throat," an investigation of the anti-annexation movement in Hawaii.

In the following sections of this chapter, I consider Michelson's journalistic career in relation to the fiction that she produced for mass-circulation magazines such as *The Saturday Evening Post*, which serialized *A Yellow Journalist*, a 1905 collection of stories featuring the author's alter ego, "girl reporter" Rhoda Massey. Analyzing Rhoda's adventures in undercover reporting (which include, among other stunts, disguising herself both as a Chinese boy and slave girl to investigate the gambling dens and brothels of San Francisco's Chinatown), I show how the interplay between Michelson's journalism and fiction adds to literary scholarship on gender and cross-racial relations. Situating Michelson's racial representations in the context of Progressive-Era politics, I argue that her writings cannot simply be dismissed as crude cultural appropriations, but need to be taken seriously as a part of an American literary tradition in which women writers from various Jewish backgrounds have spoken for, and through, people of other races. As a body of work, Michelson's fiction and journalism offer an inclusive vision of the West as a multiethnic landscape; her narratives challenge masculinist myths of the frontier, centering women and valorizing their individualistic pioneer spirit while also exposing the dark legacy of imperialism central to settler-colonial critiques of US history and ideology. Yet, in her fiction, representations of Indigenous people and others marginalized by race also serve to reinforce her protagonists' whiteness and thus validate their status as white feminist heroines. Michelson's work offers a space to interrogate how the coupling, and uncoupling, of Jewishness with whiteness occurs in tandem with formations of white feminist discourse—and often at the expense of intersectional feminism with its potential for mutually beneficial cross-racial, interethnic, and interreligious alliances.

"Oh, It Was Good to Be a Madigan!": A Nevada Childhood and the Irish-Jewish Unconscious

From Mark Twain's *Roughing It* (1872) to television's *Bonanza* (1959–73), Virginia City, Nevada, where Miriam Michelson grew up, has figured prominently in the American cultural imagination. "The sidewalks swarmed with people," wrote Twain of early 1860s Virginia City, following the discovery of the Comstock Lode, "Money was as plenty as dust; every individual considered himself wealthy, and a melancholy countenance was nowhere to be seen."[5] Although few associate the legendary Nevada mining town with Jewish women's experiences, Jeanne Abrams's book *Jewish Women Pioneering the Frontier Trail* demonstrates that Jewish women were central figures in "the highly multicultural world of the American West" during the nineteenth and early twentieth centuries. In "multifaceted" ways, according to Abrams, "Jewish women's experience in the West fostered significant opportunities for expanded female roles."[6]

Michelson's family was part of the mercantile class, and her upbringing in a Nevada mining town, as opposed to middle-class San Francisco, influenced her life and literary output in particular ways. Unlike the fiction discussed in the first two chapters of this book, Michelson's oeuvre contains few examples of conventional domestic plots; when heterosexual romance does figure into her narratives, it is usually as subplot rather than primary plotline. Nor did she herself hew to the norms of bourgeois domesticity, as Wolf and Lowenberg did in expanding the influence of the woman's sphere through their association with the club movement. Instead, Michelson shattered the notion of a separate sphere and charted an unconventional course for a woman of her time. Independent and self-supporting, Michelson chose to remain single and child-free. She followed in the path of Western male literary figures such as Twain when she began her writing career as a reporter, first in Virginia City and later in San Francisco. Michelson traded the genteel prose of Wolf's and Lowenberg's fiction for exclamatory sensationalism, jaunty vernacular, and a lighthearted, often comic tone. Like male writers of the Sagebrush School, she took frequent liberties with fact and fiction, narrating much of her journalism and stories in a conversational, first-person voice.[7]

Michelson's fame as a reporter and fiction writer made her an important, if now unacknowledged, influence on American culture at a time when men and women were navigating shifting gender ideologies. On the surface, her work may appear to lack the gravitas of female contemporaries such as Charlotte Perkins Gilman and Edith Wharton, but it deserves attention from scholars of American women's writing for the way its casual, comic tone masked serious messages. If Lowenberg's novels were overly didactic ("written for a definite cause," as one reviewer stated), Michelson sacrificed didacticism for entertainment. Critic H. L. Mencken, for example, described her work as a "literary joy ride," while an *Atlantic Monthly* reviewer delivered similarly damning praise, declaring Michelson "as popular, as 'catchy' as ragtime."[8] A commercially successful writer with crowd-pleasing appeal, Michelson operated at the nexus of literary and popular culture when modernist movements were sharpening divides between high art and low art while simultaneously troubling those distinctions. Lacking in the opaque subtleties of the avant-garde associated with Gertrude Stein and present in Levy's memoir, Michelson's work still remains decidedly ahead of its time, especially in its depiction of the modern woman. Charming, clever, and witty, her protagonists "play smart," to use a phrase adopted by Catherine Keyser to describe how women magazine writers of the 1920s and 1930s projected a "deceptive air of triviality associated with . . .

middlebrow publications to expose the anxieties riddling modern hierarchies of class identity, gender norms, and even literary reputation."[9] Michelson's distinctive, breezy voice paved the way for "middlebrow modern" writers such as Edna Ferber, Fannie Hurst, Jessie Fauset, Zona Gale, Dorothy Parker, and Anita Loos, "who ushered the literary representation of the New Woman from the era of ragtime into and through the Jazz Age."[10]

Portrait of Miss Miriam Michelson, *The World's Work* (1904).

In addition to making a significant contribution to feminist literary history, Michelson's work also captures the multiethnic and multiracial diversity of the American West. Some may question, however, whether her body of work should be understood as a contribution to *Jewish* American culture and to what extent her Jewish background shaped her experiences as a woman in the nineteenth-century West. Although Wolf and Lowenberg did not write exclusively on Jewish topics, they both published novels with Jewish protagonists, writing Jews into a national narrative through their literacy practices.[11] In contrast, when Jewish characters are present in Michelson's fiction, they are secondary players, part of the multiethnic cast that supplies backdrop and color for the adventures of her New Woman protagonists, who are ethnically indeterminate or nominally Irish.

Although the secular press identified Michelson as Jewish and the Jewish press claimed her as one of their own,[12] Michelson did not view Jewishness as a significant factor in her identity. As attuned as she was to ethno-racial divisions and tensions in the region that formed her, she maintained that her own ethnic heritage was incidental and that religion played no role in her family's life. "[Our] father and mother were born of Jewish parents, yet I should not say that ours was a religious family," she wrote in response to a question posed by her brother Albert's biographer, "I had no religious training whatever. Nor can I recall a religious discussion among us, nor a religious inhibition or compulsion. And I believe this unorthodox viewpoint would have been the case with both parents and children no matter what religious belief the former might have inherited."[13] Distancing herself from her ethno-religious heritage by two generations, Michelson does not identify her parents as Jewish, stating instead that they were "born of Jewish parents." She suggests that Jewishness—and by extension, antisemitism—was irrelevant to her upbringing in Virginia City. However, studying her life and work in its historical and cultural context presents a more complicated picture. Engaging questions of secular identity and ethno-racial difference, Michelson's writing bears the mark of her coming-of-age as the daughter of white ethnic immigrants-turned-pioneers. In fact, it is Michelson's explicit treatment of secularism—especially in her second novel, *The Madigans*—that makes her work an important addition to Jewish American literature, offering a different take on assimilationist themes while reinforcing the comparative processes of racial formation by which European immigrants became white in relation to Indigenous people and other people of color.

Michelson was born in Calaveras County, California, in 1870, shortly after Mark Twain and Bret Harte put the region on the literary map.[14] Her parents, Samuel and Rosalie (Przylubska) Michelson, had immigrated to the United States from Poland in 1855. Fleeing antisemitic persecution in their hometown of Strzelno, they arrived in New York with their first two children and initially settled on the East Side of Manhattan. Soon, however, the Michelsons were to move again. Lured by news of the Gold Rush, they traveled by ship and mule wagon across the Isthmus of Panama and then up the California coast to newly prosperous Murphy's Camp, where they made a living selling supplies to miners. By the time they left Murphy's to set up shop in another boomtown, Virginia City, the family had expanded to seven children in all, from the oldest, Albert, a physicist who began his career at the US Naval Academy and who would go on to win a Nobel Prize, to the two youngest: Charles, who became a journalist and the first publicity director of the Democratic National Committee under Franklin D. Roosevelt, and Miriam.[15]

In Virginia City, the Michelson children had a reputation for being "as industrious as they were brilliant."[16] Their mother emphasized the value of education for daughters and sons alike. As a result of her influence, "no child . . . failed to absorb an enormous respect for literature and a love of beauty in one form or another."[17] Michelson's nonfiction book *The Wonderlode of Silver and Gold* (1934) catalogs the childhood thrills that the mining town provided for her and her siblings: sledding downhill in winter into the main business district with no street cars to "block . . . one's triumphant way"; dangerously commandeering an abandoned stagecoach; bearing witness to, and at times participating in, the scuffles of boy-gangs, named for the rival mines that determined their family's livelihood; "hop-skotching over the mud and blackened, dripping snow" intoxicated by the warm mountain air that signaled the arrival of springtime; and improvising rules for games of marbles just as "the law, like other things in new Nevada, had to be made as they went along."[18]

As merchants, the Michelsons were part of the "tony bunch," as one miner's son, John Taylor Waldorf, categorized them in *A Kid on the*

Comstock, his reminiscences of growing up in Virginia City in the 1870s.[19] The siblings' academic achievements exacerbated tensions with children of miners, like Waldorf, whose gang staked a claim to a mining dump near the Michelsons' house. In her commentary on her father's recollections of his boyhood adventures, Waldorf's daughter, Dolores Waldorf Bryant, related how Albert Michelson's visits home on leave from the US Naval Academy in Annapolis, Maryland, led to class conflict and resentment. In September 1878, for example, Albert—appearing "splendid" in his naval uniform and sword, "his black hair [shining] with pomade"—was buying ice cream for his family in town, accompanied by Miriam. According to Bryant, the local gang, already harboring hostilities toward the Michelsons, whose home encroached on their territory, viewed Albert's refined appearance as "a taunt and affront to their existence" and quickly surrounded him. In a scene "prophetic of a Keystone comedy," Albert "handed his sword to Miriam and laid about him mightily with the ice cream bucket" in an effort to fight off the attacking boys.[20]

In addition to documenting class tensions in *The Wonderlode of Silver and Gold*, Michelson also acknowledged how the Comstock's racial and ethnic diversity produced animosities and divisions. The miners, she wrote, "weren't a body of men, they were individuals of twenty-eight different races, and of as strongly contrasted temperaments. . . . Italians, Germans, French, Mexicans, Irishmen, Cornishmen, Americans, each with their own racial prejudices, customs, even a particular saloon to patronize."[21] Chinese immigrants, however, bore the brunt of racial prejudice. Living in segregated camps on the outskirts of Virginia City and barred from working in the mines, the Chinese were employed primarily as domestic workers.[22] The various migrant groups also came into regular contact with nearby Paiute and Washoe tribes. In *Wonderlode*, Michelson recalls how, at age five, she became the play-wife of Black Hawk's son "at a mud-pie wedding on A Street, when the groom . . . and the bride . . . [were] both too young to protest."[23]

The sagebrush landscape's multiracial population gripped Michelson's imagination. Early short stories such as "A Touch of Civilization" (1897) and "Poker Jim's Mahala" (1900), which appeared in the *Black Cat*, were set in Nevada and featured Native American characters. The portrayals are stereotypical at times, but the stories take a mocking tone toward white settlers who viewed themselves as more civilized than

Native people. In them, Michelson attempts to see colonization from an Indigenous perspective—as she does later, too, in *The Wonderlode of Silver and Gold* when she briefly shifts the point of view to the Paiute chief Winnemucca as he spies an approaching caravan and realizes that "the unbelievable tale of white men, wandering, encroaching, closing-in upon the land, even this bitter, barren land, is true."[24] In her career as a reporter and fiction writer, Michelson showed a willingness to take on a non-white point of view, which was often critical of American expansionism and imperialism.

Despite her claims that her Jewishness was incidental to her identity, Michelson's attitude toward race and ethnicity came in part from her own sense of difference as the child of Jewish immigrants. In an oral history, Miriam's next-door neighbor, Alice Sauer, recalled the Michelsons as "foreigners" and one of the few Jewish families in town; she also noted that Samuel and Rosalie "were great friends of my parents" and that the Jews "didn't seem to have much of a society or organization, or anything like that."[25] Historians have shown that antisemitism was much less of a factor for Jews in the West as compared to other regions of the country. Due to the sparser population and the fact that pioneer families, by definition, did not have deeply established roots and traditions, Jews often functioned as an integral part of the frontier community.[26] The popular imagination constructed Western Jews as outsiders who had the potential to become insiders.[27] A 1962 episode of the long-running television Western *Bonanza* titled "Look to the Stars" inserts Miriam's brother Albert into the story of the Cartwright clan in order to teach a civil rights–era lesson about tolerance and bigotry. The episode is loosely based on facts. In 1869, shortly before Miriam's birth, seventeen-year-old Albert became the first Jew appointed to the Naval Academy. In the *Bonanza* episode, Albert, a young genius who causes trouble by conducting physics experiments in the streets of Virginia City, is expelled from school by an antisemitic teacher, who also tries to block his military appointment. At the end of the episode, the Cartwrights—who take Albert under their wing, giving him free rein to test his scientific hypotheses on the Ponderosa Ranch—publicly expose the teacher's bigotry, transforming Jews from victims of prejudice into patriotic citizens.

Miriam did not figure in the *Bonanza* episode or the real-life incidents it fictionalized. By the time of her birth, her oldest brother was already headed to the Naval Academy in Annapolis. Today, Albert Michelson's legacy overshadows that of his younger sister. His place in the annals of American history was sealed when he became the country's first Nobel Prize laureate in the sciences. (The prize recognized, among other discoveries, his invention of the interferometer, a device that was used in experiments to measure the speed of light.) In 1907, the year he won the Nobel Prize, however, many Americans would have been just as, if not more, familiar with the sister who was eighteen years his junior. One newspaper article about the Michelsons' achievements claimed that "because of her phenomenal . . . [literary] success . . . Miriam Michelson is the most widely known of the family," before going on to mention that her "brother . . . along with Rudyard Kipling were the recent winners of the Nobel prize."[28]

Miriam Michelson may now be largely obscured from the historical record, no more than a footnote in her brother's story, but in *The Madigans*, her semi-autobiographical novel about growing up in Virginia City, she eliminated her three brothers altogether. For the purposes of fiction, she transformed the coed Michelson clan of siblings into a sextet of mischievous sisters with a dead mother, laissez-faire father, and self-absorbed aunt. Left to their own devices, the Madigan girls lay claim to the mining town as their playground and stir up all sorts of trouble—mainly for each other. With its tomboy exploits appealing to a juvenile audience, *The Madigans* does away with much of the sentimentalism that made Louisa May Alcott's *Little Women* (1868–69) a classic of girls' literature. Nineteenth and early twentieth-century children's literature typically reformed and married off masculine-identified female characters like Alcott's Jo March, whose exuberant and "boyish" nature is contrasted with that of her more feminine sisters.[29] *The Madigans*, in contrast, presents a cadre of girls who revel in unladylike behavior: four-year-old Frances (known as Frank and named for their father, Francis), the twins Bessie and Florence (shortened to Bep and Fom), Irene (whose athleticism earns her the nickname "Split"), Cecilia (Sissy), and fifteen-year-old Kate, who, as the oldest, affects the "pretense of young lady-hood," mostly to antagonize her sisters.[30] In a 1907 interview for *The New York Times Saturday Review of Books*, Michelson named *The Madigans* her personal favorite among her novels. "Some of it did happen to me, and I always insist that I am Sissie [*sic*], in spite of the fact that a friend of mine insists she is," stated Michelson. "I guess it fits a good many childhoods."[31] Michelson strategically manipulates the particulars of her own upbringing to create a narrative with universal resonance and an irreverent message about gender and childhood in the late nineteenth-century West.

In addition to changing the gender make-up of her siblings, Michelson alters her family's ethno-religious identity. The episodic pieces were first serialized as "Stories of the Nevada Madigans" in *Century*, a New York–based magazine that had shed its evangelical roots for a secular outlook at the end of the nineteenth century, serializing novels such as Henry James's *The Bostonians* (1885–86) and Mark Twain's *Pudd'nhead Wilson* (1893–94). In naming her fictional family "The Madigans," the author adopts an Irish equivalent to echo her own last name, a change that further universalizes her characters while maintaining their immigrant roots. Focusing primarily on works set in the tenements of New York and Chicago, scholars such as George Bornstein and Stephen Watt have examined affinities between representations of Jews and Irish in American literature and culture. While popular comedies like Anne Nichols's *Abie's Irish Rose* (1922) united Jewish and Irish immigrant families through intermarriage plots, Watt notes that the "Irish-Jewish unconscious" also includes a trope of "surrogation," or "substitution, of one ethnic immigrant standing in proxy for another."[32] For Watt, "surrogation" produces an "uncanny" effect, encoding the familiar in the unfamiliar. Michelson's decision to make her fictional family Irish in *The Madigans* is thus a recognition of the Jewishness that the name obscures. Jewish characters, even if secularized, would make her stories an anomaly or curiosity, a Zangwillian study of a "peculiar people" set in the American West. Michelson's ethno-religious substitution, in contrast, makes her stories more familiar to *Century*'s non-Jewish readers, aligning her characters with the Comstock's dominant ethnic group (and notably, the group responsible for discovering the region's riches). While the "Irish-Jewish unconscious" pervades Michelson's fiction, with many of her protagonists appearing nominally Irish, *The Madigans* explicitly takes up questions of religious and ethnic identity. In so doing, it offers an important representation of secularism as an alternative to nineteenth-century American ideals of faith and piety and sheds light on the Michelsons' indifference toward their Jewish heritage, reinforcing the writer's statement that she and her siblings would have been unobservant "no matter what religious belief" their parents "inherited."[33]

In *Little Women*, Marmee seeks to impart Christian values to her daughters, leaving, for example, a "guide-book" for "little pilgrims" under each of her daughter's pillows on Christmas morning.[34] When Mr. Madigan takes rare interest in the education of the six daughters whom he views as a "wanton . . . outrage upon his desire" for a son, he attempts to pass on not religious values, but secular ones. Declaring Christmas "nonsense" or reminding the girls that "to kneel and kotow" in prayer "like other idiots" will get them nowhere, Mr. Madigan is "an outspoken foe to religious exercise"—though we also learn that his "aggressive skepticism" was "the tangent of excessive youthful religiosity."[35] Given that Mr. Madigan's youth was spent in Ireland—his immigrant past still evident in "the sound of his voice," which bore "the irresistible accents of the cultured Irishman"[36]—his "aggressive skepticism" becomes a feature of his new identity as an American pioneer. And it is this secular Americanism, rather than his Irish heritage, that Mr. Madigan tries to instill in his daughters.

Part of the irreverent humor of Michelson's book stems from the fact that the girls rebel against their father when they attempt to practice religious morality. "Religion," the text states, "had all the attraction of the . . . forbidden."[37] This motif is established from the first tale, "Cecilia the Pharisee," whose title refers to the ancient Hebrew sect known for its strict observance of Mosaic laws. In it, the eponymous trouble-maker resolves to act with greater kindness toward her sisters and draws up her own version of the Ten Commandments with that end in mind. In defiance of her father, she takes to prayer, searching for the forbearance to keep her commandments. But by the end of the story, eleven-year-old Cecilia is unable to abide by her program of self-improvement, finding herself "a blissful bankrupt instead of a Pharisee."[38] Like Mr. Madigan, Cecilia renounces her "youthful religiosity" for the freedom of secular thought, and together father and daughter tear up the list of commandments that did more to hinder than help her.

The Madigans' sisterly shenanigans and disdain for religious righteousness continue in stories with titles like "A Pagan and a Puritan" and "The Martyrdom of Man." In the former, Cecilia, the most "prudish" of the sisters, is falsely accused of teaching a "vulgar kissing game" to the coddled son of puritanical Mrs. Pemberton.[39] In the latter, Mr. Madigan takes an uncharacteristic interest in his daughters' education, reading aloud to them from William Winwood Reade's history *The Martyrdom of Man* (1872), a book so popular with secular intellectuals that many of them adopted it as a "substitute Bible."[40] The daughters, however, prove as impervious to Reade's Darwinian philosophy as they are to Christian dogma. One by one, they are ejected from their father's recitation for various infractions. Unrepentant, and relieved that they have been released to resume their play outdoors, the girls spend the next day making their yearly pilgrimage to the summit of Mount Davidson, which looms over Virginia City. There, they experience a pantheistic "nature-miracle," infused with the ideology of manifest destiny. Moved by the "desire to penetrate still farther and higher into the crystalline sky," the Madigans extend their claim on America, with Michelson's alter ego, Cecilia (Sissy), "stretch[ing] out her hands—a small, petticoated Balboa—to the world she had discovered." Preceded by the adjective "petticoated," Michelson's metaphor comparing Sissy to the famous Spanish explorer and conquistador imagines a woman-centered narrative of triumphant reinvention via colonization. Whereas the girls irreverently cast aside religion and scientific rationality, the West's "fresh, shining virginity of the new-created" earns the awe and respect denied to their father, allowing them to assert their identities in defiance of patriarchal definition.[41]

Mr. Madigan's ineffectualness as a father leads his children to treat their ethnic heritage with the same irreverence they devote to religion. In one of the book's chapters, "The Ancestry of Irene," the most rambunctious of the spirited lot entertains a common childhood fancy: she decides that she is not biological kin to her five sisters and that the "ordinary and humble" Mr. Madigan is, in fact, her foster father.[42] Over the course of the story, Irene concocts a number of origin tales for herself. In the story's centerpiece, she takes inspiration from hearing her older sister Kate read aloud from George Eliot's long narrative poem *The Spanish Gypsy* (1868) in which the lost gypsy child Fedalma, raised as Catholic nobility during the Spanish Inquisition, is reunited with her father, chief of the Zincalo people. Abandoning her Catholic identity and her adoptive brother-turned-lover, Fedalma chooses to return to her tribe, pledging to help them recover their lost African homeland. Her imagination ignited by Eliot's romance, Irene resets *The Spanish Gypsy* in an American context, fantasizing that she is the kidnapped papoose of Indian Jim, and that, as princess of the homeless Paiutes, she will help them to win "back their lands—and the mines, too."[43] Irene quickly becomes disenchanted with the prospect of fighting to retrieve the millions from the mines that are rightfully hers, however, and forsakes her imagined tribe for the fantasy that she is the daughter of one of the Irish bonanza kings who discovered the Comstock Lode.

In *The Spanish Gypsy*, Fedalma chooses to identify with her racial past, a decision that transforms her into a diasporic figure, an abject outsider, like Spain's Moors and Jews, who must renounce their religious beliefs or be expelled from the nation. Eliot scholars view her 1876 novel *Daniel Deronda* (a book whose title character Michelson likely used as a template for her 1906 novel, *Anthony Overman*) as a rewriting of *The Spanish Gypsy* since Deronda similarly chooses to claim his newly discovered Jewish identity.[44] Michelson's comic rewriting of *The Spanish Gypsy*, however, is more akin to a child's game of "playing Indian" or a redface performance on the vaudeville stage than a masterpiece of Victorian literature. In *Members of the Tribe: Native America in the Jewish Imagination*, Rachel Rubinstein traces representations of Native Americans in Jewish American literature and culture, arguing that "imaginative engagements with Indians pointed the way not always or only forward to an ever-elusive Americanness but also frequently 'back' to an equally dynamic Jewishness."[45] Such multidirectionality is evident in Michelson's story, further complicated by the fact that the text's "dynamic Jewishness" has been effaced by an Irish mask. "Playing Indian" served multiple purposes for Jewish (and Irish) immigrants; it allowed them to acknowledge their racial difference *and* access an American identity, especially through an imagined connection with the land. As Rubinstein explains, writers used "tropes of Jewish-Indian encounter, kinship, and resemblance" to "theatricalize, disguise, and Americanize themselves all at once."[46] Irene's fantasy that "her tribe . . . was calling her" may at first seem to point back to Jewishness, especially given Rubinstein's excavation of the millenarian belief that "the Indians of the New World were in actuality the descendants of the ten lost tribes of Israel."[47] However, if we also consider Irene's Indian princess fantasy as a revision of Eliot's *The Spanish Gypsy*, it is especially telling that Michelson eliminates the biological tie that bound Fedalma to her racial past.

Absolved of hereditary obligation, Irene, in contrast to Fedalma and Deronda, is free to forsake her tribal allegiance. Imbuing her nickname with additional meaning, Irene is "split" between identifying with the Indigenous people who have been driven from their land and the Irish immigrants who, themselves colonized by the British, are robbing that same land of its resources. Irene's temporary, imaginary identification with Indians, then, functions more like Michael Rogin's reading of blackface minstrelsy, in which Jewish and Irish performers distanced themselves from "the people they parodied"; it is a means of differentiating herself *from* Indians, positioning her on the side of the settlers rather than the colonized.[48] Irene's mercurial series of origin tales furthermore functions as a renunciation of tribalism altogether. Rather than be limited by an inherited racial, or religious, past, Irene has the freedom to choose her affiliations and continually reinvent herself. The story concludes with Irene arriving at a final epiphany about her identity:

> Oh, it was good to be a Madigan! Standing there . . . triumphant, Split [Irene] hugged herself—her very own self—her individuality, which at this minute she would not have changed for anything the world had to offer. To be a Madigan, one's birthright to laugh and do battle with one's peers; and to win, sometimes through strength, sometimes through guile, sometimes through sheer luck—but to win![49]

The story's ending at first appears to espouse the sanguine sentimentality of adolescent self-discovery, a common trope in children's literature: a young protagonist, after fantasizing about being someone and somewhere else, discovers that it is preferable to be herself.

Read more closely, the ending of "The Ancestry of Irene" is less sentimental. Irene's newfound pleasure in being "a Madigan" is not motivated by filiality; she is not identifying with the father whom she initially disowned (or the mother she barely remembers). In claiming that the Madigan "birthright [is] to laugh and do battle with one's peers," she is most closely aligning herself with her similarly competitive and free-spirited siblings, as further suggested by the passage's use of "Split," a nickname conferred upon her by her sisters, rather than Irene, the name given to her by her parents. As in the rest of *The Madigans*, the story's dominant mode is good-humored sibling rivalry, rather than sentimentalized sisterly affection. In returning to her identity as "a Madigan," Irene eschews the affective and hereditary bonds of tribalism for the individualism of the frontier myth. When she thinks, "*at this minute* she would not have changed [herself] for anything" (italics mine), she leaves open the possibility of future adaptability—especially if that is what it takes "to win." Irene ultimately chooses to identify with the immigrant pioneers who, in colonizing the West, were able to create new identities for themselves, "sometimes through strength, sometimes through guile, sometimes through sheer luck." The Madigan birthright—like the secularism passed on by their father—offers the girls the unrestricted freedom of *non*-identification, the option of making up the rules, and themselves, "as they went along."[50]

At the same time that it manipulates the trope of Jewish-Irish surrogation and the fantasy of racial interchangeability, *The Madigans* forecloses other sites of cross-ethnic identification—namely with the West's Chinese immigrant population, represented by Wong, the family's domestic servant. A stock character who makes brief appearances throughout the stories, Wong is portrayed as deferentially fearful of his master, Mr. Madigan, except on laundry days, when he appears "grim, ill-tempered, hurried, defying the world to put even the smallest additional burden on his shoulders."[51] Both Indian Jim and Wong are comic stereotypes, characterized by their simple natures and broken English (a sharp contrast with the pleasant sound of Mr. Madigan's "cultured" accent). Unlike Wong, however, Jim is depicted as educable. Trying out one of her many ancestral identities as the noble daughter of a count, for instance, Irene remembers that "a genteel interest in the lower classes is becoming to the well-born" and gives Jim a lesson in the proper usage of English gender pronouns. While "Princess Irene" goes on to imagine a romanticized identification with her pupil-turned-lost father and his wronged tribe, the Chinese are denied such empathy despite the fact that they have more in common with the Irish Madigans as fellow immigrant laborers.[52]

The girls persist in viewing Wong as strange and backward due to his superstitious beliefs. His imperviousness to enlightenment is established early on, in the book's first story, "Cecilia the Pharisee." In the middle of the night, Wong comes upon a ghostly figure: Cecilia, dressed in a nightgown "of trailing white drapery," has fallen asleep while playing the piano (a vain attempt to abide by her ninth commandment, which was to practice her music every day). Thinking that she is "de debbil," Wong flees the house, forcing Cecilia to "spe[e]d after the Chinaman [in order] to enlighten him," a pursuit that "only confirmed Wong's conception of that mission of malice which is devil's work on earth."[53] From that point forward, Wong's sole purpose in the text is to serve, and the girls' interactions with him are primarily limited to stealing provisions from his kitchen. The unenlightened "Chinaman" is more than a figure of comic relief. His subservient role and childlike belief in the supernatural establish the Madigans' superiority (despite their youth) as modern, secularized Americans. Freed of ethno-racial and religious ties, the girls can shape their selves according to their whims and their desire "to win."

Michelson offers a more complex picture of the residents of San Francisco's Chinatown in her journalism and goes on to explore the possibility of cross-racial identification with Chinese immigrants in her next book, *A Yellow Journalist* (1905). But in this group bildungsroman, where playful irreverence is the stylistic mode, the formation of the girls' identities as white Americans occurs at the expense of racialized others who are denied the freedom of self-invention. The multiethnic Western setting of Michelson's stories expands the possibilities for Jewish American writing in the Progressive Era. At the same time, through their use of local color and caricature, Michelson's stories reinforce other racial and ethnoreligious peculiarities and prejudices, unable, for instance, to imagine a space for Wong beyond the Madigans' kitchen or a Chinatown laundry.

Michelson's work demonstrates that writers from Jewish backgrounds were often engaged with questions of race, religion, and ethnicity whether or not they were writing about Jews. The absence of explicit Jewishness allows her to approach these questions about American identity from a different angle. *The Madigans*, for instance, offers a provocative alternative to the familiar assimilationist narratives of Jewish American culture. In American literature and history, Jewish assimilation is often associated with Christianization; conforming to the dominant Protestant culture might involve not only the absence of Jewish observance but also the adoption of holidays such as Christmas. Through the trope of Irish surrogation, Michelson cleverly presents a narrative of secularization in which a family becomes less *Christian*, rather than less Jewish. In the series' first installment, one of the daughters may dabble in "Christ-like charity," but by the end of their adventures, the text forthrightly and unapologetically declares that the Madigans "were not Christians."[54] The declaration does not condemn the girls for their refusal to do penance for their sins. Instead, the sisters' irreverent attitudes and exuberant personalities bind them to each other and may endear them to the reader. Michelson uses comedy, rather than sentimental didacticism, to make a case for secular American values.

When it comes to representations of gender in *The Madigans*, Michelson did not focus on exposing restrictions placed on women, as many of her better-known feminist contemporaries did. Instead, she actively imagines alternatives to conventional gender roles. Although one reviewer advised that the Madigans "deserve spanking," the book's charm derives from the author's refusal to transform the girls' misbehavior, as bratty as it is, into a morality tale.[55] To do so would be to discipline the Madigans for their unladylike conduct. In treating the sisters' high-spiritedness with unwavering good humor, *The Madigans* celebrates female feistiness over femininity. It is no coincidence, for instance, that the mine that restores the family's fortune at the end of the book is named the Tomboy. Nor are the Madigans the only residents of Virginia City to resist rigid gender roles; in several incidents, for example, boys dress as and are mistaken for girls. In *The Madigans*, as in much of Michelson's fiction set in the West, the openness of the frontier gives license to operate outside prescribed gender norms. "Some of it did happen to me," Michelson said of the Madigans' adventures. Like her young heroines, she allowed neither ethno-religious difference to define her, nor gender to confine her. Michelson's fictional tales of coming of age in Virginia City offer insight into her secular background and lack of identification with her Jewish heritage. They also illuminate the conditions that enabled her to become one of the West's pioneering women journalists, brazenly breaking through gender barriers to influence the politics and aesthetics of the Progressive-Era press.

"A Sort of Magical Human Telephone and Phonograph Combined": The Girl Reporter as Cultural Mediator

On September 30, 1897, *The San Francisco Call* devoted the first two pages of its broadsheet to an article about the United States' impending annexation of Hawaii. Heralded by the bold headline "Strangling Hands upon a Nation's Throat," the article was an impassioned plea for Hawaiian sovereignty, harsh in its condemnation of US foreign policy. "Here in Hawai'i, the best beloved, the most richly endowed of all Mother Nature's beautiful family, the old, old struggle for Anglo-Saxon supremacy is going on," the article read, "The centuries-old tragedy is being repeated upon a stage small comparatively, but with a perfection of gorgeous setting and characters whose classical simplicity gives strength to the impersonation. The only new phase in the old drama is that this time a republic is masquerading in the despot's role."[56] Although the article makes a case against annexation from the point of view of Native Hawaiians, readers would be left with no doubt as to its author. "Miriam Michelson Pens a Stirring Appeal on Behalf of the Islanders," a front-page sub-headline announced. And on the second page, a caption beneath a sketch of a young woman in pince-nez glasses identifies her as "Miss Miriam Michelson, Special Correspondent of 'The Call' at Honolulu."

"Strangling Hands upon a Nation's Throat" was Michelson's first front-page news article. But it was not the first time that her name appeared in the headlines of the articles she authored. Beginning with a four-part series on the Woman's Congress of the Pacific Coast in 1895, Michelson had established herself as *The Call*'s celebrity "girl reporter." In articles with titles such as "Viewed by a Woman: Miriam Michelson Gives Her Impression of the Congress" and "The Real New Woman: Miriam Michelson Likens Her to a Pleasant Dream, not a Nightmare," Michelson reported the news from a woman's perspective. Despite writing in an experiential first-person voice, she managed to project a degree of impartiality. She presented herself as an open-minded, sometimes even skeptical, observer of events in the process of gathering the facts in order to form impressions free of stereotypical presumptions. Employing a variety of rhetorical strategies, Michelson took readers along on her physical and mental journeys.

By most accounts, the phenomenon of the "girl reporter" began in 1887 when Elizabeth Jane Cochrane, known to readers as Nellie Bly, feigned insanity for an undercover exposé of the appalling conditions inside the Women's Lunatic Asylum on Blackwell's Island; Bly's reporting appeared first in Joseph Pulitzer's *New York World* and later in book form as *Ten Days in a Mad-House*. An early example of immersion journalism,

Bly's stunt created a media frenzy, spawning imitators—including, on the West Coast, the *San Francisco Examiner*'s Annie Laurie (Winifred Black)—and opening doors for women in the male-dominated field of journalism. Making their bodies part of the sensational spectacle of the Progressive-Era press, women broke into journalism by creating "models of self-reflexive authorship that involved not just reporting the news but *becoming* the news," as Jean Marie Lutes explains.[57] Uncovering the work of early "ladies of the press" such as Bly, Laurie, Ada Patterson, Nixola Greeley-Smith, and Elizabeth Jordan, scholars Lutes and Alice Fahs have demonstrated that women journalists played a crucial role in shaping literary and mass culture in the late nineteenth and early twentieth centuries, especially as several, like Michelson, became fiction writers.[58] Unlike Bly and Laurie, Michelson did not change her name, go undercover, or manufacture elaborate stunts. Yet there was a performative quality to her journalism, a theatrical flair befitting her status as celebrity reporter and icon of modern American culture. Like her predecessors, Michelson engaged in "self-reflexive authorship," using the first-person persona of a "girl reporter" to transform herself into a character in the stories she reported. Michelson's career lends further weight to Lutes's and Fahs's claims that women journalists, in playing up gender and the female perspective, created new paradigms of womanhood, which they publicized to readers on a daily basis through the pages of the newspaper.

Even as journalism increasingly made space for women in the late nineteenth century, Jewish women writers were largely excluded from the mainstream press. As Fahs demonstrates, women from ethnic, working-class backgrounds faced economic, educational, and language barriers, in addition to outright social discrimination, that kept them out of metropolitan newsrooms. There were, of course, "exception[s] that prove . . . the rule." Thanks to her well-publicized marriage to millionaire James Graham Phelps Stokes, New York's *Jewish Daily News* columnist Rose Pastor Stokes "briefly crossed the line between ethnic and mass-circulation newspapers," assuming the persona of the "Ghetto Girl."[59] Carol Batker, one of the few scholars to consider the work of Jewish women journalists in the Progressive Era, places them alongside Native American and Black American reformers whose journalism addressed issues of concern to their minority group. Batker's study reinforces the notion that women on the ethno-racial and ethno-religious margins primarily wrote for the ethnic press and thus for audiences of their peers.[60]

The figure of the "girl reporter" who regaled readers with her exploits in the pages of the mass-circulation dailies was, according to Lutes, "emphatically native-born and white."[61] For reporters like Bly and Laurie, ethnic difference was often a component of their stunts, as they went undercover to infiltrate spaces inhabited by poor, immigrant women. Their cross-ethnic identifications were, however, only temporary. In exposing their masquerades, they reinforced their racial whiteness and reinstated it as the dominant racial category. It is notable that Michelson shied away from undercover stunt reporting. Even as her status as a middle-class, first-generation American facilitated her entrance into newsrooms of major metropolitan papers, going undercover may have brought her closer to the ethnic roots she held at a distance. Instead, through her public performance as a "girl reporter," she crafted a persona that de-emphasized ethno-religious difference, drawing attention toward gender and away from what some might read as recognizable Jewishness. As in *The Madigans*, whiteness and secularism played significant roles in Michelson's journalistic writings, allowing her to enter spaces on the margins, to speak on behalf of other races and cultures, and to participate in public debate about progressive issues extending beyond women's rights and suffrage. Michelson may have established her career by offering a woman's viewpoint and writing about the growing presence of women in the political sphere, but she was far from a single-issue writer. Working her way from "girl reporter" to "front-page girl," she refused to be pigeonholed, as exemplified by her coverage of the Hawaiian annexation debate in 1897.

"Strangling Hands upon a Nation's Throat" serves as an example of the genre of writing often referred to disparagingly as "yellow journalism" for its tendency to sensationalize the news with the goal of selling papers as well as promoting specific political and editorial agendas. The article's provocative message was made more so by the fact that a twenty-seven-year-old unchaperoned "girl reporter" had sailed the Pacific Ocean to cover an international protest, the Hawaiian Patriotic League's petition against annexation by the US government. To many American readers in the nineteenth century, the Hawaiian Islands were the stuff of men's adventure tales, penned by writers such as Herman

Melville and Mark Twain. (Jack London, who admired Michelson's writing in the San Francisco papers, was first to arrive in the islands almost a decade after her.)[62] Yet, as Fahs shows in *Out on Assignment*, Michelson was not the only newspaperwoman to undertake such a journey. Examining travel correspondence from Hawaii and other foreign outposts, Fahs demonstrates that, in addition to mapping "new territory for women in the public sphere," female journalists extended their influence to the larger project of late nineteenth-century American expansionism. In contrast to most of the travel writings Fahs analyzes, however, Michelson did not argue for "America's right to new territories and 'possessions.'"[63] Instead, she came across as a sharp critic of American expansionism, exposing it as part of the long history of racial imperialism at home and abroad and as a betrayal of the nation's democratic ideals. Michelson's correspondence from Hawaii illustrates how the rhetorical strategies she developed while covering the rise of the New Woman in her early years at *The Call* enabled her to become a mediator across races and cultures—or, in the metaphor with which she described her reportorial presence among Native Hawaiians, "a sort of magical human telephone and phonograph combined."[64]

Michelson's newspaper writings employ narrative and stylistic techniques that today are more likely to be associated with the innovations of literary, or "new," journalism than the sensationalism of tabloid culture. In *Narrating the News: New Journalism and Literary Genre in Late Nineteenth-Century American Newspapers and Fiction*, Karen Roggenkamp demonstrates that the literary aesthetic of "new journalism," which reached its apotheosis in the 1890s when Michelson was working as a reporter, was closely intertwined with the narrative and genre conventions of American fiction. According to Roggenkamp, "The big business of urban newspapers . . . depended for its success on the reporters' narrative skills and their ability to mold information—sometimes factual and sometimes not—into dramatic and skillfully told tales."[65] To accomplish this goal, journalists used a variety of literary techniques more often associated with fiction and memoir than newspaper reporting. Michelson, for instance, carefully constructs scene and character, reproducing dialogue and deriving meaning from seemingly minor details. Writing in the first person, she simultaneously positions herself as subjective narrator and neutral outsider. Rather than following a formula, like the inverted pyramid associated with contemporary news reporting, Michelson plays with narrative structure, often with the effect of bringing her readers along on a journey and allowing them to see events unfold through her eyes.

In "Strangling Hands upon a Nation's Throat," Michelson structures the article as a series of brief vignettes with subtly pointed endings that together build to a powerful conclusion. Writing from aboard a steamship sailing out of Honolulu Harbor, Michelson begins at the end of her journey, recording her impressions of the islands she is leaving behind as the horizon "grows dimmer and dimmer." Her "strongest memories" are of the Salvation Army Hall at Hilo. In this "crude little place" with "rough, uncovered rafters" and "bare walls . . . relieved only by Scriptural admonitions in English and Hawaiian," Michelson attended a meeting of the Woman's Hawaiian Patriotic League. The stark backdrop allows Michelson to bring into relief the stately elegance of the Hawaiian women in their "black kid gloves" and "flowing trained gowns of black crepe." Embodying the "extravagance" of the lush and colorful natural landscape that Michelson had earlier described, the president of the league is identified by the "nodding red roses in her hat" and her "long, thick necklace of closely strung, deep red, coral-like, flowers, with delicate ferns interspersed." Michelson tempers the exoticism of this description by drawing parallels between the leaders of the Hawaiian anti-annexation movement and the suffrage movement at home. The dignity of the Hawaiian women and the eloquence of their speeches occasion comparison to Charlotte Perkins Stetson (Gilman), whose "simple directness" had made her "two years ago, the most interesting speaker of the Woman's Congress." By highlighting the Woman's Hawaiian Patriotic League meeting as her "strongest" and most evocative memory, Michelson once again strategically deploys the woman's angle. While the event itself is a powerful representation of women's influence on politics and the public sphere, gender identification also becomes a means of forging cross-racial understanding. Michelson's identity as a woman reporter allows her to transmit a message across languages and cultures, separating her from the American imperialism that she classifies as white and male.[66]

Covering the woman's movement in her debut series for *The Call*, Michelson wrote as a New Woman herself; her enactment of modern womanhood and belief that women belonged in the public sphere were established by her professional status as a "girl reporter." As an American journalist in the Republic of Hawaii, she found herself in a very different role. Here she had to overcome differences of language and culture in order to speak *for* the natives, tasked with representing their humanity to annexationists and countering racialized imperial discourse that portrayed them as savages incapable of self-rule. At times, Michelson's reverence for the Hawaiian people and culture veers toward romanticization. Recalling the opening benediction, she muses, "There is something wonderfully effective in earnest prayer delivered in an ancient language with which one is unfamiliar. . . . Like the Hebrew and the Latin the Hawaiian tongue seems to touch the primitive sources of one's nature, to strip away the complicated armor with which civilization and worldliness have clothed us and to leave the emotions bare." Michelson resorts to exotic stereotypes in her attempt to identify with the Indigenous population (not unlike Split Madigan, who fantasizes about being an Indian princess in "The Ancestry of Irene"). Yet, in a tacit allusion to her own ancestry, Michelson also compares "the Hawaiian tongue" to the "Hebrew and the Latin" and acknowledges that it is not "ancient language" itself, but rather one's *unfamiliarity* with the language that creates the effect of primitivism; as she explains, "tones," as opposed to "words," appeal to "feeling" above "reason."[67]

Michelson's account appeals to both feeling and reason. With the aid of an interpreter, she translates the speakers' arguments against annexation, privileging the words of the native population above her interviews with pro-annexation congressmen and other white proponents of manifest destiny. At the same time, she devotes considerable space to discussing her own position vis-à-vis the Hawaiians, rather than assuming the detached standpoint of the third-person narrator. Michelson's use of the first person adds layers to the article, transforming it into a meditation on cultural mediation in a colonial context. I quote at length to offer an example of her self-reflexive authorship:

> The woman who presided had said a few words to the people, when all at once I saw a thousand curious eyes turned upon me.
>
> "What is it?" I asked the interpreter. "What did she say?"
>
> He laughed. "'A reporter is here,' she says. She says to the people, 'Tell how you feel. Then the Americans will know. Then they may listen.'"

> A remarkable scene followed. One by one men and women rose and in a sentence or two in the rolling, broad-voweled Hawaiian made a fervent profession of faith. . . .
>
> They stood as all other Hawaiians stand—with straight shoulders splendidly thrown back and head proudly poised. Some held their roughened, patient hands clasped, some bent and looked toward me, as though I were a sort of magical human telephone and phonograph combined.
>
> I might misunderstand a word or two of the interpreted message, but there was no mistaking those earnest, brown faces and beseeching dark eyes, which seemed to try to bridge the distance my ignorance of their language and their slight acquaintance with mine created between us.[68]

Michelson depicts the political protest as a form of religious testimony in which each individual "made a fervent profession of faith" in his or her country. While the pious decorum of the crowd counters stereotypical colonial views of the natives in "heathens" in need of civilization, Michelson, in a striking reversal, further suggests that the problem of cultural translation lies with *her* ignorance, not theirs.

Through such references to her own positionality, Michelson elucidates the complex, shifting dynamics of power in a cross-cultural, colonial context. Her status as an outsider, ignorant of the national language, places her at a disadvantage; in the moment that she feels the "curious eyes turned upon," she is no longer an invisible observer, but an embodied object of the gaze. As an English-speaking American with the power of the press at her disposal, she is, at the same time, in a position of privilege, with the capacity to speak for those who have been denied the right to speak for themselves. This ability to serve as a conduit—"a sort of magical human telephone and phonograph combined"—between colonized and colonizer, between positions of power and powerlessness, is made possible by gender solidarity. As her references to the suffrage movement suggest, Michelson may not have understood the Hawaiian language, but she certainly understood the people's objections to being denied a voice in their own governance.

One of the few representations of Hawaiian anti-imperialism in the late nineteenth-century popular American press, "Strangling Hands upon a Nation's Throat" remains an important historical document. But even as historians cite the article as a source on Hawaii's anti-annexation movement, they overlook the significance of its production and its author. The article's indictment of American expansionism owes much to the conventions of new journalism and the phenomenon of the girl reporter. The import of gender on the act of cultural mediation is made clear by a scene in which a young Hawaiian girl expresses her gratitude by slipping a lei around the reporter's neck, and Michelson takes down the girl's broken English: "No one comes to—to ask us. No one listens. No one cares. Your paper will speak for us—us Hawaiians. Our voice will be heard, too. . . . The white men have ever'thing on their side. But we are right and they are wrong."[69] The dialogue may have an invented ring to it, but even so, it speaks to Michelson's awareness of her intermediary place in the colonial power structure. The synecdoche "white men" separates the girl reporter from the larger forces of American imperialism, reinforcing her neutrality as cultural mediator.

Despite our contemporary expectations that newspaper reporting maintain third-person objectivity, Michelson's subjective narration is not necessarily at odds with the stance of neutral outsider.[70] In fact, she repeatedly invoked the first person as a reminder of her supposedly impartial role as reporter—warning the girl with the lei, for instance, that she "can't do anything [to aid in the protest against annexation] except repeat what you say," or withholding a reply from the Portuguese driver who politely asked her thoughts on the fate of Hawaii because she "had come 2,000 miles to find out other people's opinions; not to express her own." In a later article published in *The Call*, Michelson revealed that she was in fact in favor of annexation until her visit to Hawaii persuaded her otherwise.[71] Michelson's self-reflexive authorship acknowledges her part in gathering and presenting information and impressions, demonstrating how the *process* of reporting led her to revise her original expectations and opinions. Replicating that process for her readers, and thus the experience of being a cultural outsider, Michelson bridges the linguistic, cultural, and geographic distance between the Hawaiian people and the American public.

Signed by 90 percent of the Hawaiian population, the Hawaiian Patriotic League's "Petition Against Annexation" (also known as the Kūʻē petitions) was a success. A Hawaiian delegation and Queen Liliʻuokalani presented the petition to Congress in December 1897, and, in early 1898, the US Senate voted against the treaty to annex the islands. But on February 15, 1898, the sinking of the battleship *Maine* in Cuba's Havana Harbor further fueled the United States' desire for expansion—and led to some of the outrageous excesses of yellow journalism, with Hearst and Pulitzer manipulating warmongering American patriotism as ammunition in their battle for readers. The ensuing Spanish-American War (April–August 1898) reinforced the strategic value of Hawaii's mid-Pacific location. The islands were annexed by joint resolution in July 1898.[72]

The argument against expansionism that Michelson presented in "Strangling Hands upon a Nation's Throat" had only a temporary effect on US foreign policy. The article, however, was to have a long-lasting impact on her career, significantly expanding her reach as a journalist and providing her with material for some of her early fiction. Much of Michelson's work for *The Call* had been limited to theater criticism, an arena deemed more suitable for women. Following her trip to Hawaii, she rose to the rank of dramatic editor. She also branched out into new territory as a reporter, covering crime, politics, and sports—all areas considered the domain of men. In the summer of 1898, Michelson moved from *The Call* to its rival, *The San Francisco Bulletin*. Under the leadership of controversial managing editor Fremont Older, she became part of a team of reporters who wielded the power of the press to expose rampant corruption in California, a state then under the control of the Southern Pacific Railroad.[73]

Michelson made her debut at the *Bulletin* with another front-page story: an obituary of San Francisco's first Jewish mayor, Adolph Sutro, who had joined the paper in its fight against the "octopus" of the railroad monopoly. Mark Twain remembered the millionaire mayor as "a fine, manly beautiful character," writing that he had "always found something of Sutro in all the Jews whom I have personally known since."[74] Michelson's article, in contrast, refrains from mentioning Sutro's Jewishness, identifying him as a Prussian-born German whose family initially settled in Baltimore, Maryland. But in Sutro's story, Michelson clearly saw parallels to her parents' journey to the United States and then westward during the Gold Rush. Her rags-to-riches account of a poor immigrant boy who made his fortune by engineering mining tunnels in her hometown of Virginia City intimates a personal connection to Sutro, whose success she attributes to "the strength of his own individuality," "the untiring activity of his body and mind," and a "bulldog tenacity which refused to be conquered."[75] Highlighting broader tropes of immigrant success, rather than the specificity of a Jewish immigrant experience, Michelson's obituary memorializes Sutro's life as a classic account of a self-made American pioneer.

Like her fictional stories of coming of age in Virginia City, Michelson's obituary of Sutro erases Jewishness, celebrates American individualism, and perpetuates white American myths of the West. Even as Michelson continued to oppose the nation's expansion beyond its borders, her writing romanticized the transformative possibilities of the frontier, sometimes extending its potential for Americanization to non-white populations. In *Sensational: The Hidden History of America's "Girl Stunt Reporters,"* Kim Todd observes that newspapers of the era, and the white women reporters who wrote for them, rarely included "concerns of Black citizens, Chinese immigrants, [and] American Indian tribes."[76] In her newspaper writings, Michelson did voice the concerns of those on the racial margins. Enabled by her whiteness and her gender, her position as a cultural mediator was likely rooted in her upbringing as the child of Jewish immigrants, despite her holding ethno-religious difference at a distance.

As circumscribed as they are by a white perspective, Michelson's writings offered a fuller and more diverse picture of the West than the work of her fellow girl reporters. Her articles about Indigenous people, Black Americans, and Chinese immigrants exposed a darker side of America's past and its present. The curious mix of racial discourses present in her reporting is heightened by the conventions of the Progressive-Era press. Local color conventions, for example, often contributed to exotic views of racial others, as is evident in Michelson's reporting from San Francisco's Chinatown.[77] Meanwhile, the journalistic practice of the interview gives her reporting a polyvocal quality, creating spaces for competing narratives. This is evident, for instance, in her article "A Military Matter in Black and White" in which she interviewed Black soldiers about the racism they faced from white soldiers during the Philippine-American War. Her reporting culminates in an unequivocal condemnation of US racism and imperialism; shifting to the second person in the article's concluding paragraph, she predicts her readers' reaction, now that they have heard the words of Black soldiers on the matter: "you'll feel rather ashamed . . . that there's anything so small in the army of the greatest of the world's republics at the very dawn of the twentieth century as race hatred; ashamed that Uncle Sam, who is preaching the democratic doctrine of equality to brown-skinned men in the tropics (with the aid of military governors on one side and bullets on the other) doesn't practice it here in San Francisco."[78] As she did in Hawaii, Michelson functioned as "magical human telephone and phonograph combined," transmitting the words of people whose voices were excluded from the mainstream press. Whereas scholars have analyzed the ways that ethno-racial minorities have created counternarratives in the ethnic press, Michelson's journalism demonstrates how the mainstream press itself mediated between competing narratives and discourses, an act of mediation made possible by the figure of the girl reporter whose performance of nonthreatening femininity allowed her access to people and places that were often off-limits to men.

"You're a Man, Rhoda, and White!": The Girl Reporter as White Feminist Heroine

The reign of the "girl reporter" was relatively short-lived. While women journalists commandeered headlines and bylines into the early twentieth century, the backlash against the excesses of the yellow press sent many scrambling for different lines of work, as girl stunt reporters became scapegoats for the wrongs of sensationalized journalism. Up until 1902, Michelson continued to cover the news. After several years at *The San Francisco Bulletin*, she temporarily moved east, where she spent two years writing for the Philadelphia *North American*, under the direction of her brother-in-law, legendary frontier journalist Arthur McEwen, who had also left the West Coast to become the paper's managing editor.[79] By the tail end of the nineteenth century, Michelson had begun to parlay her narrative journalism skills into a career as a fiction writer, publishing short stories in newspapers and mass-circulation magazines while working on a novel. Much of the raw material for her fiction had its source in her journalism. Like her reporting, her early fiction featured characters and settings that captured the multiethnic diversity of the American West. Two of these short stories, "An Understudy for a Princess" and

"The Road to Waikiki," were inspired by her trip to Hawaii, as was her unpublished novel "Ululani of Hawaii," a work of historical fiction about the founding of the Hawaiian Kingdom at the end of the eighteenth century.[80] Her reporting on San Francisco's Chinese immigrant community provided the basis for fictional sketches like "Ah Luey's Self" and "The Conversion of Choy Sing." These pieces follow Orientalized conventions of the Chinatown tale, a genre that had become a popular feature of periodical culture starting in the 1860s with Mark Twain's sketches in the Virginia City *Territorial Enterprise* and extending to works by other Western white writers as well as Asian American writers such as Edith Maude Eaton/Sui Sin Far.[81]

Michelson's breakthrough as a fiction writer came in 1904, when she published a short story, "In the Bishop's Carriage," in *Ainslee's*. Told from the first-person point of view of a streetwise pickpocket named Nance Olden, the story caught the attention of editors at the Bobbs-Merrill Company, who suggested that she expand it into a novel. The result, also titled *In the Bishop's Carriage*, was a scandalous sensation, due in part to the slangy voice of its roguish but likable criminal heroine. The book was adapted as a play and two films, and Nance became a feminist icon, a prototype for the flapper.[82] The popular success of *In the Bishop's Carriage* demonstrates how Michelson's career was shaped by the commercial demands of the mainstream literary marketplace. It is telling that her breakthrough as a novelist came with a narrative that centers a white woman's voice and experiences and shifts focus away from marginalized women of color. Set in Philadelphia, *In the Bishop's Carriage* takes place against a monoracial backdrop.[83] Her subsequent novels, *The Madigans* and *A Yellow Journalist*, continue to center white female characters; however, in relocating her heroines' adventures from the East to the West, Michelson incorporated the multiethnic landscape that had provided a backdrop for her own childhood and journalistic career.

Of all her fictional works, *A Yellow Journalist* best exemplifies the ripped-from-the-headlines quality of Michelson's writing. Narrated in an episodic format from the first-person point of view of "girl reporter" Rhoda Massey, the stories were serialized in *The Saturday Evening Post* in nine installments between January and October 1905. Each installment follows Rhoda as she covers a story for the fictional San Francisco *News*. Although the pieces are self-contained, interlocking elements link them, with some secondary characters appearing in more than one segment; such recurrences, coupled with the charismatic central figure of Rhoda and the vividness of the California setting, made for a smooth transition to novel form when D. Appleton & Company published *A Yellow Journalist* as a fourteen-chapter book at the end of 1905. Many of the characters and plotlines have parallels in real people and events, including ones Michelson herself covered while working at *The Call* and the *Bulletin*. Characters like Mammy Sinnott (based on Black abolitionist and entrepreneur Mary Ellen Pleasant) and Miss McIntosh (based on Scottish Presbyterian missionary Donaldina Cameron, famous for her rescues of Chinese women from sex slavery in San Francisco's Chinatown) would be recognizable to turn-of-the-twentieth-century readers, especially those in the West. Starting with already larger-than-life historical figures, Michelson blows them up further, giving them a cartoonish-ness befitting sensationalist fiction.

The fact that Michelson titles her series "A Yellow Journalist" and features the adventures of a "girl reporter" indicates that she was capitalizing on the kind of sensationalism that drew audiences to her debut novel about a girl thief. By the time Michelson published her series in *The Saturday Evening Post*, yellow journalism had become a well-worn catchphrase for the degeneracies of the American media, operating similarly to the phrase "fake news" today.[84] Typically used as derogatory complaint, yellow journalism critiqued the colorfulness of the American press and its ethically questionable tactics: with bold headlines and superfluous exclamation marks, papers presented the news in a hyperbolic, often lurid manner designed to attract and incite readers primarily for profit instead of aiming for nobler goals like informing the public and holding citizens accountable to a greater good.

Michelson's newspaper writings, as I have discussed, can better be understood in terms of the narrative conventions of late nineteenth-century new journalism rather than the bad rap of yellow journalism. However, for the purpose of entertaining readers through the *fictionalization* of her newspaper experiences, Michelson mobilizes the controversies surrounding yellow journalism to get a rise out of her audience and capture a mass readership. Michelson's intended provocation is made evident by the combination of her title with her protagonist's identity as a girl reporter. At the end of the nineteenth century, public outrage at yellow journalism coincided with anxieties about the corruption of femininity through association with sensationalist practices, from the bodily risks of stunt reporting to the moral taint of bending the truth. As essayist, editor, and suffragist Haryot Holt Cahoon warned, the girl reporter who "mantles her womanhood with the mud-stained garment of modern gutter journalism" sacrifices her "feminine dignity and self-respect."[85]

Still, despite the sensationalism of Michelson's fiction and her desire to entertain readers with a breezy prose style, comic interludes, and fast-paced plotting, an undercurrent of seriousness runs through *A Yellow Journalist*, especially when it comes to gender. Michelson's representation of an independent, empowered female protagonist and critiques of patriarchal institutions, from the media to marriage, qualify *A Yellow Journalist* as "feminist" in the mode of New Woman fictions produced on both sides of the Atlantic in the nineteenth and twentieth centuries. Turning away from conventional domestic fiction and the romance plot, novelists and short story writers rebelled against the constraints of Victorianism and depicted women as autonomous beings whose lives revolved around commerce and professional concerns, rather than marriage and family. New Women narratives portray middle-class female characters in workplaces and in pursuit of careers; among them are novels by Jewish women like British writer Amy Levy's *The Romance of a Shop* (1888), in which four sisters open a photography studio in London, and Annie Nathan Meyer's *Helen Brent, M.D.* (1892), in which a physician-protagonist struggles to balance her successful career at a New York hospital with her desire for romantic love and family. The figure of the newspaperwoman, in particular, offered nineteenth-century fictionists opportunities to explore how women were writing their way into the public sphere, with examples ranging from Fanny Fern (Sarah Payson Willis)'s semi-autobiographical novel *Ruth Hall* (1855) to Elizabeth Garver Jordan's story collection *Tales of the City Room* (1898).[86]

Unlike Cahoon and other critics who cautioned women away from newspaper work out of fear that the grittiness of the media industry would blemish femininity, Michelson maintained that women belonged in journalism. For her, the problem lay not with sensationalism and its threat to womanly ideals, but with gender inequality; what ultimately needed reforming was a patriarchal system in which women were treated differently from men. In *A Yellow Journalist*, she directs her critique at the prejudices and patriarchal practices that curtailed women's opportunities. At the same time, aware that such systems are slow to change, she empowers white women to overcome the odds stacked against them. Michelson strategically used fiction to offer a behind-the-scenes look at the industry, including the hypermasculine space of the newsroom, through a woman journalist's point of view. Fiction gives Michelson a cover, allowing her to explore issues she could not address directly in her nonfiction due to cultural taboos and threat of recrimination. Fiction also provides her with a dual and refracting lens: *A Yellow Journalist* gains legitimacy from the fact that its author is drawing from personal and eyewitness experiences, while the first-person adventures of her imaginary alter ego, Rhoda Massey, grant license to exaggerate and dramatize, with the effect of emphasizing certain gendered and racial realities.

Michelson's investment in exploring gender dynamics is evident from the outset. In "The Pollexfen Story," the first installment of *A Yellow Journalist*, readers are introduced to Rhoda through her competition with Ted Thompson, a male reporter at a rival newspaper. Rhoda eagerly embraces her first out-of-town assignment: a sordid and convoluted Gilded-Age domestic scandal involving money, murder, a hypnotized matriarch, and rumors of elopement. Arriving at the Pollexfen family's secluded home in pursuit of interviews, she encounters her rival reporter on the track of the same story, leading her to muse, "Everybody knows that Thompson doesn't consider a newspaper woman a foeman worthy of his steel—he's said so often enough. So, I bowed stiffly and resentingly and, in my heart, fearfully. But this last, of course, he couldn't see, and I'd have died before letting him know it. Oh, to beat Thompson on a story!"[87] The use of the compound word "foeman" (rather than simply "foe")—as well as avoidance of the compound word "newspaperwoman"—underscores Thompson's misogynistic belief in women's inferiority: only a man could be a worthy competitor. Rhoda's determination to get the scoop is about more than advancing her career. Her wishful exclamation "Oh, to beat Thompson on a story!" indicates that breaking the story would be a triumph for her gender; she would revel in proving him wrong about women's journalistic abilities.

Later, when Rhoda does, in fact, beat Thompson to the story, Michelson conveys her heroine's irrepressible pleasure in the success of her career. Rhoda informs us that the congratulatory telegram she received from her editor, McCabe, after breaking the Pollexfen story remains a cherished possession: "I've got it yet—that telegram. It's like wedding cake or a baby's shoe—it's so precious!"[88] The simile comparing her boss's words of praise to keepsakes associated with marriage and motherhood presents an alternative to domesticity. Rhoda becomes a mouthpiece for Michelson's message that women can find fulfillment in professional accomplishments. When Pollexfen's fifteen-year-old niece Dorothea, harboring her own aspirations for a career in the theater, inquires curiously and admiringly about Rhoda's vocation, it sends the journalist off on a long, gushing monologue about the joys of newspaper work: "I love the local room just before each of us goes out to bag his story. I love it when we all get back at night and pencils fly over the paper and typewriters click and the telephone bells go whirring. I love it when the paper's gone to press."[89] Rhoda's passion for her work contrasts sharply with her ambivalence about the path that many of the male characters, including Ted Thompson, prescribe for her: one that would lead to marriage and family.

While on the Pollexfen case, Rhoda receives an education in how her gender can operate as both an obstacle and asset to women's professional achievement. During an interview with Mr. Pollexfen, she is repeatedly identified in gendered terms; in the space of less than a page, she is called "a charming girl," "a pretty little woman," and "a beautiful lady journalist."[90] Rhoda recoils from the supposed flattery, recognizing the attempt to undermine her professional authority: "Ugh! I wasn't a charming girl. I wasn't a girl at all just then; I was only a reporter, a creature with eyes and ears and possessed by curiosity—and to be set back into my skirts that way made me tingle with distaste."[91] Although Rhoda articulates a desire for neutrality—to be viewed solely in terms of her profession, rather than as a "*lady* journalist"—she discovers that her gender can also be used to her advantage. Earning the admiration and trust of Dorothea and her sister, Mary, allows Rhoda to break the Pollexfen story; reassured that Rhoda, "a girl like myself . . . wouldn't hurt us," Mary supplies the girl reporter with the information that eluded Ted Thompson and his fellow male reporters.[92] Throughout *A Yellow Journalist*, Rhoda forms identificatory bonds with other women that enable her success as a reporter.

Her gender proves a boon in other ways, too, as she learns that a woman's body grants her access to people and places unattainable for men. In an episode from "The Ex-City Editor's Club," for instance, Rhoda, newly promoted to city editor and frustrated by the *News* employees' resistance to taking orders from a woman, delegates the slenderest male reporter to sneak on to a window ledge at the chamber of commerce in order to eavesdrop on a grand jury deliberation. When the reporter fails to fulfill her directive (in a display of toxic masculine rebellion, he ends up at a saloon, drinking with colleagues instead), Rhoda, rather than stewing over the disrespect, immediately regroups. She realizes that her own small stature makes her the one best suited to the daring stunt. Slipping her "light little body . . . along the cornice and . . . below the ledge," Rhoda finds herself "in heaven—the heaven of the reporter where you see things from the inside" with the prospect of giving secrets "away in a glorious, self-conscious, jubilating scoop!"[93]

Despite Rhoda's dislike of being "set back in her skirts," her outward feminine appearance allows her to orchestrate performances of womanliness that gain her access to sources and incriminatory evidence. In one scene, she ingratiates herself with a male informant simply by laughing. "A woman's laugh [is] a mighty good weapon when she's dealing with a man," she observes, "It sounds so light, so giddy, so altogether silly, that he wouldn't for a moment suspect her of having brains or purpose."[94] Indeed, in the ethically suspect manner of the yellow journalist, her strategies often involve disguising her intellectual ability, journalistic motives, and professional identity. She not only plays up femininity, but also takes on various traditional female roles—for instance, a nurse and a bride—as she investigates leads. In the chapter titled "A Dream Trousseau," she infiltrates the all-female space of a convent and gets in the good graces of a key source, a seamstress-nun, by pretending that she is a fiancée in need of a trousseau. Affecting a feminine act to win the nun's sympathies, she blushes and cries, noting, "I found I could be as silly and hysterically without reason as any woman I've ever interviewed."[95] This performance is a "strong contrast to the Rhoda who rides on a wagon through a volley of gunshots with a murderer early in her adventures and to the Rhoda who chooses to pursue her exciting career as a reporter rather than become an actual bride to the handsome rival reporter who courts her."[96] The chapter title, "A Dream Trousseau," with its subtitle

"Which Miss Massey Ordered," exudes irony. Earlier, in response to Ted Thompson's "bold-faced conceit" that Rhoda would eventually come around to the idea of family and marriage (and specifically, marriage to *him*), she replies, in a sassily accented retort, "I'm wedded to me art."[97]

The plot of *A Yellow Journalist* does capitulate to market demands for heterosexual romance by pairing off Rhoda and Ted, whose rivalry lessens in intensity when they end up working for the same paper. But the romance plotline remains secondary to Rhoda's adventures as a reporter, is played largely for laughs, and feels entirely unconvincing. While Rhoda occasionally and somewhat grudgingly admits her attraction to Ted (which reads more as a desire to emulate his journalistic prowess), the relationship is mostly one-sided; he professes his adoration for her, as she repeatedly pushes him away and maintains a stronger commitment to the thrill of her career. In one comic interlude, she is so intent on chasing a story that she forgets a date she made with Ted to celebrate their engagement; apparently, the fact that she had finally agreed to marry Ted also slipped her mind, and the episode ends with her leaving him behind as she elatedly rushes off to stop the presses with her "stunner" of a front-page story.[98] Michelson offers readers a rare depiction of an ambitious professional woman who is rewarded, rather than punished, for finding her job more exciting and fulfilling than she does her beau.

Rhoda's relationship with Ted should not only be understood as Michelson giving in to expectations of heteronormativity; the plotline can also be read as an important component of the author's critique. Especially by today's standards, Ted's aggressive and relentless pursuit of Rhoda smacks of sexual harassment, interfering with her attempt to do her job. Michelson treats unwanted romantic overtures and sexual advances as some of the many indignities that women face in the male-dominated workplace. In "The Milpitas Maiden" (an installment that appeared in *The Saturday Evening Post*, but for unknown reasons was not included when *A Yellow Journalist* was published as a stand-alone book), an incompetent male reporter, who is inebriated on the job, tries to "make love" to Rhoda while they are both covering a suffrage convention. The scene is played for comic effect; for example, an unwelcome kiss from her colleague makes Rhoda want to "box his ears," which she is unable to do only because she is holding the phone with her right hand

and is "not left-handed."[99] However, the underlying gravity of such episodes would not be lost on women readers. As I have argued elsewhere, the early twentieth-century writings of women such as Michelson and Elizabeth Jordan functioned as a prelude to the #MeToo movement, as "it became common practice for women journalists to pen fictional narratives based on their real-life adventures and to incorporate . . . encounters with powerful, predatory men in their fiction."[100]

#MeToo, along with other feminist movements of the twentieth and twenty-first centuries, has come under attack for overwriting women of color and privileging the voices and concerns of white, middle-class women.[101] Similar critiques could be leveled at Michelson's brand of pop feminism and can be illuminated by considering how racialized language infuses the gender dynamics of her fiction as well as by examining how people of color are represented in her literary imagination. As was the case for the Madigan sisters, Rhoda's triumphs as a feminist heroine are inextricable from her white identity. Her empowerment is conveyed through the use of colloquial metaphors that promote both masculinity and whiteness as aspirational ideals. At the same time that Rhoda comes to view her gender as an asset in her work as a yellow journalist, she aspires to be accepted by her colleagues as if she were one of the boys. Continually fighting to be treated by the same standards her colleagues apply to one another, Rhoda believes that "the sweetest thing in a working girl's life was to earn men's praise for doing men's work in a workmanlike way."[102] This overdetermined statement ("*men's* praise," "*men's* work," "work*man*like") equates masculinity with professional rewards, even when a woman is the one achieving them. When Rhoda does succeed in earning hard-won praise from men, their admiration is expressed in linguistic terms that are both gendered *and* racialized. For example, after she impresses her boss by exposing a gambling racket in Chinatown, she becomes known at the office as "McCabe's White-headed Boy," denoting her status as the editor-in-chief's pet reporter (and implying her coworkers' resentment of her success). The phrase "white-headed boy" confers upon Rhoda a provisional male identity and marks her rising rank in the office's hierarchical power structure. It also has racialized implications. Here and elsewhere in *A Yellow Journalist*, the metaphorical use of the word "white" carries favorable connotations, indicating superiority. "Black," in contrast, has negative connotations;

it is used in the text synonymously with "blackguard," identifying characters' behavior as suspect and dishonorable. The adjective in "white-headed boy" reasserts Rhoda's whiteness, which is necessary in light of her masquerade as "a Chinese boy" when she went undercover for the Chinatown investigation.[103]

The use of gendered and racialized language to signify Rhoda's increasing acceptance by men culminates in an exchange that takes place in the final chapter of the book. In this episode, which is titled "Some Japanese Prints," Rhoda uncovers corruption in the highest echelons of her own paper. The consequences for the security of Rhoda's career are grave: her whistleblowing results in the loss of her job. But her investigative skill and moral commitment to exposing the unjust exercise of power do merit the esteem of a formerly hostile male reporter named Frank McGowan, who had frequently made Rhoda the butt of a misogynistic joke ("What's the difference between Rhoda of the *News* and the bulldog I named after her? Well, the four-footed Rhoda *will* give up after a time").[104] While McGowan previously viewed ambitious determination in a woman as excessive, abnormal, and even inhuman, he signals his newfound acceptance of her as his equal with the "brotherly squeeze" of a handshake and declares, "You're a man, Rhoda, and white!"[105] McGowan's metaphors communicate his respect—and elevate Rhoda from a "white-headed *boy*" to a grown "*man*" who is "white." In McGowan's colloquial speech, "white" means that Rhoda is honorable, deserving of high regard. Paired with "man," it further emphasizes his opinion of Rhoda's superior qualities.

In earning her an honorary position among the dominant, white, male class, Rhoda's work ethic simultaneously legitimates her standing as a white feminist heroine—one who has emerged victorious by using her smarts and her femininity to her advantage, laboring at least twice as hard as her male colleagues to prove herself and overcoming discrimination that they did not face. But Rhoda does not rise to the top of the power hierarchy and gain full entrance into the old white boys' club. Instead, in exposing the corruption and injustice at the very heart of the media's power structure, she ends up excised from it. *A Yellow Journalist* concludes on an ambiguous note, leaving the reader with uncertainty about the future of Rhoda's career. Will she return to newspaper work or leave "the arena of noisy, sensational journalism" for "the rather more quiet and genteel field of the newspaper magazine," as the text implies is an option? This ambiguity is further enhanced by the uncharacteristically sentimental final page, which finds Rhoda "walk[ing] home under the stars" with Ted Thompson, whose reputation she had saved by proving that he had been made into "a whipping boy" and taken the fall for the crimes of the newspaper's proprietor. The romantic coda feels tacked on and out of character for Rhoda. Could such a spirited heroine, who had so boldly expressed her exuberance about newspaper work, possibly allow Ted's "tenderness" to "hush" her "as though [she] were a child"?[106] Yet, even if Michelson was bowing to literary convention and the exigencies of the marketplace in domesticating Rhoda as she draws her heroine's adventures to a close, the text undermines familiar romance tropes; it does so by depicting its female protagonist (Rhoda) as the savior of a helpless man (Ted). Rhoda's heroic act of clearing Ted's name is especially interesting in light of the fact that Michelson explores tenuous alliances between her heroine and women of color who appear in the text, but resists valorizing the Progressive-Era journalist as a white savior.

By marking feminism as "white," critiques of white feminist ideology make clear that the dominant strain of feminism remains invested in white American supremacist ideals, including individualism and capitalism. White feminism maintains an allegiance to a racial hierarchy that supersedes allegiances to women of color and neglects to acknowledge intersectional barriers that make gender equality impossible to achieve. Historically, white feminists have failed to recognize the urgency of interracial alliances, as when white suffragists in the National Women's Party, led by Alice Paul, decided it was not in their best interest for Black suffragists to march alongside them—a decision that journalist and activist Ida B. Wells bravely defied.[107] In several chapters of *A Yellow Journalist*, Michelson incorporates experiences of Black and Asian women who are allied with Rhoda in some way. While Michelson's racial representations at times run counter to expectation and stereotypical convention, these women are not fully developed as characters; their purpose is largely to contribute to the text's local color and to enable Rhoda's ascent as a journalist. The inclusion of women of color as secondary characters in a narrative that centers Rhoda exposes the text's racial blind spots, compelling qualification of the protagonist's status as feminist heroine: she is a *white* feminist heroine. Examining a series of three chapters that appear consecutively in the book version—"The Pencil Will," "The Fascination of

Fan-Tan," and "In Chy's Restaurant"—further brings to light this racialized dimension of Rhoda's heroism.

"The Pencil Will," the third installment of *A Yellow Journalist*, contains the series' first significant representation of racial difference. It introduces the character of Mammy Sinnott, who is based on Black abolitionist and businesswoman Mary Ellen Pleasant. Known to the public as "Mammy Pleasant," the moniker used by the mainstream press, Pleasant became a legendary figure in the history of Victorian-era San Francisco for her financial acumen, civil rights activism, and influence over wealthy white families. In the late nineteenth century up until her death in 1904 (shortly before *A Yellow Journalist* was published), Pleasant was embroiled in high-profile scandals and courtroom dramas that provided sensationalist fodder for the San Francisco papers. In newspaper articles such as "Dark-Skinned Lion-Tamer in the House of Mystery," Michelson herself contributed to the myth of Pleasant and replicated the racist practice of referring to her as "Mammy."[108] Similarly, in "The Pencil Will," Michelson does not give her fictional version of Pleasant a forename other than "Mammy," a sign that the characterization is likely to be one-dimensional. Indeed, with her dialect-ridden speech and maternal devotion to her young white charge, Sinnott is, in many ways, a stock mammy character, legible according to tropes established by the postbellum plantation romance.

A closer look, however, at the relationship between Rhoda and Sinnott suggests that the text is not only perpetuating racial stereotypes. Sinnott is one of the few female characters in *A Yellow Journalist* to display intelligence and agency. The real-life Pleasant objected to being called "mammy," but employed the mammy role as a cover; through savvy acts of self-invention and self-presentation, she was often taken to be the servant of the white families with whom her fortunes were linked, and she strategically used such assumptions to operate in the white world. Sinnott, too, appears to be subservient at first. She may work as a nursemaid for a white family and protect their interests, but she is shown to be the household authority in the absence of its deceased patriarch. In "The Pencil Will," Sinnott exerts control over the other characters and drives most of the story's action. It is she who enlists Rhoda as an ally, realizing that a partnership between a Black woman and a white "girl reporter" could be mutually advantageous.

Contributing to a pattern throughout *A Yellow Journalist*, the plot of "The Pencil Will" depends on bonds formed between women. The chapter explores how patriarchal culture attempts to disrupt those bonds and pit women against each other. At the opening of the chapter, which centers on a trial over a contested will, Rhoda observes that the male lawyers and some of the reporters covering the story have amplified the rivalry between the sisters-in-law who are on opposing sides of the case. In his coverage, for example, Frank McGowan dramatizes the conflict as "The War of the Widows."[109] Even Rhoda is initially tempted to heighten the tension and construct her story so that her readers would take the side of one woman against the other. By the end of the chapter, however, the two Mrs. Dilworths are shown to have the same interest at heart: the welfare of the sole Dilworth heir, Baby Jim, who is in Sinnott's care and whose affectionate disposition has won over Rhoda. The evolution of the relationship between the Dilworth widows parallels that between Rhoda and Sinnott. Although they begin as adversaries, with Rhoda determined to extricate family secrets that Sinnott works to conceal, they are ultimately aligned. As it turns out, both Rhoda and Sinnott are most concerned about Baby Jim's future, and all four women are connected by an ethic of maternal care that sets them apart from the men—even as they are problematically united around the figure of a white male child. Rhoda becomes a somewhat unwitting participant in Sinnott's plan to conspire against the male reporters. Sinnott manipulates the men by feeding them contradictory information that they go on to print in their papers, justifying her deceit by declaring, "'Tain't no lie to lie to a newspaper reporter that gets a livin' by tellin' lies!"[110] Rhoda does not end up with much of a story for her editors, deciding that it would harm Baby Jim to print the scandalous truth she uncovers about his paternity. But Sinnott has, in a sense, salvaged Rhoda's career by sparing her the humiliation that she doled out to the men and which, for Rhoda, may have meant her downfall, given that she is a woman.

In subverting the servile mammy stereotype with a portrayal of a strong Black female character who wields control over men, the text runs the risk of depicting Black power as nefarious.[111] In their coverage of the Dilworth trial, the male journalists villainize Sinnott as an "evil genius," with one reporter, for instance, inserting frequent "allusion[s] . . . to The Sinister Black Hand" in his stories.[112] Rhoda, in contrast, comes to respect

Sinnott's shrewd intelligence and offers a counternarrative. She recognizes that the Black woman acts out of desire for what is right and just, not with sinister intent.

The portrait of Sinnott as a commanding force, deserving of respect, has its precedent in Michelson's journalistic writings. In "Dark-Skinned Lion-Tamer in the House of Mystery," Michelson turned her inability to secure an interview with Pleasant into material for a character study of the Black woman and her influence in San Francisco society. Making multiple visits to Pleasant's home only to be repeatedly turned away, Michelson confessed, "My interview with Mammy Pleasant should rightly be written up under the head, 'People I Haven't Met.'" She goes on to elaborate:

> If a foreign Prince comes to San Francisco your managing editor, through an influential friend, may arrange a short meeting for you, when only stereotyped questions may be asked. If a famous murderer is to be hanged soon you may talk to him, provided your questions are not too personal or indelicate. If a great lady's daughter is to be married she will grant you an interview, if you will be sufficiently grateful. But tell me, ye gods of pull, what is the magic string that will open Mammy Pleasant's door and Mammy Pleasant's lips![113]

At the end of the article, Michelson succeeds in opening "Mammy Pleasant's door and Mammy Pleasant's lips," but is still not granted the desired interview. After Michelson is admitted to the "House of Mystery" by another woman (presumably Pleasant's servant), "a deep, imperious voice" instructs her, from the top of the staircase, to leave. Pleasant admonishes, "If I want you, I'll send for you." Michelson includes a variation on this encounter in "The Pencil Will." With "an imperiousness" that made Rhoda "feel like a child," Sinnott sends the girl reporter away from the Dilworth home, telling her "When I want yo,' Rhody Massey, I'll send fo' yo.'"[114] The use of dialect in the short story version underscores how Michelson's fictionalization of Pleasant conforms to the mammy type. Yet, both the newspaper article and the short story alter the expected racial power hierarchy: here, it is the white woman who is made subservient, instructed to come only when the Black woman calls for her.

As a character who appears in only one installment of *A Yellow Journalist*, however, Sinnott operates in the service of the white heroine's story. Although one of the Mrs. Dilworths and her lawyer make appearances in later episodes, Sinnott drops out of the series, contained to "The Pencil Will." Scholars in African American studies have cited the historical erasure of Mary Ellen Pleasant as evidence of the ways that Black voices and experiences have been elided from the history of the American West. In recent decades, Pleasant has been reclaimed as "the Mother of Civil Rights in California" and recognized for her activism and philanthropy, which included donating $30,000 to support John Brown's raid on Harpers Ferry. Pleasant remains grounded more in myth than in fact due to deliberate acts of subterfuge and self-mythologizing, which have produced contradictory versions of her life story. Since Michelson penned "The Pencil Will," Black writers have found rich material in Pleasant's enigmatic past. In both Michelle Cliff's novel *Free Enterprise: A Story of Mary Ellen Pleasant* (1993) and Denise Nicholas's play *Buses* (1991), for example, Pleasant appears as a fictionalized historical figure; both Cliff and Nicholas imagine her in intra-racial, pan-African-diasporic alliances with other extraordinary Black women from folklore and history. In the hands of Black women writers, Pleasant becomes a heroine in her own story and in the ongoing, collective fight for racial justice. Michelson's Black secondary character may enact revenge upon white male reporters for their racist treatment of her, but she lacks the radicalism that marks the career and fictional afterlives of her historical counterpart. Even as Michelson's multiethnic West makes space for Black Americans, her representation of Sinnott speaks to the limits of the white racial imagination. Sinnott's character serves largely to bring into relief Rhoda's whiteness—and, in the process, aligns Michelson with the white feminist ideology that permeates many representations of female empowerment in mainstream American popular culture.

"Out-Yellowing Your Master": The Girl Reporter as Chinese Impersonator

When *A Yellow Journalist* was published in book form, it contained several new installments in Rhoda's adventures, including two chapters set in San Francisco's Chinatown. Although it is unclear why "The

Fascination of Fan-Tan" and "In Chy Fong's Restaurant" were omitted from the series' magazine run, it is possible that the content of these stories was deemed too risqué for *The Saturday Evening Post*, with its reputation of all-American wholesomeness.[115] The chapters depict Rhoda's most elaborate and provocative performance of stunt-girl reporting: she goes undercover first as a Chinese boy at a gambling house and then as a Chinese slave girl in a brothel to investigate networks of vice and rumors of graft in Chinatown. Placed consecutively after the episode with Mammy Sinnott, these two chapters complicate the text's racial dynamics, disrupting the Black-white binary established in "The Pencil Will." Rhoda's undercover stunts destabilize her whiteness, as she becomes "a yellow journalist" in quite another sense; the text plays with racialized meanings of its title, using "yellow" interchangeably to refer to Rhoda's sensationalist methods of reporting and to Orientalist delineations of Asian difference.

While the Chinatown chapters of *A Yellow Journalist* need to be read in the specific context of girl stunt reporting, they also participate in a broader American cultural tradition of cross-racial performance and appropriation that includes forms of masquerade, ventriloquism, and passing. As scholars such as Jennifer Glaser and Jonathan Freedman have shown, cross-racial performances and identifications are ubiquitous in Jewish-authored texts, generating a complex set of often contradictory meanings that simultaneously couple Jewishness with whiteness and construct Jews in terms of racial difference.[116] When Karen Skinazi and I initiated the process of recovering Michelson's work by reprinting "In Chy Fong's Restaurant" in the journal *MELUS*, we chose the story because its narrative of racial impersonation "adds to a rich archive of texts that allow us to explore cross-racial, cross-ethnic, and interreligious relations in the United States" and "offers ways to expand upon and complicate the inquiries of scholars . . . who have situated Jewish writers within the framework of comparative race and ethnic studies." "In Chy Fong's Restaurant," we noted, is "one of Michelson's most intriguing articulations of 'passing,' a recurring theme in her work" and exemplifies how her "stories of New Women intersected with her interest in telling stories about people of different ethno-cultural backgrounds dwelling in, and on the outskirts of, America."[117] Here, I expand on our claims to demonstrate how Michelson's fiction mobilizes the spectacle of girl stunt reporting to undermine another dangerous racial binary: one that justified American ideologies of exclusion and imperialism by positioning white, Christian values as righteously superior to an exotic, degenerate, and threatening East Asia.

When Rhoda initially ventures into Chinatown, garbed and made up as a "queued" Chinese boy on his way to a fan-tan game, her views of her surroundings and the Chinese population are circumscribed by Orientalized notions of Asian difference. "The risk and terror of Chinatown were upon me," Rhoda thinks, as she takes in "the dirt and the glamour of the East," the "noisome, narrow streets where the big lanterns swing[,] and the Chinese children, playing in the entrances to subterranean dwellings . . . like gaudy dragon flies lighting up the squalor."[118] Concerned about the dangers that Chinatown posed for a woman alone, even one in male disguise, Rhoda's editor assigns two white chaperones for her protection; she is accompanied by an inexperienced male reporter named Forbes and Sergeant Wyss, a police officer who heads the Chinatown squad. Rhoda's initial perception of Chinatown as an exotic underworld overrun by violent gangs is fueled by Wyss, who refers to the neighborhood's residents as "crafty devils" and "Chinks."[119] Chinatown becomes a spatial embodiment of the "Yellow Peril," expressing racist fears of Asian power as a threat to white Western dominance and existence.

Rhoda's perceptions of Chinatown as a space of filth, terror, and inscrutability, wherein her very presence invites risk of bodily harm, shift over the course of her investigation. As she pursues her journalistic mission of rooting out the facts and distinguishing them from myth, she comes to suspect that the police sergeant Wyss—and the white, masculinist "law and order" he represents—pose greater danger than the so-called Yellow Peril. "The Fascination of Fan-Tan" hints early on that Wyss, supposedly there for Rhoda's protection, is a sexual threat—a narrative that runs counter to sensationalized tales of Chinese men holding white women captive as sex slaves.[120] Noting "the flirtatious glint" in Wyss's eyes and the "challenging hint" in his voice, Rhoda deduces that her Chinese boy persona is a turn-on (a subtle critique of white heterosexual masculinity); she reminds herself that men "can't resist" either "the subtle influence of the Orient" or "the suggestiveness of feminine disguise . . . so the combination must be a hard one for a mere police sergeant to go up against." While she pushes aside her initial discomfort about Wyss because "that hasn't anything to do with the case," her suspicion that the police sergeant is an untrustworthy scoundrel proves to be correct.[121]

As it turns out, Wyss is in cahoots with the Chinatown highbinders and warns them in advance of the undercover reporter he is escorting into their midst. The Chinese gamblers hide evidence of illegal activity and transform their fan-tan game into an "orderly, sociable, quiet meeting of half a dozen Chinamen, sitting amiably chatting in sing-song Chinese, drinking tea and smoking their pipes."[122] Rhoda easily sees through the act. Ditching Wyss, she joins forces with a Chinese woman named Gum Tai, whose young son Rhoda had protected from the "little white urchins" who terrorized him. Gum Tai takes Rhoda back to the gambling den, where she witnesses a raucous, illegal game of fan-tan in the same room she had left shortly before. During the ensuing raid, made possible by Gum Tai's clever trick of dropping pebbles so the gamblers are unable to shut the doors to keep out the police, Rhoda once again comes face-to-face with Wyss: "His eye caught mine, and for a second I had an absurd sensation of being in peril . . . of feeling what a hypnotized subject must feel when it is suggested to him that he is being knocked down—beaten—trampled upon."[123] Although Rhoda's exoticized view of Chinatown remains largely intact, "The Fascination of Fan-Tan" subverts the racial binary that positions the white man in opposition to the threat of the "Yellow Peril" and as the guardian of white womanhood. It is Wyss, not the Chinese men, who proves a menace to Rhoda, instilling in her, and in the reader, a "sensation" of "peril" and fear of physical endangerment. In contrast, Gum Tai, with her "amazing celerity" and "cool-headed nerve," emerges as Rhoda's formidable accomplice.[124]

"In Chy Fong's Restaurant" further explores alliances between Rhoda and women of color while continuing and intensifying the narrative of immersion journalism. After Wyss denies the allegations of graft printed by her paper, Rhoda plans to obtain undeniable proof by going undercover as a Chinese "sing-song girl" in a Chinatown parlor house, hoping to spy an exchange of money between the police sergeant and his Chinese coconspirators. She pursues the daring stunt in defiance of McCabe, her editor and mentor in the techniques of sensational journalism. "You're out-yellowing your master," McCabe cautions her after she outlines her scheme. On the one hand, he is concerned that she will put herself in jeopardy, unconvinced that she can sustain a performance as a "Chinawoman." On the other, he appears uncomfortable with the idea of a woman surpassing his own journalistic feats; in response to Rhoda's confidence in her ability to pull off the masquerade, he questions, "Am I the News Editor of this paper or am I merely the home secretary for your foreign—very foreign—affairs, you conceited and rampant little yellow journalist?"[125] Without the support of McCabe, who fears Rhoda's unchecked rise to the top will undermine his masculinity, turning him from boss into her "secretary," Rhoda once again enlists the help of Gum Tai. The Chinese woman trains Rhoda for her role, giving her lessons in properly docile comportment: "No talk. No look see. No turn head. No move."[126] Like Mammy Sinnott's dialect in "The Pencil Will," Gum Tai's use of pidgin English verges on racist caricature. Rhoda also models her behavior on the slave girl Ah Oy, who appears as stereotypically "passive" as a "China doll."[127] Less submissive than she first seems, Ah Oy, too, forms a strategic alliance with Rhoda and ends up serving as her protector, thus countering historical accounts of Chinatown rescues, in which white, Christian missionaries, acting as moral authorities, saved Chinese women from enslavers and traffickers.

Michelson's fictional treatment of human trafficking, a topic familiar to her from her work as a journalist, needs to be understood in light of the history of Chinese women and immigration in America as well as the ways that Asian women have been portrayed in American culture. In *Unbound Feet: A Social History of Chinese Women in San Francisco*, Judy Yung explores how the experiences of Chinese American women were shaped by a variety of historical and social conditions, including patterns of immigration and labor; patriarchal control and sexism in both China and the United States; and anti-Asian racism, which led, in turn, to anti-Chinese legislation such as the Page Act of 1875 and the Chinese Exclusion Act of 1882. As a result of these converging factors, significant numbers of Chinese women were transported to San Francisco's Chinatown in the nineteenth century and forced to work without pay as prostitutes in seedy cribs and parlor houses, which catered to an elite clientele of white and Chinese men. Although immigration restrictions such as the Page and Chinese Exclusion Acts were designed in part to curtail prostitution and sexual exploitation, they had the opposite effect and worsened circumstances for Chinese women. As Yung explains,

"By making it more difficult for Chinese women to immigrate and by successfully reducing their numbers, the laws inadvertently increased the demand and raised the value of prostitutes, but still did not stop the lucrative trade."[128] Because the titillating topic of sex trafficking lent itself well to the sensationalist discourse of the nineteenth-century press, the association between Asian women and prostitution came to dominate American culture, with Chinese women often treated as sexually and morally suspect.

Michelson wrote her Chinatown chapters against this historical backdrop.[129] As voyeuristic narratives that allow readers to follow along with Rhoda as she infiltrates Chinatown's alluring and forbidden spaces, these chapters participate in Orientalist discourse that fueled anti-Chinese sentiment. For example, the fact that "In Chy Fong's Restaurant" takes place in a brothel disguised as a restaurant and discloses sexual slavery as central to Chinatown's economy reinforces the linkage of Chinese immigration with illicit sexuality and patriarchal abuse. In employing the journalistic practice of undercover reporting, however, Rhoda engages in acts of racial impersonation that at least temporarily upend the relationship between cultural insiders and outsiders. Her exploits offer a shift in perspective that complicates familiar racial tropes, exposing white complicity and resisting a stance of white moral superiority. "In Chy Fong's Restaurant" may replicate the cultural tendency to situate Asian women in sexualized contexts, but the story does not depict its Chinese female characters as solely or innately submissive. In fact, Ah Oy and the other sing-song girls engage in "lifelong rehearsals" in order to perfect their Lotus Blossom personae.[130] Because Rhoda, too, learns to enact stereotypes of Asian femininity in order to go undercover, her racial impersonation denaturalizes their identities, exposing elaborately staged acts of gendered and racialized performances.

What is further notable about "In Chy Fong's Restaurant" is its avoidance of a moralizing tone—especially when we consider Michelson's writing in relation to turn-of-the-twentieth-century Chinatown tales by writers such as Helen F. Clark, who employed the genre to promote the work of Christian missions in saving Chinese women. *A Yellow Journalist* resists positioning the liberated American woman in opposition to the oppressed and passive Chinese victim. Instead of having Rhoda become the savior of Ah Oy and the other Chinese prostitutes through her investigative reporting, for instance, Michelson's story allies Rhoda and the Asian women against Miss McIntosh, a zealous white missionary. Miss McIntosh foils Rhoda's investigation by staging a raid on Chy Fong's restaurant, arriving just as the disguised reporter is about to witness Wyss receive a bribe. In this scene, Ah Oy acts as Rhoda's guardian. Signaling Rhoda with a "swift, enigmatic glance—imploring, confiding, searching," Ah Oy leads her out onto the balcony so that she can escape discovery during the raid—before disappearing herself.[131] Because we remain confined to Rhoda's first-person perspective, the text leaves us with an intriguing ambiguity surrounding Ah Oy's actions; it is unclear whether she had been secretly cooperating with Miss McIntosh to plan her escape from the brothel or whether she was trying to elude the missionary, perhaps even using Rhoda as a decoy. Either way, the cross-racial identification between Ah Oy and the "yellow journalist" is humorously reinforced at the end of the story when Rhoda finds herself captured by Miss McIntosh, who is under the assumption that her new rescue is a helpless "sing-song girl" rather than a fearless girl reporter. The comedy of the story's denouement hinges on the ludicrousness of cross-racial identification and mistaken identity, thus reifying boundaries between white and Asian as much as challenging them.

Through Rhoda's interactions with Miss McIntosh, "In Chy Fong's Restaurant" further resists the widely accepted idea that, for Chinese women, the alternative to sex work was a life of austere Christian morality with adherence to the repressive, patriarchal codes of white Victorian femininity. The text avoids becoming a polemic for American moral superiority by creating fictionalized versions of historical women who figured prominently in turn-of-the-twentieth-century discussions about Chinese prostitution and infusing the characters' interactions with comedic rather than sentimental overtones. Ah Oy, for example, evokes the historical figure of Ah Toy, the most famous nineteenth-century Chinese American woman due to the fact that she accumulated enough wealth as a prostitute to buy her own brothel; wielding considerable influence in San Francisco society, Ah Toy—much like Mary Ellen Pleasant—occupies a mythic space in California history.[132]

The character of Miss McIntosh similarly has a historical referent. She is based on Scottish American missionary crusader Donaldina Cameron, who ran the Presbyterian Mission House and claimed to have saved more than 1,500 Chinese girls from sex slavery. Cameron's efforts to rescue and reform Chinese women who had been forced into prostitution earned her the nickname "Chinatown's Angry Angel." But Cameron's religious mission often had dire consequences for the Chinese women she saved, who were "pressured into adopting gender roles that emphasized female purity, piety, and Christian home life." As Yung writes, the efforts of Presbyterian missionaries were "flawed by an unyielding belief in the superiority of Victorian cultural values, to the point of self-righteous condescension."[133] Cameron was revered and glorified as a white crusader in mainstream American discourse for her daring raids and efforts to reform and civilize Chinese women, but to others, especially the Chinese Americans she worked to control, she symbolized American imperialist ideology, forcing the women to submit to Western, Christian lifestyles or face deportation to China.[134] Rhoda responds to her rescue with frustration and disappointment, crying out that she "longed to beat" Miss McIntosh.[135] For the story's white heroine, the stakes are low; Miss McIntosh may have impeded the girl reporter's big scoop but she quickly releases Rhoda upon discovering her identity. Beneath the comic denouement, however, lies the implication that not all Chinese women sought rescue by white missionaries.

To some extent, Rhoda's yellowface performances reinforce her status as a white feminist heroine, one capable of "out-yellowing" her "master." However, in playing Rhoda's fictional adventures for laughs, often at the protagonist's own expense, rather than narrating events with earnestness or sentimentality, the text stops short of glorifying its protagonist, presenting her instead as humorously flawed. Rhoda's elaborate scheme is in many ways a failure; "In Chy Fong's Restaurant" does not resolve with the grand exposé of graft that Rhoda hoped to publish. Instead, she takes smaller satisfaction in thwarting the missionary's efforts and rebelling against the self-righteous forces of Christian imperialism. Rhoda refuses to give voice to the narrative of white moral authority by choosing not to "write up the story of the slave girls and the Mission" for her paper, a decision that Miss McIntosh "never can understand."[136] Moreover, the story's ending bears similarities to Michelson's sympathetic appeal on behalf of Hawaiians in "Strangling Hands upon a Nation's Throat," in which she endeavored to represent the humanity of a people whom many white Americans viewed as "heathens" in need of civilization. Like

Michelson's performance of racial ventriloquism in serving as a "magical human telephone and phonograph combined," Rhoda's act of racial impersonation highlights her allyship with women of color in opposition to white, Christian hegemony and "Anglo-Saxon supremacy."[137] The Chinatown chapters of *A Yellow Journalist* operate within and at times reproduce Orientalist ideology, but they also offer readers opportunities to see beyond it. Rhoda's Chinese personae and alliances with Asian women offer a different perspective than the typical voyeuristic, touristic gaze, leading to the realization that white, masculinist, capitalist greed—represented by Wyss, the corrupt white police sergeant—and misguided, self-righteous Christian morality—represented by the plan-bungling Miss McIntosh—are greater threats than the "Yellow Peril." In so doing, these chapters contribute to a broader cultural tradition of writings by Jewish women that appropriate narratives of other races to advance a feminist critique of whiteness.[138]

Rhoda's skepticism about white religious morality links her to the Madigans, who displayed similar irreverence for Christian values, and, in turn, to Michelson's own secular Jewish background. Although Michelson usually expresses her devout secularism by maintaining a distance from her ethno-religious heritage, scrubbing her writing clean of explicit Jewish references, *A Yellow Journalist* proves an interesting exception to Michelson's general reticence to identify her writing with Jewishness. It contains one of the few unmediated representations of Jewishness in Michelson's oeuvre. In a series of consecutive episodes, Rhoda investigates a scandal that her editor at first refers to obliquely as "the Lowenthal *ménage à trois*."[139] As more details emerge, readers are introduced to three generations of Lowenthals: the father, David, an influential theatrical manager; his son, Leo Lothal, who "dropped a syllable of his father's name" in order to follow in the family artistic tradition and pursue a stage career; and the matriarch, Gran'ma Lowenthal.[140]

The Lowenthal family dysfunction is caused by intermarriage, linking Michelson's representations of Jewish life to those in Wolf's and Lowenberg's novels. It unfolds that as David achieved professional success and fame as an artistic manager, he traded up his loyal "little Jewish wife," Leo's mother, for a non-Jewish actress, Evelyn Randall, "bewitched" by "the power of her bad, beautiful face."[141] The second marriage causes a conflict with "old-fashioned" Gran'ma Lowenthal, who took an instant dislike to this "daughter-in-law of another religion, a different caste," concerned that the "'outlandish woman'" was "lightly contemptuous of the man who was sacrosanct in that clean, simple temple [of] his mother's heart." Gran'ma's fear that Evelyn would "trail . . . her husband's honor in the dust" proves to be correct.[142] The family drama comes to a climax when it is revealed that Evelyn is having a very public affair, hence the rumors of a "Lowenthal *ménage à trois*," and Leo is subsequently accused of murdering his stepmother's lover. Rhoda's reporting on the case turns public opinion against young Lothal. This time, however, despite the "thundering scoop" that earns her a front-page headline ("Rhoda Massey Finds the Missing Revolver") and a promotion, Rhoda is unable to savor her success. She grows remorseful for having deceived the kind, elderly Jewish grandmother in order to get her story. Moved by Gran'ma Lowenthal's defense of her grandson and her interest in "befriend[ing]" the girl reporter, Rhoda is persuaded to prove Leo's innocence and clear the Lowenthal family name.[143]

Michelson's Jewish characters are worth consideration for several reasons. For one, the text's representation of a sophisticated and acculturated Jewish family presents an alternative to the dialect-speaking immigrants who appear in better-known, canonical texts, reminding us of Annie Nathan Meyer's call for a wider range of representation as well as her specific suggestion that Jewish patrons of the arts would make a good subject for fiction.[144] David Lowenthal is described as "a man all poetry, all sensuous delight in beautiful things, a dreamer, not a man of action or business, like his business partners, but an artist in whom the genius of his wonderful race manifested itself in stage productions that were embodied masterpieces."[145]

Like many of the characters in *A Yellow Journalist*, David Lowenthal has a historical parallel. At the turn of the twentieth century, Jewish impresarios such as San Francisco's own David Belasco were very much in the public eye. When David Lowenthal is first mentioned in the text, he is described as a member of the Theatrical Syndicate. The historical Theatrical Syndicate comprised a group of Jewish owners who banded together to consolidate operations of theaters across the country. At the time that Michelson wrote *A Yellow Journalist*, the Theatrical Syndicate was taking heat for its monopolistic business practices, but the criticisms were usually couched in not-so-thinly-veiled antisemitic attacks that drew upon economic stereotypes of unscrupulous greed and myths of Jewish commercial dominance. The syndicate was vilified in the press, often referred to as the Jewish Trust, the Jewish Syndicate, or even the "Sheeniedicate." In political cartoons, syndicate members were drawn with grotesque features, including hooked noses. *A Yellow Journalist* appeared in *The Saturday Evening Post* concurrently with drama critic James Metcalfe's series of virulently antisemitic articles targeting the syndicate in *Life* magazine. Read in this context, Michelson's sensitive portrayal of the Lowenthals and Rhoda's efforts to exonerate the family and restore their reputation take on new meaning.[146] Whereas Michelson largely erased Jewish specificity from *The Madigans* and from her journalism, Jewishness figures explicitly into her depiction of a multiethnic West in *A Yellow Journalist*.

Like other secondary characters in *A Yellow Journalist*, the Lowenthals take a backseat to the protagonist. It is Rhoda's adventures as a New Woman that knit together these varied ethno-racial representations. Toward the end of "In Chy Fong's Restaurant," just before her capture by Miss McIntosh, Rhoda stands on the balcony of the Chinatown brothel and looks out over the city and the bay below: "I stretched out my arms toward it all," she states, "it was beautiful; it was American; it was Western; it was mine."[147] The moment brings us back to a similar scene in *The Madigans*, where another of Michelson's alter egos, Sissy, "stretched out her hands—a small, petticoated Balboa—to the world she had discovered." In both cases, Michelson's protagonists challenge the masculinism of the frontier. Speaking while in the guise of a Chinese immigrant woman, the heroine of *A Yellow Journalist* also performs an act of racial ventriloquism. An exaggerated and sensationalized version of the cultural mediation enacted by Michelson in her journalism, Rhoda's declaration boldly asserts the right of those on the ethno-racial margins to lay claim to the nation's story.

A Yellow Journalist exposes the vexed nature of white allyship that crosses the line into troubling appropriation. Rather than categorically dismissing such messy texts by Jewish American women as offensive and out-of-sync with our times, this chapter operates from the premise that the writers' racial blind spots are themselves worth examination. When read closely in their historical context, Michelson's sensationalist fictions illuminate the complex dynamics of cross-ethnic and cross-racial representation in Jewish American women's writing—especially when we consider her background as a reporter in the era of yellow journalism and the way her engagement with suffrage and other progressive causes informed her representations of women and her treatment of race and gender.[148] Prolific in multiple popular genres, Michelson evinces the rarely acknowledged range of Jewish women's writing in the turn-of-the-twentieth-century United States. In the following chapter, I widen that range further by considering the career of Anna Strunsky, a writer whose literary and journalistic endeavors had direct ties to the leftist activism and bohemian subculture of the San Francisco Bay Area.

5
Letters of a Girl Socialist

Literary Collaboration and Bay Area Bohemia

On October 10, 1904, Anna Strunsky appeared before the women of the Philomath Club. Strunsky was nearing the end of a series of speaking engagements on the California women's club circuit, where she presented passionate addresses about the leading socialist figures of the day. Strunsky's October 10 address might seem to mark a collision between two San Francisco subcultures: Jewish high society, represented by the affluent, immaculately dressed matrons of the Philomath Club, whose families had been established on the West Coast since the Gold Rush, and the bohemian world of the unconventional, "attractively disheveled" Strunsky, a young Russian immigrant whose family had arrived in California at the end of the century. Having made a name for herself as the "Girl Socialist of San Francisco" by the time she was nineteen, Strunsky had dropped out of Stanford and was pursuing a career as a writer and activist. In 1903, her first book, *The Kempton-Wace Letters*, a novelistic collaboration with Jack London, made public her tumultuous romance with the adventurous, working-class rebel of Western American letters. An adventurer herself, Strunsky ran with "The Crowd," a circle of hard-drinking intellectuals and artists, and had recently returned from a trip to Europe with her friend Gelett Burgess, where she met with socialist leaders such as Prince Peter Kropotkin, the subject of her Philomath address. As she explained in a letter to her publisher, thanking him for the advance that financed her trip abroad, the goal of her journey was to gather material for "a book which will be the *Uncle Tom's Cabin* of the capitalist regime."[1]

Contrary to expectations, Strunsky's radicalism failed to scandalize the Philomath women, and her speech did not become an explosive site of clashing worlds. Instead, Strunsky "held her audience spellbound" by telling stories about Kropotkin, a Russian prince who had renounced his noble birthright and was now living in exile for writing and disseminating socialist propaganda. According to *The San Francisco Call*, the Philomath women sat "rapt" during Strunsky's "earnest address," which "brought her a deserved ovation." Unlikely to forgo their own wealth and privilege for the greater good of humanity, Lowenberg and the other clubwomen were certainly not proponents of the Kropotkin school of socialism, nor would they have tolerated their own daughters trekking to Europe in the company of an eccentric man like Burgess, editor of the San Francisco humor magazine *The Lark*. But they clearly respected the charismatic, idealistic, and intellectual woman who stood before them and whose "magnetic enthusiasm . . . yet simple language . . . lent . . . charm" and power to her message.[2]

In *The Iron Heel* (1908), Jack London imaginatively drew upon Strunsky's speaking engagement, in addition to his own experiences lecturing to bourgeois audiences, for a key scene in his dystopian socialist novel. In a chapter titled "The Philomaths," London's working-class protagonist, Ernest Everhard, gives a fiery and combative speech to a San Francisco club of that name. Described as "the most select on the Pacific Coast," London's Philomath Club is the "creation of Miss Brentwood, an enormously wealthy old maid," and its members are "the wealthiest in the community." London's fictional club differs from San Francisco's historical Philomaths in significant ways: its membership is not Jewish nor does it consist solely of women, despite being founded by a woman, whose wealth and social clout call to mind Bettie Lowenberg's.[3]

Underscoring and complicating the gender dynamics of the novel, London stages the verbal battle between his working-class, socialist hero and the capitalist elite against the backdrop of a love story. Like most of *The Iron Heel*, the episode is narrated by Ernest's future wife, Avis, who attends the meeting because her father is a Philomath. Avis views the speech as a turning point in her romance with Ernest, as it "vanish[es]" her "last doubt of the completeness of [her] love for him." This realization effects a change in Avis's status in society, as older women begin to view her as a "a too-forward and self-assertive young woman with a mischievous penchant for . . . interference in other persons' affairs."[4] Avis's conversion to the socialist cause, her investigative activism, and her love for the novel's revolutionist hero mark her as not only a traitor to her class, but also a transgressor of traditional gender roles.

London's gender displacements become increasingly complex when considered in the context of the novel as a whole. In this scene, the Philomaths are displaced by a male-dominated version of the San Francisco women's club, and Anna Strunsky, the "girl socialist" known for her debating skill, is transformed into a virile socialist spokesman, the aptly named Ernest Everhard. Interestingly, however, *The Iron Heel* centers the voice of a woman by telling its tale of violent socialist revolution from Avis's first-person point of view. Using the conceit of a found manuscript written by Avis to record her husband's exploits as leader of the revolt against the oligarchic "Iron Heel," the novel is London's "most sustained and complete effort to impersonate a female narrator, at once a fully imagined character as well as the tale's recorder and commentator."[5] London's impersonation of a female narrator creates multiple layers of gender transposition since Avis's written reminiscences not only focus on her husband, immortalizing him as the narrative's hypermasculine hero, but are also framed by the mediating voice of London's fictional male historian, Anthony Meredith, whose footnotes explain, comment upon, and correct Avis's manuscript. In the opening paragraph of the foreword, Meredith justifies his copious annotations to the published version of the "Everhard Manuscript." "To the historian," he writes, the document "bristles with errors—not errors of fact, but errors of interpretation. Looking back across the seven centuries that have lapsed since Avis Everhard completed her manuscript, events, and the bearings of events, that were confused and veiled to her, are clear to us. She lacked perspective. She was too close to the events she writes about. Nay, she was merged in the events she has described." The book thus opens by undercutting the female narrator whose words we are about to read, privileging the male historian's account as more reliable. Meredith's foreword concludes by informing us, "Of Avis Everhard there is no further record," and London extends his literary conceit to the end of the book, where Avis's manuscript "breaks off abruptly," silencing her mid-sentence.[6]

A dystopian science fiction story doubling as socialist tract, *The Iron Heel* was not London's first formal experiment in creating a multivocal, cross-gendered narrative.[7] The book can be placed effectively in dialogue with *The Kempton-Wace Letters*, the novel London coauthored with Strunsky. Inspired by their real-life correspondence, the 1903 novel uses an epistolary form to debate love, sex, and marriage. Throughout,

London maintains the voice of an American male correspondent, Herbert Wace, a young man contemplating marriage and who closely resembles the novelist himself. Strunsky played a more complex role in the novel's creation. She composed the text written by Wace's middle-aged friend, a British man named Dane Kempton, whose epistles combine philosophical debate with fatherly advice. Strunsky also wrote the correspondence of Wace's fiancée, Hester Stebbins, whose letters appear at the end of the book. First published anonymously, *The Kempton-Wace Letters* was assumed initially to be the work of London alone. When the Macmillan Company subsequently published an edition with author attribution, only London's name appeared on the spine of the book, although both authors' names were included inside on the title page. Even today, some critics make the error of attributing the novel solely to London or of viewing Strunsky's contributions as incidental despite the fact that she wrote more than half the text.[8] As in *The Iron Heel*, women's writing, even when temporarily given center stage, ends up being enveloped and eclipsed by men's.

Unsurprisingly, this gender dynamic extends to Strunsky's treatment in scholarship. Such framing is evident, for example, in the finding aid for her papers at the Yale University Archives, which begins by stating, "The life of Anna Walling, an advocate of socialism and the cause of labor, was molded by three prominent socialists: Jack London, William English Walling, and Leonard Abbott. The papers of Anna Walling, acquired by the Yale University Library from Walling's family in 1980, are most significant for understanding Walling's relationships with these three men." Although Strunsky initially kept her maiden name (a decision that made headlines in the news of her time) and the collection is officially titled the Anna Strunsky Walling Papers, reflecting her later decision to append her husband's last name to her own, the author of the finding aid refers to her as "Anna Walling." After detailing the wide-ranging activities of her long life, all of it chronicled in the extensive collection of published and unpublished manuscripts, diaries, correspondence, and memorabilia, the finding aid sums up with the declaration that "hers was a life made interesting by the people she loved rather than by the work she produced."[9] While it is true that some of Strunsky's work centers on the men in her life and in the socialist movement more broadly, it would be more accurate to say that these three men—Walling,

London, and Abbott—were equally "molded" by her. Furthermore, this framing of her papers downplays the significance of her many writings on women, including her novel *Violette of Père Lachaise* (1915), which features a socialist artist as its heroine, and her unpublished manuscript *Revolutionary Lives*, much of which is devoted to profiling women leaders of the Russian Revolution. Like Avis's "Everhard Manuscript" in *The Iron Heel*, Strunsky's writings are deemed valuable for the ways that they support a phallocentric version of history.

This effacement is especially noticeable in literary studies, where considerations of her life and work are relegated to scholarship on London, whether in the few critical essays that examine *The Kempton-Wace Letters*, biographical criticism that hypothesizes how the women London knew inspired his heroines, or works of literary biography that discuss his relationship with Strunsky as a youthful episode of his short life.[10] Strunsky has fared better, especially recently, in historical scholarship, even as most historians have focused primarily on her marriage in 1906 to socialist intellectual and reformer William English Walling, which at the time was one of several well-publicized intermarriages between Jewish women and Christian philanthropists who shared political views. In his comprehensive biographical study, *Revolutionary Lives: Anna Strunsky and William English Walling* (1998), which takes its main title from Strunsky's unpublished manuscript, James Boylan notes, "Where twenty or thirty years ago I, like many of my contemporaries, might have dismissed half the tale—Anna's half—as irrelevant or inconsequential, it is now possible to study the two of them on equal terms, and justifiably so. We can explore more freely now the links between domestic and public spheres, between personal acts and social consequences."[11] Two other monographs similarly provide thoughtful considerations of Strunsky's place in history; both Steven Zipperstein's *Pogrom: Kishinev and the Tilt of History* (2018) and Julia Mickenberg's *American Girls in Red Russia: Chasing the Soviet Dream* (2017) devote chapters to considering the links between her personal and political lives. Mickenberg, for instance, situates Anna's and her sister Rose's experiences as correspondents in Russia in the context of the larger phenomenon of young American women whose attraction to the socialist revolution abroad coincided with the twentieth-century crusade for gender equality.[12]

While extending the current direction of historical scholarship, this chapter also aims to contribute to feminist and Jewish literary scholarship by examining Strunsky's early writings. Although Strunsky herself was part of the late nineteenth-century migration of eastern European Jews that was responsible for producing the genre of ghetto fiction, her writing rarely fits into the familiar paradigms of Jewish American literature. To assess how the culture of the West Coast shaped Strunsky's life and work, I begin with her biographical background. Situating her first book, *The Kempton-Wace Letters*, in the context of Bay Area bohemian literary culture, I read it alongside her real-life correspondence with Jack London as well as in relation to critical debates about the meaning of intermarriage in the American literary imagination. Although Jewishness is not mentioned explicitly in the novel (an erasure that is itself significant), *The Kempton-Wace Letters* offers insight into historical views on race and reproduction, including the eugenicist beliefs that kept London from marrying his Jewish collaborator despite their erotically charged intellectual partnership. As this chapter demonstrates, Strunsky's contributions to American literary culture were defined by her background as a Russian Jewish immigrant woman immersed in the leftist intellectual and artistic life of turn-of-the-twentieth-century San Francisco—an environment that proved to be at once liberating and constricting for her development as a writer.

In Bohemia

Anna Strunsky's connection to Russia would prove a defining force in her life. She was born on March 21, 1877, in Babinots, a *shtetl* now known as Babinovitch in what is now Belarus. Her father, Elias, was a businessman, and her mother, Anna, was the daughter of Rabbi Lasser Horowitz. Anna Strunsky was the fourth of the couples' six children; their oldest son, Albert, had been born in 1870, followed by Hyman in 1871 and Max in 1873. Breaking from the Ashkenazi custom of naming children for deceased relatives, the Strunskys named their first daughter after her mother. (Anna and her husband, William English Walling, were later to continue the family's tradition, giving one of their daughters the name "Anna.") Because both Anna's birth date and her mother's coincided with Purim, the joyous festival became a special family occasion; even when

Anna was an adult, the Strunskys would gather together, celebrating both Annas and the liberation of the Jews from persecution thanks to the brave deeds of the beautiful Queen Esther.[13]

The Purim story would have resonated strongly for the Strunskys as Jews living in the Russian Empire. Later, upon witnessing the immediate aftermath of the Homel massacre as a journalist in Russia in 1906, Anna recognized how lucky her family was compared to the many Russian Jews who fell victim to brutal, antisemitic violence.[14] Despite racial and religious prejudices against Jews under Czarist rule, Elias became a successful and respected merchant who held contracts with the government during the Russo-Turkish War (1877–78). By the time Anna's sister, Rose, was born in 1884, however, rising antisemitism and the eruption of pogroms following the 1881 assassination of Alexander II made life in Russia untenable, and the family decided to emigrate, joining the mass migration of eastern European Jews to the United States. They arrived in New York on September 20, 1886, when Anna was nine.

Even as she became an American citizen and spent most of her life in the United States, Strunsky identified strongly with her Russian roots. "From childhood, I felt the spell of Russia, the call of her sorrows," she wrote in her unpublished manuscript *Revolutionary Lives*, "There was Russia which I held by a slender thread of memory, by a hot and full throb of the pulse of my being."[15] Unlike fellow Russian immigrant Mary Antin, who described the process of becoming "a new being" in her autobiography *The Promised Land* (1912), Strunsky did not seek "release . . . from the folds of [her] clinging past."[16] Instead, she embraced her identity as a "foreigner." In her poem "Foreign-born," she speaks of the "Glorious, miraculous fate that deprives me of a country. / . . . Foreign-born, I bring with me my inseparable memories, my haunting instincts, my far-reaching thought."[17] Yet Strunsky's childhood memories of Russia remained hazy, her "only recollection" being

> a long village street and barefoot children and rambling hovels. I remembered myself a little child standing in a patch of sunlight and poking my fingers into a wall and finding it soft as sand. I dug and dug and let the fine red dust slip into my fist and laughed to think I had the stuff of which houses were made,—weak, powdery stuff, unstable as water. Later this afforded me an analogy for

> the whole fabric of Czardom, the age-old conceptions of kingship, crumbling to fine dust in the sunlight of a new day.

Like her father and her sister, Rose, who became a translator of Russian literature, Strunsky maintained her connection to her homeland through books. "I did not remember the beauty, but I remembered the intellectual aspects of Russia," she wrote, "They crowded around me in visions of books and authors, the Russia of Tolstoi and Turgenieff, of Gogol, Pushkin."[18]

The Strunskys initially settled in Manhattan, where they lived on East Thirty-Ninth Street and Elias ran a grocery and liquor store. The Strunskys' last child, Morris, was born soon after their arrival, in 1887. When Elias became an American citizen in 1892, the Yiddish poet Morris Rosenfeld, who would give voice to the experience of Jewish immigrant laborers in his *Songs from the Ghetto* (1898), served as witness to his naturalization. Elias's business interests met his family's material needs, allowing the family to live more comfortably than less fortunate immigrants depicted in Rosenfeld's poetry. Strunsky's father was thus able to prioritize his children's education and intellectual sustenance. Elias may have listed his occupation as "grocer" on his naturalization application, but to his daughter, her father was "an artist." "Whatever he does he does with vision and inspiration," Strunsky wrote in the toast she gave in honor of her parents' golden wedding anniversary, "His reverence for the inner life was unlimited, and it seemed almost that he respected books a little too much because they were made out of the thought of man." Passing on his bibliophilism to his daughter, Elias gave Anna her first book, an anthology of early American poets, feeding her love for poetry, which "even then in [her] childhood, was the greatest passion of [her] life."[19]

Anna's passion for language made her a child prodigy at Public School 49 in New York. By her early teens, she was sending her writings to magazines and succeeded in publishing articles in the *Twentieth Century*, a radical newspaper. In 1894, her academic accomplishments were featured in an article on the woman's page of *The New York Herald*, accompanied by a sketch of the young, studious "Annie Strunsky," clasping schoolbooks. "She is as gentle and amiable as she is brilliant," her school principal told the reporter, "Although only six years in America her knowledge of English is accurate and comprehensive, and her diction is choice and even classic. She reads the best authors in several languages."[20] In addition to learning German in school and speaking Yiddish at home, Strunsky spent her evenings studying French and reading literature in English and Russian.

The Strunsky home functioned as a salon for fellow émigrés, and Anna credited her parents' openness to people and ideas for providing an education that surpassed her formal schooling: "This was my best school and from these personalities I got more than I ever got out of books or halls of learning. Here were truly formative forces—meeting people in intellectual councils; budding geniuses, refugees, revolutionists; broken lives and strong lives, all made welcome, all met with reverence and with warmth. Here was a school for fellowship and for love that could not be equaled."[21] Strunsky's childhood memories reveal that Elias treated his daughter as an intellectual equal; neither youth nor gender kept her from being considered a participant in the political and literary conversations that were dominated by adult men. From these gatherings, too, Strunsky developed her leftist politics and an ease speaking with people from all walks of life, which would serve her well when she returned to Russia as a journalist. Her journey, however, would not be a straightforward one back and forth between New York and Russia. Instead, the Strunskys would find themselves part of another historic nineteenth-century migration, relocating to the West Coast, where their family's values transplanted well to the bohemian, socialist subculture of San Francisco in the Gay Nineties.

Soon after Strunsky became a minor celebrity in New York thanks to the *Herald* article, Elias, suffering from weakened health, decided to move the family westward, swayed by campaigns extolling the salutary benefits of the Golden State. The family initially lived in a roomy house on Golden Gate Avenue before moving to Sutter Street, and Elias founded the Strunsky Wine and Liquor Company, a business that prospered until 1906, when it was destroyed in the earthquake and fire. The Strunskys were a vital part of San Francisco's Russian émigré community, which was significantly smaller than the Russian Jewish community they had left behind in New York. Elias was on the board of trustees of Nevah Zedeck, a small Russian congregation on Mission Street, and was elected chairman of its Zionist committee.[22] He was also a council member of the International Jewish League, founded by Rabbi Jacob Voorsanger of Temple Emanu-El to defend the rights of Jews worldwide following the Kishinev massacre in 1903.[23] As in New York, the Strunskys maintained their commitment to intellectual exchange and democratic principles, welcoming Jews and non-Jews alike into their home and emphasizing the importance of education for their daughters as well as their sons.

If Strunsky was formed by her Russian past, her future was molded by the culture of Progressive-Era California, where she spent the formative years of adolescence and young womanhood. Writing of her San Francisco days almost two decades later, she found herself transported "back in that city of . . . teeming hopes and dreams and resolutions, back on the gay and romantic battlefield of my youth, back upon those streets which once echoed the resounding steps of my girlhood."[24] Growing up in San Francisco gave Strunsky educational opportunities that were not as readily available to women elsewhere in the country. She graduated from the state's oldest public high school, Lowell High School, formerly Boys' High, which had begun integrating girls into its college preparatory program in the late 1880s. At a time when women were not expected to attend college, she continued her education at Stanford University.

Founded by Senator Leland Stanford, a railroad tycoon, and his wife, Jane Lathrop Stanford, as a memorial to their son, Stanford University opened in Palo Alto in 1891. One of few coeducational universities in the country at the end of the nineteenth century, Stanford took a progressive stance when it came to gender; while other coed institutions maintained some form of sex segregation, such as prohibiting women from studying the sciences, Stanford allowed women to enroll in all courses and majors. The university also prized women's "physical vigor," encouraging them to become active in sports and other extracurricular activities.[25]

Although Strunsky ultimately did not graduate from Stanford, she entered with the class of 1900. The years she spent there as an English major from 1896 to 1899 were a heyday for women undergraduates; during that time, women dominated campus life in ways they would not after Jane Stanford amended the institution's founding grant to limit the number of women students out of concern that the large number of women drawn to the university would transform it into "The Vassar of the West."[26] In her 1903 article titled "Stanford Women in the Ranks of Literature," published in an annual "Woman's Edition" of the *Stanford Daily* (not incidentally, sister Rose was on the special issue's all-female editorial board), Strunsky described the headiness of being a Stanford woman during the university's first decade. "At Stanford the winds of freedom blow," she wrote from New York, where she was at work on her second novel after completing the manuscript of *The Kempton-Wace Letters*, "The tints of the intellectual life are as variegated . . . as the emblazoned clouds that hang at sunset over the purple hills. . . . At Stanford no one laughs at the aspirant, everybody encourages . . . Men and women here woo ideas with the beautiful openness of . . . courtships." Strunsky moves on from this grandiose vision of Stanford as a natural and intellectual paradise to recall a specific scene: "It is 'eleven fifteen' Monday morning in room 25 at Stanford, and a teacher who is truly a teacher is reading Milton, in a memorable way. Only a few seats in the back of the room are occupied by men,—the class is one of women." Her recollection of this woman-dominated classroom led her to predict that women would soon assume a more significant role in American society, due to increased educational opportunities like those offered at Stanford.[27]

In college, Strunsky's literary aspirations were encouraged by her male professors as well as by the rare woman faculty member. She made an impression on William James, who was a visiting lecturer at the university in 1898 and encountered Strunsky in a psychology seminar. After listening to her "maintain . . . that Conversion from religion to free thought was also a religious experience, or could be," James invited her to contribute an essay to his forthcoming book, *Varieties of Religious Experience*.[28] (The essay did not end up being published and was subsequently lost.) She also developed a close friendship with one of her English professors, Melville Best Anderson, a Dante scholar. The friendship lasted until the end of his life, with Strunsky coming to view Anderson as a second father, calling him "Daddy" in their extensive correspondence, which ranged widely in subject matter from Italian literature and the Sacco-Vanzetti trial to Strunsky's personal struggles balancing motherhood and her desire to write.

If Anderson became a paternal figure for Strunsky, history professor Mary Sheldon Barnes, the first woman appointed to Stanford's faculty, played a maternal role. In letters addressed to "Madonna Marie," Strunsky called Barnes her "friend, sweetheart, mother."[29] Barnes, who began her college teaching career at Wellesley, was known for her innovative pedagogy, supplying students with primary source material so that they could arrive at their own interpretations. In a letter to students that serves as an introduction to her textbook *Studies in General History*, Barnes outlines a teaching philosophy that links the making of history to citizenship, expressing the hope that students will "learn how to judge and interpret what you see before you in your own country, and to help to make America that of which she may become,—the strongest, noblest, finest nation in all the world."[30] When Barnes passed away in Strunsky's junior year, Strunsky envisioned creating a memorial monograph for her teacher. Like many of the writing projects Strunsky planned, this one never came to fruition.[31]

Strunsky's recollections in "Stanford Women in the Ranks of Literature" offer a hint of her active social life, which simultaneously fueled and interfered with her intellectual endeavors. The student entering Stanford will find "no dearth of friends," she notes.[32] Strunsky's "courtships" were not only with ideas; there were also flirtations with men. In her autobiography *Living My Life*, Emma Goldman, who befriended Anna and Rose Strunsky as a guest in their parents' San Francisco home in 1897, claims that Anna's flaunting of Victorian gender proprieties may have led to her failure to graduate. "Among the most interesting people I met in San Francisco were two girls, the Strunsky sisters," wrote Goldman, "[Anna] had been suspended from Leland Stanford University because she had received a male visitor in her room instead of in the parlour. I told Anna of my life in Vienna and of the men students with whom we used to drink tea, smoke, and discuss all through the night."[33] Strunsky biographer James Boylan believes that Goldman invented or embellished the anecdote, perhaps projecting her own nonconformity onto her friend, and that Strunsky's failure to graduate was more likely due to academic troubles. In correspondence with Jack London and others, Strunsky refers to her difficulties earning passing grades on exams, and while she was an assiduous writer, filling pages and notebooks, the Bancroft, Yale, and Huntington archives bear ample evidence of her struggle to bring writing projects to completion. (Copies of her printed articles in her papers are often marked by her handwritten edits as well, indicative of her impulse to revise her writing continually, even after publication.)

If Strunsky did not live up to her great promise as a student, she became a pathbreaker in an intensely competitive arena of late nineteenth-century academic life: college debate. She was a member of Stanford's Saturday Night Club, a women's debating society. She also broke a significant gender barrier when, in 1897, as a sophomore, she became the first woman chosen to represent Stanford in the yearly debate with rival University of California, Berkeley for the Carnot Medal. The competition was rigorous, and participants did not find out the topic of the debate until one week before, drawing lots to determine the position they would argue. In response to the resolution "that in the light of experience, further extension of the French colonial system would be impolitic," Strunsky argued the affirmative, calling "colonization a delusion and a snare and contrary to the genius of the French people."[34] Although the prize was awarded to a male competitor from Berkeley, Strunsky had made her mark. Years later, other Stanford women continued to take pride in her accomplishment, viewing her as a pioneer for her oratorical talent and her fearlessness in taking the platform alongside men.

At the same time that she was attempting to fulfill her obligations as a student, Strunsky's activities extended beyond Stanford to the Socialist Labor Party (SLP), which she had joined in her senior year of high school. Active in the United States since the 1870s, the SLP had been revitalized in the 1890s. In 1896, the SLP met in New York City on the Fourth of July to reaffirm its platform, resolving to "call upon the people to organize with a view to the substitution of the co-operative commonwealth for the present state of planless production, industrial war and social disorder—a commonwealth in which every worker shall have the free exercise and full benefit of his faculties, multiplied by all the modern factors of civilization."[35] Unlike Jack London, who found socialism "hammered into" him based on his firsthand experiences working alongside America's "submerged tenth," Strunsky believed her socialist ideals to be innate.[36] In an oral history interview conducted four years before her death, she claimed, "You are born a socialist. You are born with music, or poetry or painting or science. You can't really become a socialist unless you're born that way."[37]

While Strunsky's political beliefs can be traced back to her origins in Russia, her lifelong infatuation with socialism was more likely due to a combination of environmental factors and intellectual study. Her papers and writings reveal not only the breadth of her reading, but also the depth with which she grappled with ideas as well as her compassion for others and sense of public duty when it came to speaking out against injustice and inequality. While she was raised by leftists, who welcomed socialist leaders like Goldman into their home, she did not simply adopt her parents' ideological beliefs as her own. She recalled, "[M]y father [was] rather critical" when "[i]n that first youth of mine when hardly more than a child I joined the Socialist Party." Although father and daughter "clashed passionately" over her alignment with the SLP, which Elias did not believe was "radical enough," the disagreement did not diminish their strong connection. Rather Anna understood that her father's willingness to spar with her over politics was a sign of his love and respect.[38]

From the beginning of her time at Stanford, Strunsky was gaining significant notoriety as a public speaker and socialist activist, and her commitments beyond the university may have interfered with her ability to keep up with her academic work. San Francisco's vibrant club movement provided her with a forum to espouse her views before bourgeois audiences of men and women. Whether she was addressing a mixed audience or a woman's club, her lectures typically centered on important men: socialist thinkers such as William Morris, Karl Marx, and Ferdinand Lassalle or Victorian poets such as Robert Browning and Algernon Charles Swinburne. One female observer described her oratorical style: "In lecturing, she seems to lose all self-consciousness in the interest of her subject, and at times has spoken at great length and with an enthusiasm and intensity remarkable in one of her frail and delicate physique. Her fluency and her unhesitating flow of beautiful English are most unusual, especially when one stops to consider that Miss Strunsky is still in the younger twenties . . . [O]ften times out of sympathy with the subject matter, Miss Strunsky's animation becomes contagious, and her audiences find themselves, willy-nilly, in their seats when the lecture is over."[39] Strunsky had a mesmeric ability to connect with her listeners, and, as with her 1904 talk before the Philomath Club, audiences found that she defied their expectations for a socialist speaker. "Somewhat fearful lest she would wave a red flag and provoke a riot," the members of Sequoia Club, for instance, were relieved to discover that "Anna Strunsky is not Emma Goldman, and her lecture [on 'Underground Russia'] was far from being anarchistic."[40] Strunsky knew how to tailor her message to her audience.

Newspaper reports of Strunsky's speeches reveal that her gender made her an object of fascination and opened her up to critique and ridicule. For example, a short notice in Utah's *Deseret Weekly* about the activities of the SLP in San Francisco read, "Up to the present time the spreading of their doctrine has been entrusted to men with strong lungs, but of late a young woman barely past her teens, has sprung up among them, like a Jean d'Arc, to lead their forces on to imaginary victory. Her name is Anna Strunsky. . . . Her lectures on the ethics of socialism show clearly that she is familiar with the subject, though she is not thoroughly grounded and seems to get confused in open debate; but as she has just recently been introduced to the public, her inability to hold her own may be due to stage fright and time will improve her." Ending with the question, "What next will woman attempt?," the paragraph acknowledges that Strunsky's performance is emblematic of a larger shift in American culture and politics, as women increasingly wielded their voices and intellectual power on the public stage.[41]

Strunsky's youthful appearances on the San Francisco lecture circuit also led to encounters with the yellow press. In 1897, Hearst's *San Francisco Examiner* ran a profile with the headline "Girl Socialist of San Francisco" and a pictorial sketch of Strunsky speaking to a predominantly male audience. Strunsky's depiction conveys her seriousness of purpose with one arm raised beseechingly to her audience; her single female interrogator, however, appears as a witch-like figure, dressed all in black and floating ominously above the heads of the men. The article's sensationalism derives from the spectacle of a woman speaking publicly on matters thought to be outside the feminine sphere. The *Examiner*'s reporter, John Hamilton Gilmour, writes, "It gives one queer feelings to hear a young girl whom it would naturally be supposed was occupying her mind with things more in accord with her years, lecturing on the ethics of socialism." The article praises her eloquence and intelligence, noting her use of "classical allusions, gathered at the Stanford University." It also devotes considerable space to her appearance. Before revealing the content of her speech, for instance, Gilmour notes that she is "but a slip of a girl" and "singularly picturesque." Strunsky's Russian Jewish immigrant background adds to her allure. "The blood that surges within her is yet hot with the oppressions endured by her ancestors," Gilmour writes, "Her whole aspect is foreign—from her coloring to her pronunciations."

Gilmour's descriptions gain detail as the article continues: "She has the rich coloring of the Orient, the dark skin, brightened by red, and the lustrous black hair which is the heritage of the women of the East. Her eyes are distinctly Oriental. . . . It is from that dreaming, sentimental type of womanhood that the nihilists found the greatest help in their destructive work."[42]

Published at a time when anti-immigration sentiment, especially against the Chinese, was at a height in San Francisco, the article employs Orientalist discourse to cast Strunsky as exotic, vaguely threatening, and sexually alluring due to her eastern roots. In later years, the yellow press would go even further, transforming her into a hot-blooded temptress; in 1904, for example, journalists falsely outed her as the woman who broke up Jack London's first marriage, and, in 1911, coverage of her husband William English Walling's trial for breach of promise to Bertha Grunspan depicted Strunsky in a negative and salacious light. Rather than wholly condemning yellow journalism in her 1911 *Collier's* article, "A Tribute to the Yellow Press: Its Virtues and Its Vices as Estimated by a Victim," Strunsky defended the value of a free press, arguing that "despite the temporary unpleasantness of being reviled and hounded, despite the utter misrepresentation and lies, there is something basically true and democratic both in the process and in the effect of yellow journalism."[43] The sensationalizing coverage of Strunsky's lectures in the 1890s expose another benefit, proving the adage that any publicity is good publicity. From her Stanford days up until the time she left the West Coast for Russia in 1905, the "girl socialist of San Francisco" could depend on steady speaking engagements.

Having grown up in a home that brought her into daily contact with lively political debate, radical ideas, and literary-minded people, Strunsky gravitated toward San Francisco's bohemian counter-culture. Her social circle comprised free-thinking, left-leaning writers and artists who called themselves "The Crowd." It included George Sterling, a poet and the ringleader of the group; painters Xavier Martínez and Maynard Dixon; photographer Arnold Genthe; critic Porter Garnett; humorist Gelett Burgess; fiction writer Herman Whitaker; Harry Lafler, editor of *The Argonaut*; socialist lawyers Austin Lewis and Cameron King; and its most famous member, Jack London. The Crowd ebbed and flowed over the years, as members came and went, with several of them, like London and Strunsky, taking off on overseas adventures. The locations of their gatherings also varied. They met at members' flats and studios, from San Francisco and the East Bay cities of Oakland, Berkeley, and Piedmont to the artist colonies of Carmel and Monterey. They frequented eating and drinking establishments that served late night clientele, like Coffee Dan's, a basement cabaret known for its pint-sized cups of coffee (and later, during Prohibition, for continuing to serve alcohol), and Coppa's, an Italian restaurant that became a popular tourist destination after The Crowd decorated its walls with eclectic chalk murals. They also held meetings under the auspices of the Bohemian Club. Founded in 1872 as a drinking club for newspapermen, this invitation-only club billed itself as "an association of gentlemen connected professionally with literature, art, music, the drama"; it held an annual bacchanalian encampment among the redwoods of Sonoma on a piece of land that became known as Bohemian Grove.[44] In 1898, the socialist men of The Crowd founded the Ruskin Club, a philosophy club with ties to the arts and crafts movement named for British art critic John Ruskin.

The activities of the Bay Area bohemians ranged from political debate and socialist pamphleteering to readings of pre-Elizabethan plays and, at Burgess's urging, sessions in which they would write "down whatever came in our minds for a set period and then read . . . it to one another."[45] There were also riotous parties fueled by whiskey, whimsy, and entertaining hijinks. In his essay "Where is Bohemia?," Burgess defined Bohemia as a "mental fairyland" whose "charm" came from its status as an uncharted frontier. "There are no roads in all Bohemia!" exclaimed Burgess, "One must choose and find one's own path, be one's own self, live one's own life."[46] Strunsky's short, unpublished sketch titled "In Bohemia" depicts a New Year Eve's celebration at a flat ruled over by the "Queen of Bohemia," an honorific bestowed upon *Examiner* feature writer Isabel Fraser. Strunsky captures the spontaneity of bohemian life and its cooperative spirit. Since the cook "had spent too much time over a poem which refused to come to a climax," all of the guests, despite having donned evening dress, contributed to a motley dinner of "beef-tea for soup, canned frankfurters, canned tongue, canned beans, little sealed envelopes of salt and pepper, miniature bottles of sauce, embryonic boxes of Ghirardelli chocolates." She imbues the scene with a raucous conviviality, reminiscent of Puccini's namesake opera, *La Bohème*:

Photograph of Anna Strunsky by Arnold Genthe, 1914. Courtesy of the Genthe Collection, Library of Congress, Prints and Photographs Division.

"We sang songs and recited poems and poured out our love like wine. We drank standing toasts to our friends and the friends of our friends." Strunsky suggests that the toast-making and drinking went on for some time: "It was early morning when we rose and crossed hands around the table singing For Auld Lang Syne. We were in the grasp of youth and its splendid gaiety and tenderness. We were on the crest of surging hopes. Our souls stirred and our hearts dreamed. We went our way, a little band of patriots consecrated to the eternal defense of Bohemia."[47]

As much as the bohemians thumbed their noses at convention, The Crowd's gender politics were simultaneously progressive and retrograde. Wives and girlfriends were often included, as were a select group of female intellectuals like the Strunsky sisters, writer Mary Austin, socialist activist Jane Roulston, and newspaper reporters Isabel Fraser and Mary Edith ("Maizie") Griswold. When the socialist cohort formed the California Society of the Friends of Russian Freedom, Strunsky, the lone female member of its executive committee, was chosen as "chairman."[48] The all-male Bohemian and Ruskin Clubs occasionally invited women to events held in their clubrooms. The Ruskin Club, which hosted a farewell dinner for Strunsky before she left for Russia, was thought to be especially progressive; it held an annual "ladies' night" to which they invited speakers such as Jessica Peixotto, a professor of social economics at the University of California, Berkeley.[49] Still, other events, like the Bohemian Grove outing, were viewed as sacred spaces for male bonding. The group's institutions and social dynamics inevitably cultivated a culture of what today we would call "toxic masculinity." Sexism and misogyny were prevalent. Not a few of the men developed reputations for excessive drinking and womanizing. When a new woman was introduced to the group, the men rated her appearance, taking a secret vote under the table to determine whether she should be invited again. Mary Austin, for example, "rated a thumbs-down." According to one male member of the group, "She was writing beautiful stuff but she wasn't pretty. The pretty ones didn't have to write very much to get in again."[50]

Delicate and feminine, Strunsky's beauty thus gave her an advantage, earning her entrée into male-dominated spaces. After leaving Stanford, she became a regular and popular attendee at Crowd get-togethers. Elsie Whitaker Martínez (Herman's daughter who married artist Xavier Martínez when she was eighteen and he was thirty-seven) described Strunsky's magnetic presence in an oral history interview. "Women admired Anna but resented the attraction their men felt for her," Elsie recalled, "The Israelite woman can be completely irresistible without the taint of a flirt. She was beautiful—fine features, smoldering eyes, a wide, generous mouth, and above all a soft vibrant voice. She had a deep messianic feeling, whether for socialism or woman's rights, that was appealing and compelling and to which even the women responded."[51]

By today's standards, The Crowd may not reflect the full diversity of the American West, but at the time, its bohemian credentials derived in part from its multiethnic intermixing. In her 1907 *Pacific Monthly* article, "The Story of a Famous Fraternity of Writers and Artists," Agnes Foster Buchanan wrote, "Like everything else in San Francisco, the personnel of the 'Coppa Crowd' was cosmopolitan and diverse—more so, perhaps, than would be found in any other similar gathering in the world. Here we find Martinez standing for Spanish traditions and influence; [Jimmy] Hopper who is French-Irish; the Russian Jewess, Anna Strunsky; Whitaker, and Austin Lewis, who are Cornishmen; and Jack London, George Sterling and Gelett Burgess, who are the Americans."[52] Like Martínez, who wore his long hair in a headband as a tribute to his Indigenous roots and taught his friends to sing French revolutionary songs "with a Latin rhythm," Strunsky brought exotic flair to the group, and her ethnoracial difference was partially the source of her attraction.[53] Elsie Whitaker Martínez continually returns to this theme in her remembrances of Strunsky. Her generalization about "Israelite women" persists in her description of the first meeting between two "vivid people," Anna Strunsky and Jack London. According to Elsie, "Anna's was the burning spirit that matched Jack's—that inner burning spirit of the Jewish people." Elsie's recollections further reveal that members of the group, despite their seeming openmindedness, held to notions of white racial superiority. She notes that "Jack had once confided to Sterling that he wouldn't marry her [Strunsky] because he was pure Anglo-Saxon and she was Semitic, although he loved her."[54] Such contradictory attitudes toward race and gender politics not only form the basis of the real-life affair between Jack London and Anna Strunsky, but also the literary work that arose from their erotic and intellectual relationship, *The Kempton-Wace Letters*.

"Love Letters of a Socialist"[55]

Socialism brought Jack London and Anna Strunsky together. In one of several versions of the story that Strunsky tells, they met in March 1899 at San Francisco's Turk Street Temple, a popular site for socialist lectures located a short walk from Anna's Sutter Street home. The occasion was the SLP's celebration of the 1871 Paris Commune uprising, and the future collaborators were introduced by Frank Strawn-Hamilton, a street-corner orator who had mentored London, transforming him into the "Boy Socialist of Oakland."[56] "Frank Strawn Hamilton, who had introduced Jack to me, had introduced Jack to socialism," wrote Strunsky in her unpublished memoir, pleased by the symmetrical consistency created by the pair of introductions.[57] Elsewhere in the memoir, Strunsky narrates her first sighting of London, which took place following an inspiring speech by Marxist Austin Lewis:

> [Jack] rose from a seat well towards the front and walked towards the platform. I too was on the way to the speaker. Then someone introduced him: "Jack London!" What a curious and beautiful name! About twenty-three, he seemed at once younger and older than his years. There was that about him that made one feel that one would always remember him. He seemed the incarnation of the Platonic ideal of man, the body of the athlete and the mind of a thinker.
>
> He was proud, he said, that we had men like Austin Lewis with us. Already some of the best and finest had crossed the barriers of class to side with the people. Then he hurried away to catch the last ferry for Oakland where he lived with his mother.[58]

Soon after their initial meeting, London called on Strunsky at her parents' home, where Anna and her siblings were gathered with extended family. They sat in front of the fire, talked of the books he was reading with an eye toward giving "himself a university education," and planned to form a small club devoted to reading the works of Karl Marx. But a hint of tensions to come lurks behind Strunsky's romantic recollections of London's first visit to the Strunsky residence. As the conversation turned to Rudyard Kipling and imperialism, London picked up a copy of *The Seven Seas* and declared that "Anglo-Saxons were the salt of the earth," seemingly unfazed by the fact that he was a guest in the home of Russian Jewish immigrants.[59]

Nor were London's freely expressed notions of Anglo-Saxon superiority a turn-off for Strunsky. In the months that followed their first encounter, the two literature-loving socialists frequently spent time together: at her house, on walks around the city, and with The Crowd. In a passage that she planned to excise from the full-length memoir, Strunsky conveys how comfortable London was in her family's home: "He came across the Bay, let himself in—our doors were never locked—and went to sleep on the floor on the bear rug in the room where my brother received his patients. The next morning at breakfast he drank cup after cup of coffee and smoked innumerable Mexican cigarettes, rolling them himself and lighting one from the other."[60] The Strunsky family provided an audience for London's adventure stories, allowing him to sharpen his skills as a raconteur; he wove tales about his itinerant travels as a tramp, for example, that would later find their way into his published writings.

By December 1899, London and Strunsky had also become regular correspondents, extending conversations begun in person to often lengthy letters. Although it is mostly London's side of the correspondence that has survived, saved by Strunsky and now housed with his papers at the Huntington Library, the letters offer valuable windows into both of their early writing careers and their relationship. Largely written between 1899 and 1904, the period that marked London's rise from struggling amateur to literary celebrity with the publication of *The Call of the Wild* in 1903, these letters—numbering close to one hundred—depict two aspiring young writers in conversation about their craft. Strunsky and London exchanged manuscripts in progress, offering each other feedback, advice, and encouragement. They recommended writers and texts to one another. They exchanged clippings of other writers' stories and poems as well as books. Their decision to collaborate on an epistolary novel grew out of their correspondence and became a further extension of it. Functioning as a joint apprenticeship for both writers, the process of coauthoring *The Kempton-Wace Letters* created an additional forum in which they could read, admire, comment on, and edit each other's work. Based on the extant one-sided correspondence, it appears that London was more often in the mentorship role, but there is ample evidence that they both played this role for each other. Strunsky was far more than a muse-like inspiration for London's heroines. With more formal schooling under her belt, she strongly influenced his writing, bringing her keen intelligence and considerable knowledge to bear on his work while also critiquing his representations of women and Jews.

The relationship between Strunsky and London is further revealing for what it tells us about the gendered structures of authorship, literary markets, and intellectual collaboration at the turn of the twentieth century. The correspondence captures an early stage in the careers of two literary aspirants who had the talent and ambition to become famous and prolific writers. Only one of them went on to achieve this goal. When Jack London died at age forty, he had published over fifty books, including novels, collections of short stories, and nonfiction. Several of these works became classics and continue to be taught in schools. Most of his books are still in print, and he further enjoys an international reputation as one of the best-known American writers around the globe. Strunsky lived more than twice as long as Jack London, passing away at age eighty-six. She never stopped writing over the course of her long life and was a contributor to a variety of periodicals, from socialist journals to popular magazines. In contrast to London, however, she published only two novels, one of them in collaboration with him, the other no longer in print. It is rare to find someone today who has read any of her work. This comparison is not simply about Jack London and Anna Strunsky. Rather, their contrasting legacies emblematize the unrealized promise of many women writers in American literary history.

The London-Strunsky correspondence contains other intriguing elements as well. The letters London wrote to Strunsky allow us to trace the evolution of their relationship, from the sexual innuendos of his early infatuation to his outright declarations of love, from her rejection of him upon realizing the extent of his profligacy and untrustworthiness to the platonic warmth of a bicoastal friendship that lasted until his untimely death. Their romantic attraction was complicated by London's involvements with other women, especially his first wife, Elizabeth "Bess" Maddern, whom he married unexpectedly in April 1900, at the same time that his relationship with Strunsky was deepening. "For a thousand reasons I think myself justified in making this marriage," London wrote in a letter to Strunsky after he announced his engagement, reassuring her, and himself, that "[i]t will not, however, interfere much with my old life or my life as I had planned it for the future."[61] Indeed, it seems that London, who took a scientific and pragmatic approach to marriage, describing his decision as "open[ing] transactions for a wife," fully intended to carry on his extramarital flirtation with Strunsky.[62] His eager requests to see her, and to commune over literature, continue to appear in his letters. In a letter dated three months after his marriage, he signs off by asking, "And when are we to read 'The Flight of the Duchess'? And when are you coming over?"[63]

The change in London's marital status did not prove a strong deterrent for Strunsky either, and collaboration on *The Kempton-Wace Letters* began during the first summer of the Londons' marriage. According to Strunsky's unpublished memoir, the two writers arrived at the idea to coauthor a book "while he, his wife Bessie, and I were out for a sail in his little boat *The Spray*."[64] Throughout the collaborative process, their lives remained closely intertwined, with Strunsky extending her affection to Bessie and their first child, Joan.[65] Per London's suggestion, Strunsky also, for a time, moved into the Londons' home, so that the two authors could work more efficiently on the revisions to their novel. The love triangle is titillating, of course, in its sexual intrigue. However, it is of particular interest here because the obstacle in this star-crossed romance was not simply another woman; more significant were the ideological and ethnoreligious differences dividing the would-be lovers. London was drawn to Strunsky in part because of her foreignness and her fierce idealism, but he refused to compromise his beliefs in white racial purity and Anglo-Saxon superiority. This intimate conflict supplied a source of ongoing intellectual debate, which Strunsky and London decided to make public in fictional form via *The Kempton-Wace Letters*. The composition of the novel, in turn, provided a pretense for spending time together and maintaining their correspondence.

London's first letter to Strunsky, written on December 19, 1899, makes clear the erotic charge of their intellectual connection. "Seems as if I have known you for an age—you and your Mr. Browning," he begins, referring to her favorite Victorian poet. From the outset, London uses their shared literary aspirations as an excuse to get to know Strunsky better, offering to advise her on "the more prosaic" aspects of the profession, such as manuscript submission. He also attempts to pin her down as a person and a writer: "As I sat there listening to you, I seemed to sum you up in this way: A woman to whom it is given to feel the deeps and heights of emotion in an extraordinary degree; who can grasp the intensity of transcendental feeling, the dramatic force of situation, as few women, or men either, can." London's flattering impression of Strunsky is tempered by his questions about whether she has the diligence to make it as a writer. "Has she the 'dig,' the quality of application, so that she might attain it [literary technique]?" London asks, writing to Strunsky of herself in the third person. Then he shifts to the second person, directly posing the question to her: "In a nut-shell, you have the material, which is your own soul, for a career: have you the requisite action to hew your way to it?"[66]

These initial letters flew quickly back and forth between Strunsky's home in San Francisco and London's in Oakland, where both correspondents were living with their parents. Two days later, on December 21, 1899, London penned a reply to a now missing letter from Strunsky. Quoting her words in order to respond to them, London's reply gives us a rare glimpse of Strunsky's writing to him and demonstrates the debate-like nature of their epistolary exchanges. Strunsky did not take kindly to London's attempt to "sum [her] up" and calls him out on the way that gender limits his perceptions. "Somehow it is a new note to me, that of being seen as 'aimless, helpless, hopeless,' and I am uneasy under it all," she wrote, inserting a quotation from Robert Browning's poem "Epilogue."[67] Conceding to her request that he refrain from misreading her based on preconceived notions of femininity, London presents her with a complimentary analogy: "As I had spoken to a man who came out of nowhere, shared my bed and board for a night, and passed on, so did I speak to you."[68] Intended to reassure Strunsky of the equality between them, London's defense of his words sexualizes their relationship, while also recasting it in homoerotic terms, akin to a fleeting nighttime encounter between two men.

Such sexual innuendo continues in the letter dated December 27, 1899, where he signs off with another request to spend time with her: "Typewriters, while very excellent in their way, are a very poor medium for conversation. The mouth were better formed for expression than the finger-tips. May I see you next Friday night? Candidly, I may some time steal you or certain portions of you for exploitation between covers, unless you hasten to get yourself copyrighted."[69] As scholars have pointed out, London did "steal" Strunsky for use between the "covers" of his books; aspects of her character define unconventional heroines like Frona Welse in *A Daughter of the Snows* (1902) and Maud Brewster in *The Sea-Wolf* (1904) who are not only men's intellectual equals, but also prove their courage and physical parity when faced with extreme conditions on land and sea.[70] With references to "exploitation" and "copyright," London employs the language of social economics to align himself—the dominant, male figure in their relationship—with the capitalist class, suggesting that he is a threat to Strunsky unless she takes legal action to protect herself and her individual interests. The multilayered innuendo further exemplifies how the verbal play between them conflated the language of authorship (the covers of books) with the language of sex (covers as bed linen). In his desire to use his mouth rather than his fingertips and to "exploit" her "between covers," London alludes to the eroticization of their intellectual exchanges, which grew more intimate when they began sharing work. Anxiously awaiting her response to a box of his manuscripts, London wrote to remind her "that I have disclosed myself in my nakedness," before going on to chastise himself for "getting nervous and soft as a woman"—a simile sure to provoke a reply from Strunsky.[71]

This deepening intimacy, and London's part in ensuring its development, can also be traced through the salutations used in the correspondence. London's initial letters are addressed "My dear Miss Strunsky," but on January 21, 1900, a month into the correspondence, he openly rejects formalities, following "Dear Miss Strunsky" with "O Pshaw! Dear Anna."[72] Strunsky holds on to convention a bit longer, as evidenced by London's letter on February 20. "Now I feel comfortable," he tells her, "Nobody ever 'Mr. London's' me, so every time I opened a letter of yours I felt a starched collar draw round my neck. Pray permit me softer neckgear for the remainder of our correspondence."[73] As London's salutations change over time, they reflect the complexity of their relationship and the many things they are to one another. By the end of 1900, he addresses Strunsky as "Comrade Mine," at once a testament to the socialist cause that binds them and to what he calls in the letter "a white beautiful friendship . . . between a man and a woman."[74] While in the throes of working on *The Kempton-Wace Letters*, Strunsky becomes "My Little Collaborator," and, when offering her advice on a marriage proposal she received from another man, she becomes "Sister." But as London falls deeply in love, he addresses her simply with "Dear You."

As their relationship moves toward its dramatic climax, London's signature also varies. In the summer of 1902, shortly before he is to leave on a trip to England to conduct research for *The People of the Abyss*,

London takes on the lovesick persona of "Sahib," signing off, "Your very miserable Sahib," "Sahib," and "The Sahib." It is as "Sahib" that London comes closest to overcoming his white supremacist beliefs and committing to Strunsky (albeit, such a commitment was dependent on his ability to extricate himself from his overhasty marriage). Although its origins can be found in the Arabic word for "companion," suggesting that London is effectively sacrificing his racial purity for the sake of love, the term has a more complex usage. In the colonial context, "Sahib" was used in India as a respectful form of address for European imperialists; the word came to signify the higher status of white men in relation to their colonial subjects. Early in their correspondence, London similarly asserted his dominance over Strunsky with an allusion to her Jewish heritage. Agreeing to Strunsky's request that he serve as her "taskmaster" and help her to become a more disciplined writer, London, who himself followed a strict writing regimen, drew a metaphor from the Book of Exodus. "I love power, to dominate my fellows," he wrote, "I shall stand over you with a whip of scorpions and drive you to your daily toil. Like Pharaoh of old, I shall hold you in bondage, and in the end, you will send plagues upon me, and amid signs and portents and great tumult, depart, leaving behind a wake of devastation and terror."[75] The Old Testament reference, which again imbues their common desire for artistic production with sexual frisson, illuminates a power dynamic that is similarly embedded in London's use of the term "Sahib." Even if the term is intended to indicate equality or her hold over him, the signature draws attention to the racialization of their relationship and effectively highlights *her* difference—for it is only in relation to Strunsky that London becomes "Sahib."

That Strunsky's ethno-religious difference not only circumscribes their romantic relationship but also underlies their intellectual collaboration is evident in London's correspondence with other men. In October 1900, London wrote to his friend Cloudesley Johns about his plans for *The Kempton-Wace Letters*:

> A young Russian Jewess of 'Frisco and myself have often quarreled over our conceptions of love. She happens to be a genius. She is also a materialist by philosophy, and an idealist by innate preference, and is constantly being forced to twist all the facts of the universe in order to reconcile herself with her self. So, finally, we

> decided that the only way to argue the question out would be by letter. Then we wondered if a collection of such letters should happen to be worth publishing. Then we assumed characters, threw in a real objective love element, and started to work.[76]

Rather than identifying his coauthor by name, London once again attempts to "sum her up" by describing her as a "young Russian Jewess of 'Frisco"; that she also "happens to be a genius" asserts her distinctiveness and her potential to move beyond the constraints of this identity. Focusing on the flaws in Strunsky's logical reasoning ("being forced to twist all the facts of the universe in order to reconcile herself with her self"), his letter is interesting for the information it leaves out: namely, that London himself was "being forced . . . to reconcile" his love for Strunsky with his own materialist philosophy, which included the belief that human beings had a responsibility to social evolution and could improve the race through eugenics. Perhaps because London was unwilling to implicate himself publicly in a romance that violated the taboo on racial mixing, his feelings for Strunsky are similarly omitted from the diegetic narrative of *The Kempton-Wace Letters*. This erasure, however, takes a different form, one well-suited to Strunsky's argument that love transcends the materialism of identity. In the novel, the character that Strunsky assumes—that of a fifty-something, British man, Dane Kempton—effectively disguises her youth, Russianness, Jewishness, and gender, the very elements of her identity that London used to define her in his letter to Johns. Although London claims that they "threw in a real objective love element," *The Kempton-Wace Letters* maintains a degree of abstraction; the published text itself never reveals that the "quarrel" that led to its inception was grounded in racial and ethno-religious differences between the two authors and was not simply a matter of philosophical debate.

Tracing the evolution of *The Kempton-Wace Letters* from the London-Strunsky letters (supplemented by Strunsky's archival papers, especially in the absence of her side of the correspondence) allows us to see that she did more than try to persuade London of her "conception of love." She also challenged his pseudo-scientific belief in race difference, effecting a change in London's perception of her, from "Russian Jewess" to "protean" self. Early exchanges between the correspondents indicate that in addition to pushing back against his assumptions about gender, she also questioned his tendency to generalize about Jews. For instance, when they began to exchange manuscripts, Strunsky offered London blunt feedback on a short story whose central characters were a poor Jewish shopkeeper named Jaky and his wife, Leah. The story—whose Jewish themes are signaled by its title, which London changed from "The God of Abraham" to "Two Children of Israel"—was long thought to be lost in its entirety, but a four-page fragment was later identified by Jay Williams, having been mislabeled in the Jack London Papers at the Huntington Library, and subsequently published in *Studies in American Naturalism* under the title "Life in Jewish Oakland." In it, Jaky and Leah (presumably immigrants, although, unlike other characters in the story, their dialogue is rendered in unaccented English) are trying to improve themselves by studying mathematics and reading literature aloud at night. The plot of the story centers on Jaky's induction to socialism, with much of the fragment describing his experiences as he accompanies a friend to a political meeting. It is unclear whether London sent Strunsky this particular story because he believed her experience as a "Russian Jewess" qualified her to comment on the story's Jewish characters and themes. Regardless, he was hoping that her feedback would help him improve the story, which had already been rejected by a number of magazines, including *McClure's* and *The Atlantic Monthly*.[77]

Strunsky's opinion of the story aligned with that of the magazine editors. Expressing his gratitude to Strunsky for giving him a "clearer vision" of what was wrong with the story, London wrote, "It is you who are the missionary. I am down in the dust to Jaky for an unpardonable wrong. But my extenuation is my youth and inexperience. . . . Not only have you shown me my main flaw, but you have exposed a second—the lack of artistic selection."[78] The extant fragment of the story contains a brief scene of marital harmony with sympathetic, if idealized, characterizations of Jaky and Leah; the latter, for example, is described with hair "rippl[ing] in waves of jet to her waist, the brilliant lights of her face accentuated by the ebony halo."[79] Yet, Strunsky worried that the depiction of Jewish shopkeepers veered too close to economic stereotypes that were prevalent in Anglophone fiction, noting, "Only not all Jews haggle and bargain." As usual, London cited Strunsky's objection back to her and went on to defend himself against this particular critique by arguing that

Jaky and his wife were based on an actual Jewish couple who ran a secondhand store in Oakland and whom London had helped learn English. Once again expressing his desire to deepen their friendship and to get to know her better ("Still, from the little I have seen of you, my lips have been moistened, my head lifted"), London did, however, acknowledge a connection between his initial misreading of Strunsky and his unsuccessful attempt to bring these Jewish characters to life. "I have misunderstood you a score of times and trampled rough-shod over as many sensibilities," he wrote, even as he insists, perhaps a bit facetiously, that his "glittering adumbrations bespoke far more than" one-note Jewish stereotypes.[80]

London ended up retiring his short story about Jewish life in Oakland, and subsequent letters show his attempt to arrive at a better understanding of the multidimensional experiences of Jewish immigrants in America through his relationship with Strunsky. In a letter written in January 1900 in response to Strunsky's news that she had left Stanford due to academic difficulties but was planning to enroll in courses at Berkeley, he enclosed a portrait of Mary Antin with little commentary beyond his wish that the picture "were not [in] profile."[81] London's very next letter (the same one in which he first addressed his recipient as "Dear Anna" in an effort to get "the friendship down to a comfortable basis") provides context for the photograph. This time, he enclosed a review of Antin's first book, *From Plotzk to Boston* (1899). Based on letters Antin had written to her uncle in Yiddish at age thirteen chronicling her family's migration from Russia to America, the book had been published recently in English translation with an introduction by Israel Zangwill. "Had I not known you I could not understood the little which I do," London wrote to Strunsky, "How I would like to know the girl, to see her, to talk with her, to do a little toward cherishing her imagination."[82]

London's desire to know Antin—which explains his preference for a close-up picture rather than a profile—is, of course, another expression of his interest in furthering his relationship with Strunsky and "cherishing her imagination" through literary mentorship. Here London notes the similarities between Strunsky and Antin, both Russian immigrants who were celebrated as child prodigies and exemplary products of the American education system. But London would also come to see that the experiences and literary sensibilities of the two "Russian Jewesses" diverged in significant ways. Antin's nonfiction narrative of her physical and spiritual journey from the Russian Pale of Settlement to "the Promised Land" of America would serve as a rehearsal for her more famous 1912 autobiography and would help establish some of the most familiar tropes of Jewish immigrant writing: the exceptional individual who successfully undergoes the process of Americanization and rises triumphantly, newly formed, from the slums to take her place in the nation as a model minority. Immigrant narratives like Antin's resonated because they fit into well-established paradigms of American literature, specifically the autobiographical tradition of upward mobility, individualism, and self-education spanning from Benjamin Franklin to Frederick Douglass and beyond. In its broadest outlines, Strunsky's story contained similar strains; she, too, fled tyranny and antisemitism in Russia, landing at Stanford. But the bohemian culture of the West Coast gave a different shape to her story, and her writing deviated from the kind of work associated with Anglophone Jewish writers of the period such as Antin and Zangwill.

Like her later published and unpublished writings, Strunsky's early attempts at fiction do not adhere to the American narratives of the "melting pot" and immigrant opportunity; instead, the themes of her surviving short stories include socialism, unrequited love, and the trials of female authorship. A fragment of a story titled "Alexei Grigorevitch—Fatalist," for example, opens by describing a "little group of Russian immigrants" who hold an impromptu socialist meeting on a tenement roof in New York: "These were theorists, and to their sensitive, imaginative minds the matters of idea were of deeper and closer significance than the matters of fact—theorists who were poor and misplaced and disappointed, who had come to America led not by the Golden Finger but rather by an Aurora of fervid dreams." The story's eponymous protagonist is a promising law student in Russia who found his eyes opened to socialism at the university; thus, "Russia became intolerable, and on coming to New York he had neither the means to pursue his studies nor the interest in them to make the effort worth while." The story incorporates a love triangle, with the character of Vera choosing another socialist, Sergei Mardfin, over Alexei, leading Alexei to travel west by train in search of a "rebirth of the spirit." In the last paragraph of the story, Vera reads a newspaper account of Alexei's death, possibly by suicide while en route to California, and the story concludes with a gloomy image of "a fate-driven man lying dead on a track, lying dead of loneliness."[83] Unlike Antin, Strunsky does not offer American democracy as an easy antidote to Russian oppression.

Another of Strunsky's early stories, "With Bigamous Intent," similarly resists a conventional happy ending. Set in San Francisco, the story centers on an aspiring male playwright, Leonidas Masson, who discovers an intelligent young woman, Laura Stanislaus, working as a maid in his aunt's house. Laura's Slavic last name, which means "achieving glory or fame," signals her promise, and Leonidas leads "his rose of democracy," as he calls Laura, "into a world of books and men." Thinking herself unworthy of Leonidas's love and recognizing that, as a woman, she cannot fulfill her dream of becoming a writer, Laura becomes engaged to another man instead. Leonidas, in turn, begins to publish his own work under Laura's name, hoping to keep his dream of his prodigy's potential alive. As the plays that he authors in her name become famous, people "surmised that Leonidas Masson was Laura Stanislaus," but "these [individuals] drew ridicule upon themselves, for there was something personal in the plays that coquetted with the reader and awakened in him the unholy literary passion of seeking the author behind the lines and that was held to be absolute intensive evidence that a woman wrote them." Although Leonidas eventually has the opportunity to reunite with the real Laura, he prefers the fantasy that he has created within himself. The story concludes with his decision not to reveal the charade of authorship to Laura Stanislaus's faithful fans, who "never ceased to question him concerning the woman who refused so persistently to come before the curtain when the audience cried author." Reminiscent of Strunsky's relationship with London, "With Bigamous Intent" explores the gendered power dynamics of authorship and intellectual collaboration, complicated by love. "They walked together and read together and besieged each other with their moods. It was an excellent comradeship and lasted until Laura fell in love with Leonidas," the story reads.[84] Although the fiction is borrowed from fact, Laura and Leonidas do not map neatly onto Strunsky and London. Both characters are instead composites. The story suggests that the successful artist must, too, be a composite figure who defies expectations about gender.[85]

Given the ways that Strunsky continually challenged his assumptions about gender and race, it is no surprise that London—as he got to know her better, read her work in progress, and began to collaborate with her—was forced to reconsider his belief that "the human might be filed into categories." In his best-known letter to Strunsky, now excerpted in several editions of famous love letters, he wrote: "You elude me. I cannot place you, cannot grasp you. . . . Were ever two souls, with dumb lips, more incongruously matched! We may feel in common—surely, we oft-times do—and when we do not feel in common, yet do we understand; and yet we have no common tongue. Spoken words do not come to us . . . We have, flashed through us, you and I, each a bit of the universal, and so we draw together. And yet we are so different."[86] Whereas London previously believed that Strunsky's Jewishness was the primary obstacle to their union, here he is no longer able to "categorize" her or the differences between them, which have become ineffable. He believed that this indefinable quality had the potential to make her a great writer, if she could find the means to translate it into words. "O, Anna," he exclaimed in another letter, inquiring about her progress on a now lost manuscript titled "Consciousness of Kind," "if you will only put your flashing soul with its protean moods on paper! What you need is the form, or in other words, the expression."[87]

Gender and Authorship in *The Kempton-Wace Letters*

If Strunsky's early solo-authored manuscripts did not provide the form for her "flashing soul with its protean moods," *The Kempton-Wace Letters* did. The book consists of thirty-nine chapters, each written in the form of a letter, with dates spanning over the course of sixteen months. The first thirty-seven chapters document an exchange between two men, prompted by Dane Kempton's response to the sudden news of Herbert Wace's engagement. The news takes Kempton by surprise, causing him to wonder why Wace did not write earlier given that "the great event was not when you found your offer of marriage accepted, but when you found you had fallen in love."[88] In reply, Wace reveals that he has not fallen in love; rather, he has decided to marry the "sensible" Hester Stebbins, a graduate of Stanford, out of procreative duty, explaining that "biologically, it [marriage] is an institution necessary for the perpetuation of the species."[89] Both epistolary novel and philosophical treatise, *The Kempton-Wace Letters* translates its coauthors' ongoing debates about the reasons for marriage—she on the side of love, he on the side of science—into fictional form with Strunsky and London playing the respective parts of Kempton and Wace. In her unpublished memoir, "Jack London," Strunsky credits London with the initial idea to coauthor a book as a means of working through their disagreement: "Jack proposed that we write a book together on eugenics and romantic love. The moon rose, paled, and faded from the sky. Then the night came awake and our sails filled. Before we landed we had our plot, a novel in letter form in which Jack was to be an American, an economist, and I an Englishman, a poet, who stood in relation to him of father to son."[90]

Setting the novel's romantic, moonlit origin story on London's boat, Strunsky makes only brief reference to the presence of his wife, Bessie, who had accompanied them on the summer sailing excursion. She offers no insight into Bessie's contribution to the debate, what she made of her husband's pragmatic approach to marriage, and how she responded to the strong intellectual and literary affinity—not to mention sexual tension—between London and Strunsky. As its title suggests, *The Kempton-Wace Letters* is similarly dominated by a dialogue between two individuals. Unlike Bessie in Strunsky's telling, however, Wace's fiancée, Hester Stebbins, does emerge as a physical presence and is ultimately given a voice in the narrative. Beginning as a transatlantic exchange between Kempton's home in London, England, and Wace's in Berkeley, California, the correspondence bridges the geographic distance between the letter writers when Kempton arrives, in letter XXXII, to lecture on "Literature and Democracy" at Stanford University and meets Hester for the first time. It is Hester who brings the book to its conclusion. Composed by Strunsky in the voice of the young fiancée, the final two letters—one written to each of the male correspondents—tell of Hester's decision to break off the engagement after she learns that Wace is devoid of romantic feeling for her. By most reckonings, it seems that Kempton (that is, Strunsky) has won the debate.

In his introduction to the 1990 edition of *The Kempton-Wace Letters*, Douglas Robillard calls the plot "straightforward" and the "device a simple one that allows the authors to dispense with most of the conventions of fiction as they carry on their discussion of eugenics and romance."[91] In ascribing predictability to the text, Robillard appears to have in mind the long tradition of epistolary fiction, whose origins can be traced back to the origin of the novel itself. As exemplified by Aphra Behn's *Love-Letters Between a Noble-Man and His Sister* (1684) and Samuel Richardson's writing from the first-person point of view of his eponymous character in *Pamela* (1740), the form is closely tied to notions of female authorship and voice. The relationship between form and content in *The Kempton-Wace Letters* adds to the seeming straightforwardness of the plot. Love supplied the most common topic for epistolary fiction, and authors often used it as a pretext for exploring philosophical questions, as in Jean-Jacques Rousseau's *Julie, or the New Heloise* (1761), based on the tragic medieval love story of Heloise and Abelard. Strunsky herself described the method of writing the novel as "simple" with the authors actually exchanging letters as Kempton and Wace, sending them back and forth between "her house in San Francisco" and London's "in the beautiful town of Piedmont across the Bay."[92] But both the novel's plot and epistolary device become increasingly complex when we carefully consider this collaborative process and specifically Strunsky's role in the text's creation.

As much as the dialogic form of epistolary fiction seems to lend itself to collaboration, coauthored epistolary novels are rare, and it is the collaborative, cross-gendered aspect of *The Kempton-Wace Letters* that marks it as a work of literary experimentation. A modern text in the trappings of traditional form, addressing the timeless topic of love and marriage, the novel is very much a product of California's bohemian culture. It was constructed with an awareness of its specific place and time, which are identified in the headings of each letter. (Although the specific year is left blank, the use of "19—," coupled with the copyright date of 1903, clearly situates the work in the context of a new century.) Not only was the text composed by sending letters across the San Francisco Bay, but the address line on Wace's letters reads "The Ridge, Berkeley, California," and Stanford University provides the setting for the book's final chapters, with the vibrant intellectual life of the Bay Area bringing the three characters together. As a collaborative, cross-gendered, epistolary text, the book's precedents include *The American Diary of a Japanese Girl*, written by another Bay Area bohemian, Yone Noguchi, with significant editorial input from Blanche Partington, a drama critic who would later have a brief affair with London. The 1901 novel, which initially masqueraded as an anonymously published diary, is now considered a pioneering work of

Asian American and queer literature in which Noguchi, a Japanese-born man, takes on the identity of "Miss Morning Glory," a young woman newly arrived in San Francisco from Japan.[93] Artistic inspiration can also be found in The Crowd's playful group writing sessions orchestrated by Gelett Burgess, and the later spontaneous decision to turn the walls of Coppa's into a collaborative canvas testifies to a similar creative impulse in which artists gave new meaning to old forms by working collectively.

On the surface, *The Kempton-Wace Letters* addresses an ideological debate about marriage. As we know from the book's backstory, however, the debate was sparked by Strunsky's Jewishness, which London viewed as a racial difference that made their union unviable. It is important to keep in mind, then, that London's side of the argument depends upon a spurious claim: that race constitutes a biological difference. As I demonstrated in the previous section, Strunsky repeatedly challenged his essentializing assumptions. Likewise, in *The Kempton-Wace Letters*, Strunsky does not simply confront London's argument about marriage; despite the fact that the text does not explicitly invoke Jewishness, she succeeds in destabilizing his—and the reader's—underlying beliefs about identity. She achieves this largely through form and process. The text's premise allows her to take on a protean identity, writing from the perspective of Dane Kempton, a non-Jewish, non-American man. At the end of the text, she shape-shifts again, assuming the identity of another non-Jewish character, Hester Stebbins. More closely resembling her creator in terms of gender and age, Hester is also a complex character, who, like Strunsky, defies categorization.

In what follows, I analyze the various gender transpositions that take place in the text, from Strunsky's literary drag performance as Dane Kempton to her removal of drag to assume the voice of Hester in the conclusion. I argue that *The Kempton-Wace Letters* addresses the contemporary discourse about race and intermarriage, while also offering a commentary on gender and authorship. The joint artistic undertaking gave Strunsky the space to write as a man, to put her "protean moods" on paper in a way that eluded her when she wrote alone. It also allowed her to publish *with* a man, one whose literary star was on the rise and who was forging important connections in the male-dominated publishing industry. With this in mind, I consider how the marketing, material production, and reception of *The Kempton-Wace Letters*—from its initial anonymous publication and the subsequent revelation of London and Strunsky's authorship to scholarship today—both subverted and reinforced gender binaries. Strunsky's writing career ended up being defined less by her collaboration with Jack London on *The Kempton-Wace Letters*, and more by the ways that critics, readers, and scholars downplayed and erased her role in the novel's creation.

If Strunsky graciously credited London with the idea for *The Kempton-Wace Letters* in her unpublished memoir, his letters reveal that she was the one who acted upon the proposal and initiated the writing process. London's letter dated August 30, 1900, contains the first reference to the project in his correspondence: "I hardly know where you have got those *Letters* to already in your impetuous way. You only have given me hints in your notes, and I don't know where you have traveled to. We must have a long talk about it. Some afternoon or evening by ourselves, preferably at my place. . . . We must have fully discussed it, and have everything thoroughly mapped out before we commence."[94] As usual, their literary endeavors give London an excuse to see Strunsky—and in this case, to spend time with her alone, rather than with their friends. London's desire to get "everything thoroughly mapped out before we commence" is typical of his rigorous work ethic, which he often tried to impose on Strunsky, who struggled to be a disciplined writer. In this case, however, the prospect of taking on a male role proved liberating, and Strunsky seemed to have no problem sitting down to work. Scolding her for beginning the project in her "impetuous way" and without his oversight, London expresses his discomfort with Strunsky's taking control of the narrative. His letter, including his stated preference for meeting at his place, reads as an attempt to wrest back control.

Nevertheless, Strunsky persisted, forging ahead with the project. A few weeks later, on September 15, London's correspondence indicated that he had received the first of Dane Kempton's letters. He praised Strunsky's "splendid phrasing" as well as her ideas, including her proposal that the book conclude with two letters from Hester—"one to me and one to you," as London wrote, dropping their Kempton-Wace characters. The September 15 letter also offers insight into their process of collaborative creation, as London described his editing of her work: "You will find I have altered Dane Kempton's letters somewhat, here and there, in little places. But I have striven to do so O so slightly. Only where I deemed strength and ambiguity demanded." Going on to reassure Strunsky that "these alterations are not irrevocable," he explained, "I must not cramp you for the very truth of it. It is impossible that there be the slightest common ring in the letters of Dane Kempton and the letters of Herbert Wace. We must be ourselves. So see, girl, that whatever alterations I make, I make with this understanding. And in the end, even on such things, your verdict shall be final."[95] Typical of the power play between them, London both asserts and relinquishes control. (Recall, for instance, that when London offered to play the dominant role of Strunsky's Pharaoh-like "taskmaster," he ended with the prediction that she would "send plagues upon" him and "depart, leaving behind a wake of devastation and terror.") London's description of the collaborative process is further interesting for its attempt to achieve realism, an objective that blurs the line between the writers and their characters. "We must be ourselves," he cautioned. Reading London's letter, it is easy to see why Robillard claimed that they "dispense[d] with most of the conventions of fiction." Yet, this is much more the case for London than for Strunsky, whose performance as a man necessitated an explicit engagement with the fictions of gender.

Although the power dynamic between them would be further complicated by their male publisher's editing and marketing of *The Kempton-Wace Letters*, London's promise to give Strunsky the "final" say held to an extent. As the author of the book's opening and closing letters, Strunsky dominated and framed the text. The book's opening paragraph, written in the voice of Dane Kempton, contains a number of shifts that draw attention to the text's intricate gender play:

> Yesterday I wrote formally, rising to the occasion like the conventional happy father rather than the man who believes in the miracle and lives for it. Yesterday I stinted myself. I took you in my arms, glad of what is and stately with respect for the fulness of your manhood. It is to-day that I let myself leap into yours in a passion of joy. I dwell on what has come to pass and inflate myself with pride in your fulfillment, more as a mother would, I think, and she your mother.[96]

To begin, Strunsky-as-Kempton takes on a dual male identity in relation to Wace: Kempton is not only a close friend but also a surrogate father, having assumed the parental role following the death of the younger man's parents. By the third sentence, however, the relationship of Kempton to Wace sounds more like that of a lover, imagining an embrace "stately with respect for the fulness of your manhood" that becomes increasingly passionate. Strunsky's male disguise and the physical distance between the letter writers allow her a space to express such erotic overtones. While the paragraph opens with Strunsky slipping into her masculine role as "the conventional happy father," by its end, she has partially unveiled her female identity, with Kempton behaving "more as a mother would." This moment takes on greater significance as the book continues and it is revealed that Wace has not only lost both his parents but that Kempton had had an affair with Wace's mother, Ellen, in his youth; in his maternal and paternal relationship to Wace, Kempton has merged the identity of the woman he loved and the man who was his rival for her affections. The end of the letter reasserts a masculine identity as Kempton signs off, "Ever your devoted father."[97] Importantly, however, none of the identities that Kempton takes on—father, mother, lover, friend—are scientifically based. Even Kempton's claims of kinship with Wace are determined by emotional ties and shared history. Through this series of slippages, Strunsky's character begins *The Kempton-Wace Letters* by posing a challenge to binary and biological notions of identity.

While Kempton sets out to argue "that it is wrong to marry without love," his argument contains a subtext about the limits of biological determinism and the dangers of scientism that is made more explicit as the correspondence continues. "I must not fall into your mistake of dividing men into categories," Kempton writes to Wace in chapter IX, "Men are not either intellectual or emotional; they are both. It is a rounded not an angular development which we follow. Feeling and thinking are not mutually exclusive, and the great personality feels deeply because he thinks highly, feels keenly because he sees widely."[98] Kempton's fictional letter echoes the real-life correspondence between the two authors. Likely citing Strunsky's language back to her, London opened his now famous love letter of April 3, 1901, by posing and answering a question: "Did I say that the human might be filed in categories? Well, and if I did, let me qualify—not all humans. You elude me."[99] Kempton's letter, authored by Strunsky, reads as a rebuke to London's qualification and its logic of exceptionalism. Kempton extends the conclusion to all humanity, refraining from "dividing men into categories." The subtle shift in language—from "human" in London's letter to the seemingly universal use of the word "men" in Kempton's—may seem counterintuitive at first, but employing the gendered term allows Kempton/Strunsky to deconstruct the category of "man" and expose the limits of masculinity. As demonstrated in the book's opening letter, the gendered category "man" proved inadequate for defining Kempton's relationship to Wace and response to the news of Wace's marriage; feeling "stinted" by his initial attempt to respond "formally," according to the cultural dictates of fatherhood and manliness, Kempton refuses to deny himself the full complexity of human feeling. Instead, he takes up his pen again. Confessing that his response to the news was emotional and passionate, he embraces these traits in himself, despite the fact that such sentiments are typically associated with womanliness and maternity.

Although most of the text is given over to a dialogue between Kempton and Wace, it is Hester Stebbins who emerges as the most complex character. Much more than a pawn in an intellectual contest between two men, she becomes an active participant in the debate—thanks to Strunsky's astute suggestion that the text should conclude with Hester's own letters. But Hester, interestingly, is not solely Strunsky's invention. She is a collaborative creation and a composite figure. Both scientist and poet, she combines elements of Wace and Kempton. And it is London, writing as Wace, who supplies the initial characterization of Hester. Wace may not be in love, but the description of Hester included in his first letter to Kempton evinces his respect for her and her intellect. Explaining that their scientific studies brought them together as undergraduates, when he was a "cocksure junior" at Berkeley and she a "far maturer" freshman at Stanford, Wace hopes to endear his fiancée to his literary-minded father figure by revealing her poetic aspirations. "How shall I describe her?," Wace writes,

> Perhaps as a George Eliot, fused with an Elizabeth Barrett, with a hint of Huxley and a trace of Keats. I may say she is something like all this, but I must say she is something other and different. There is something about her a certain lightsomeness, a glow or flash almost Latin or oriental, perhaps Celtic. Yes, that must be it—Celtic. But the high-stomached Norman is there and the stubborn Saxon. . . .

> She is unafraid, and wide-looking and far-looking, but she is not over-looking. The Saxon grapples with the Celt, and the Norman forces the twain to do what the one would not dream of doing and what the other would dream beyond and never do.[100]

This initial description of Hester attests to Wace's difficulty summing her up, echoing London's early failed efforts to "sum up" Strunsky. A few sentences into the passage, Wace acknowledges the impossibility of the task: "I may say she is something like all this, but I must say she is something other and different." His repetition of the vague word "something" speaks to the ways Hester eludes language and cannot be pinned down. Yet, despite this acknowledgment, Wace goes on to attempt an ethnological analysis of her personality. This, too, fails to capture Hester; the various racial categories, like gendered ones, prove inadequate as a means of definition.

With the writer's own words often undermining his scientific claims, *The Kempton-Wace Letters* issues a multipronged attack on the pro-eugenics argument voiced by Wace. Wace's description of Hester relies on a logic of racial hierarchy, with the historically powerful groups—Norman and Saxon—coming to dominate over the course of the passage. Although Hester's personality bears metaphorical traces of "the Latin or oriental, [or] perhaps Celtic," Wace would be uninterested in marriage were it not for her Anglo-Saxon heritage. According to Wace's principles of "domestic selection," Hester's fitness for marriage and reproduction derives from her genetic make-up and specifically her white racial purity. "She has health and strength and beauty and youth, and she will certainly make a most charming wife and excellent mother," he reasons, making clear his rationale for choosing her.[101]

The Kempton-Wace debate, however, is not simply a matter of poetry and emotion over science and intellect. The strength of Kempton's rebuttal comes from his ability to combine his romantic inclinations with rational thought, presenting his anti-eugenicist case via intellectual reasoning. He recognizes, for example, that a purely scientific approach to marriage devalues women, depriving them of agency and reducing them to receptacles for reproduction. While Wace would like to believe that his scientific view is more evolved than the older man's starry-eyed faith in romance, Kempton makes a persuasive case for the opposite; he demonstrates that it is the younger man who holds outdated views, especially of women. "Woman is new-born in strength and dignity, and the highest chivalry the world has ever known is in blossom," writes Kempton, channeling the feminist mindset of his creator, "She is an equal, a comrade . . . She is no longer a means but an end in herself, not alone fit to mother men but fit to live in equality with men. . . . Because of the greater and more general emancipation of woman the subtlety of modern love has become possible."[102] In addition to using Kempton as a mouthpiece for gender equality, Strunsky also arms him with reinforcement in the form of a minor female character, Herbert's sister, Barbara Wace, who lives near her foster father in England. Not only does Barbara share Kempton's beliefs, calling Wace's antipathy to emotion "unnatural," but she has made her own life choices according to anti-eugenicist principles; Barbara married the man she loves, despite his chronic illness and the fact that this disability may prevent him from supporting her and having children.[103]

Discovering that Wace has not revealed his philosophy of marriage to Hester, Kempton becomes her champion and defender. "You do not love Hester," the older man pleads with Wace, pressuring him to tell his fiancée the truth, "You want her to mother your children, and you install her in your life for the purpose before the need."[104] Kempton describes Wace's decision to marry in impersonal and businesslike terms (much like London's statement that he "opened transactions for a wife" when he became engaged to Bess Maddern). Criticizing Wace for trying to "install" Hester in his life with little regard for emotion or individuality, Kempton demonstrates that Wace's scientific thinking will not advance humanity, but is an act of dehumanization. In this respect, Wace's argument is much more than an idealist's defense of romance. It is also a materialist—and feminist—defense of women.

Given that Hester is a joint product of her coauthors' imaginations, it is useful to consider her character in light of Strunsky's critique of London's previous representations of women. Among Strunsky's earliest published articles are reviews of London's first two books, the short story collections *The Son of the Wolf*, published in 1900, and *The God of His Fathers*, published one year later in 1901. In her review of the second collection, Strunsky praised her friend's fiction, calling the work "a classic." Toward the end of the review, however, Strunsky issued a critique of London's gender portrayals. Allowing for exceptions, like "The Grit of Women," Strunsky observed that "the women in the book are built up as types rather than individuals. Where woman is brought into the action prominently, it is still obviously for the purpose of developing the hero's character."[105] *The Kempton-Wace Letters* manages to avoid falling into this trap, despite its title and conceit and even as Wace's reasons for marrying Hester threaten to reduce her to a type. "You betrothed yourself not because Hester is different from everybody in the world, but because she is like," Kempton writes to Wace after meeting Hester for the first time at Stanford. Just as Strunsky's review criticizes London for failing to develop his female characters, Kempton accuses Wace of taking Hester "for what is typical in her, not for what is individual."[106] As Kempton comes to know and love Hester, his opposition to the marriage grows, and he repeatedly urges Wace to inform her of his motives. Kempton's conviction is no longer purely philosophical. Instead, he sees it as his duty to preserve Hester's individuality. If the text has a male hero, it is Kempton. Wace, in fact, absolves himself from action. Rather than confronting Hester, he grants Kempton permission to do so before signing off his final letter. "Tell her, then, tell her all you wish, you dear old fluttery, mothery poet father—as though it made any difference," writes Wace, unmoved by his foster father's appeal and coldly indifferent to the heartbreak he may cause his fiancée.[107]

The novel may depict Hester as an individual rather than a type, but it would fall short of redressing Strunsky's critique of London's work if it were not for the decision to disrupt the text's dialogic structure as an exchange between two male correspondents. Rather than having Kempton play the role of Hester's savior, sweeping in at the end to rescue her from a loveless marriage, the book endows Hester's character with voice and agency. Hester is not only "brought into the action prominently," but also takes over the narrative, emerging as its central figure. Early in the correspondence, Wace promises to send Kempton samples of Hester's poetry, writing of her work, "She is waiting for a stronger voice and sings softly as yet."[108] These words are evocative of a letter London wrote to Strunsky on May 2, 1900, before their collaboration began, in which he advised her, "You will have to shout loud, for the world is rather deaf, and you may have to shout long."[109] Hester's voice, and Strunsky's, get stronger and louder over the course of the novel. Whereas Wace/London first introduced Hester's character, once Kempton gets to know her, he turns the tables on Wace, "endeavoring to make [him] acquainted with" the woman to whom he is betrothed and writing multiple letters a week for that purpose.[110] Beginning with chapter XXXI, Kempton sends Wace five letters in a row, labeled "From the Same to the Same." Strunsky's writing thus begins to dominate the text. Impersonating a man grants her an opportunity to strengthen her voice, but, as in the book's first paragraph, a gradual slippage occurs. In his final letter, Wace reminds us of Kempton's nonbinary gender identity when he calls Strunsky's alter ego a "mothery poet father." By the end of the novel, Strunsky has removed the male drag, writing her last two letters in the persona of Hester, the main female character.

Hester's first letter, written to Wace, reveals that she is the one who takes action and drives the denouement, making the decision to end the engagement when she learns that Wace does not love her. "You have not changed, but my faith in you has," she tells him.[111] Her words allude to her ex-fiancé's lack of development over the course of the novel. Wace is a static character; even his location, identified in the address line of the correspondence, remains the same throughout (a noticeable contrast with Kempton, who travels between London and California). As the friendship between Kempton and Hester grows, their conversations taking place on walks around Stanford's campus, Wace remains isolated on "The Ridge," his ranch in nearby Berkeley. The final chapter consists of a letter "From Hester Stebbins to Dane Kempton," with Strunsky performing a dual role as writer and recipient, woman and man. Whereas *The Kempton-Wace Letters* offers no glimpse of Wace's future beyond the narrative, Hester reveals that she has another suitor, a "youth . . . who loves me," and ends her letter to Kempton—and the book—with these words: "Do you ask what is left me, dear friend? Work and tears and the intact dream. Believe me, I am not pitiable."[112] In spite of the pain caused by her unrequited love for Wace, Hester is not defeated. She still has her science, her art, and her dreams. She is a heroine who refuses to be defined solely by love and her relationships with men.

"The Woman's Side of the Question"

Throughout their collaboration on *The Kempton-Wace Letters*, both Strunsky and London were also working on a number of solo writing efforts. If they began their friendship and collaboration as unknown writers, London was well on his way to literary fame by the time their coauthored novel was published in 1903. After years of frequent rejection, his stories had found increasing acceptance among editors of prestigious publications like *The Atlantic Monthly* and *McClure's*. By the beginning of the new century, he had produced a sufficient number of high-quality stories to comprise two collections: *The Son of the Wolf* in 1900 and *The God of His Fathers* in 1901. His debut novel, *A Daughter of the Snows*, appeared in print in 1902, although critics agreed that it did not live up to the promise of his short stories and London himself called it his "failure-novel."[113] The following year marked a significant turn in his fortunes. The 1903 publication of *The Kempton-Wace Letters* would be dramatically overshadowed by a novella with an unlikely canine protagonist. First serialized in *The Saturday Evening Post* and subsequently published in book form by Macmillan, *The Call of the Wild* became a bestseller, earning London popular and critical acclaim that continues to this day.

At a time when London was rousing the literary establishment with his virile, violence-driven adventure stories set in the harsh conditions of the northland, Strunsky's fictional interests were tamer and more genteel, as evidenced by her "Book of Ideas," in which she jotted down notes and outlines for various projects. The first entry, dated February 19, 1901, displays her persistent attraction to the epistolary form. In it, she sketches a plan for a piece of prose about "a woman of between fifty and sixty harkening back to her youth, telling out the joy and the glory . . . in letters to a granddaughter." Next to an entry outlining chapters for "Windlestraws," an unpublished novel now held at the Yale University Archives, appears an idea for an autobiographical tale: "A story, beautiful, pathetic. The love and loss, the struggle and hope and failure of a young girl meant for great things . . . scene at Stanford . . . Dedicated 'To Rose, my sister.' How I love her!" A few pages later another entry stands out, written in bolder ink. Dated May 12, 1901, it reads: "Love letters written by J. L. and me. Real, spontaneous letters between two young literary persons. Fictitious, of course, since we are not lovers."[114] It is difficult to know what to make of this entry. Is Strunsky referring to *The Kempton-Wace Letters*, which she and London were in the midst of writing? Perhaps the bolder ink and definitiveness of this entry indicate a project in process. Or is Strunsky considering the possibility of another novelistic discourse on love, one in which she might play a character more like herself, a "*young* literary person," rather than a middle-aged man? If so, perhaps *The Kempton-Wace Letters* had given her the confidence to imagine, at least privately, another collaboration with her "not-lover," an additional opportunity to sublimate their feelings into fiction and a space in which they could overcome the taboos of racial mixing and adultery that confronted them in real life.

The entries that open Strunsky's diary are revealing in terms of gender, artistic inspiration, and literary production. The ideas that never came to fruition—the letters from a grandmother to granddaughter and the story of a "young girl meant for great things" with its dedication to her sister—are centered on women. "Windlestraws" has a male protagonist named John Torrance. Similarly, Strunsky succeeded in writing and publishing a book of "love letters" by collaborating with a man and taking on a male identity for most of the text herself. The blank pages in Strunsky's "Book of Ideas" are equally illuminating on matters of women and authorship. At some point in 1902, Strunsky stopped jotting down notes (at least in this particular diary), and almost one hundred blank pages appear in the middle of the book. Years later, one of her children came across the idea book and momentarily broke the silence of those empty pages. On the page dated June 28, an entry in her daughter's hand reads:

> *This is mother Idea book* [sic]
> *mother shouldn't write any ideas because she hasn't any time.*

On the page headed June 30, the same hand makes another notation: "Mother is the darlingest mother in the world but she always wants to write and never gets there."[115] Strunsky's other diaries tell us why she "hasn't any time" and "never gets there." Once she marries and has children, Strunsky's ideas for her writing are superseded by a record of family matters—nursing schedules for her babies; her often rocky relationship with her husband, English; musings on her love for her sister, Rose. Occasionally, ideas for writing projects do crop up again. At 4:00 a.m. one December day, for example, Strunsky began cataloging "Memories of Jack for my book."[116] These memories form the basis of her manuscript "Jack London," an unpublished memoir that is at once a biography of a great male author and a testament to the unrealized dreams of a woman writer.

Anna Strunsky's archive is a palimpsest. Beneath the relatively small number of published writings lie traces of the work she might have produced had circumstances been different, an untold story of what she might have accomplished had she been unconstrained by gender. Later in life, family intervened, and she often put aside her own work in support of her husband's writings and travels and her children's upbringing. But *The Kempton-Wace Letters*, published when Strunsky was young and single, also bears traces of what could have been. As plans for the book progressed, Strunsky developed even greater ambitions for her female character and proposed to London that they intersperse letters from Hester throughout and open the book with a prologue written from her first-person point of view. Strunsky went so far as to pen a prologue, a four-page, handwritten document in Hester's voice expressing the character's doubts about her impending marriage and inserted an additional plot twist: her suspicion that Wace is in love with his friend's wife and that Hester is not his first choice. Thus, archival clues reveal that Strunsky was angling for an approach that would more fully flesh out "the woman's side of the question."[117] Concluding the book with Hester Stebbins's letters was a step in that direction.

Strunsky's suggestions to feature Hester more prominently were nixed by London and their Macmillan editor, George Brett. Scrawled across the top of Strunsky's drafted prologue in the Huntington Library archives is a single sentence, most likely written in London's hand: "I am very doubtful about this prologue."[118] While London initially approved Strunsky's plan to include a prologue, their editor, George Brett, persuaded him otherwise. "I have thought the matter over and have decided against the Prologue," London wrote to Brett in January 1903, after implementing the editor's proposed revisions. London presented himself to Brett as unilaterally in charge of *The Kempton-Wace Letters*, as suggested by his use of the first-person singular in this sentence, as well as the businesslike statement that follows. "Miss Strunsky has been informed of this," London wrote next, turning to the passive voice to indicate that the decision was official and no further action was required.[119] Brett went on to make another decision that would have a disastrous effect on Strunsky's career: to publish the book anonymously and thus to diminish—if not entirely erase—her role in the narrative.

* * *

In 1905, two years after *The Kempton-Wace Letters* was published, first anonymously and subsequently with the authors' names attached, Strunsky said her farewells to San Francisco. She was headed back to Russia, accompanied by her sister, where they would work as journalists, reporting on the ongoing revolution for a news syndicate organized by wealthy Chicago socialist William English Walling. The following year, Anna Strunsky and Walling were married, and the couple went on to spend most of their years in New York and Connecticut.[120] San Francisco was never again to be Strunsky's permanent home. Yet the culture of turn-of-the-twentieth-century Northern California proved a defining influence on her career. It enabled her early experimental collaboration, *The Kempton-Wace Letters*, setting a course for a Jewish immigrant writer to produce innovative work that transcended the conventions of the ghetto genre and the constraints of gender. At the same time, the novel and its production history have much to tell us about the often insurmountable obstacles to women's literary production, even within the supposedly progressive culture of Bay Area bohemia.

Coda

From its opening chapter titled "Two Victorian Sisters," Frances Bransten Rothmann's family memoir, *The Haas Sisters of Franklin Street*, originally republished in 1979 and reissued in 2017, evokes the atmosphere of a fairy tale to describe her privileged background as a descendant of San Francisco's German Jewish elite. "Once upon a time, in the long ago 1880s, San Francisco's Franklin Street was a fashionable residential district," Rothmann begins, continuing to map her family tree on to an altered neighborhood that bears vestiges of its storied past:

> On this street, within the radius of three blocks bounded by California and Jackson Streets, lived three married Greenebaum sisters. These women, my grandmother and two great-aunts, lived out their stately, orderly lives in spacious Victorian mansions. Today, Franklin Street is a busy one-way thoroughfare. The homes of my great-aunts, Carrie Walter and Stella Simon, were demolished and replaced by stucco apartment buildings. But two family homes remain on Franklin Street. The one at 2007 Franklin Street was built for my grandparents, the William Haases, in 1886; it is a tall, grey Victorian with turrets, bay windows, intricate carvings, and a Queen Anne tower. The other at 1735 Franklin Street was built in 1902 and is a red brick, ivy-covered Edwardian with imposing white pillars. This home was a wedding gift to my parents from my grandparents.[1]

Rothmann's recollection of the Gilded-Age grandeur of "spacious Victorian mansions" contrasts sharply with literary depictions of congested streets and cramped tenements contained in some of the best-known works of Jewish American autobiography and fiction. For decades, scholars have considered the ghetto genre—represented by immigrant writers such as Abraham Cahan, Mary Antin, and Anzia Yezierska—as Jewish American literature's principal contribution to turn-of-the-twentieth-century American letters. This book has demonstrated that Jewish writers were simultaneously influencing American literary culture west of the ghetto. In turn, I have explored how regional particularities of the American West shaped the careers and literary sensibilities of a diverse group of Jewish American women writers linked by their ties to the city of San Francisco.

As a multigenerational history of a Bay Area family whose affluence and social status date back to California's heady Gold Rush beginnings, Rothmann's autobiographical account, like many of the texts I have considered here, nuances familiar tropes of Jewish immigration and assimilation. Despite their smooth integration into San Francisco high society, where the financial success of mercantile ventures rendered them seemingly indistinguishable from their non-Jewish counterparts, Rothmann's parents and grandparents, she informs us, were "proudly loyal to their Jewish origins."[2] She depicts her family's involvement in Temple Emanu-El as existing in harmony, rather than tension, with the Easter egg hunts and lavishly decorated Christmas celebrations hosted at her grandparents' Franklin Street home. The structure of *The Haas Sisters of Franklin Street* further complicates linear narratives of Jewish assimilation. Rothmann concludes with an epilogue in which she explains how "the pendulum has swung back to the synagogue" with her children's generation. She describes, for example, how her son returns home on Friday evenings after services wearing "a *yarmulke*"—the head covering that, in the 1880s, was banned by the Reform rabbi of Temple Emanu-El in an effort to downplay Jewish difference and conform to Christian practices.[3] Of observing Shabbat with her adult children, Rothmann writes, "I treasure this weekly ritual that never before existed for me."[4]

In other ways, too, Rothmann's memoir encapsulates some of the preoccupations of this study. The first part of the memoir's title, which identifies the sisters by their maiden names, reflects Rothmann's prioritizing of her maternal line; the story of her family unfurls around the key figures of her mother, Florine Haas Bransten, and her aunt, Alice Haas Lilienthal. *The Haas Sisters of Franklin Street* thus constructs a matrilineal history, just as *West of the Ghetto* counters masculinist and patriarchal tendencies within Jewish American literary scholarship by uncovering a cohort of Jewish women writers who dominated the Western literary landscape during the Gilded Age and Progressive Era. Exemplified in the memoir's opening passage, which is quoted above, Rothmann's spotlighting of her female relatives coincides with her emphasis on the domestic realm as setting; her title identifies the sisters by their home, yoking them to their Franklin Street addresses. Like Harriet Lane Levy, whose memoir *920 O'Farrell Street* was discussed in chapter 3, Rothmann imbues the neighborhood and its Victorian architecture with symbolism, notably class signifiers, finding meaning in what can only be remembered as well as in what physically remains. Attention to space, place, and region reorients our relationship to the past, whether we are considering the legacy of a family or the literary legacies I explored throughout this book. Unlike Levy's O'Farrell Street home, replaced by the end of her memoir with a Cadillac dealership (and today with a movie theater parking lot), some of the residential properties that comprise Rothmann's family inheritance have endured as indelible parts of San Francisco's landscape—including her grandparents' Queen Anne mansion, the Haas-Lilienthal House, now a historic landmark that stands as the city's only example of Gilded-Age architecture open for the public to tour.

Rothmann's palimpsestic description of Franklin Street, documenting what remains side by side with what once was, also resonates with the project of literary recovery that animates *West of the Ghetto*. At first, my search for forgotten Jewish women writers of Old San Francisco yielded faint traces—enough for an article, maybe two, I thought. But this neglected literary tradition expanded and came more sharply into focus as I dug into available archives and assembled my own from microfilm, periodical databases, and digitized resources like Google Books. I chose to focus on five representative writers whose works and careers offer rich and varied opportunities for literary study—opportunities that I hope will extend beyond the pages of this book.

As I have shown, these women made distinct contributions to American and transnational literature, but they were not anomalous. They existed in relation to a larger literary culture and participated in networks, partnerships, and movements that can serve as trailheads for future scholarship. In addition to *The Haas Sisters of Franklin Street* and *920 O'Farrell Street*, for example, other autobiographical works published in the post–World War II period nostalgically recall Jewish life in Old San Francisco. Ruth Bransten McDougall's *Under Mannie's Hat*, a family memoir by Rothmann's cousin, was initially published in 1964 and appeared in a revised version as *Coffee, Martinis, and San Francisco* in 1978. These family memoirs join a tradition of San Francisco Jewish women's life-writing, which includes Flora Jacobi Arnstein's privately published fictionalized autobiography, *No End to Morning*, and Annette Rosenshine's unpublished "Life's Not a Paragraph," as well as autobiographical texts by Rebekah Bettelheim Kohut, Gertrude Stein, and Alice B. Toklas (all briefly discussed in this book) that address how the authors were impacted by formative years spent in the Bay Area.[5]

In pairing stories of two sisters, Rothmann's memoir signals yet another potential avenue for future research on San Francisco Jewish women writers, many of whose careers thrived due to familial bonds and networks. Several of the writers I consider here had siblings in the same profession, including Emma Wolf, whose sister Alice S. Wolf published short stories in *The Argonaut* and a novel, *A House of Cards* (1896), prior to her marriage. Anna Strunsky may be best remembered today for her relationships with prominent socialist men such as Jack London and William English Walling, but the most important, constant, and intimate relationship in her life was with her sister, Rose Strunsky (Lorwin), who shared her political and literary leanings. Joining Anna on a fateful trip to Russia in 1905 to report on the revolution, Rose went on to make her career as an author, journalist, literature professor, and translator of Russian classics. The sisters Jessie and Emma Kaufman, whom I did not have space to consider in this book, were part of a literary salon organized by one of California's most famous, non-Jewish novelists of the period, Gertrude Atherton.[6] Jessie, who also wrote under a pseudonym, set some of her fiction in Hawaii, including her 1912 novel, *A Jewel of the Seas*, while Emma wrote short stories, plays, and journalism, most notably the full-length work of nonfiction *Cuba at a Glance* (1898), a collaboration with suffragist writer Anne O'Hagan.[7] Also deserving of study are the careers of sisters-in-law Flora Jacobi Arnstein and Helen Arnstein Salz, artist-educators who combined visual arts and poetry and founded San Francisco's progressive Presidio Open Air School.

The writers discussed in this book were allied with others through their involvements in political movements across the ideological spectrum, occasioning further consideration of the symbiotic relationship between social reform and San Francisco's literary culture. Bettie Lowenberg's Philomath Club operated as a training ground and platform for artistically minded women like Wolf and Levy, while other members produced writing that served explicitly political purposes. Florence Prag

Kahn, for instance, wrote regular newspaper columns for the *San Francisco Chronicle* prior to becoming the first Jewish congresswoman in 1925. Like Miriam Michelson, Selina Solomons, who came from a Sephardic family, was a well-known activist for women's rights who wrote suffrage texts such as *How We Won the Vote in California* (1912) and the play *The Girl from Colorado: Or, the Conversion of Aunty Suffridge* (1911).[8]

By the early decades of the twentieth century, other Jewish San Francisco women were following in Michelson's footsteps, including Blanche Upright, whose work as a newspaper reporter led to a career as a novelist in the 1920s, and Pauline Jacobson, a reporter for *The San Francisco Bulletin* whose literary journalism about the city's early years was subsequently collected in *City of the Golden 'Fifties* (1941).[9] Of course, the influence of these writers extends well beyond their region. Michelson, for instance, was the first of many popular Jewish American women writers—including Midwestern-born novelists Edna Ferber and Fannie Hurst—whose work similarly features irrepressible female protagonists and feminist plotlines. In her autobiography *A Peculiar Treasure* (1939), Ferber acknowledged the impact that Michelson had on her, citing the *Yellow Journalist* series in *The Saturday Evening Post* as the reason she herself became a "girl reporter." For Ferber, too, journalism served as entrée into fiction writing. In novels such as *Cimmaron* (1930) and *Giant* (1952), she—like Michelson before her—captured the nation's sweeping, multiethnic panorama, simultaneously contributing to and complicating myths of the American West.[10]

To gather the stories of pioneering Jewish women writers whose families journeyed westward in the nineteenth century, I embarked on a long and often circuitous journey of my own. My journey took place through time as well as space. I traveled into the past through the archives, seeking voices of women whose histories and literary contributions have been erased and overlooked. In recovering these women's voices, *West of the Ghetto* offers alternatives to the foundational Jewish American literary canon and challenges how the story of Jewish literary history in the United States has long been told. My hope is that this new genealogy proves elastic and capacious, clearing space for a range of Jewish writers from diverse backgrounds whose work expands our understanding of literary Jewishness and its relationship to American culture.

Notes

Introduction

1 Rebekah Bettelheim Kohut, *My Portion* (T. Seltzer, 1925), 37–38.

2 Harriet Lane Levy, *920 O'Farrell Street: A Jewish Girlhood in Old San Francisco* (Heyday, 1996), 63. As the title of the 2013 documentary film *American Jerusalem: Jews and the Making of San Francisco* makes clear, many Jewish Bay Area families viewed San Francisco as a new Promised Land. In a 2014 panel discussion of the film sponsored by the Leo Baeck Institute and the Center for Jewish History, filmmaker Jackie Krentzman explained that her documentary's title came from San Francisco Jews' practice of substituting "San Francisco" for "Jerusalem" at the Passover seder; this practice dates back to the 1870s. See https://www.youtube.com/watch?v=vtlolSgs490. A similar sentiment is expressed in a short play titled *The Spell of the Spanish Shawl*, coauthored by Ada Goldsmith and Emma Wolf, which was performed at the annual breakfast of the San Francisco Section of the National Council of Jewish Women on October 14, 1926. The play concludes with a song titled "That Old Spanish Shawl" (sung to the tune of the patriotic march "Columbia, Gem of the Ocean"), which celebrates Columbus as the "first Zionist," implying that many of the San Francisco Jewish women who participated in the event viewed the United States as a Jewish homeland. See "Spell of the Spanish Shawl—Scripts and Programs, 1926," National Council of Jewish Women, San Francisco Section Records, 1897–2010, Carton 7, Folder 44, Bancroft Library, University of California, Berkeley. On the end of the Jewish diaspora, see Caryn Aviv and David Schneer, *New Jews: The End of the Jewish Diaspora* (New York University Press, 2005).

3 Lillian Wald, "American Jewry's First Lady," *Wisconsin Jewish Chronicle*, November 15, 1935, 1. For a brief biography of Kohut, see Joyce Antler, *The Journey Home: Jewish Women and the American Century* (Free Press, 1997), 40–54.
4 Kohut, *My Portion*, 61–62.
5 Ruth Sapin, "A Mother in Israel," *Menorah Journal* 11 (June 1925): 307–9.
6 James Luby, "Romantic Career of a Vicarious Mother in Israel," *New York Times*, April 26, 1925, BR5.
7 Henrietta Szold, introduction to *My Portion*, xi.
8 On the shifting meanings of the word "ghetto," which initially referred to compulsory segregated Jewish enclaves in Europe and later to voluntary Jewish immigrant neighborhoods in the United States (and has most recently taken on associations with Black American urban experiences), see Daniel B. Schwartz, *Ghetto: The History of a Word* (Harvard University Press, 2019).
9 Albert Halper, "Notes on Jewish American Fiction," *Menorah Journal* 20 (1932): 61–69.
10 Michael P. Kramer, "Against the Tide: Re-Discovering Early Jewish American Literary History," *Studies in American Jewish Literature* 33, no. 1 (2014): 2, 3. See also Michael P. Kramer, "The Wretched Refuse of Jewish American Literary History," *Studies in American Jewish Literature* 31, no. 1 (2012): 61–75.
11 The biblical reference to Jews as a "peculiar people" as a means of denoting chosen-ness took on new associations with Jews of the Victorian ghetto when Zangwill subtitled *Children of the Ghetto* "A Study of a Peculiar People" in 1892. For an excellent consideration of how non-Jewish writers in the late nineteenth century drew on Christian typology and contributed to a Hebraic myth in which Jewishness was associated with an anachronistic past, see Sharon B. Oster, *No Place in Time: The Hebraic Myth in Late-Nineteenth-Century American Literature* (Wayne State University Press, 2019). For more on the controversy surrounding the ghetto genre, see Lori Harrison-Kahan, "Ghetto Realism—and Beyond," in *The Oxford Handbook of American Literary Realism*, ed. Keith Newlin (Oxford University Press, 2019), 201–18, and Lori Harrison-Kahan, "'Truth-Telling Should Be an Author's Religion': Jewish Fiction and American Literary Realism," in *Yearning to Breathe Free: Jews in*

Gilded Age America, eds. Adam D. Mendelsohn and Jonathan D. Sarna (Princeton University Press, 2023), 189–216.

12 For an important corrective to this literary historical narrative, see Ayelet Brinn, *A Revolution in Type: Gender and the Making of the American Yiddish Press* (New York University Press, 2023).

13 For more on how Jewish American literary history has been viewed through the distorting lenses of patriarchy and misogyny, see Annie Atura Bushnell, Lori Harrison-Kahan, and Ashley Walters, introduction to *Matrilineal Dissent: Women Writers and Jewish American Literary History*, eds. Annie Atura Bushnell, Lori Harrison-Kahan, and Ashley Walters (Wayne State University Press, 2024). For a critique of the "golden age" narrative in Jewish American literary studies, see Benjamin Schreier, *The Rise and Fall of Jewish American Literature: Ethnic Studies and the Challenge of Identity* (University of Pennsylvania Press, 2020). For a recent work of scholarship that complicates the "golden age" narrative through attention to American writers from the USSR, many of whom are women, see Karolina Krasuska, *Soviet-Born: The Afterlives of Migration in Jewish American Fiction* (Rutgers University Press, 2024).

14 For a helpful discussion of how attention to Jewish life in the American West (where white Jewish Americans regularly came into contact with Indigenous, Latinx, and Asian American people in addition to Black Americans) complicates comparative race and ethnic paradigms that rely on Black-white binaries, see Ellen Eisenberg, introduction to *Jewish Identities in the American West: Relational Perspectives* (Brandeis University Press, 2022), 189–214.

15 Kohut, *My Portion*, 39.

16 Kohut, *My Portion*, 39.

17 David S. Koffman, *The Jews' Indian: Colonialism, Pluralism, and Belonging in America* (Rutgers University Press, 2019), 5. On Native Americans in the Jewish American literary imagination, see also Rachel Rubinstein, *Members of the Tribe: Native America in the Jewish Imagination* (Wayne State University Press, 2010) and Jennifer Glaser, *Borrowed Voices: Writing and Racial Ventriloquism in the Jewish American Imagination* (Rutgers University Press, 2016), especially chapter 5.

18 For an important recent consideration of the relationship between Jews and Native people in the American West, see Rebecca Clarren,

The Cost of Free Land: Jews, Lakota, and An American Inheritance (Penguin Random House, 2023).

19 See, for example, Koffman, *The Jews' Indian* for a historical approach and Rubinstein, *Members of the Tribe* for a literary approach.

20 Exceptions include Miriam Michelson's short story "The Cross-Eyed Saint of Guasapadi," *Black Cat*, July 1, 1903, 1–10; and (Mrs. I.) Bettie Lowenberg, "The Tragedy of La Purisama Concepcion," *Club Life* 3 (May 1905): 8–10, 12. A currently lost story by Lowenberg titled "The Rose of San Fernando," which was published in *Club Woman* in December 1903, may deal with similar themes; I mention it here with the hope that someone else may have better luck than I did tracking it down.

21 Literary scholarship on Jewish-Irish relations includes George Bornstein, *The Colors of Zion: Blacks, Jews, and Irish from 1845–1945* (Harvard University Press, 2011) and Stephen Watt, *"Something Dreadful and Grand": American Literature and the Irish-Jewish Unconscious* (Oxford University Press, 2015). For an interesting discussion of how early twentieth-century Jewish women proletarian writers similarly displaced Jewishness with Irishness, see Ashley Walters, "Women Who Wouldn't: Early Twentieth-Century Jewish Women's Proletarian Literature and Ethnoracial Displacement," in Atura Bushnell, Harrison-Kahan, and Walters, *Matrilineal Dissent*, 29–69.

22 See, for example, Cathy Schlund-Vials, *Modeling Citizenship: Jewish and Asian American Writing* (Temple University Press, 2011); Caroline Rody, *The Interethnic Imagination: Roots and Passages in Contemporary Asian American Fiction* (Oxford University Press, 2009); Jonathan Freedman, *Klezmer America: Jewishness, Ethnicity, Modernity* (Columbia University Press, 2008), especially chapter 7; and Judith Oster, *Crossing Cultures: Creating Identity in Chinese and Jewish American Literature* (University of Missouri Press, 2003). For an example of recent scholarship that considers Jewish cultural appropriations of Asian identity, see Samantha M. Cooper, "'To See What Lovely Japanese Our Young People Can Be': American Jewish Community Performance, Racial Appropriation, and Gilbert and Sullivan's *Mikado*, 1885–1939," *The Opera Quarterly* 39, nos. 1–2 (2023): 1–29.

23 For an overview of Jews and Orientalist discourse, see Ivan Davidson Kalmar and Derek J. Penslar, "Orientalism and the Jews: An

Introduction," in *Orientalism and the Jews*, eds. Ivan Davidson Kalmar and Derek J. Penslar (Brandeis University Press, 2005), xiii–xl.

24 On Asian Jews today, see, for example, Rachel Gross, "Part Asian-American, All Jewish?," *NPR Code Switch*, February 10, 2015, https://www.npr.org/sections/codeswitch/2015/02/10/384069013/part-asian-american-all-jewish; Gen Xia Ye Slosberg, "Asian Jews Deserve Better," *Hey Alma*, March 3, 2021, https://www.heyalma.com/asian-jews-deserve-better/; Helen Kim and Noah Leavitt, *JewAsian: Race, Religion, and Identity for America's Newest Jews* (University of Nebraska Press, 2016); and Samira Mehta, "Asian American Jews, Race, and Religious Identity," *Journal of the American Academy of Religion* 89, no. 3 (2021): 978–1005.

25 Kohut, *My Portion*, 57.

26 This book thus continues a project I began in my first monograph, *The White Negress: Literature, Minstrelsy, and the Black-Jewish Imaginary* (Rutgers University Press, 2011).

27 For an article-length consideration of Jewish American literature and the Western frontier that considers Rachel Calof's *My Story: Jewish Homesteader on the Northern Plains*, see Debra Shein, "Isaac Raboy's *Der Yiddisher Cowboy* and Rachel Calof's *My Story*: The Role of the Western Frontier in Shaping Jewish American Identity," *Western American Literature* 36, no. 4 (2002): 359–80.

28 This scholarship includes monographs such as Koffman's *The Jews' Indian*; Shari Rabin's *Jews on the Frontier: Religion and Mobility in Nineteenth-Century America* (New York University Press, 2017); Sarah Imhoff's *Masculinity and the Making of American Judaism* (Indiana University Press, 2017); Jeanne Abrams's *Jewish Women Pioneering the Frontier Trail: A History in the American West* (New York University Press, 2006); Fred Rosenbaum's *Cosmopolitans: A Social and Cultural History of the Jews of the San Francisco Bay Area* (University of California Press, 2009); and Deborah Dash Moore's *To the Golden Cities: Pursuing the American Dream in Miami and L.A.* (Free Press, 1994) in addition to edited volumes such as *Transnational Traditions: New Perspectives on American Jewish History* (Wayne State University Press, 2014), edited by Ava F. Kahn and Adam D. Mendelsohn; *Jews of the Pacific Coast: Reinventing Community on America's Edge* (University of Washington Press, 2010), edited by Ava F. Kahn, Ellen Eisenberg, and

William Toll; *California Jews* (Brandeis University Press, 2003), edited by Ava F. Kahn and Marc Dollinger; and *Jewish Life in the American West: Perspectives on Migration, Settlement, and Community* (University of Washington Press, 2002), edited by Ava F. Kahn. See also Harriet Rochlin and Fred Rochlin, *Pioneer Jews: A New Life in the Far West* (Houghton Mifflin, 1984).

29 Rosenbaum, *Cosmopolitans*, 69–100.

30 Rosenbaum, *Cosmopolitans*, 69.

31 Ava F. Kahn, introduction to *Jewish Voices of the California Gold Rush: A Documentary History, 1849–1880*, ed. Ava F. Kahn (Wayne State University Press, 2002), 38. See also Robert Levinson, *The Jews in the California Gold Rush* (Ktav, 1978).

32 For demographic data, see Jackie Krentzman, dir., *American Jerusalem: Jews and the Making of San Francisco* (National Center for Jewish Film, 2013) and its accompanying website https://www.americanjerusalem.com/story-summary, accessed July 17, 2024.

33 Moses Rischin, "The Jewish Experience in America: A View from the West," in *Jews of the American West*, eds. Moses Rischin and John Livingston (Wayne State University Press, 1991), 32.

34 Kahn, introduction to *Jewish Voices of the California Gold Rush*, 39–40.

35 Rabin, *Jews on the Frontier*, 7.

36 Abrams, *Jewish Women Pioneering the Frontier Trail*, 19, 12, 20.

37 On Ray Frank, see Shari Rabin, "'The Advent of a Western Jewess': Rachel Frank and Jewish Female Celebrity in 1890s America," *Nashim* 22 (2011): 111–35; Reva and William M. Kramer. "The Girl Rabbi of the Golden West: The Adventurous Life of Ray Frank in Nevada, California, and the Northwest," *Western States Jewish History*, 28, no. 2 (1986): 99–111, 223–36, 336–51; and Antler, *The Journey Home*, 8–10.

38 Abrams, *Jewish Women Pioneering the Frontier Trail*, 11.

39 Edward Zerin, *Jewish San Francisco* (Arcadia Publishing, 2006), 19. For further discussion of antisemitism in the United States and particularly in San Francisco, see Peter Decker, *Fortunes and Failures: White-Collar Mobility in Nineteenth-Century San Francisco* (Harvard University Press, 1978), especially chapters 5 and 9; Tony Fels, "Religious Assimilation in a Fraternal Organization: Jews and Freemasonry in Gilded-Age San Francisco," *American Jewish History* 74, no. 4 (1985): 369–403; Naomi Cohen, *Encounter with Emancipation: The German Jews in the United*

States, 1830–1914 (JPS, 1984): 224–31; Naomi Cohen, "Anti-Semitism in the Gilded Age: The Jewish View," in *Essential Papers on Jewish-Christian Relations in the United States*, ed. Naomi Cohen (New York University Press, 1990); Leonard Dinnerstein, *Anti-Semitism in America* (Oxford University Press, 1994); Ralph Mann, "Frontier Opportunity and the New Social History," *Pacific Historical Review* 53, no. 4 (1984): 463–91; Michael Dobkowski, *The Tarnished Dream: The Basis of American Anti-Semitism* (Greenwood Press, 1979); and Warren C. Wood, "S. An-Sky's *The Dybbuk* and the Process of Jewish American Identity in 1920s San Francisco," *California History*, 99, no. 2 (May 2022): 32–58.

40 Marc Dollinger, foreword to Zerin, *Jewish San Francisco*, 7.

41 Kohut, *My Portion*, 62.

42 See Harley Erdman, *Staging the Jew: The Performance of an American Ethnicity, 1860–1920* (Rutgers University Press, 1997). Several of the essays in Michael Shapiro and Edna Nahshon's *Wrestling with Shylock: Jewish Responses to "The Merchant of Venice"* (Cambridge University Press, 2017) deal with the popularity of *The Merchant of Venice* in the United States; see, for example, Nahshon, "The Anti-Shylock Campaign in America," 33–48. Emma Wolf, for example, certainly had the stage Jew in mind when she crafted her own Jewish characters. In a pivotal scene in her first novel, *Other Things Being Equal*, the characters attend a performance of *The Merchant of Venice* starring Edwin Booth as Shylock. This episode in the novel was likely inspired by Booth's famous 1889 performance as Shylock at the California Theater, which Wolf attended.

43 For an examination of visual representations of Jews in the American press of the period, see Matthew Baigell, *The Implacable Urge to Defame: Cartoon Jews in the American Press, 1877–1935* (Syracuse University Press, 2017).

44 See Donald Pizer, *American Naturalism and the Jews: Garland, Norris, Dreiser, Wharton, and Cather* (University of Illinois Press, 2008). See also Pizer, "A Note on S. Behrman as a Jew in Frank Norris's *The Octopus*," *Studies in American Naturalism* 6, no. 1 (Summer 2011): 88–91.

45 Frank Norris, *McTeague: A Story of San Francisco* (1899; repr., Signet, 1981), 37–38.

46 Elisa New, "My Favorite Anti-Semite: Frank Norris and the Most Horrifying Jew in American Literature," *Tablet*, October 24, 2013, https://

www.tabletmag.com/sections/arts-letters/articles/mcteague-frank-norris, accessed July 17, 2024.

47 Josephine Lazarus, "Judaism, Old and New," in Lazarus, *The Spirit of Judaism* (Dodd, Mead, 1895), 70–71. Notably, the decades immediately following the Civil War saw the emergence of a Jewish American poetic tradition dominated by the work of women poets such as Emma Lazarus, Penina Moise, Minna Cohen Kleeberg, and Adah Isaacs Menken (whose Jewish ancestry is uncertain).

48 On feminist literary recovery as an ongoing project, see Sharon M. Harris, "'Across the Gulf': Working in the 'Post-Recovery' Era," *Legacy* 26, no. 2 (2009): 284–98.

49 See Tillie Olsen, *Silences* (Feminist Press, 2003) as well as the similarly influential *How to Suppress Women's Writing* (University of Texas Press, 2018), which was originally published in 1983 by Jewish American feminist science fiction writer Joanna Russ.

50 On Kessler-Harris's discovery of Yezierska, see Tony Michels, Lara Vapnek, and Annie Polland, "An Interview with Alice Kessler-Harris," *Jewish Social Studies* 24, no. 2 (Winter 2019): 72–105. Yezierska's status as *the* foremother of Jewish American fiction has been challenged by recovery efforts centering on Emma Wolf as well as Jonathan Sarna's recent work on Cora Wilburn. Sarna's recovery of Wilburn's serialized 1860 novel *Cosella Wayne; Or, Will and Destiny* (University of Alabama Press, 2019) points to periodical culture as an untapped resource for piecing together a more comprehensive genealogy of Jewish American women's writing. On Wolf, see, for example, Barbara Cantalupo and Lori Harrison-Kahan, introduction to Emma Wolf, *Heirs of Yesterday* (Wayne State University Press, 2020): 1–79; Lori Harrison-Kahan, "'A Grave Experiment': Emma Wolf's Marriage Plots and the Deghettoization of American Jewish Fiction," *American Jewish History* 101, no. 1 (January 2017): 5–34; Jessica Kirzane, "Women, Love, and the Reform Jewish Mission: Jewish-Christian Marriage in Emma Wolf's *Other Things Being Equal* and Its Literary Successors," *American Jewish History*, 104, nos. 2–3 (April–July 2020): 289–322; and Josh Lambert, "The Jewish Jane Austen Whose Novels Were Almost Forgotten," *Lilith* 46, no. 1 (Spring 2021): 23–25. For an earlier consideration of Wolf alongside other nineteenth-century Jewish American women writers, see Diane Lichtenstein, *Writing Their Nations: The Tradition*

of Nineteenth-Century American Jewish Women Writers (Indiana University Press, 1992). On *Cosella Wayne*, see Jonathan D. Sarna, "The Forgetting of Cora Wilburn: Historical Amnesia and *The Cambridge History of Jewish American Literature*," *Studies in American Jewish Literature* 37, no. 1 (Spring 2018): 73–87.

51 See, for example, Lichtenstein, *Writing Their Nations*; Janet Handler Burstein, *Writing Mothers, Writing Daughters: Tracing the Maternal in Stories by American Jewish Women* (University of Illinois Press, 1996); Ellen Serlen Uffen, *Strands of the Cable: The Place of the Past in Jewish American Women's Writing* (Peter Lang, 1992); and Ann Shapiro, ed., *Jewish American Women Writers: A Bio-Bibliographical and Critical Sourcebook* (Greenwood, 1994).

52 Rachel Rubinstein, "'Oyb me zukht gefint men': Translating Yiddish Literature Hidden in Plain Sight," in Atura Bushnell, Harrison-Kahan, and Walters, *Matrilineal Dissent*, 149. See also Anita Norich, "Translating and Teaching Yiddish Prose by Women," *In geveb*, April 2, 2020, https://ingeveb.org/blog/translating-and-teaching-yiddish-prose-by-women, accessed July 18, 2024.

53 Atura Bushnell, Harrison-Kahan, and Walters, introduction to Atura Bushnell, Harrison-Kahan, and Walters, *Matrilineal Dissent*, 3.

54 Allison Schachter, *Women Writing Jewish Modernity, 1919–1939* (Northwestern University Press, 2021), 4.

55 See Lori Harrison-Kahan, "Pioneering Women Writers and the Deghettoisation of Early Jewish American Fiction," in *The Edinburgh Companion to Modern Jewish Fiction*, eds. David Brauner and Axel Stähler (Edinburgh University Press, 2015), 19–32; and Kirzane, "Women, Love, and the Reform Jewish Mission: Jewish-Christian Marriage in Emma Wolf's *Other Things Being Equal* and Its Literary Successors," 289–322.

56 Emma Wolf, *Other Things Being Equal* (1892; repr., Wayne State University Press, 2002), 254.

Chapter 1

1 William Dean Howells, "Editor's Easy Chair," *Harper's Monthly Magazine*, May 1915, 959.

2 William Dean Howells, "New York Low Life in Fiction," *New York World*, July 26, 1896, 18.

3 In the late nineteenth and early twentieth centuries, Jewish American writers were accused of contracting "Zangwillitis." See, for example, "Jewish Writers in the New World," *Public Opinion*, December 14, 1904, 753–54.

4 Quoted in "Chronicle and Comment," *Bookman*, January 1900, 428–29.

5 Annie Nathan Meyer, "Concerning Sensitive Epiderms," *Bookman*, February 1900, 532–34. Meyer was to come back to this topic four years later when she published a letter in *The New York Times Book Review* in response to Edith Wharton's depiction of a money-grubbing Jewish art dealer in her 1904 story "The Pot-Boiler." Questioning why "the mediaeval Jew of letters" still dominates literature of the day, Meyer called for a writer who possessed "the delightful certainty of Mrs. Wharton's art" to paint a realistic portrait, suggesting, for example, that the Jewish patron of the arts would make a suitable and more accurate subject for literature. See Annie Nathan Meyer, "Shepson in 'The Pot-Boiler,'" *New York Times*, December 10, 1904, 871.

6 Meyer, "Concerning Sensitive Epiderms," 534. Neither of Meyer's two novels features explicitly Jewish characters, but some of her short stories do. See, for example, Annie Nathan Meyer, "Henry Brooke, Jr.," *The American Jewess*, December 1895, 123–27, which is about an upper-class Jew who passes for gentile in order to be admitted to his college's drama club, and Annie Nathan Meyer, "The Shoe Pinches Mr. Samuels," *The Crisis*, January 1935, 8–9, 24–25, which features a Southern rabbi who must convince his congregation to speak out against the lynching of African Americans before Jews become the next target of racial violence. For more on Meyer's representations of Jewishness, see Lori Harrison-Kahan, "Where the Shoe Pinches: Appropriation and Allyship in Annie Nathan Meyer's Anti-Lynching Literature," in *Matrilineal Dissent: Women Writers and Jewish American Literary History*, eds. Annie Atura Bushnell, Lori Harrison-Kahan, and Ashley Walters (Wayne State University Press, 2024), 71–109.

7 "Miss Wolf's New Story," *Jewish Messenger*, December 14, 1900, 1.

8 Israel Zangwill, "A New Jewish Novelist," *The Jewish Chronicle*, February 5, 1897, 19; "Book Brieflets," *The American Jewess*, February 1897, 236.

9 For notable exceptions, see Jessica Kirzane, "Women, Love, and the Reform Jewish Mission: Jewish-Christian Marriage in Emma Wolf's

Other Things Being Equal and Its Literary Successors," *American Jewish History*, 104, nos. 2–3 (April–July 2020): 289–322; Barbara Cantalupo, "Discovering Emma Wolf, San Francisco Author," *CCAR Journal: A Reform Jewish Quarterly* 51, no. 1 (Winter 2004): 77–84; Barbara Cantalupo, "Emma Wolf's *Heirs of Yesterday* and the Jewish Community in the Late Nineteenth Century," *Studies in American Jewish Literature* 22 (2003): 145–53; and Diane Lichtenstein, *Writing Their Nations: The Tradition of Nineteenth-Century American Jewish Women Writers* (Indiana University Press, 1992). There is also evidence that Wolf received attention during her lifetime from scholars interested in Jewish fiction. For instance, her work was included on a syllabus for a course on "Jewish Characters in Fiction" for the Jewish Chautauqua Society, which was first published in 1903 and revised in 1911 by Rabbi Harry Levi; see Harry Levi, "Lesson XIV: 'The Heirs of Yesterday,' Emma Wolf," *Jewish Characters in Fiction: English Literature* (Jewish Chautauqua Society, 1911), 138–49.

10 See, for example, Clare Virginia Eby, *Until Choice Do Us Part: Marriage Reform in the Progressive Era* (University of Chicago Press, 2014). For a discussion of marriage plots in nineteenth- and twentieth-century Jewish literature, see Naomi Seidman, *The Marriage Plot: Or, How Jews Fell in Love with Love, and with Literature* (Stanford University Press, 2016).

11 See Anne C. Rose, *Beloved Strangers: Interfaith Families in Nineteenth-Century America* (Harvard University Press, 2001) and Keren R. McGinity, *Still Jewish: A History of Women and Intermarriage in America* (New York University Press, 2009).

12 See Paul R. Spickard, *Mixed Blood: Intermarriage and Ethnic Identity in Twentieth-Century America* (University of Wisconsin Press, 1989).

13 Most rabbis, including Isaac Mayer Wise, architect of the Reform movement, did not sanction intermarriage. Although Jacob Voorsanger, the rabbi of Wolf's synagogue, Temple Emanu-El, was known to perform intermarriages, they were rare among the congregation's elite Jews. See Fred Rosenbaum, *Visions of Reform: Congregation Emanu-El and the Jews of San Francisco, 1849–1999* (Judah L. Magnes, 2000), 61, 84.

14 Most existing surveys of prewar Jewish American fiction position ghetto narratives as an origin point. See, for example, Jules Chametzky, "Main Currents in American Jewish Literature from the

1880's to the 1950's (and Beyond)," *Ethnic Groups* 4 (1982): 85–101; Stanley Chyet, "Three Generations: An Account of American Jewish Fiction (1896–1969)," *Jewish Social Studies* 34, no. 1 (1972): 31–41; Leslie Fiedler, "Genesis: The American-Jewish Novel Through the Twenties," *Midstream* 4 (Summer 1958): 21–33; David Fine, "In the Beginning: American-Jewish Fiction, 1880–1930," in *Handbook of American Jewish Literature*, ed. Lewis Fried (Greenwood, 1988), 15–34; Solomon Liptzin, *The Jew in American Literature* (Bloch, 1966); Louis Harap, *Creative Awakening: The Jewish Presence in Twentieth-Century American Literature, 1900–1940s* (Greenwood, 1987); Louis Harap, *The Image of the Jew in American Literature: From Early Republic to Mass Immigration* (Jewish Publication Society of America, 1974); Sanford Marovitz, "Images of America in American-Jewish Fiction," in Fried, *Handbook of American Jewish Literature*, 315–56; Sanford Marovitz, "New York and Others: Regionalism in Early American-Jewish Literature," *Yiddish* 7, no. 4 (1990): 19–27; and Sanford Sternlicht, *The Tenement Saga: The Lower East Side and Early Jewish American Writers* (University of Wisconsin Press, 2004). For some interesting early attempts to offer more comprehensive and diverse surveys of early Jewish American writing, see Ludwig Lewisohn, "A Panorama of a Half-Century of American Jewish Literature," *Jewish Book Annual* 9 (1951): 3–10, and Florence Kiper Frank, "The Presentment of the Jew in American Fiction," *Bookman* 71, no. 3 (1930): 270–75.

15 On Wolf's fame as an early Jewish American novelist, see Josephine Lazarus, *The Spirit of Judaism* (Dodd, Mead, 1895), 70–100, and D. G. Myers, "Emma Wolf's Stories," http://dgmyers.blogspot.com/2010/05/emma-wolfs-stories.html, accessed July 17, 2024. Myers argues that Wolf is "the mother of American Jewish fiction," since *Other Things Being Equal*, published by the "Christian-owned house of A. C. McClurg," was "the first American novel written by a Jew, on a Jewish subject, but aimed at a general audience." This designation has since been challenged by Jonathan Sarna's recovery of Cora Wilburn's work, especially her novel *Cosella Wayne*, which was serialized in the spiritualist journal *Banner of Light* in 1860. See Sarna, "The Forgetting of Cora Wilburn: Historical Amnesia and *The Cambridge History of Jewish American Literature*," *Studies in American Jewish Literature* 37, no. 1 (Spring 2018): 73–87.

16 Rosenbaum, *Visions of Reform*, 16. In addition to conducting services primarily in English, nineteenth-century Reformers instituted the use of the organ during services, loosened or eliminated dietary restrictions, and expanded the role of women in the synagogue, allowing mixed seating and counting women in a minyan.
17 Marc Lee Raphael, "Rabbi Jacob Voorsanger of San Francisco on Jews and Judaism: The Implications of the Pittsburgh Platform," *American Jewish Historical Quarterly* 63, no. 2 (1973): 191, 192, 203.
18 Alan Silverstein, *Alternatives to Assimilation: The Response of Reform Judaism to American Culture, 1840–1930* (Brandeis University Press, 1994). See also Fred Rosenbaum, *Cosmopolitans: A Social and Cultural History of the Jews of the San Francisco Bay Area* (University of California Press, 2009) and *Visions of Reform*.
19 See Barbara Cantalupo, introduction to Emma Wolf, *Other Things Being Equal* (1892; repr., Wayne State University Press, 2002), 9–53, and William Tornheim, "Pioneer Jews of Contra Costa," *Western States Jewish History* 16, no. 1 (1983): 3–22.
20 For more on how Wolf's disability enabled her career, see Lori Harrison-Kahan, "We Shouldn't Ignore This Groundbreaking Jewish Novelist's Disability," *Hey Alma* (June 21, 2021), https://www.heyalma.com/we-shouldnt-ignore-this-groundbreaking-jewish-novelists-disability/, accessed July 17, 2024.
21 Emma Wolf, "One-Eye, Two-Eye, Three-Eye," *The American Jewess*, January 1896, 279–90.
22 Given the dates, it is unlikely that Alice's marriage to a Christian directly inspired *Other Things Being Equal*, as Barbara Cantalupo claims in her introduction to *Other Things Being Equal*, but the existence of the novel and the fact of her sister's marriage together suggest the timeliness of the intermarriage theme. One announcement of Alice's marriage, for example, stated that it was "proof of [Emma Wolf's] theory" in *Other Things Being Equal* "that religious scruples must give way before the impulses of the human heart." See "MacDonald Will Marry To-morrow," *San Francisco Chronicle*, July 19, 1898, 11.
23 See Emma Wolf, *Fulfillment: A California Novel* (Henry Holt, 1916).
24 Wolf, *Other Things Being Equal*, 184.
25 Wolf, *Other Things Being Equal*, 254.

26 Fiedler, "Genesis," 21–33.

27 Frederic Cople Jaher, "The Quest for the Ultimate *Shiksa*," *American Quarterly* 35, no. 5 (1983): 518–42. Such tropes have made a comeback in popular culture today; the 2024 Netflix romantic comedy *Nobody Wants This* (which was originally titled *Shiksa*), for example, has generated fierce debate about the way it depicts Jewish women as undesirable marriage partners for Jewish men (in this case, a rabbi), pitting them against "shiksas." See, for instance, Esther Zuckerman, "Nobody Wants This Mean-Spirited Depiction of Jewish Women in *Nobody Wants This*," *Time*, September 26, 2024, https://time.com/7023404/nobody-wants-this-netflix-jewish-women/, accessed January 4, 2025.

28 Anzia Yezierska, *Salome of the Tenements* (1923; repr., University of Illinois Press, 1995), 26.

29 Yezierska, *Salome of the Tenements*, 147.

30 Adam Sol, "Longings and Renunciations: Attitudes Towards Intermarriage in Early Twentieth Century Jewish American Novels," *American Jewish History* 89, no. 2 (2001): 215–30.

31 See also Kirzane, "Women, Love, and the Reform Jewish Mission"; Ann Shapiro, "The Ultimate *Shaygets* and the Fiction of Anzia Yezierska," *MELUS* 21, no. 2 (1996): 79–88; and Josh Lambert, *Unclean Lips: Obscenity, Jews, and American Culture* (New York University Press, 2014), 118–30. Ted Merwin offers a useful consideration of the meanings of intermarriage in American popular culture; see Merwin, "The Performance of Jewish Ethnicity in Anne Nichols' *Abie's Irish Rose*," *Journal of American Ethnic History* 20, no. 2 (Winter 2001): 3–37.

32 Wolf, *Other Things Being Equal*, 266.

33 Wolf, *Other Things Being Equal*, 253–54.

34 Wolf, *Other Things Being Equal*, 70.

35 Wolf, *Other Things Being Equal*, 64, 68.

36 Eric L. Goldstein, *The Price of Whiteness: Jews, Race, and American Identity* (Princeton University Press, 2006), 5.

37 Goldstein, *The Price of Whiteness*, 20.

38 Goldstein, *The Price of Whiteness*, 99. In his 1914 afterword to *The Melting Pot*, Zangwill addressed this common misinterpretation of his melting pot theory, differentiating "the process of American amalgamation" from "assimilation or simple surrender to the dominant type." Instead, he describes the amalgamation of the melting pot in

terms more often associated with theories of transnationalism and pluralism, as "an all-around give-and-take by which the final type may be enriched or impoverished." See Zangwill 's afterword reprinted as appendix E of *From the Ghetto to the Melting Pot: Israel Zangwill's Jewish Plays*, ed. Edna Nahshon (Wayne State University Press, 2006), 379–82.

39 Wolf, *Other Things Being Equal*, 267. It is worth noting, however, that this final line was one of the few additions that Wolf made when she published the revised edition of *Other Things Being Equal* in 1916, a change that seems to leave readers with some uncertainty about the couple's future. Thanks to Barbara Cantalupo for pointing out the difference between the two versions.

40 Wolf, *Other Things Being Equal*, 184.

41 Wolf, *Other Things Being Equal*, 194.

42 Wolf, *Other Things Being Equal*, 238.

43 Meyer, "Concerning Sensitive Epiderms," 533.

44 Wolf, *Other Things Being Equal*, 104.

45 Annie Josephine Levi, "Intermarriage," *The American Hebrew*, May 22, 1896, 73.

46 On Wolf's popularity among women's clubs, see Anne Ruggles Gere, *Intimate Practices: Literacy and Cultural Work in U.S. Women's Clubs, 1880–1920* (University of Illinois Press, 1997), 220–21.

47 "Writes About Home: Emma Wolf and Her Two Books," *San Francisco Chronicle*, July 15, 1894, 2.

48 Wolf seems to have had some difficulty publishing her Jewish-themed work. According to Jonathan Sarna, the Jewish Publication Society (JPS) rejected one of Wolf's manuscripts in 1894 because "some of the characters [are] immoral and the Rabbi hero impossible . . . whenever a traditional Jewish custom is discussed in the book, the Rabbi declares himself conscientiously unable to observe it." Quoted in Jonathan D. Sarna, *JPS: The Americanization of Jewish Culture, 1888–1988* (Jewish Publication Society, 1989), 80. Sarna further notes that Wolf submitted one of her works to a JPS prize competition for "the best story relating to a Jewish subject suited to young readers" in 1897; though Wolf's story was one of the top two submissions, the committee could not reach a consensus and decided not to award a prize. Quoted in Sarna, *JPS*, 86.

Neither of the two manuscripts Sarna mentions made their way into print, and the manuscripts are no longer extant. For a fuller discussion of Wolf's attempts to publish Jewish-themed work with the JPS, see Barbara Cantalupo and Lori Harrison-Kahan, introduction to Emma Wolf, *Heirs of Yesterday* (Wayne State University Press, 2020), 25–50.

49 Mrs. I. Lowenberg, "The Philomath Club," in *Western Jewry: An Account of the Achievements of Jews and Judaism in California* (Temple Emanu-El, 1916), 57–58.

50 "The Philomath Club: Its First Open Meeting at the Palace Yesterday," *The San Francisco Call*, January 15, 1895, 12.

51 Later, the San Francisco branch of the NCJW provided a platform for her literary endeavors, as evidenced by her collaboration with fellow member Ada Goldsmith on *The Spell of the Spanish Shawl*, a patriotic play celebrating the United States as an American Zion. Ada Goldsmith and Emma Wolf, "Spell of the Spanish Shawl—Scripts and Programs, 1926," National Council of Jewish Women, San Francisco Section Records, 1897–2010, Carton 7, Folder 44, Bancroft Library, University of California, Berkeley.

52 Barbara Cantalupo, "The Letters of Israel Zangwill to Emma Wolf: Transatlantic Mentoring in the 1890s," *Resources for American Literary Study* 28 (2002): 121–38.

53 On Zangwill, see, Meri-Jane Rochelson, *A Jew in the Public Arena: The Career of Israel Zangwill* (Wayne State University Press, 2008).

54 Israel Zangwill to Emma Wolf, December 2, 1896. All of Zangwill's letters to Wolf cited in this chapter can be found in Cantalupo, "The Letters of Israel Zangwill to Emma Wolf," 121–38.

55 Zangwill, "A New Jewish Novelist," 19.

56 Israel Zangwill, "In the World of Art and Letters," *Cosmopolitan*, April 1897, 690.

57 Israel Zangwill to Emma Wolf, February 5, 1897. For evidence that Wolf had already thought to try the *Jewish Publication Society*, see Cantalupo and Harrison-Kahan, introduction to Emma Wolf, *Heirs of Yesterday*, 25–50.

58 Israel Zangwill to Emma Wolf, August 22, 1897.

59 See Horace Kallen, "Democracy Versus the Melting-Pot," *The Nation*, February 25, 1915, 217–20.

60 Israel Zangwill, *The Melting Pot* (1908), in *From the Ghetto to the Melting Pot: Israel Zangwill's Jewish Plays*, ed. Edna Nahshon (Wayne State University Press, 2006), 271.
61 Zangwill, *The Melting Pot*, 288.
62 Zangwill, *The Melting Pot*, 363.
63 Werner Sollors, *Beyond Ethnicity: Consent and Descent in American Culture* (Oxford University Press, 1986), 72.
64 Zangwill, *The Melting Pot*, 332.
65 Zangwill, *The Melting Pot*, 363.
66 Israel Zangwill to Emma Wolf, December 12, 1900.
67 Emma Wolf, *Heirs of Yesterday* (A. C. McClurg, 1900), 7.
68 Israel Zangwill, *Dreamers of the Ghetto* (Jewish Publication Society, 1898), 20.
69 Wolf, *Heirs of Yesterday*, 35, 37, 35.
70 Wolf, *Heirs of Yesterday*, 32–33.
71 Abraham Cahan, *The Rise of David Levinsky* (1917; repr., Harper Torchbooks, 1960), 194.
72 Wolf, *Heirs of Yesterday*, 63, 52.
73 Wolf, *Heirs of Yesterday*, 59.
74 Wolf, *Heirs of Yesterday*, 100.
75 Wolf, *Heirs of Yesterday*, 128.
76 Wolf, *Heirs of Yesterday*, 144.
77 Wolf, *Heirs of Yesterday*, 235. On Reform Judaism, see also Dana Evan Kaplan, *American Reform Judaism: An Introduction* (Rutgers University Press, 2003) and Jonathan D. Sarna, *American Judaism* (Yale University Press, 2004), 82–88 and 144–51. The reference to Friday night services is significant, given the likelihood that Wolf's congregation, Temple Emanu-El, was the first synagogue in the United States to hold services on the evening of the Sabbath. See Rosenbaum, *Visions of Reform*, 46.
78 Wolf, *Heirs of Yesterday*, 285.
79 Sollors, *Beyond Ethnicity*, 72.
80 Zangwill, *The Melting Pot*, 363.
81 Israel Zangwill to Emma Wolf, May 14, 1898.
82 Wolf, *Heirs of Yesterday*, 285.
83 Jeanne Abrams, "Remembering the Maine: The Jewish Attitude Toward the Spanish-American War as Reflected in *The American Israelite*," *American Jewish History* 76, no. 4 (June 1987), 440, 444.

84 Wolf, *Heirs of Yesterday*, 261.

85 Seymour "Sy" Brody, *Jewish Heroes and Heroines of America* (Frederick Fell, 2004), 104; "Col. Joseph M. Heller Dies; Doctor in Two U.S. Wars," *Washington Post*, October 12, 1943, 8.

86 Wolf, *Heirs of Yesterday*, 268, 263–64.

87 Wolf, *Heirs of Yesterday*, 275.

88 Wolf, *Heirs of Yesterday*, 100, 109.

89 See Matthew Frye Jacobson, *Whiteness of a Different Color: European Immigrants and the Alchemy of Race* (Harvard University Press, 1998); Michael Rogin, *Blackface, White Noise: Jewish Immigrants in the Hollywood Melting Pot* (University of California Press, 1996); and Lori Harrison-Kahan, *The White Negress: Literature, Minstrelsy, and the Black-Jewish Imaginary* (Rutgers University Press, 2011).

90 William R. Handley, *Marriage, Violence, and the Nation in the American Literary West* (Cambridge University Press, 2002), 4.

91 Frederick Jackson Turner, *The Frontier in American History* (Henry Holt, 1920), 2–3.

92 Wolf, *Other Things Being Equal*, 61.

93 "Emma Wolf, Author of Fulfillment," *Chicago Daily Tribune*, May 6, 1916, 7.

94 "Emma Wolf, Beloved S. F. Author, Dead," *San Francisco Chronicle*, August 31, 1932, 9. In actuality, Wolf's confinement was probably not as extreme as this obituary suggests. She may have become more reclusive with time, but there is evidence that she maintained her connection to Jewish life and culture in particular. She was involved in the San Francisco branch of the NCJW through the 1920s, and she presented on the topic of literature at the Western Assembly of the Jewish Chautauqua Society in 1920. As late as 1922, she continued to be listed as an associate member of the Philomath Club.

Chapter 2

1 See Jewish Women's Congress, *Papers of the Jewish Women's Congress [Held at Chicago, September 4, 5, 6, and 7, 1893]* (Jewish Publication Society of America, 1894); Deborah Grand Golomb, "The 1893 Congress of Jewish Women: Evolution or Revolution in American Jewish Women's History?" *American Jewish History* 70, no. 1 (September

1980): 52–67; and Faith Rogow, *Gone to Another Meeting: The National Council of Jewish Women, 1893–1993* (University of Alabama Press, 1993).

2 Mrs. I. Lowenberg, "The Philomath Club," in *Western Jewry: An Account of the Achievements of Jews and Judaism in California* (Temple Emanu-El, 1916), 57–58.

3 "The Philomath Club: Its First Open Meeting at the Palace Yesterday," *The San Francisco Call*, January 15, 1895, 12. As I discuss in the following chapter, Levy was well known at the time as a writer of social sketches for *The Wave*, the weekly literary journal that also gave Frank Norris his start. Later in life, she published poetry and a memoir, *920 O'Farrell Street: A Jewish Girlhood in Old San Francisco* (Heyday Books, 1996).

4 This chapter thus contributes to scholarship that offers new perspectives on Jewish American literature, Jewish American writers, and the relationship between Jewishness and American literature through institutional analyses. For recent examples, see Josh Lambert, *The Literary Mafia: Jews, Publishing, and Postwar American Literature* (Yale University Press, 2022), and chapter 1 of Laura R. Fisher, *Reading for Reform: The Social Work of Literature in the Progressive Era* (University of Minnesota Press, 2019), which focuses on the institution of the settlement house as a site of Jewish literary production.

5 "Not All Natives," *Town Talk*, October 26, 1918, in Bettie Lowenberg Scrapbook (1915–), Oversize Box 1, Bancroft Library, University of California, Berkeley.

6 See John P. Marschall, *Jews in Nevada: A History* (University of Nevada Press, 2008).

7 On Isidor Lowenberg's business ventures, see Michael Harris, *Jeans of the Old West* (Schiffer, 2016), 117–18. In 1879, for example, Isidor Lowenberg applied for a patent for overalls in an effort to differentiate his jeans from those of Levi Strauss.

8 "In a Bower of Blossoms," *The San Francisco Call*, March 25, 1896, 13; "Splashes," *The Wave*, January 18, 1896, 11.

9 Albert Nelson Marquis, ed., *Who's Who in America*, vol. 9 (A. N. Marquis, 1916–17), 1523; Lowenberg, "The Philomath Club," 57–58; "The Philomath Club," *The San Francisco Call*, January 15, 1895, 12.

10 Karen J. Blair, *The Clubwoman as Feminist: True Womanhood Redefined, 1868–1914* (Holmes and Meier, 1980), 1, 5.

11 Anne Ruggles Gere, *Intimate Practices: Literacy and Cultural Work in U.S. Women's Clubs, 1880–1920* (University of Illinois Press, 1997), 2, 44, 53. Like Gere's *Intimate Practices*, Barbara Sicherman's *Well-Read Lives: How Books Inspired a Generation of American Women* (University of North Carolina Press, 2010) includes Jewish women and Jewish women's clubs in its consideration of the literacy practices of nineteenth-century American women, but neither scholar addresses the club movement in California specifically.

12 See Evelyn Brooks Higginbottom, *Righteous Discontent: The Women's Movement in the Black Baptist Church, 1880–1920* (Harvard University Press, 1994) and Elizabeth McHenry, *Forgotten Readers: Recovering the Lost History of African American Literary Societies* (Duke University Press, 2002).

13 Selma Berrol, "Class or Ethnicity: The Americanized German Jewish Woman and Her Middle Class Sisters in 1895," *Jewish Social Studies* 47 (Winter 1985): 23. On Jewish women's clubs, see also William Toll, "A Quiet Revolution: Jewish Women's Clubs and the Widening Female Sphere, 1897–1920," *American Jewish Archives* 41, no. 1 (Spring–Summer 1989): 7–26; and Pamela Nadell, "The Pioneers: The Oldest Jewish Women's Book Club in America," *Paper Brigade Daily*, May 11, 2020, https://www.jewishbookcouncil.org/pb-daily/the-pioneers-the-oldest-jewish-womens-book-club-in-america, accessed July 18, 2024.

14 Gere, *Intimate Practices*, 6, 23.

15 Gere, *Intimate Practices*, 87, 92.

16 Lowenberg, "The Philomath Club," 57–58.

17 "The Philomath Club," *The San Francisco Call*, January 15, 1895, 12.

18 Florence Collins Porter, ed., "Chats About Clubs and Club Women," *Los Angeles Herald*, January 27, 1901, 3.

19 Sarah Comstock, "The Best Known Club Women of the Pacific Coast," *The San Francisco Call*, November 24, 1901, 7.

20 Charles G. Bush, "Sorosis, 1869," *Harper's Weekly*, May 15, 1869, 312. For an image of the cartoon, see https://www.masshist.org/database/viewer.php?item_id=5887&mode=large&img_step=1&&pid=41, accessed July 18, 2024.

21 See Florence Collins Porter, ed., "Chats About Women and Women's Clubs," *Los Angeles Herald*, February 16, 1902, 3; and "Color Line

Drawn by Club Women," *Los Angeles Times*, February 8, 1902, 3. On racism within white women's clubs, especially in the American South, see, Jean Lee Cole et al., introduction to *Parole Femine: Words and Lives of the Woman's Literary Club of Baltimore* (Apprentice House, 2019), xxiii–xxv.

22 Gere, *Intimate Practices*, 80.

23 *The Daily Palo Alto* (now the *Stanford Daily*) included notices when professors lectured to women's clubs. "Quads," *Daily Palo Alto*, September 13, 1897, 4; "Quads," *Daily Palo Alto*, November 5, 1897, 1; "Quads," *Daily Palo Alto*, October 12, 1899, 1; "Quads," *Daily Palo Alto*, February 7, 1898, 4; "Quads," *Daily Palo Alto*, March 16, 1898, 1; "Quads," *Daily Palo Alto*, October 18, 1900, 1.

24 See "Kahn Tells of Washington Life: Interesting Lecture by the Congressman Before Philomath Club," *San Francisco Chronicle*, November 11, 1902, 12; Laura Bride Powers, "California Club Is Reconciled to New Officers," *The San Francisco Call*, May 9, 1904, 5; and "U.S. Will Be Paying War Debt for 100 Years, Says Kahn," *San Francisco Chronicle*, October 11, 1921, 6. In 1903, Florence Prag Kahn was elected as the club's second president and Lowenberg was made honorary president. See "Mrs. Lowenberg Honored," *San Francisco Chronicle*, September 15, 1903, 10. In 1925, Florence Prag Kahn became the first Jewish woman to serve in Congress when she took over her deceased husband's seat.

25 "Slaves of the Theater and Not Patrons of the Drama," *San Francisco Chronicle*, November 23, 1915, 9. It is notable that when rabbis were invited to speak at the Philomath, they tended to address literary rather than solely religious topics. In 1921, for example, Lowenberg's daughter, Mrs. Abraham Lincoln Brown, invited Rabbi Martin Meyer of Temple Emanu-El to speak on "Recent Contributions of Jewish Poets" as part of a program on "Current Literary Thought." See "Philomath Club to Have Literary Feast," *San Francisco Chronicle*, January 24, 1921, 9.

26 "Philomath Club to Hear Service Chaplain Speak," *San Francisco Chronicle*, October 21, 1917, S6; "Philomath Club's Knitting Bee Gives Occasion for Fine Programme of Songs," *San Francisco Chronicle* (30 September 1917), S6.

27 "Earnest Address by Anna Strunsky," *The San Francisco Call*, October 11, 1904, 3.

28 Laura Bride Powers, "Activity in the Clubs Is a Cure for 'Nerves,'" *The San Francisco Call*, December 12, 1904, 7. The club later named a scholarship after Mary Prag.
29 Gere, *Intimate Practices*, 35, 39.
30 Mrs. I. Lowenberg, "Report of Vice-President of S. F. District," *Club Life*, March 1903, 4.
31 See, for example, "San Francisco: The Religious Congress," *American Israelite*, May 3, 1894, 3.
32 "Earnest Address by Anna Strunsky," 3. In contrast, an article published in *Emanu-El* on Strunsky's lecture before the San Francisco chapter of the National Council of Jewish Women did make much of her Jewish identity; see Maurice Brodzky, "Council of Jewish Women: Anna Strunsky," *Emanu-El*, September 29, 1905, 63–64.
33 Quoted in "Were Called 'Heathens'," *The American Hebrew*, June 11, 1897, 176.
34 "San Francisco Ministers Protest," *San Francisco Chronicle*, September 12, 1899, 2.
35 On the linkage between stereotypes of Jewish women and cultural anxieties about assimilation, see Riv-Ellen Prell, *Fighting to Become American: Assimilation and the Trouble Between Jewish Women and Jewish Men* (Beacon Press, 1999).
36 Harriet Watson Capwell, "The Philomath Club an Object of Admiration," *San Francisco News Letter*, August 21, 1909, 8, in Bettie Lowenberg Scrapbook, Oversize Box 2, Bancroft Library, University of California, Berkeley.
37 Capwell, "The Philomath Club an Object of Admiration," 8.
38 Her article echoes the words of San Francisco novelist Gertrude Atherton:

> San Francisco had always prided herself on having the finest class of Jews of any city in the United States. They were not too many, and they were highly educated, traveled, honorable, dignified, public-spirited, and of outstanding ability. They were eminent at the bar, on the bench, in finance, in business. They and their wives were active in charities, generous patrons of music, art, education, lectures. San Francisco attracted only the best, it told itself proudly. The women patronized the best

> dressmakers in San Francisco, New York, Paris. Their children went to the fashionable private schools. And although they were clannish and formed a distinguished social group of their own, they were welcome in the best society. Their dwellings were as handsome as any, but without ostentation.

See Atherton, *The Horn of Life* (Appleton, 1942), 282.

39 Florence Collins Porter, ed., "Chats About Clubs and Club Women," *Los Angeles Herald*, January 27, 1901, 3.

40 "A Golden Gate Pioneer," *The Land of Sunshine*, April 1898, 241–42.

41 Mrs. I. Lowenberg, "The Unsolved Problem," *Club Life*, February 1903, 5, 7–8. Lowenberg also read a version of this paper before the California Federation of Women's Clubs in 1899.

42 "Club Ladies Breakfast," *The San Francisco Call*, November 23, 1895, 16.

43 Mrs. I. Lowenberg, "Americanization," *Emanu-El*, September 10, 1920, Bettie Lowenberg Scrapbook, Oversize Box 2, Bancroft Library, University of California, Berkeley.

44 "Club Ladies Breakfast," *The San Francisco Call*, November 23, 1895, 16.

45 "An Anti-Suffrage Club," *The San Francisco Call*, November 25, 1895, 16.

46 Comstock, "The Best Known Club Women of the Pacific Coast," 7.

47 Comstock, "The Best Known Club Women of the Pacific Coast," 7.

48 Beth Wenger, "Jewish Women and Voluntarism: Beyond the Myth of Enablers," *American Jewish History* 79, no. 1 (Autumn 1989): 16–36.

49 "Scientist Says That Woman Is Eternal Savage," *Sausalito News*, July 3, 1909, 1.

50 "The Burden of Conversation: A Symposium—By Mrs. Mary Jarboe, H. G. Platt, Mrs. I. Lowenberg, and Willis Polk," *The Wave*, December 21, 1895, 12.

51 Laura Bride Powers, "Activity in the Clubs Is a Cure for 'Nerves,'" 7.

52 Mrs. I. Lowenberg, "Report of Vice-President of S. F. District," 4.

53 "Wise Words from Leading San Francisco Club Women on the Twentieth Century Girl," *The San Francisco Call*, January 7, 1900, 8.

54 Agnes Thernau, "Women Candidates for Second Place," Clipping, Bettie Lowenberg Scrapbook, Oversize Box 2, Bancroft Library, University of California, Berkeley.

55 Jeanne Abrams, "Remembering the Maine: The Jewish Attitude Toward the Spanish-American War as Reflected in *The American*

Israelite," *American Jewish History* 76.4 (June 1987): 439–55. On the work of Jewish Red Cross volunteers, including Lowenberg, see "Israel's Tithe to America," *The San Francisco Call*, July 24, 1898, 19.

56 Sally Sharp, "Lowenberg Tea on Saturday for Clubhouse," *The San Francisco Call*, February 18, 1904, 3.

57 "Israel's Tithe to America"; "Seeks Books and Games for Use of Soldiers," *The San Francisco Call*, January 9, 1902, 12; American National Red Cross, *A Record of the Red Cross Work on the Pacific Slope* (Pacific Press Publishing, 1902).

58 On Lowenberg's efforts to ensure women's participation in the planning of the exposition, see Anna Pratt Simpson, *Problems Women Solved: Being the Story of the Woman's Board of the Panama-Pacific Exposition; What Vision, Enthusiasm, Work and Cooperation Accomplished* (The Woman's Board, 1915), 4–5. For a history of the exposition, see Abigail Markwyn, *Empress San Francisco: The Pacific Rim, the Great West, and California at the Panama-Pacific International Exposition* (University of Nebraska Press, 2014).

59 Nan Towle Yamane, "Pacific Coast Women's Press Association, 1890–1941," in *Women's Press Organizations, 1881–1999*, ed. Elizabeth V. Burt (Greenwood Press, 2000), 189–97.

60 Josephine Clifford McCrackin, "Ina Coolbrith Invested with Poets' Crown," *Overland Monthly*, November 1915, 448–50.

61 See, for example, Mrs. I. Lowenberg, "Social Service," *Emanu-El*, September 29, 1916, Bettie Lowenberg Scrapbook (1915–), Oversize Box 1, Bancroft Library, University of California, Berkeley. On the history of *Emanu-El*, which is now *J.: The Jewish News of Northern California*, see Maya Mirsky, "'All Hail': 127 Years Ago This Newspaper's First Issue," *J.: The Jewish News of Northern California*, November 22, 2022.

62 "Philomath Club," *City and County Federation of Women's Clubs San Francisco Yearbook, 1918–1920* (City and County Federation of Women's Clubs, 1920), https://legacy.sfgenealogy.org/sf/women/wczzh.htm, accessed May 28, 2025.

63 Bettie Lowenberg, "Then and Now," Bettie Lowenberg Scrapbook, Oversize Box 2, Bancroft Library, University of California, Berkeley.

64 "Second Edition Needed," *Overland Monthly*, July 1920, 86.

65 Annie Josephine Levi, "Intermarriage," *The American Hebrew*, May 22, 1896, 73. On Wolf's popularity among women's clubs, see Gere, *Intimate*

Practices, 220–21. As Barbara Cantalupo points out in an unpublished biography of Wolf, the 1916 reprint of *Other Things Being Equal* is further evidence of the book's enduring popularity into the twentieth century.

66 See Anne C. Rose, *Beloved Strangers: Interfaith Families in Nineteenth-Century America* (Harvard University Press, 2001) and Keren R. McGinity, *Still Jewish: A History of Women and Intermarriage in America* (New York University Press, 2009).

67 Eric L. Goldstein, *The Price of Whiteness: Jews, Race, and American Identity* (Princeton: Princeton University Press, 2006), 20.

68 As Gere points out, the subject of naming was often debated among clubwomen; see Gere, *Intimate Practices*, 7–8. In 1893, Julia Ward Howe made this distinction: that in formal society a woman should be identified by her husband's name, but in "literary life" by "her own baptismal name." See "Opinions About Names," *Woman's Exponent*, April 15 and May 1, 1893, 1.

69 Advertisement for *The Irresistible Current* in *The American Hebrew and Jewish Messenger*, December 25, 1908, 211; advertisement for *The Irresistible Current* in *Overland Monthly*, July 1908, 25.

70 On Roosevelt's response to Zangwill's *The Melting Pot*, see *From the Ghetto to the Melting Pot: Israel Zangwill's Jewish Plays*, ed. Edna Nahshon (Wayne State University Press, 2006), 241–43.

71 Mrs. I. Lowenberg, *The Irresistible Current* (Broadway, 1908), 24.

72 Lowenberg, *Irresistible Current*, 33, 32.

73 Lowenberg, *Irresistible Current*, 36–37.

74 Lowenberg, *Irresistible Current*, 80.

75 Lowenberg, *Irresistible Current*, 40, 141; Wolf, *Other Things Being Equal*, 194.

76 Lowenberg, *Irresistible Current*, 397, 547.

77 Maurice Brodzky, "An Intellectual Woman Interviewed: Mrs. I. Lowenberg," *Emanu-El*, April 28, 1905, 6.

78 Lowenberg, *Irresistible Current*, 110.

79 Lowenberg, *Irresistible Current*, 536.

80 "Review of Recent Books," *Los Angeles Herald*, December 21, 1908, 8.

81 "Announcements of New York Books," *New York Times*, April 4, 1908, 192.

82 Review of *The Irresistible Current* in *The Jewish Tribune*, August 28, 1908, Bettie Lowenberg Scrapbook, Oversize Box 2, Bancroft Library, University of California, Berkeley.

83 "Book Notes," *Emanu-El*, August 7, 1908, Bettie Lowenberg Scrapbook Oversize Box 2, Bancroft Library, University of California, Berkeley.

84 Rabbi M. Friedlander, "The Irresistible Current," *Emanu-El*, September 4, 1908, Bettie Lowenberg Scrapbook, Oversize Box 2, Bancroft Library, University of California, Berkeley.

85 Benny Kraut, "Judaism Triumphant: Isaac Mayer Wise on Unitarianism and Liberal Christianity," *AJS Review* 7–8 (1982–83): 179–230.

86 "*The Irresistible Current*," *Overland Monthly and Out West Magazine*, November 1908, 12.

87 "Mrs. Lowenberg's 'Irresistible Current,'" *Sunset*, November 1908, 668.

88 "Mrs. Lowenberg's Book Discussed," *The San Francisco Call*, February 10, 1909, 7; see also "Mrs. I. Lowenberg Given Reception," *The San Francisco Call*, October 8, 1908, 9.

89 "Mrs. Lowenberg's 'Irresistible Current,'" 668.

90 *Other Things Being Equal* was followed by *A Prodigal in Love* (1894) and *The Joy of Life* (1896). In 1900, Wolf returned to Jewish themes with *Heirs of Yesterday*. As I discuss briefly in the previous chapter and at length in the introduction to the 2020 edition of *Heirs of Yesterday*, coedited by Barbara Cantalupo, there is evidence that Wolf may have had more difficulty publishing her Jewish-themed work.

91 Mrs. I. Lowenberg, "The Uniform Divorce Law," *The Woman Citizen: A Home Journal for Western Women*, August 1912, 16.

92 Mrs. I. Lowenberg, *A Nation's Crime* (Neale Publishing Company, 1910), 378.

93 Advertisement for *The Voices* in *Overland Monthly* (July 1920), 96.

94 Mrs. I. Lowenberg, *The Voices* (Harr Wagner, 1920), 82, 264.

95 "The Voices: A Book of Knowledge as well as Romance," *Overland Monthly and Out West Magazine*, April 1920, 336.

96 Mariana Bertola, "Betty [*sic*] Lowenberg," eulogy delivered at the S. F. District Convention at Petaluma, April 23, 1925, Bettie Lowenberg Papers, Box 1, Bancroft Library, University of California, Berkeley.

97 William Toll, "From Domestic Judaism to Public Ritual," in *Women and American Judaism*, eds. Pamela S. Nadell and Jonathan D. Sarna (Brandeis University Press, 2001), 142.

Chapter 3

1 Allen Lesser, "Life with Mother Too," *Menorah Journal* 35 (1947): 319.
2 Harriet Lane Levy, "920 O'Farrell Street: The Front Bedroom," *Menorah Journal* 25 (Winter 1937), 69. The second excerpt is Harriet Lane Levy, "Neighbors (Including Alice Toklas)," *Menorah Journal* 25 (Spring 1937): 183–94.
3 Lesser, "Life with Mother Too," 319, 322.
4 On the Jewish Publication Society and the politics of print culture, see Barbara Cantalupo and Lori Harrison-Kahan, introduction to Emma Wolf, *Heirs of Yesterday*, eds. Barbara Cantalupo and Lori Harrison-Kahan (Wayne State University Press, 2020) and Jonathan D. Sarna, *JPS: The Americanization of Jewish Culture, 1888–1988* (Jewish Publication Society, 1989).
5 As of January 5, 2025, a search for Mary Antin's *The Promised Land* in the MLA International Bibliography alone yields sixty results. In contrast, a search for *920 O'Farrell Street* yields a single result: an article-length version of this chapter that I authored. Some historians, however, have used Levy's memoir as a primary source for scholarship on Jewish life in the American West, and literary biographers refer to it in work on Gertrude Stein, Alice B. Toklas, and their circle.
6 The scholarship on spatiality in Woolf's prose is extensive. See, for example, Elizabeth Evans and Sarah Cornish, eds., *Woolf and the City: Selected Papers from the Nineteenth Annual Conference on Virginia Woolf: Fordham University, New York, New York, 4–7 June 2009* (Clemson University Press, 2010); Jennie-Rebecca Falcetta, "Geometries of Space and Time: The Cubist London of *Mrs. Dalloway*," *Woolf Studies Annual* 13 (2007): 111–36; Georgia Johnston, "Politics of Retrospective Space in Virginia Woolf's Memoir 'A Sketch of the Past'" in *Mapping the Self: Space, Identity, Discourse in British Auto/Biography*, ed. Frédéric Regard (Université de Saint-Etienne, 2003), 285–96; Victoria Rosner, *Modernism and the Architecture of Private Life* (Columbia University Press, 2005), especially chapters 3 and 5; Julie Robin Solomon, "Staking Ground: The Politics of Space in Virginia Woolf's *A Room of One's Own* and *Three Guineas*," *Women's Studies* 16 (1989): 331–47; Susan Merrill Squier, *Virginia Woolf and London: The Sexual Politics of the City* (University of North Carolina Press, 1985); Tone Selboe,

"Virginia Woolf and the Ambiguities of Domestic Space" in *Exploring Textual Action*, eds. Lars Sætre, Patrizia Lombardo, and Anders Marcussen Gullestad (Aarhus Universitetsforlag, 2010). 283–310; and Christina Stevenson, "'Here Was One Room, There Another': The Room, Authorship, and Feminine Desire in *A Room of One's Own* and *Mrs. Dalloway*," *Pacific Coast Philology* 49, no. 1 (2014): 112–32. For an analysis of Jewish space in Woolf's work, see Phyllis Lassner and Mira Spiro, "A Tale of Two Cities: Virginia Woolf's Imagined Jewish Spaces and London's East End Jewish Culture," *Woolf Studies Annual* 19 (2013): 59–82. For a reading of Gertrude Stein's work in relation to the spaces of avant-garde literary production (and specifically the space of her Paris home/salon, 27 rue de Fleurus, which figures importantly in Levy's own encounters with modernism), see Sara Blair, "Home Truths: Gertrude Stein, 27 Rue de Fleurus, and the Place of the Avant-Garde," *American Literary History* 12, no. 3 (2000): 417–37.

7 Maren Linett, "Introduction: Modernism's Jews/Jewish Modernisms," *Modern Fiction Studies* 51, no. 2 (2005): 249.

8 See Amy Feinstein, *Gertrude Stein and the Making of Jewish Modernism* (University Press of Florida, 2020) as well as "Goy Interrupted: Mina Loy's Unfinished Novel and Mongrel Jewish Fiction," *Modern Fiction Studies* 51, no. 2 (2005): 335–53, and the introduction to Gertrude Stein, "The Modern Jew Who Has Given Up the Faith of His Fathers Can Reasonably and Consistently Believe in Isolation," *PMLA* 116 (2001): 416–21. As Feinstein notes in her introduction to *Gertrude Stein and the Making of Jewish Modernism*, scholar Maria Damon was instrumental in "launch[ing] the study of Stein's Jewish identity" (4). See Maria Damon, "Gertrude Stein's Jewishness, Jewish Social Scientists, and the 'Jewish Question,'" *Modern Fiction Studies* 42, no. 3 (Fall 1996): 489–506, and Maria Damon, "Gertrude Stein's Doggerel 'Yiddish': Women, Dogs, and Jews," in *The Dark End of the Street: Margins in American Vanguard Poetry* (University of Minnesota Press, 1993), 202–35. See also Allison Schachter, *Women Writing Jewish Modernity, 1919–1939* (Northwestern University Press, 2021) for a consideration of modernist writings by women in Hebrew and Yiddish.

9 In a meditation on regionalism and American identity in *Everybody's Autobiography* (Virago, 1938), Gertrude Stein explained that she called herself "a Californian because there [she] was from six to eighteen,"

growing up in East Oakland and San Francisco. She goes on to state, "when Alice Toklas a Californian and Pat Bruce a Virginian used to talk about what was American I always said that Richmond and San Francisco did not make anybody know what was American, it was just Virginia and California and is California that now no not now" (215).

10 Annette Rosenshine, "Life's Not a Paragraph," unpublished memoir, Annette Rosenshine Collection, Bancroft Library, University of California, Berkeley.

11 "Died: Levy," *The San Francisco Call*, June 10, 1900, 30.

12 Harriet Lane Levy, *920 O'Farrell Street: A Jewish Girlhood in Old San Francisco* (Heyday, 1996), 70, 88, 96.

13 Levy, *920 O'Farrell Street*, 89, 93.

14 "Commencement Exercises at Berkeley of the Class of '86," *Daily Alta California*, July 1, 1886, 1. "Wanted" was later published in *The Wave*; see Harriet Levy, "Wanted," *The Wave*, July 16, 1892, 6–7.

15 Levy, *920 O'Farrell Street*, 70.

16 On Cosgrave's high estimation of Levy as a writer, see Toklas to W. G. and Mildred Rogers, July 22, 1948, in Alice B. Toklas, *Staying on Alone: Letters of Alice B. Toklas* (Liveright, 1973), 128.

17 Harriet Levy, "To San Francisco," *Prosit: A Book of Toasts* (Paul Elder, 1904), 79.

18 On the conversation with Zangwill, see Levy, *Paris Portraits: Stories of Picasso, Matisse, Gertrude Stein, and Their Circle* (Heyday, 2011), 7.

19 Levy, *920 O'Farrell Street*, 195.

20 Levy, *920 O'Farrell Street*, 17, 19, 20.

21 Levy, *Paris Portraits*, 4.

22 See Shari Benstock, *Women of the Left Bank, 1900–1940* (University of Texas Press, 1986) and Andrea Weiss, *Paris Was a Woman: Portraits from the Left Bank* (Counterpoint, 2013).

23 Levy, *Paris Portraits*, 83.

24 Levy, *Paris Portraits*, 85.

25 Levy, *Paris Portraits*, 55.

26 See John J. Appel, "Christian Science and the Jews," *Jewish Social Studies* 31, no. 2 (1969): 100–121.

27 Levy, *Paris Portraits*, 55.

28 Gertrude Stein, *Portraits and Prayers* (Random House, 1934), 105–7. Another word portrait titled "Harriet Fear," written around 1908 but

not published until 1951 after Stein's and Levy's deaths, takes aim at Levy's timidity; it is a character study of an individual too reticent to experience life to its fullest, "one who was completely afraid in being living" and thus "never undertook to do anything." See Gertrude Stein, *Two: Gertrude Stein and Her Brother and Other Early Portraits [1908–12]* (Yale University Press, 1951), 343. In her introduction to this collection of previously unpublished writings that includes "Harriet Fear," Janet Flanner recalls Stein's own ideas about the series of early portraits, noting that "the names of the people of whom these portraits were made she [Stein] considered of no interest or little interest" and explaining that Stein set out to create portraits "of people who were not very important people and were not very interesting" (x–xi).

29 "Society by the Outsider," *The San Francisco Call*, August 7, 1910, 42.

30 Toklas to Harriet Lane Levy, Jan 8, 1917, Harriet Lane Levy recollections, BANC MSS, C-H 11, Bancroft Library, University of California, Berkeley.

31 Sylvia Salinger to her family, October 28, 1912, in Sylvia Salinger, *Just a Very Pretty Girl from the Country: Sylvia Salinger's Letters from France, 1912–1913*, ed. Albert S. Bennett (Southern Illinois University Press, 1987), 9.

32 Levy, *Paris Portraits*, 100.

33 Toklas to Harriet Lane Levy, 29 IV '35, Harriet Lane Levy Recollections, BANC MSS, C-H 11, Bancroft Library, University of California, Berkeley.

34 Gertrude Stein, *The Autobiography of Alice B. Toklas*, in *Selected Writings of Gertrude Stein*, ed. Carl Van Vechten (Vintage, 1990), 18.

35 Gertrude Stein scholars have also pointed out that her brother Leo Stein, who lived with her and played an important role in her life, is virtually written out of *The Autobiography of Alice B. Toklas*, including the parts that recount Gertrude's early life; this erasure was a result of the estrangement between Gertrude and Leo that occurred in 1910 around the time that Alice moved in with them, replacing Leo, who moved out. See, for example, Brenda Wineapple, *Sister Brother: Gertrude and Leo Stein* (G. P. Putnam's Sons, 1996).

36 Alice B. Toklas, *What Is Remembered* (1963; repr., North Point, 1985), 61. Toklas appears to make an error in her autobiography, naming the

Matisse painting *La Femme Aux Yeux Bleus* (The Woman with Blue Eyes).

37 Toklas to Louise and Redvers Taylor, August 18, 1947, in Toklas, *Staying on Alone*, 74–75.

38 Levy, *920 O'Farrell Street*, 17.

39 Toklas to W. G. and Mildred Rogers, July 22, 1948, in Toklas, *Staying on Alone*, 127.

40 For a discussion of Toklas's conflict over writing her own memoirs, see Linda Simon, *The Biography of Alice B. Toklas* (University of Nebraska Press, 1991).

41 Toklas to Louise and Redvers Taylor, May 1, 1949, in Toklas, *Staying on Alone*, 159.

42 Levy, *Paris Portraits*, 27.

43 "Harriet Lane Levy," *New York Times*, September 17, 1950, 104.

44 On *The Autobiography of Alice B. Toklas*, see, for example, Carolyn Barros, "Getting Modern: *The Autobiography of Alice B. Toklas*," *Biography* 22, no. 2 (1999): 177–208, and Leigh Gilmore, *Autobiographics: A Feminist Theory of Women's Self-Representation* (Cornell University Press, 1994), 199–223. Phoebe Stein Davis argues against the experimentalism of *The Autobiography of Alice B. Toklas*, especially when it comes to national identity; see Davis, "Subjectivity and the Aesthetics of National Identity in Gertrude Stein's *The Autobiography of Alice B. Toklas*," *Twentieth Century Literature* 45, no. 1 (1999): 18–45.

45 Levy, *920 O'Farrell Street*, 2.

46 Many scholars have examined the relationship between literature and the visual arts in modernist cultural production. For an approach that specifically addresses Jewish modernism, see Barbara Mann, "Visions of Jewish Modernism," *Modernism/Modernity* 13, no. 4 (2006): 673–99.

47 On the house as a repository of memory, especially in works of literature, see Gaston Bachelard, *The Poetics of Space*, trans. Maria Jolas (Penguin, 2014).

48 Levy, *920 O'Farrell Street*, 1.

49 Levy, *920 O'Farrell Street*, 99.

50 Joseph Frank, "Spatial Form in Modern Literature," *The Sewanee Review* 53, no. 2 (Spring 1945): 225.

51 Levy, *920 O'Farrell Street*, 61.

52 Levy, *920 O'Farrell Street*, 63.

53 Levy, *920 O'Farrell Street*, 1.
54 Levy, *920 O'Farrell Street*, 1.
55 Levy, *920 O'Farrell Street*, 2.
56 Levy, *920 O'Farrell Street*, 3.
57 In comparison, other memoirists have described a fluidity between Jewish and non-Jewish spaces in San Francisco, especially in comparison to Eastern cities. See, for example, Mary Prag, "Early Days," unpublished memoir, Florence Prag and Julius Kahn Papers, Bancroft Library, University of California, Berkeley; Kohut, *My Portion*; and Rosenshine, "Life's Not a Paragraph."
58 Levy, *920 O'Farrell Street*, 12.
59 Levy, *920 O'Farrell Street*, 9.
60 Levy, *920 O'Farrell Street*, 11.
61 Levy, *920 O'Farrell Street*, 13.
62 Levy, *920 O'Farrell Street*, 24, 25, 24.
63 Levy, *920 O'Farrell Street*, 5.
64 Levy, *920 O'Farrell Street*, 119, 122.
65 Levy, *920 O'Farrell Street*, 125.
66 Levy, *920 O'Farrell Street*, 121.
67 Levy, *920 O'Farrell Street*, 123, italics added.
68 Levy, *920 O'Farrell Street*, 123.
69 Levy, *920 O'Farrell Street*, 124.
70 Levy, *920 O'Farrell Street*, 140.
71 Levy, *920 O'Farrell Street*, 141.
72 Levy, *920 O'Farrell Street*, 124.
73 Levy, *920 O'Farrell Street*, 136.
74 Levy, *920 O'Farrell Street*, 137.
75 Levy, *920 O'Farrell Street*, 137.
76 Mary Antin, *The Promised Land* (1912; repr., Penguin, 1997), 196.
77 Levy, *920 O'Farrell Street*, 141.
78 Levy, *920 O'Farrell Street*, 143.
79 Levy, *920 O'Farrell Street*, 145.
80 Levy, *920 O'Farrell Street*, 145, 146.
81 Levy, *920 O'Farrell Street*, 106, 108, 112.
82 Levy, *920 O'Farrell Street*, 113.
83 Levy, *920 O'Farrell Street*, 112.
84 Gilmore, *Autobiographics*, 200.

85 Nora Doyle, "Gertrude Stein and the Domestication of Genius in The Autobiography of Alice B. Toklas," *Feminist Studies* 44, no. 1 (2018): 44, 69.
86 Barbara Will, *Gertrude Stein, Modernism, and the Problem of "Genius"* (Edinburgh University Press, 2000), 7.
87 Sidonie Smith, "Performativity, Autobiographical Practice, Resistance," *a/b: Auto/Biography Studies* 10, no. 1 (1995): 29.
88 In addition to rumors about Levy's relationship with married sculptor David Edstrom in Europe, Harriet's great-nephew Albert Salinger Bennett prefaces his published collection of his mother's correspondence from France with a story about Harriet's "rendezvous with a gentleman friend" that went sour when she discovered that he was married. According to Bennett, the meeting preceded her trip to France as a chaperone for Bennett's mother, Sylvia, and "when Harriet informed [Sylvia] about the rendezvous, she turned purple with rage—the first time Sylvia had witnessed such a phenomenon." See Bennett, *Just a Very Pretty Girl from the Country*, 1. In my meeting with Albert Bennett on March 24, 2019, in New York City, he recalled memories of Levy, his great-aunt, who was frequently escorted by a man he called her "beau."
89 Yet, it is important to keep in mind that while Stein's sexuality and her relationship with Toklas are openly acknowledged today and "were common knowledge among . . . their . . . modernist acquaintances in Paris and beyond, . . . no reference was made in print to this knowledge until after Alice B. Toklas's death in 1967." See Marianne Dekoven, "Modernism and Gender," in *The Cambridge Companion to Modernism*, ed. Michael Levenson (Cambridge University Press, 2006), 185.
90 Levy, *Paris Portraits*, 96–97, 98.
91 For more on the ways that modernism dovetails with queerness, see Laura Doan and Jane Garrity, "Modernism Queered," in *A Companion to Modernist Literature and Culture*, edited by David Bradshaw and Kevin J. H. Dettmar (Blackwell, 2006), 542–50.
92 Levy, *920 O'Farrell Street*, 190, 192.
93 Levy, *920 O'Farrell Street*, 192, 194.
94 Levy, *920 O'Farrell Street*, 194.
95 Levy, *920 O'Farrell Street*, 195–96, italics added.
96 Stein, *Everybody's Autobiography*, 289.

97 Levy, *920 O'Farrell Street*, 196.
98 Hana Wirth-Nesher, "Introduction: Jewish-American Autobiography," *Prooftexts* 18, no. 2 (1998): 114.

Chapter 4

1 In 1947, the same year that Levy published *920 O'Farrell Street*, Grabhorn Press also printed Levy's only book of poetry, *I Love to Talk About Myself & Other Verses Concerning God & Man & Me*, in a limited edition of five hundred copies. Levy's mother, Henrietta (Yetta) Michelson, and Miriam Michelson's father, Samuel Michelson, were siblings. The families were in close contact since Miriam's brother Albert lived with the Levys while attending high school in San Francisco. As fellow writers, Harriet and Miriam were both part of the Round Table Club, which gathered together some of San Francisco's professional women writers. The two cousins' religious upbringings differed significantly. While Levy recounts her religious upbringing in her memoir *920 O'Farrell Street* (as I discussed in the last chapter), Miriam grew up in a secular home and did not identify as Jewish (as I will discuss in this chapter). Those differences in religious observances may be due in part to where the families settled. San Francisco provided the Levys with a robust Jewish community and access to Jewish institutions; this was not the case for the Michelsons, who settled in Virginia City, Nevada.
2 On "girl stunt reporters," see Kim Todd, *Sensational: The Hidden History of America's "Girl Stunt Reporters"* (Harper, 2021); and Jean Marie Lutes, *Front-Page Girls: Women Journalists in American Culture and Fiction, 1880–1930* (Cornell University Press, 2006). For an overview of women in American journalism history, see Brooke Kroeger, *Undaunted: How Women Changed American Journalism* (Knopf, 2023).
3 My edited volume of Michelson's journalism and fiction, *The Superwoman and Other Writings by Miriam Michelson* (Wayne State University Press, 2019), reintroduced her to contemporary readers and unearthed her writings as important artifacts of turn-of-the-twentieth-century literary and periodical culture. See also Lori Harrison-Kahan, "Miriam Michelson's *The Superwoman* and the Future of Feminist Recovery," in *Jewish Women Science Fiction*

Writers Create Future Females: Gender, Temporality—and Yentas, ed. Marleen S. Barr (Rowman & Littlefield, 2025), 9–23, and two articles that I published in collaboration with Karen E. H. Skinazi: "Miriam Michelson's Yellow Journalism and the Multi-Ethnic West," *MELUS* 40, no. 2 (Summer 2015): 182–207, which was accompanied by a reprint of Michelson's story "In Chy Fong's Restaurant: Where Miss Massey Meets a Missionary" from *A Yellow Journalist* (1905); and "The Girl Reporter in Fact and Fiction: Miriam Michelson's New Women and Progressive Era Periodical Culture," *Legacy* 34, no. 2 (December 2017): 321–38, which was accompanied by reprints of Michelson's "The Real New Woman," a piece of journalism that appeared in *The San Francisco Call* in 1895, and her short story "The Milpitas Maiden," which appeared as part of the "Yellow Journalist" series in *The Saturday Evening Post* in 1905.

4 "Jewish Women in Our History," *Washington Post*, December 3, 1905, SM6. For an example of similar coverage in the Jewish press, see "Some Jewesses Who Have Attained Distinction," *The Sentinel*, July 12, 1918, 11.

5 Mark Twain, *Roughing It* (1872; repr., Signet, 2008), 225.

6 Jeanne Abrams, *Jewish Women Pioneering the Frontier Trail: A History in the American West* (New York University Press, 2006), 2, 19. On the role of women in Virginia City, see *Comstock Women: The Making of a Mining Community*, eds. Ronald M. James and C. Elizabeth Raymond (University of Nevada Press, 1998). On the Jewish presence in Virginia City, see John P. Marschall, *Jews in Nevada: A History* (University of Nevada Press, 2008).

7 On the Sagebrush School, see Lawrence I. Berkove, "The Sagebrush School Revived," in *A Companion to the Regional Literatures of America*, ed. Charles L. Crow (Blackwell, 2003), 324–43; and Lawrence I. Berkove, ed., *The Sagebrush Anthology: Literature from the Silver Age of the Old West* (University of Missouri, 2006). Michelson 's writings add an important gender perspective to understandings of the Sagebrush School, which, as Berkove notes, was dominated by male writers and has been characterized by an "ideal of manliness." See Berkove, "The Sagebrush School Revived," 326.

8 H. L. Mencken, "The Last of the Victorians," Smart Set, November 1909, 156; Mary Moss, "Notes on New Novels," *Atlantic Monthly*, January 1906, 47.

9 Catherine Keyser, *Playing Smart: New York Women Writers and Modern Magazine Culture* (Rutgers University Press, 2011), 7.

10 Harrison-Kahan and Skinazi, "Miriam Michelson's Yellow Journalism and the Multi-Ethnic West," 198. On middlebrow moderns, see Lisa Botshon and Meredith Goldsmith, eds., *Middlebrow Moderns: Popular American Women Writers of the 1920s* (Northeastern University Press, 2003).

11 As discussed earlier, after taking on ethno-religious prejudice in *The Irresistible Current* (1908), Lowenberg turned her attention to social inequalities based on gender and class in *A Nation's Crime* (1910) and *The Voices* (1920), while three of Wolf's five novels were set in secular contexts. Readers of Wolf's writing in the magazine *The Smart Set*—to which she contributed ten stories between 1902 and 1911—may have been unlikely to categorize her as a Jewish writer at all, given the absence of Jewish content in the fiction that appeared with her byline. See Barbara Cantalupo, ed., *Emma Wolf's Short Stories in "The Smart Set"* (AMS Press, 2010).

12 In addition to the article in *The Washington Post*, see Frances Maule Bjorkman, "Fair and Famous Jewish Women," *Broadway Magazine*, November 1907, 203–8, for an example of how Michelson was covered in the secular press. For an example of how Michelson was covered in the Jewish press, see "Some Jewesses Who Have Attained Distinction."

13 Robert A. Millikan, *Biographical Memoir of Albert A. Michelson (1852–1931)* (National Academy of Sciences, 1938), https://www.nasonline.org/wp-content/uploads/2024/06/michelson-a-a.pdf

14 See, for example, Mark Twain's "The Celebrated Jumping Frog of Calaveras County," which was first published in *The Saturday Press* in 1865, and Bret Harte's *The Luck of Roaring Camp and Other Sketches* (Fields, Osgood, and Company, 1870).

15 The most complete account of the family's history can be found in Dorothy Livingston, *Master of Light: A Biography of Albert A. Michelson* (University of Chicago Press, 1973).

16 Dolores Waldorf Bryant, commentary in John Taylor Waldorf, *A Kid on the Comstock: Reminiscences of a Virginia City Boyhood* (American West Publishing Company, 1970), 118.

17 Livingston, *Master of Light*, 17.
18 Miriam Michelson, *The Wonderlode of Silver and Gold* (Stratford Company, 1934), 52, 108, 133.
19 Bryant, *A Kid on the Comstock*, 114.
20 Bryant, *A Kid on the Comstock*, 119.
21 Michelson, *Wonderlode of Silver and Gold*, 170.
22 Chinese immigrants experienced employment discrimination and were prevented from working in the mining trade. For more on the Chinese presence in Virginia City, see George M. Blackburn and Sherman I. Richards, "The Prostitutes and Gamblers of Virginia City, Nevada: 1870," *Pacific Historical Review* 48, no. 2 (May 1979): 239–59, and Sue Fawn Chung, *The Chinese in Nevada* (Arcadia, 2011).
23 Michelson, *Wonderlode of Silver and Gold*, 72. On Native Americans in Virginia City, see Eugene M. Hattori, "'And Some of Them Swear like Pirates': Acculturation of American Indian Women in Nineteenth-Century Virginia City," in James and Raymond, *Comstock Women*, 229–45.
24 Michelson, *Wonderlode of Silver and Gold*, 9. For more on the complexity of Michelson's views of Native Americans and United States assimilation policy, see, for example, Miriam Michelson, "Changing a Bad Indian into a Good One," *The San Francisco Call*, April 24, 1898, 25, reprinted in Harrison-Kahan, ed., *The Superwoman and Other Writings*, 183–89.
25 Mary Ellen Glass, "Alice E. Sauer: Reminiscences of Life in Virginia City and Washoe Valley, Nevada," in *University of Nevada Oral History Archive* (University of Nevada Oral History Program, 1969), 9. Marschall's study of Jews in Nevada contradicts this to an extent. Although there were no Jewish congregations in Virginia City, there were two Jewish benevolent societies, including a B'nai B'rith Lodge, by the time Miriam was born. See also James and Raymond, *Comstock Women*, 188.
26 On antisemitism in the American West, see Abrams, *Jewish Women Pioneering the Frontier Trail*, 11; and Ellen Eisenberg, Ava F. Kahn, and William Toll, *Jews of the Pacific Coast: Reinventing Community on America's Edge* (Seattle: University of Washington Press, 2009), 7. Historians have shown that the residents of Virginia City tended to live and socialize in ethnic clusters. In *Jews in Nevada*, John P. Marschall notes

that while "Jews [were] spread through the Germanic-European section of town," several Jewish families, including the Michelsons, lived within close proximity to each other on A Street. Marschall is careful to point out, however, that the neighborhood "was not a ghetto" (72). In contrast, for example, to Chinese immigrants, Jewish merchants were well integrated into the community, with many of their children attending school alongside other Euro-Americans. That Chinese immigrants and Jews faced different degrees of popular prejudice is clear from Mary McNair Mathews's memoir *Ten Years in Nevada; Or, Life on the Pacific Coast* (Baker, Jones, and Company, 1880). Mathews dehumanizes Chinese immigrants, describing Virginia City's Chinatown as "a loathsome, filthy den . . . breed[ing] . . . pestilential disease" and "John Chinaman" as "truly the curse of the Pacific Coast." While she also harbors negative views of the town's Jewish shopkeepers, whom she depicts as greedy and untrustworthy, she admits to having "seen many" Jews whom she "thought were nice people" (249, 169, 53).

27 Edward Meeker's vaudeville song "I'm a Yiddish Cowboy" (1908), for example, derives its humor from the incongruity of Western life and Jewish identity, but allows for the possibility that the "Yiddish cowboy" can become American, notably by creating a distinction between himself and Indians. In the chorus, "Tough Guy Levi" sings, "I don't care for Tomahawks or Cheyenne Indians, oi, oi / I'm a real live 'Diamond Dick' that shoots 'em till they die / I'll marry squaw or start a war, for I'm a fighting guy." For more, see Rachel Rubinstein, *Members of the Tribe: Native America in the Jewish Imagination* (Wayne State University Press, 2010); David S. Koffman, *The Jews' Indian: Colonialism, Pluralism, and Belonging in America* (Rutgers University Press, 2019); and Alan Trachtenberg, *Shades of Hiawatha: Staging Indians, Making Americans, 1880–1930* (Hill and Wang, 2004).

28 *The Anaconda Standard*, February 16, 1908, 19.

29 Louisa May Alcott, *Little Women* (1868–69; repr., W. W. Norton, 2004), 13.

30 Miriam Michelson, *The Madigans* (Century, 1904), 299.

31 Otis Notman, "Popular Writers from the Far West," *The New York Times Saturday Review of Books*, June 1, 1907, BR356.

32 Stephen Watt, *"Something Dreadful and Grand": American Literature and the Irish-Jewish Unconscious* (Oxford University Press, 2015), 54.

33 On secularism as universal religion, see Susan Jacoby, *Freethinkers: A History of American Secularism* (Henry Holt, 2005).
34 Alcott, *Little Women*, 18.
35 Michelson, *The Madigans*, 22, 128, 31, 28.
36 Michelson, *The Madigans*, 271.
37 Michelson, *The Madigans*, 194.
38 Michelson, *The Madigans*, 38.
39 Michelson, *The Madigans*, 89, 77.
40 Warren Sylvester Smith, *The London Heretics, 1870–1914* (Dodd, Mead & Company, 1968), 5.
41 Michelson, *The Madigans*, 290, 282.
42 Michelson, *The Madigans*, 149.
43 Michelson, *The Madigans*, 175.
44 On *The Spanish Gypsy* as a dress rehearsal for *Daniel Deronda*, see Deborah Nord, "George Eliot's Notes for *The Spanish Gypsy*," *Princeton University Library Chronicle* 72, no. 2 (Winter 2011): 471–76; and David Kurnick, "Unspeakable George Eliot," *Victorian Literature and Culture* 38, no. 2 (2010): 489–509.
45 Rubinstein, *Members of the Tribe*, 9. On the cultural appropriation of Native American identity, see also Philip Deloria's classic study *Playing Indian* (Yale University Press, 1999).
46 Rubinstein, *Members of the Tribe*, 58.
47 Michelson, *The Madigans*, 162; Rubinstein, *Members of the Tribe*, 10.
48 Michael Rogin, *Blackface, White Noise: Jewish Immigrants in the Hollywood Melting Pot* (University of California Press, 1996), 57. Michelson's representations of Indigeneity also fit well into the paradigm of ambivalent Jewish-Indian identification discussed by David Koffman in *The Jews' Indian*. Koffman, as well as Sarah Imhoff in *Masculinity and the Making of American Judaism* (Indiana University Press, 2017), focus largely on the way Jewish actors used identification with and distancing from Indigenous people to construct American masculinity; Michelson's work indicates that similar dynamics apply to Jewish women's imaginings of Native people in the American West.
49 Michelson, *The Madigans*, 187.
50 Michelson, *Wonderlode of Silver and Gold*, 133.
51 Michelson, *The Madigans*, 338.
52 Michelson, *The Madigans*, 157, 151.

53 Michelson, *The Madigans*, 33–34.
54 Michelson, *The Madigans*, 5, 249.
55 "Madigans Deserve Spanking," *The San Francisco Call*, October 23, 1904, 6.
56 Miriam Michelson, "Strangling Hands upon a Nation's Throat," *The San Francisco Call*, September 30, 1897, 1–2, reprinted in Harrison-Kahan, ed., *The Superwoman and Other Writings*, 162.
57 Lutes, *Front-Page Girls*, 5. On Annie Laurie, see Katherine H. Adams and Michael L. Keene, *Winifred Black/Annie Laurie and the Making of Modern Nonfiction* (McFarland, 2015).
58 The phrase "ladies of the press" comes from the title of Ishbel Ross's survey of women in journalism, *Ladies of the Press: The Story of Women in Journalism by an Insider* (Harper & Brothers, 1936).
59 Alice Fahs, *Out on Assignment: Newspaper Women and the Making of Modern Public Space* (University of North Carolina Press, 2014), 26, 25.
60 See Carol J. Batker, *Reforming Fictions: Native, African, and Jewish American Women's Literature and Journalism in the Progressive Era* (Columbia University Press, 2000).
61 Lutes, *Front-Page Girls*, 24.
62 See, for example, Jack London to Cloudesley Johns, May 18, 1899, in *The Letters of Jack London*, eds. Earle Labor, Robert C. Leitz III, and I. Milo Shepard, vol. 1 (Stanford University Press, 1988), 76.
63 Fahs, *Out on Assignment*, 233.
64 Michelson, "Strangling Hands upon a Nation's Throat," in Harrison-Kahan, ed., *The Superwoman and Other Writings*, 167.
65 Karen Roggenkamp, *Narrating the News: New Journalism and Literary Genre in Late Nineteenth-Century American Newspapers and Fiction* (Kent State University Press, 2005), xiv.
66 Michelson, "Strangling Hands upon a Nation's Throat," in Harrison-Kahan, ed., *The Superwoman and Other Writings*, 161–64.
67 Michelson, "Strangling Hands upon a Nation's Throat," in Harrison-Kahan, ed., *The Superwoman and Other Writings*, 164.
68 Michelson, "Strangling Hands upon a Nation's Throat," in Harrison-Kahan, ed., *The Superwoman and Other Writings*, 165–68.
69 Michelson, "Strangling Hands upon a Nation's Throat," in Harrison-Kahan, ed., *The Superwoman and Other Writings*, 168.

70 On newspaper reporting and the emerging convention of third-person objectivity, see Michael Schudson, *Discovering the News: A Social History of American Newspapers* (Basic Books, 1981).

71 See Miriam Michelson, "Perkins Talks upon Annexation," *The San Francisco Call*, October 7, 1897, 3.

72 For a history of Hawaii's annexation, see Noenoe K. Silva, *Aloha Betrayed: Native Hawaiian Resistance to American Colonialism* (Duke University Press, 2004).

73 "There never was a better newspaper fight than the *Bulletin*'s," Michelson wrote to Older years later. Miriam Michelson to Fremont Older, undated, Fremont Older Papers, 1907–1941, Box 1, Bancroft Library, University of California, Berkeley. In her three years at *The San Francisco Bulletin*, Michelson also found a home for some of her earliest published fiction, as well as the flexibility to experiment with journalistic form (going so far, in one instance, to publish an article in verse). In March 1899, the paper reprinted "The Awakening of Zojas"; inspired by Edward Bellamy's *Looking Backward* (1888), the science fiction tale was first published anonymously in *Macmillan's Magazine* of London under the title "A Strange Experiment, and What Came of It." On December 24, 1899, in addition to publishing a critique of Christmas consumerism and the way it highlighted the gap between rich and poor ("Amid the Merry Throng of Christmastide Shoppers"), Michelson contributed to the Christmas edition of the *Bulletin* with three Christmas-themed pieces, "The Conversion of Choy Sing and Other Sketches."

74 Letter from Mark Twain to Charles Erskine Scott Wood, 1885, quoted in Shelley Fisher Fishkin, "Mark Twain and the Jews," *Arizona Quarterly* 61, no. 1 (Spring 2005): 142.

75 Miriam Michelson, "Adolph Sutro Passes Away," *The San Francisco Bulletin*, August 8, 1898, 2.

76 Todd, *Sensational*, 250.

77 See, for example, Miriam Michelson, "Where Waves the Dragon Flag," *The San Francisco Bulletin*, February 12, 1899, 1, reprinted in Harrison-Kahan, ed., *The Superwoman and Other Writings*, 194–201.

78 Miriam Michelson, "A Military Matter in Black and White," *The San Francisco Bulletin*, December 3, 1899, 9, reprinted in Harrison-Kahan, ed., *The Superwoman and Other Writings*, 215–19.

79 Michelson had also begun her career working for McEwen; from 1894 to 1895, she contributed mostly theater criticism to the "Amusements" column of his weekly newspaper, *Arthur McEwen's Letter*, before moving to *The San Francisco Call* in 1895. McEwen, who had married Miriam's sister Bessie in 1883, was responsible for coining the term "Gee Whiz Journalism" to describe the sensationalist tactics of the Progressive-Era press. He famously stated, "Any issue the front page of which failed to elicit a 'Gee Whiz!' from its readers was a failure, whereas the second page ought to bring forth a 'Holy Moses!' and the third an astounded 'God Almighty!'" Quoted in Ben Procter, *William Randolph Hearst: The Later Years, 1911–1951* (Oxford University Press, 2007), 5.

80 Evidence of the novel about Hawaii exists only in the form of a 1900 reader's report from publisher Houghton Mifflin, which rejected the manuscript as "a dull story of Hawaii a century ago, with Kamehameha for hero, told in a stiff, inverted style" (Miriam Michelson. Category: Fiction; received: Mar. 6, 1900; sent to editor: Mar. 7, 1900; decision: Mar. 11, 1900; letter sent: Mar. 12, 1900. Houghton Mifflin Company reader reports on manuscripts submitted for publication, MS Am 2516, (7915)–(8279), (8043). Houghton Library, Harvard College Library). The Houghton Mifflin editor may have had legitimate qualms with Michelson's prose but almost certainly mischaracterized the plot of the manuscript. The title indicates that the book was not primarily about Kamehameha I, the founder of the Kingdom of Hawaii. Instead, the manuscript appears to have been a work of historical fiction centered on a remarkable *heroine*: the Hawaiian high chiefess Ululani of Hilo (also known as "Ululani the Great"). In Michelson's short story "An Understudy for a Princess," *Black Cat* 70 (July 1901): 1–16, she drew on the controversy over expansionism that she wrote about in *The San Francisco Call* as backdrop for an interracial romance involving a white adventurer who falls in love with a Hawaiian woman impersonating the Crown Princess Ka'iulani. For a reprint of the story, see Harrison-Kahan, ed., *The Superwoman and Other Writings*, 265–80.

81 On Twain, see Hsuan L. Hsu, *Sitting in Darkness: Mark Twain's Asia and Comparative Racialization* (New York University Press, 2015). Harte's "Wan Lee, the Pagan" (1876)—like his poem "Plain Language

for Truthful James" (1870), also known as "The Heathen Chinee"—attempts to offer a sympathetic portrait of Chinese immigrants; as is often the case with Chinatown tales, such attempts go awry because the writings are so infused with racial stereotypes that they end up fueling Sinophobia. In the 1890s, Frank Norris published stories set in Chinatown in the San Francisco journal *The Wave*. The most famous of these stories, "The Third Circle" (1897), was a sensational tale about a white woman kidnapped and enslaved by Chinese traffickers. See Karen A. Keely, "Sexual Slavery in San Francisco's Chinatown: 'Yellow Peril' and 'White Slavery' in Frank Norris's Early Fiction," *Studies in American Naturalism* 2, no. 2 (2007): 129–49. Women writers also gravitated to the Chinatown genre, and like men, saw it as a chance to write about the titillating topic of sex trafficking. Mary Austin, for instance, published one of her first short stories "The Conversion of Aw Lew Sing" (1897) in the *Overland Monthly*. While Norris's plots revolve around white men rescuing white women from sexual enslavement by Chinese men, Austin's story features a poor Chinese vegetable gardener who rescues a beautiful Chinese woman from both the highbinders who enslave her and the missionaries who attempt to Christianize her, feigning his own conversion as a means of making her his legal wife. Other white women, like New York missionary Helen F. Clark, author of *The Lady of the Lily Feet and Other Stories of Chinatown* (1900), took conversion more seriously, writing Chinatown tales to promote the success of the missions in saving Chinese women. Today, the best-known purveyor of the Chinatown tale is Edith Maude Eaton, who published as "Sui Sin Far" among other Chinese-sounding pen names. Born of an English father and a Chinese mother, Eaton, who lived in both Canada and the United States, is celebrated as the first Asian North American fictionist. She published Chinatown journalism and short fiction in a variety of periodicals. As scholars have shown, Eaton adopted Orientalist motifs in her work and in her writing persona, but simultaneously deployed tricksterism and other subversive techniques to challenge anti-Chinese sentiment and traditional East-West binaries. See, for example, Dominika Ferens, *Edith and Winnifred Eaton: Chinatown Missions and Japanese Romances* (University of Illinois Press, 2002).

82 Shortly after the release of the book, playwright and director Channing Pollock purchased the dramatic rights in order to adapt it for the stage. In his autobiography, *Harvest of My Years* (Bobbs-Merrill, 1943), Pollock confessed that he wrote the play without having read Michelson's novel because he "never had time" and "success in dramatizing a novel depended on not knowing too much about it" (169). The fact that Pollock knew the story of *In the Bishop's Carriage* well enough to adapt it without reading the book speaks to the popularity of the novel and how the plot and characters were very much part of general cultural knowledge at the time. Later, the emergent medium of moving pictures gave *In the Bishop's Carriage* new life. The 1913 screen adaptation made cinema history. Directed by Edwin S. Porter (of *Great Train Robbery* fame), *In the Bishop's Carriage* marked the full-length feature debut of silent film star and Hollywood legend Mary Pickford, who played Nance Olden. In 1920, a remake titled *She Couldn't Help It* featured actress Bebe Daniels. *In the Bishop's Carriage*, too, had roots in Michelson's journalism. In an article that she published in the Philadelphia *North American*, "Motives of Women Who Commit Theft" (1902), she explored the social conditions of female criminality, a topic that had gotten much play at the end of the nineteenth century by women journalists such as Elizabeth Jordan, who reported on the Lizzie Borden murder trial; see Miriam Michelson, "Motives of Women Who Commit Theft," reprinted in Harrison-Kahan, ed., *The Superwoman and Other Writings*, 257–9.

83 The setting is not, however, monocultural. There is a white ethnic immigrant sensibility to the characters in *In the Bishop's Carriage*, and Nance's scoundrel boyfriend, Tom Mogan, is explicitly identified as Irish.

84 The term "yellow journalism" was coined in 1897. Its origins lie in a slang-speaking, comic-strip character named "The Yellow Kid" who first appeared in Pulitzer's New York *World* and later in Hearst's New York *Journal*. For more on yellow journalism, see Joseph W. Campbell, *Yellow Journalism: Puncturing the Myths, Defining the Legacies* (Praeger, 2001).

85 Haryot Holt Cahoon "Women in Gutter Journalism," *Arena* 17 (1896–97): 570, 574.

86 On Fanny Fern, see Joyce W. Warren, "*Legacy* Profile: Fanny Fern (1811–1872)," *Legacy* 35, no. 2 (2018): 210–20. On Jordan, see

Elizabeth Garver Jordan, *The Case of Lizzie Borden and Other Writings*, eds. Jane Carr and Lori Harrison-Kahan (Penguin, 2024) and Sharon M. Harris, *Her Life in Ink: Elizabeth Jordan, Journalist, Editor, and Mystery Author* (Lyons Press, 2026). Michelson's writings also make an interesting comparison to those of early twentieth-century Yiddish journalist and fiction writer Miriam Karpilove, whose 1926 novella *A Provincial Newspaper* similarly features a journalist-protagonist who writes for and edits the woman's page of a Yiddish newspaper called *The Pathfinder*; see Miriam Karpilove, *A Provincial Newspaper and Other Stories*, trans. Jessica Kirzane (Syracuse University Press, 2023).

87 Michelson, *A Yellow Journalist*, 1. Unless otherwise indicated, all citations to *A Yellow Journalist* will refer to the book version, published by D. Appleton and Company in 1905, rather than *The Saturday Evening Post* series.

88 Michelson, *A Yellow Journalist*, 24.

89 Michelson, *A Yellow Journalist*, 9. Michelson professed similar ideas in her journalism. For example, in an interview with Phoebe Couzins, one of the nation's first woman lawyers, Michelson and her subject debated the merits of the "single life and an independent career." While fifty-two-year-old Couzins expressed some regret at pursuing the law at the expense of marriage and children, twenty-five-year-old Michelson opined that the "woman who remains single . . . may miss much joy, but she misses more unhappiness." See Miriam Michelson, "What Say Ye Women to This?: Miss Phoebe Couzins on Single Life and an Independent Career," *Arthur McEwen's Letter*, February 9, 1895, 5.

90 Michelson, *A Yellow Journalist*, 6–7.

91 Michelson, *A Yellow Journalist*, 6.

92 Michelson, *A Yellow Journalist*, 21.

93 Michelson, *A Yellow Journalist*, 258–59.

94 Michelson, *A Yellow Journalist*, 148.

95 Michelson, *A Yellow Journalist*, 217.

96 Harrison-Kahan and Skinazi, "Miriam Michelson's Yellow Journalism and the Multi-Ethnic West," 193.

97 Michelson, *A Yellow Journalist*, 125.

98 Michelson, *A Yellow Journalist*, 169.

99 Miriam Michelson, "The Milpitas Maiden," *The Saturday Evening Post*, June 24, 1905, reprinted in Harrison-Kahan, ed., *The Superwoman and Other Writings*, 363, 361.

100 Lori Harrison-Kahan, "The Seeds of #MeToo Started Growing 100 Years Ago," *CNN*, November 2, 2019, https://www.cnn.com/2019/11/02/opinions/me-too-movement-history-jordan-michelson-harrison-kahan/index.html, accessed July 22, 2024.

101 The hashtag #MeToo, which went viral in 2016 in the wake of sexual assault allegations against Harvey Weinstein and others was a co-optation of work begun by Black activist Tarana Burke, who has since been credited for the role she played in igniting the movement. See Tarana Burke, *Unbound: My Story of Liberation and the Birth of the MeToo Movement* (Flatiron, 2021) and Mikki Kendall, *Hood Feminism: Notes from the Women That a Movement Forgot* (Viking, 2020).

102 Michelson, *A Yellow Journalist*, 242, 247.

103 Michelson, *A Yellow Journalist*, 87. For an example of the use of "black," see Michelson, *A Yellow Journalist*, 274.

104 Michelson, *A Yellow Journalist*, 230.

105 Michelson, *A Yellow Journalist*, 296.

106 Michelson, *A Yellow Journalist*, 308, 315, 270, 315.

107 On white feminism, see Koa Beck, *White Feminism: From the Suffragettes to Influencers and Who They Leave Behind* (Atria, 2021); Kyla Schuller, *The Trouble with White Women: A Counterhistory of Feminism* (Bold Type, 2021); and Rafia Zakaria, *Against White Feminism: Notes on Disruption* (W. W. Norton, 2021).

108 See, for example, Isabel Fraser, "Mammy Pleasant: The Woman," *The San Francisco Call*, December 29, 1901, 4. It is worth noting that Black writers also referred to her as "Mammy," including W. E. B. Du Bois who identifies her as "Mammy Pleasants" in *The Gift of Black Folk* (Stratford, 1924), 271–72. Some historians understand the mammy role and performance as a cover that Pleasant embraced in order to access white spaces and get close to white people. For more on Pleasant, see Lynn Hudson, *The Making of Mammy Pleasant: A Black Entrepreneur in Nineteenth-Century San Francisco* (University of Illinois Press, 2008).

109 Michelson, *A Yellow Journalist*, 58.

110 Michelson, *A Yellow Journalist*, 77.

111 See Carly Severn, "How a Heroine Became a 'Demon' in Victorian San Francisco," December 28, 2018, https://www.kqed.org/news/11701126/how-a-heroine-became-a-demon-in-victorian-san-francisco, accessed May 3, 2025.

112 Michelson, *A Yellow Journalist*, 58.

113 Michelson, "Dark-Skinned Lion-Tamer in the House of Mystery," *The San Francisco Call*, October 10, 1897, 29, reprinted in Harrison-Kahan, ed., *The Superwoman and Other Writings*, 180–81.

114 Michelson, *A Yellow Journalist*, 74.

115 On *The Saturday Evening Post*, see Jan Cohn, *Creating America: George Horace Latimer and "The Saturday Evening Post"* (University of Pittsburgh Press, 1989). In general, given Rhoda's determination and pluck, Michelson's series was a good fit for *The Saturday Evening Post*, a magazine that appealed to the "average American" by combining "nineteenth-century" virtues—especially the value of hard work—with "twentieth-century opportunities" (28).

116 Jonathan Freedman, *Klezmer America: Jewishness, Ethnicity, Modernity* (Columbia University Press, 2007), and Jennifer Glaser, *Borrowed Voices: Writing and Racial Ventriloquism in the Jewish American Imagination* (Rutgers University Press, 2016).

117 Harrison-Kahan and Skinazi, "Miriam Michelson's Yellow Journalism and the Multi-Ethnic West," 185–86.

118 Michelson, *A Yellow Journalist*, 88–89.

119 Michelson, *A Yellow Journalist*, 87, 88.

120 See Brian Donovan, *White Slave Crusades: Race, Gender, and Anti-Vice Activism, 1887–1917* (University of Illinois Press, 2006); and Karen A. Keely, "Sexual Slavery in San Francisco's Chinatown: 'Yellow Peril' and 'White Slavery' in Frank Norris's Early Fiction," *Studies in American Naturalism* 2, no. 2 (Winter 2007): 129–49.

121 Michelson, *A Yellow Journalist*, 88.

122 Michelson, *A Yellow Journalist*, 91.

123 Michelson, *A Yellow Journalist*, 96, 98.

124 Michelson, *A Yellow Journalist*, 99.

125 Michelson, *A Yellow Journalist*, 102.

126 Michelson, *A Yellow Journalist*, 101.

127 Michelson, *A Yellow Journalist*, 113.

128 Judy Yung, *Unbound Feet: A Social History of Chinese Women in San Francisco* (University of California Press, 1995), 33.
129 The Chinese Exclusion Act was extended indefinitely in 1904, shortly before *A Yellow Journalist* was published.
130 Michelson, *A Yellow Journalist*, 102.
131 Michelson, *A Yellow Journalist*, 113.
132 On Ah Toy, see Yung, *Unbound Feet*, 33–34, and Elizabeth Sinn, *Pacific Crossing: California Gold, Chinese Migration, and the Making of Hong Kong* (Hong Kong University Press, 2013), 219–64.
133 Yung, *Unbound Feet*, 36.
134 On Cameron, see Mildred Crowl Martin, *Chinatown's Angry Angel: The Story of Donaldina Cameron* (Pacific Books, 1977), Carol Green Wilson, *Chinatown Quest: The Life Adventures of Donaldina Cameron* (Stanford University Press, 1931), and Donovan, *White Slave Crusades*.
135 Michelson, *A Yellow Journalist*, 117.
136 Michelson, *A Yellow Journalist*, 118.
137 Michelson, "Strangling Hands upon a Nation's Throat," in Harrison-Kahan, ed., *The Superwoman and Other Writings*, 167, 162.
138 I have described how this cultural tradition of Jewish women's racial appropriation produces a feminist critique of whiteness in *The White Negress: Literature, Minstrelsy, and the Black-Jewish Imaginary* (Rutgers University Press, 2011).
139 Michelson, *A Yellow Journalist*, 105.
140 Michelson, *A Yellow Journalist*, 150.
141 Michelson, *A Yellow Journalist*, 157, 156.
142 Michelson, *A Yellow Journalist*, 159.
143 Michelson, *A Yellow Journalist*, 169, 177.
144 Annie Nathan Meyer, "Shepson in 'The Pot-Boiler,'" *New York Times*, December 10, 1904, BR871. In the hands of non-Jewish writers, the figure of the Jewish art patron, however, has lent itself to antisemitic stereotypes; see, for example, Willa Cather's depiction of Siegmund Stein in "Scandal," a short story published in *Century* in August 1919.
145 Michelson, *A Yellow Journalist*, 149–50.
146 On antisemitism, David Belasco, and the Theatrical Syndicate, see for example, Harley Erdman, *Staging the Jew: The Performance of an American Ethnicity, 1860–1920* (Rutgers University Press, 1997), 93–117; and Mark Hodin, "The Disavowal of Ethnicity: Legitimate Theatre

and the Social Construction of Literary Value in Turn-of-the-Century America," *Theatre Journal* 52 (2000): 211–26. As Hodin points out, Metcalfe singled out David Belasco as different from the other Jewish theater managers, viewing him as a cultured Jew. Michelson's portrait of Lowenthal may align with this view of Belasco but also operates as a composite of several managers.

147 Michelson, *A Yellow Journalist*, 114.

148 For additional examples, see Harrison-Kahan, *The White Negress*, and Harrison-Kahan, "Where the Shoe Pinches: Appropriation and Allyship in Annie Nathan Meyer's Anti-Lynching Literature" in *Matrilineal Dissent: Women Writers and Jewish American Literary History*, eds. Annie Atura Bushnell, Lori Harrison-Kahan, and Ashley Walters (Detroit: Wayne State University Press, 2024): 71–109.

Chapter 5

1 James R. Boylan, *Revolutionary Lives: Anna Strunsky and William English Walling* (University of Massachusetts Press, 1998), 33; John Hamilton Gilmour, "Girl Socialist of San Francisco," *San Francisco Examiner*, October 3, 1897, 10; Anna Strunsky to George Brett, June 3, 1903, Macmillan Company Records, Manuscripts and Archives Division, New York Public Library, Astor, Lenox, and Tilden Foundations.

2 "Earnest Address by Anna Strunsky," *The San Francisco Call*, October 11, 1904, 3.

3 Jack London, *The Iron Heel* (1908; repr., Penguin, 2006), 57.

4 London, *The Iron Heel*, 57, 75.

5 Jonathan Auerbach, introduction to *The Iron Heel*, ix.

6 London, *The Iron Heel*, 5, 8, 251. The historical notes appended to Margaret Atwood's dystopian novel *The Handmaid's Tale* (1985) bear striking resemblances to the foreword to *The Iron Heel*, especially in the way that a fictional male historian intervenes to comment on a woman's historical testimony and to question its reliability as a source.

7 Strunsky would later call *The Iron Heel* "prophetic on a vast scale" for its prediction of the rise of twentieth-century fascism. She also sees London as the obvious model for Ernest Everhard. See Anna Strunsky, "Jack London," Anna Strunsky Walling Papers (MS 1111), Manuscripts and Archives, Yale University Library.

8 In 2016, SeaWolf Press began the process of reissuing all fifty of Jack London's books, including *The Kempton-Wace Letters*, in honor of the centennial of his death. In marketing materials that list all of the reissued titles for the Jack London 100th Anniversary Collection, there is no mention of the fact that *The Kempton-Wace Letters* was a coauthored novel by Anna Strunsky.

9 Guide to the Anna Strunsky Walling Papers, MS 1111, April 1982, Yale University Library, Manuscripts and Archives, https://archives.yale.edu/repositories/12/resources/4483, accessed July 23, 2024.

10 Some of these works are blatantly sexist; see, for example, Robert Brainard Pearsall, "Elizabeth Barrett Meets Wolf Larsen," *Western American Literature* 4, no. 1 (Spring 1969): 3–13. Others—most notably Clarice Stasz's *Jack London's Women* (University of Massachusetts Press, 2001)—attempt to offer correctives. In chapter 5 of *Male Call: Becoming Jack London* (Duke University Press, 1996), Jonathan Auerbach offers an in-depth analysis of the production of *The Kempton-Wace Letters* that does justice to the complexity of Strunsky's role in the collaboration and, like my own reading, acknowledges the "profound implications" of her "gender shift" (162).

11 Boylan, *Revolutionary Lives*, 2.

12 For another recent example of historical scholarship, see Ashley Walters, "'Oriental Leaven': Anna and Rose Strunsky in the Unpublished Writings of Jack London and Sinclair Lewis," *American Jewish History* 104, nos. 2–3 (April–July 2020): 323–45.

13 In addition to mentions of family Purim celebrations in Strunsky's family papers, an article in *Emanu-El* reported on one such event at the home of the Strunskys' Sutter Street neighbors, where Anna's father "discussed learnedly on the origin of Purim" while one of her brothers "spoke pleasantly on the position of women which has not changed for centuries as we find now, just as in the time of Queen Esther, that women's influence prevails in the highest places." See "Social News," *Emanu-El*, March 16, 1906, 17.

14 For Strunsky's experiences as witness to the Homel massacre, see Anna Strunsky, *The Homel Massacre: An Address Delivered Before the New York Section Council of Jewish Women* (National Council of Jewish Women, 1914).

15 Anna Strunsky, "Revolutionary Lives," Anna Strunsky Walling Papers, BANC MSS C-H 95, Bancroft Library, University of California, Berkeley.
16 Mary Antin, *The Promised Land* (1912; repr., Penguin, 1997), 1, 3.
17 Anna Strunsky Walling, "Foreign-born," *The Conservator* 28, no. 5 (July 1917): 68.
18 Strunsky, "Revolutionary Lives," Bancroft Library.
19 Anna Strunsky, "Golden Wedding," Anna Strunsky Walling Papers, BANC MSS C-H 95, Bancroft Library, University of California, Berkeley.
20 "Contributors to Magazines: Annie Strunsky, of Grammar School No. 49, Is a Gifted Pupil," *New York Herald*, February 24, 1894, 11.
21 Strunsky, "Golden Wedding," Bancroft Library.
22 "Directory of Local Organizations," *The American Jewish Year Book*, vol. 1 (American Jewish Committee, 1900), 114; "The Zionist Movement," *Emanu-El*, February 4, 1898, 8.
23 "National Organizations," *The American Jewish Year Book*, vol. 8 (American Jewish Committee, 1906), 115.
24 Anna Strunsky Walling, "He Was Youth Incarnate," *Labor Unity*, November 27, 1924, 3.
25 Stanford University, "Admission of Women," *Annual Report of the President of the University* (1919), 47.
26 Nancy Weiss Malkiel, *"Keep the Damned Women Out": The Struggle for Coeducation* (Princeton University Press, 2016), 5.
27 Anna Strunsky, ex-'00, "Stanford Women in the Ranks of Literature," *Stanford Daily*, April 22, 1903, 5.
28 Anna Strunsky to Hilda Abel, June 16, 1958, Box 1, Anna Strunsky Walling Papers, BANC MSS C-H 95, Bancroft Library, University of California, Berkeley.
29 Quoted in Boylan, *Revolutionary Lives*, 9.
30 Mary Sheldon Barnes, *Studies in General History* (Heath, 1885), viii. See also Will S. Monroe, "Death of Mary Sheldon Barnes," *Journal of Education*, September 15, 1898, 175.
31 Boylan, *Revolutionary Lives*, 9.
32 Strunsky, "Stanford Women in the Ranks of Literature," 5.
33 Emma Goldman, *Living My Life* (1931; repr., Pluto Press, 1987), 227.
34 "Fryer Wins the Honors," *San Francisco Chronicle*, February 12, 1898, 10.

35 "Socialist Labor Party Platform," *The World Almanac and Encyclopedia* (Press Publishing Co., 1896), 94.
36 Jack London, "How I Became a Socialist" (1903) in *London's Essays of Revolt*, ed. Leonard D. Abbott (Vanguard, 1928), 57, 59.
37 Interview with Anna Strunsky Walling, June 6, 1960, Oral History of the Left, Tamiment Library, New York University, quoted in Norma Fain Pratt, "Anna Strunsky Walling," *Shalvi/Hyman Encyclopedia of Jewish Women* (Jewish Women's Archive), https://jwa.org/encyclopedia/article/walling-anna-strunsky, accessed April 28, 2025.
38 Strunsky, "Golden Wedding," Bancroft Library.
39 Agnes Foster Buchanan, "The Story of a Famous Fraternity of Writers and Artists," *Pacific Monthly*, January 1907, 74–75.
40 "The Perfervid Miss Strunsky," *Town Talk*, October 28, 1905, 21.
41 "Our San Francisco Letter," *Deseret Weekly*, October 23, 1897, 579.
42 Gilmour, "Girl Socialist of San Francisco," 10.
43 Anna Strunsky Walling, "A Tribute to the Yellow Press: Its Virtues and Its Vices as Estimated by a Victim," *Collier's*, April 22, 1911, 32.
44 Quoted in Hannah Sampson, "What Is Bohemian Grove?," *Washington Post*, April 6, 2023, https://www.washingtonpost.com/search/?query=Bohemian+Grove, accessed May 16, 2025.
45 Anna Strunsky, "Jack London," Anna Strunsky Walling Papers (MS 1111), Manuscripts and Archives, Yale University Library.
46 Gelett Burgess, "Where Is Bohemia?," in *The Romance of the Commonplace* (Paul Elder and Morgan Shepard, 1902), 129.
47 Anna Strunsky, "In Bohemia," c. 1906, Anna Strunsky Walling Papers (MS 1111), Manuscripts and Archives, Yale University Library.
48 Statement of the California Society of the Friends of Russian Freedom, Anna Strunsky Walling Papers (MS 1111), Manuscripts and Archives, Yale University Library. In her unpublished memoir of Jack London, Strunsky remembers London being president and she the secretary of the society, which is not reflected in the promotional materials.
49 Zoe Green Radcliffe, "Football Games Forgotten for Home Dinners," *The San Francisco Call*, November 13, 1904, 40.
50 Warren Unna, *The Coppa Murals: A Pageant of Bohemian Life in San Francisco at the Turn of the Century* (Book Club of California, 1952), 8–9. Mary Austin shot back at the male bohemians in her autobiography *Earth Horizon* (Houghton Mifflin, 1932), wryly writing "of

the liability of men of genius to find their subjective activities on their way to fruition so largely at the mercy of the effect on them of women. I never needed a love affair to release the sub-conscious in me, nor did Nora May French, who was the only other woman of our circle whose gifts approached Sterling's or London's" (303). For more on the gender dynamics of The Crowd, see Catherine Jean Prendergast, *The Gilded Edge: Two Audacious Women and the Cyanide Love Triangle That Shook America* (Dutton, 2021).

51 Elsie Whitaker Martínez, "San Francisco Bay Area Writers and Artists," interview by Franklin D. Walker and Willa Klug Baum, 1964, Bancroft Library, University of California, Berkeley.

52 Buchanan, "The Story of a Famous Fraternity of Writers and Artists," 66.

53 Ed Herny, Shelley Rideout, and Katie Wadell, *Berkeley Bohemia: Artists and Visionaries of the Early 20th Century* (Gibbs Smith, 2008), 135.

54 Whitaker Martínez, "San Francisco Bay Area Writers and Artists," interview.

55 The title of this section comes from a poem London wrote to Strunsky about their collaboration on *The Kempton-Wace Letters*, in which he implores her to "come write to me and be my Love," modeling his verse on Christopher Marlowe's "The Passionate Shepherd to His Love." The stanza in question reads: "These tender things we'll put in print / Sweetheart, there may be millions in't / The public simply can't resist / 'Love Letters of a Socialist.'" A full transcription of the poem can be found in Auerbach, *Male Call*, 176–77.

56 "Jack London, the Boy Socialist: Once an Industrial Tramp, Now a High-School Student," *San Francisco Chronicle*, February 16, 1896, 20.

57 Details of Strunsky's account vary. In "The Meaning of Jack London" (*The New York Call Magazine*, November 28, 1920, 3–4), she does not mention the Paris Commune and says she cannot remember whether they were introduced by Frank Strawn-Hamilton or Cameron King. Several biographers note that their first meeting likely took place in December 1899, not March, based in part on the fact that their correspondence begins in December 1899; if this were the case, the occasion of their meeting would not be the commemoration of the Paris Commune, which took place in March.

58 Anna Strunsky, "Jack London," Yale University Library. In the memoir, Strunsky interestingly edits herself out of this scene. In her 1920 article

"The Meaning of Jack London," which appeared in *The New York Call Magazine*, she not only notes that King or Strawn-Hamilton asked if she wanted to meet London before introducing them, but also adds this detail: "We shook hands and remained talking to each other. I had a feeling of wonderful happiness. To me it was as if I were meeting in their youth Lasalle, Karl Marx or Byron, so instantly did I feel that I was in the presence of a historical character. . . . This certainty with which he inspired me was the vital subjective fact about our meeting" (3).

59 Strunsky, "Jack London," Yale University Library.

60 Strunsky, "Jack London," Yale University Library.

61 London to Strunsky, April 6, 1900, in *The Letters of Jack London*, eds. Earle Labor, Robert C. Leitz III, and I. Milo Shepard, vol. 1 (Stanford University Press, 1988), 179.

62 London to Ninetta Eames, April 3, 1900, in Labor, Leitz, and Shepard, *Letters of Jack London*, vol. 1, 178.

63 London to Strunsky, July 31, 1900, in Labor, Leitz, and Shepard, *Letters of Jack London*, vol. 1, 198.

64 Strunsky, "Jack London," Yale University Library.

65 Later, Strunsky also developed a friendship with Charmian Kittredge London, London's second wife. Their extensive correspondence continued after London's death.

66 London to Strunsky, December 19, 1899, in Labor, Leitz, and Shepard, *Letters of Jack London*, vol. 1, 134.

67 Browning's stanza reads, "Oh to love so, be so loved, yet so mistaken! / What had I on earth to do / With the slothful, with the mawkish, the unmanly? / Like the aimless, helpless, hopeless, did I drivel /—Being—who?" James Boylan points out that London must have missed the literary reference since he replied that he did not recall using the words "aimless, helpless, hopeless" to describe her.

68 London to Strunsky, December 21, 1899, in Labor, Leitz, and Shepard, *Letters of Jack London*, vol. 1, 135–36. This letter ends with a passage that Strunsky later quotes to open the eulogy she publishes in the socialist periodical *The Masses* after London's death: "Take me this way: a stray guest, a bird of passage, splashing with salt-rimed wings through a brief moment of your life—a rude and blundering bird, used to large airs and great spaces, unaccustomed to the amenities of confined existence." The beautiful language presages the prose style

and youthful, rebellious persona for which London would come to be known. See Anna Strunsky Walling, "Memoirs of Jack London," *The Masses*, July 1917, 13.

69 London to Strunsky, December 27, 1899, in Labor, Leitz, and Shepard, *Letters of Jack London*, vol. 1, 137.

70 In her "Jack London" manuscript, Strunsky names herself as the influence for Frona. For more on London's representations of Strunsky in his fiction, see Walters, "'Oriental Leaven.'"

71 London to Strunsky, March 15, 1900, in Labor, Leitz, and Shepard, *Letters of Jack London*, vol. 1, 173.

72 London to Strunsky, Jan 21, 1900, in Labor, Leitz, and Shepard, *Letters of Jack London*, vol. 1, 144.

73 London to Strunsky, February 20, 1900, in Labor, Leitz, and Shepard, *Letters of Jack London*, vol. 1, 161.

74 London to Strunsky, December 26, 1900, in Labor, Leitz, and Shepard, *Letters of Jack London*, vol. 1, 228, 229. London includes a discussion of "white friendship" between Frona and Vance Corliss in *A Daughter of the Snows* (1902; repr., SeaWolf, 2017), 278–9.

75 London to Strunsky, February 13, 1900, in Labor, Leitz, and Shepard, *Letters of Jack London*, vol. 1, 156.

76 London to Cloudesley Johns, October 17, 1900, in Labor, Leitz, and Shepard, *Letters of Jack London*, vol. 1, 214. A similar example occurs in a letter London later writes to Macmillan editor George Brett who published *The Kempton-Wace Letters*. Notifying Brett of Strunsky's impending trip to New York and her plans to visit the Macmillan offices, London pens a letter of introduction on Strunsky's behalf dated November 9, 1902: "I am sure you will find her charming. She is a young Russian-Jewess, brilliant, a college-woman, etc." (London to George P. Brett, November 9, 1902, in Labor, Leitz, and Shepard, *Letters of Jack London*, vol. 1, 315).

77 For more on this story, see Jay Williams, *Author Under Sail: The Imagination of Jack London, 1902–1907* (University of Nebraska Press, 2021), 60–63.

78 London to Strunsky, December 29, 1899, in Labor, Leitz, and Shepard, *Letters of Jack London*, vol. 1, 138.

79 Jay Williams, "Life in Jewish Oakland: A Lost Short Story by Jack London," *Studies in American Naturalism* 10, no. 1 (Summer 2015): 83.

80 London to Strunsky, December 29, 1899, in Labor, Leitz, and Shepard, *Letters of Jack London*, vol. 1, 138. In 1911, London contributed to a symposium on "The Jew in English Fiction" in *The American Hebrew and Jewish Messenger*; in his statement, he defended his portrayal of Jewish characters in his fiction and wrote, "I am a terrific admirer of the Jews; I have consorted more with Jews than with any other nationality; I have among the Jews some of my finest and noblest friends . . . it is as unfair for a writer to make villains of all races except the Jews, as it is to make villains only of Jews. To ignore the Jew in the matter of villainy is so invidious an exception as to be unfair to the Jews." See Jack London, "The Jew in English Fiction," *American Hebrew and Jewish Messenger*, September 22, 1911, 609.

81 London to Strunsky, January 21, 1900, in Labor, Leitz, and Shepard, *Letters of Jack London*, vol. 1, 144.

82 London to Strunsky, January 21, 1900, in Labor, Leitz, and Shepard, *Letters of Jack London*, vol. 1, 145.

83 Anna Strunsky, "Alexei Grigorevitch—Fatalist," Anna Strunsky Walling Papers (MS 1111), Manuscripts and Archives, Yale University Library.

84 Anna Strunsky, "With Bigamous Intent," Anna Strunsky Walling Papers (MS 1111), Manuscripts and Archives, Yale University Library.

85 Strunsky's papers also include extensive notes for a play with a similar plotline, although in that case a male author turns out to be a woman.

86 London to Strunsky, April 3, 1901, in Labor, Leitz, and Shepard, *Letters of Jack London*, vol. 1, 244. This letter appears in the following volumes: Cathy N. Davidson, ed., *The Book of Love: Writers and Their Love Letters* (Plume, 1996); David H. Lowenherz, ed., *The 50 Greatest Love Letters of All Time* (Gramercy, 2005); and John C. Kirkland, ed., *Love Letters of Great Men*, vol. 1 (John C. Kirkland, 2008). The letter was written shortly after London announced his wife Bess's first pregnancy, writing to Strunsky that he was praying the baby would be a boy.

87 London to Strunsky, July 31, 1900, in Labor, Leitz, and Shepard, *Letters of Jack London*, vol. 1, 198.

88 Jack London and Anna Strunsky, *The Kempton-Wace Letters* (NCUP, 1990), 1.

89 London and Strunsky, *The Kempton-Wace Letters*, 4, 3.

90 Strunsky, "Jack London," Yale University Library.

91 Douglas Robillard, introduction to *The Kempton-Wace Letters*, v.
92 Strunsky, "Jack London," Yale University Library.
93 See Laura E. Franey, introduction to Yone Noguchi, *The American Diary of a Japanese Girl*, eds. Edward Marx and Laura E. Franey (Temple University Press, 2007).
94 London to Strunsky, August 30, 1900, in Labor, Leitz, and Shepard, *Letters of Jack London*, vol. 1, 202.
95 London to Strunsky, September 15, 1900, in Labor, Leitz, and Shepard, *Letters of Jack London*, vol. 1, 205.
96 London and Strunsky, *The Kempton-Wace Letters*, 1.
97 London and Strunsky, *The Kempton-Wace Letters*, 2.
98 London and Strunsky, *The Kempton-Wace Letters*, 14, 24.
99 London to Strunsky, April 3, 1901, in Labor, Leitz, and Shepard, *Letters of Jack London*, vol. 1, 244.
100 London and Strunsky, *The Kempton-Wace Letters*, 4–5.
101 London and Strunsky, *The Kempton-Wace Letters*, 19.
102 London and Strunsky, *The Kempton-Wace Letters*, 49.
103 London and Strunsky, *The Kempton-Wace Letters*, 6. In a letter dated November 15, 1900, London reveals that he, or his Wace persona, has angered Strunsky by calling women "the creature of a lower evolution, weaker, inferior, unfit," which she sees as "an insult to every woman in the world." London to Strunsky, November 15, 1900, in Labor, Leitz, and Shepard, *Letters of Jack London*, vol. 1, 219.
104 London and Strunsky, *The Kempton-Wace Letters*, 114.
105 Anna Strunsky, review of *The God of His Fathers* by Jack London, *Impressions Quarterly* 2, no. 4 (October 1901): 60. In a letter to Strunsky, London expressed his appreciation of this review. London to Strunsky, October 3, 1901, in Labor, Leitz, and Shepard, *Letters of Jack London*, vol. 1, 255–56.
106 London and Strunsky, *The Kempton-Wace Letters*, 113.
107 London and Strunsky, *The Kempton-Wace Letters*, 113.
108 London and Strunsky, *The Kempton-Wace Letters*, 5.
109 London to Strunsky, May 2, 1900, in Labor, Leitz, and Shepard, *Letters of Jack London*, vol. 1, 183.
110 London and Strunsky, *The Kempton-Wace Letters*, 110.
111 London and Strunsky, *The Kempton-Wace Letters*, 116.
112 London and Strunsky, *The Kempton-Wace Letters*, 118–19.

113 London to Strunsky, April 1, 1902, in Labor, Leitz, and Shepard, *Letters of Jack London*, vol. 1, 287.
114 Diary no. 1, Box 23, Folder 300, Anna Strunsky Walling Papers (MS 1111), Manuscripts and Archives, Yale University Library. Note that she used a Sunset Diary from 1900 for this purpose but changed the dates to 1901 and 1902.
115 Diary no. 1, Box 23, Folder 300, Anna Strunsky Walling Papers (MS 1111), Manuscripts and Archives, Yale University Library.
116 Diaries and Writings, Anna Strunsky Walling Papers (MS 1111), Manuscripts and Archives, Yale University Library. This list of memories of Jack London appears on a diary page dated Friday, July 27, 1928, but the date is crossed out and the handwritten date "Dec. 4" (without a year) appears below. Strunsky used the 1928 diary between 1929 and 1932, so the notes were probably recorded during that four-year period.
117 This line appeared in advertisements for *The Kempton-Wace Letters*. For example, an advertisement in the *New York Tribune* on May 31, 1903, which lists the author as anonymous, describes the book as a "discussion in the letters of two men on 'the one great interest of life,' through which runs and reappears the woman's side of the question" (41).
118 Anna Strunsky, unpublished prologue to *The Kempton-Wace Letters*, Jack London Papers, The Huntington Library, San Marino, California.
119 London to George Brett, January 20, 1903, in Labor, Leitz, and Shepard, *Letters of Jack London*, vol. 1, 337.
120 For a detailed account of the Strunsky-Walling marriage, see Boylan, *Revolutionary Lives*.

Coda

1 Frances Bransten Rothmann, *The Haas Sisters of Franklin Street: A Look Back with Love* (Judah Magnes Museum, 1979), 2.
2 Rothmann, *The Haas Sisters of Franklin Street*, 70. See also Fred Rosenbaum, "Jewish Americans: Religion and Identity at 2007 Franklin Street" (San Francisco Heritage, May 2017), https://www.haas-lilienthalhouse.org/_files/ugd/abba95_926bd9fa8b54458f9c600aada5437604.pdf, accessed January 1, 2025.
3 Rothmann, *The Haas Sisters of Franklin Street*, 75; Rosenbaum, "Jewish Americans," 14. This detail is also suggestive since, in the late

nineteenth century, the Reform congregation at Temple Emanu-El became one of the first in the country to prioritize Friday evening services for Shabbat in order to leave Saturday mornings open for secular activities.

4 Rothmann, *The Haas Sisters of Franklin Street*, 75.

5 Flora Jacobi Arnstein, *No End to Morning* (self-published, no date), Annette Rosenshine Collection, Bancroft Library, University of California, Berkeley; Annette Rosenshine, "Life's Not a Paragraph," unpublished memoir, Annette Rosenshine Collection, Bancroft Library, University of California, Berkeley. See also Flora Arnstein, "Growing Up in the Nineties," *San Francisco Chronicle* (1976), Flora J. Arnstein Papers, Bancroft Library, University of California, Berkeley. On Kohut's *My Portion* (1925), see the introduction to this book. On Stein's and Toklas's autobiographical writings, see chapter 3.

6 Gertrude Atherton, *Adventures of a Novelist* (Liveright, 1932), 112.

7 For examples of the Kaufman sisters' short stories, see Jessie Kaufman, "A Hawaiian Expedient," *Overland Monthly*, January 1900, 10–18 and Emma B. Kaufman, "The Friends," *Lippincott's*, May 1892, 609–20.

8 On Prag Kahn, see Glenna Matthews, "'There Is No Sex in Citizenship': The Career of Congresswoman Florence Prag Kahn," in *We Have Come to Stay: American Women and Political Parties, 1880–1960*, eds. Melanie S. Gustafson, Kristie Miller, and Elisabeth I. Perry (University of New Mexico Press, 1999), 131–40. On Solomons, see M. K. Silver, "Selina Solomons and Her Quest for the Sixth Star, 1862–1942," *Western States Jewish History* 35, nos. 3–4 (2003): 211–23.

9 On Upright, see Landon Haynes, "Her First Book Made Her Famous," *Los Angeles Times*, January 25, 1925, 10. Jacobson also published a biography of Jewish mayor Adolph Sutro; see Jacobson with Carl Glasscock, *Miner, Merchant, and Mayor* (Society of California Pioneers, 1933).

10 Edna Ferber, *A Peculiar Treasure* (Doubleday, Doran, 1939), 115. For more on Ferber and Hurst, see Lori Harrison-Kahan, *The White Negress: Literature, Minstrelsy, and the Black-Jewish Imaginary* (Rutgers University Press, 2011), chapters 2 and 3. For an analysis of Ferber's writing that considers the relationship between Jewishness and Western geography, see Michael Hoberman, *A Hundred Acres of America: The Geography of Jewish American Literary History* (Rutgers University Press, 2018), chapter 3.

Index

Note: Page numbers appearing in *italics* refer to figures.